NO PYRRHIC
VICTORIES

Vice Admiral Sir Roger Keyes.

NO PYRRHIC VICTORIES

THE 1918 RAIDS ON
ZEEBRUGGE AND OSTEND

A RADICAL REAPPRAISAL

E.C. COLEMAN

Other History Press books by E.C. Coleman

Captain Vancouver: North-West Navigator
The Travels of Sir John Mandeville
The Royal Navy in Polar Exploration: From Frobisher to Ross
The Royal Navy and Polar Exploration. Vol. 2: From Franklin to Scott
Scraps: The Wit of the Victorians
The Pig War: The Most Perfect War in History
The Grail Chronicles: Tracing the Holy Grail from the Last Supper to its
Current Location

Frontispiece: The 1918 sketch 'Vice Admiral Sir Roger Keyes KCB,
CMG, CVO, DSO', by Glyn Warren Philpot.

First published 2014
by Spellmount, an imprint of The History Press
The Mill, Brimscombe Port
Stroud, Gloucestershire, GL5 2QG
www.thehistorypress.co.uk

British Library Cataloguing in Publication Data.
A catalogue record for this book is available from the British Library.

ISBN 978 0 7509 5849 3

Typesetting and origination by The History Press
Printed in Great Britain

Contents

Foreword by Josephine Keyes		06
Foreword by Commander Ralph Wykes-Sneyd		08
Acknowledgements		10
Introduction		11
1	The Problem	23
2	The Answer	41
3	The Challenge	58
4	The Plan	70
5	The Muster	91
6	The Trial by Patience	111
7	The Ostend Raid	123
8	The Inferno	137
9	The Mole	151
10	The Blockships	170
11	Preparations for the Second Ostend Raid	190
12	The Reckoning	210
13	The Defence Against Disenchantment	230
	Epilogue	260
	Select Bibliography	313
	Index	315

Foreword
by Josephine Keyes

I was very pleased to be invited to write a foreword to *No Pyrrhic Victories*, an expert reassessment of the success (or otherwise) of my grandfather Roger Keyes' naval actions at Zeebrugge and Ostend in 1918.

Ernest Coleman has cast his wonderfully sceptical eye over yet another 'accepted version' and come to some very interesting conclusions. Indeed he proves that the idea that the raid was a failure was based entirely on German propaganda, which successfully persuaded everyone that the channel was not obstructed by the sunken block ships for long, and indeed that a submarine left the base a day later. A great deal of effort and sleight of hand appears to have been employed to this end but, crucially, there is no photographic evidence at all that it did.

Coleman puts forward a series of intriguing theories about how this trick was achieved including: 'It would have been a small thing to have put UB16 onto a barge, covered her with tarpaulins, and towed her to the North Sea whilst persuading the Dutch to look the other way' for instance. The other theory, again backed up with considerable evidence, is that UB16 was never in the base in the first place. The families of the brave warriors, so many of whom gave their lives, will be immensely relieved to hear this and I heartily recommend they read the book.

In this year of remembrance for all who were killed in the First World War, the actions of the Royal Navy are often forgotten. Indeed, as Coleman points out, it was not a naval war. So it is fitting that this book sets the record straight now. The National Portrait Gallery came to a similar conclusion when it dug out a huge, sagging, damaged and neglected portrait of the naval leaders of the First World War, including Roger Keyes, and had it beautifully restored to hang in pride of place, and tour the country. My grandfather's status as a forgotten hero appears to be shifting.

By a strange chance, three out of four of my children's grandfathers were at Zeebrugge, so it is particularly pleasing that this book is now in print to help them understand their family history more positively. Their paternal grandfathers, Captain Bryan Adams and Lieutenant Edward Hilton Young, met for the first time during the battle. It is said that when Young was wounded in the arm, it was Adams who sent him below, thereby probably saving his life, as Young had no intention himself of ceasing his 'self-appointed duty of cheering everybody up'. Young's arm was subsequently amputated, demonstrating the seriousness of the wound. The two gallant gentlemen did not meet again until their children, Elizabeth Adams and Wayland Young, fell in love.

Last year we went to Ostend for the unveiling of the beautifully restored *Vindictive* memorial. The King and Queen attended, and my youngest laid wreaths. It is intensely moving to see how the grandfathers', and all the other brave men's actions are remembered and honoured in Belgium, when they are either forgotten or misrepresented here.

Coleman wears his learning and diligent research lightly, while never underestimating the seriousness of his subject matter. I particularly liked this on the 'inaccuracy' of German reporting of the action: 'The vessel was so completely destroyed that no fragment remained, either in German or in British, records.'

I am sure I speak on behalf of all the descendants when I say that we are grateful that the record has been straightened up, in proper naval fashion, in such a conclusive and learned way.

Josephine Keyes, granddaughter of Admiral of the Fleet, Lord Keyes

Foreword
by Commander Ralph Wykes-Sneyd

As the country turns its attention to events of 100 years ago, the Great War, Ernest Coleman's comprehensive account and detailed analysis of the Zeebrugge Raid is a timely and well-researched contribution.

Since Trafalgar, 100 years before, Great Britain had enjoyed the security that accompanied supremacy of the high seas, the benefits of the greatest maritime trading empire the world had seen and the prosperity that went with it. The Royal Navy remained predominate but had become complacent, preoccupied with spit, polish and protocol to the detriment of fighting efficiency. In 1914 the nation regarded the Home Fleet as the bastion of its security but neither Britain nor Germany relished an Armageddon of their Grand Fleets for fear of the consequences of losing. Both were ill prepared to deal with the threat from a weapon system considered at the outbreak of war to be of marginal importance, at least in Britain; the submarine and the U-boat in particular.

In February 1915, following Germany's declaration of unrestricted U-boat warfare, the support lifelines to the empire and neutral America as well as to the Allied armies in France were critically threatened. Unrestricted warfare also raised the risk to shipping of neutral countries, and would inevitably garner support for the Allied cause. Could Britain be brought to submission through starvation before American muscle was brought to bear in Europe?

The Chiefs of Staff were without answer to the crippling and unsustainable losses from U-boat attrition of Atlantic shipping. In 1917 food reserves fell to less than six weeks: Britain was being brought inexorably to the brink of defeat. Desperate measures were needed to disrupt the U-boat menace, including denying U-boats their bases and extending their transit to the Atlantic. If their ports could not be engaged by land, the objective of the third battle of Ypres was the expulsion of the Germans from Flanders and the capture of Zeebrugge and Ostend, then they must be harassed from sea.

The Zeebrugge Raid was astonishingly audacious and meticulously planned with impressive examples of British inventiveness. My grandfather, Ralph Sneyd, who in *Thetis* led the blockships, was wholly convinced the operation was necessary. He, like the others, was a volunteer but all had been told that this was not an operation from which they could expect to return. It was a highly risky but feasible operation. Moreover it offered the Navy, who in the mind of the British public had had a comparatively quiet war, the opportunity to rekindle and demonstrate its traditional appetite for offensive action, in Nelsonian style.

As one is gripped by Coleman's telling of the story, one cannot be other than hugely impressed by the valour, devotion, dedication and outstanding competence of those who took part, and all underpinned by superb seamanship and exceptional courage in the most demanding of circumstances. The cost in lives was alarmingly high, even by standards of the time and inevitably consumed the thoughts of those who returned. We do appreciate, however, that the Great War and all that it involved changed our society forever, arguably, more so than any other event in our island's history. We are right to reflect today on our debt to the generation that included those who went to Zeebrugge on St George's Day in 1918.

Historians have argued, at times inconclusively it seems, about the success of the Zeebrugge Raid, and personal agendas have loomed large in many assessments.

Nevertheless, success there was; first, the objective to disrupt the U-boats and their bases was achieved and thereafter the U-boats were on the back foot for the remainder of the war. The effect would have been even greater, in consolidation, by bombing the German craft bottled up in the canals. Of course, by then, the Navy no longer controlled its own air power.

Second, the result was a huge boost to British and Allied morale; a rare and desperately needed victory when Germany's spring offensive on the Western Front threatened to collapse the Allied lines; war weariness was beginning to set in at home.

Third, the raid was inspirational and nurtured the Royal Navy's appetite for offensive action; Zeebrugge was the prelude to the raids to St Nazaire, Bordeaux, and the fjords of Norway enshrined in the notion 'They can because they think they can'.

Commander Ralph Wykes-Sneyd AFC RN, Grandson of Vice-Admiral Ralph Wykes-Sneyd, the leader of the Zeebrugge blockships.

Acknowledgements

This story could not have been told without the willing help of a number of people and organisations. In particular, I wish to thank the Royal Marines Museum archivist Matthew Little, and other members of the museum's staff who helped me get started. I am also grateful for the help provided by the Fleet Air Arm Museum and Chief Petty Officer Edmund Coleman who acted as my local 'runner'. All images are part of my collection unless otherwise credited.

I am deeply indebted for their help and encouragement to Josephine Keyes, the granddaughter of Admiral of the Fleet, the Lord Keyes; to the Dowager Lady Kennet, the daughter of Captain Bryan Adams and daughter-in-law of Commander Edward Hilton Young; to Commander Ralph Wykes-Sneyd AFC RN, the grandson of Vice Admiral R. Wykes-Sneyd; to Muffet Billyard-Leake and Richard Britten-Long Laird, both descendants of Captain E.W. Billyard-Leake, and especially to his daughter Mrs Mary Fox. I am equally grateful to the Reverend Sir John Alleyne for allowing me access to his father's personal account of the Ostend action.

I would also like to thank Commander Denis Maly of the Belgian Royal Naval Reserve, and Vice-President of the Port of Zeebrugge Technical Department, for his kind assistance and encouragement. Also Eric Stabbinck Van Parijs of the Zeebrugge Port Authority for the information given and tolerance shown during our detailed tour of the mole and the lighthouse extension.

The important assistance given by Mrs Susan Breeson, whose rigidly non-naval reading of the manuscript was of vital help, and also to Mike Ingham (formerly of the Merchant Navy), whose commonsense advice on matters of conflicting nature was of great value. Also to my wife, Joy, for turning a blind eye to an eternity of gardening and household-repair delays.

Finally, I am deeply grateful to those men of the Zeebrugge and Ostend raids who lost their lives, or suffered grievous injuries, in the cause of freedom. The price they paid must never be devalued.

Introduction

In August 1914 the majority of the people of Great Britain and her overseas empire firmly believed that the war against Germany and her Austrian allies would be 'over by Christmas'. The only difficulty would be working out the date that the Rhine would be crossed by the victorious British forces.

The people of Britain had good reason to think this way. The Royal Navy, with its tradition of victory, was, ton for ton, more than twice the size of the German Navy, and no one expected much of a threat from the Austrians at sea. Germany had a powerful army but much of her manpower would be directed towards the east, where the Russians, with their seemingly unlimited resources, presented a formidable foe. The British Army was smaller than the German, but professionally trained by men who had experienced combat in the Boer War and supported, not just by the French and the Belgians, but also by men from her overseas dominions and colonies. Moreover, the cause itself was good. Germany had flagrantly attacked Belgium in defiance of a treaty between the two countries, and Britain intended to honour her own part in that same treaty – to come to Belgium's aid if that country was attacked.

Over three-and-a-half years later, however, things looked decidedly different. Instead of being over by Christmas, the war had seen four Christmases come and go. With the high rate of attrition in the trenches along the Western Front, confidence in the outcome of the war had been severely dented. The threat of food shortages, failure on the field of battle, the high rate of casualties, and the rise of the 'Disenchantment School' (based upon the proposal that 'victory is not worth the price'), caused morale to fall away.

The year 1917 and the early months of 1918 had proved especially trying. The end of 1916 had seen the arrival of a new prime minister, David Lloyd George. He did not take long to wake up to the fact that the people would soon start to blame him for the casualties, particularly on the Western Front. An 'Easterner' by preference, he had convinced himself that the answer to the stalemate in the trenches was to send enough troops to the eastern Mediterranean to knock Turkey out of the war. This would allow Russia, and her resources, access to the Mediterranean and a supply route that would benefit both her and Great Britain.

For a time it seemed as if Lloyd George's eastern proposal held the answer to the war's outcome. Kut-al-Amara was recaptured in February 1917 and Baghdad two weeks later. Shortly after General Allanby began his Palestine offensive in October the same year, Jerusalem was back in Christian hands for the first time since the Crusades. Two months later, Jericho was added to the victories in the east.

The chief problem with Lloyd George's plan, however, was that the generals on the Western Front, in particular the British commander-in-chief, Field Marshal Sir Douglas Haig, did not agree, and refused to give up troops that could be sent to the east. Haig and his commanders, fully supported by the French, were firm in their belief that the decisive theatre of war was in France, and that any weakening of their strength risked a German breakthrough that could result in an Allied defeat. In addition, the sending of hundreds of thousands of troops and supplies through the Mediterranean could easily place their ships in the periscope crosswires of German submarines – the wide-ranging and effective 'U-boats'.

Lloyd George's response to his military leader's reluctance to fall in with his ideas was to cause shock and consternation throughout the army. As the bulk of the fighting was taking place on French soil, it seemed entirely reasonable to allow the French military leadership to control the overall strategy. In effect this meant that the British Army would, whenever possible, act in a coordinated manner with the French yet, at the same time, retain its independence. Lloyd George, however, handed over complete control of the British Army to the French.

It took considerable, desperate, renegotiating for the British military leadership to re-establish its relationship to the French high command. Eventually it was agreed that the British Army would come under the control of the French commander-in-chief, General Nivelle, solely for the duration of his 1917 spring offensive. Lloyd George, nevertheless, had managed to poison his relations with his own military leaders for the remainder of the war – an unexpected bonus for the enemy.

In the outcome, however, Nivelle's plans turned into disaster. Only on the British section of the front with the Canadians at Vimy Ridge and the British themselves at Arras was any progress made. The French, buoyed up with great expectations, had achieved little beyond a few gains where the enemy had retreated to pre-prepared positions and from where they refused to be moved. The effect of this failure was such that mutinies broke out in the French Army.

More bad news came from the Italian front. The Italian Army had managed to hold its own against the Austrians but had failed to produce any decisive actions. The Germans, alarmed at the Austrians' failure to advance against the Italians, decided to send reinforcements and, in late October 1917, led an attack centred around the town of Caporetto. Unused to such ferocity, the Italians fell back with such rapidity that, within a few days, they had lost almost a third of a million men – mainly as prisoners – along with most of their artillery, and had retreated to within 20 miles of Venice. The Austro-German army, however, fell victim to its own success. So fast, and so far, had been the retreat, that the advancing forces stretched their supply lines to breaking point. They had no choice but to halt and consolidate their gains. This, in turn, allowed time for the arrival of six French and five British divisions – troops who were desperately needed in France.

There had seemed to be at least one bright hope in the gloom of events in 1917. Woodrow Wilson, the president of the United States of America, was a pacifist by nature and a neutral by inclination, but he was shaken to the core when, thanks to British naval intelligence carefully brought to his attention, he learned that the Germans were encouraging the Mexicans across his southern border to attack the United States. In return for keeping the Americans out of the European war, the Germans offered the Mexicans military and financial aid that would lead to the return of New Mexico, Arizona, and Texas. There had been considerable American loss of life at sea due to submarine attacks and in March 1917, another five US ships were sunk as a result of the German policy of unrestricted submarine warfare. These losses, along with the attempt to coerce Mexico into an attack on the US, persuaded President Wilson to declare war on Germany despite a strong opposition from German and Irish groups, and a Chief of Naval Operations who declared that he 'would as soon fight the British as the Germans'.

The Germans themselves were of the opinion that the United States was wholly unprepared for war and would take so long to get involved that Germany could secure a victory before the potential might of America could be brought to bear. By the end of 1917 and the beginning of 1918, it seemed as if the Germans were to be proved right.

In order to be seen as strictly neutral 'in thought and deed', Wilson had kept the US Army at peacetime levels with no preparation for war. Even if he doubled its size by adding the National Guard, the combined force would have been outnumbered twenty to one by the German Army. Consequently, even a year after its entry into the war, and despite great promise shown in minor engagements, the USA had still not taken a decisive part in the fighting.

As if to balance the entry of the USA into the war, the early months of 1917 saw dramatic changes on the Eastern Front. The Russian Army, after few victories and many defeats, starved of food and equipment, and with men deserting in their hundreds of thousands, saw its morale crumble to the point of total ineffectiveness. In the capital, Petrograd, the local garrison was ordered to confront strikers and rioters, but the soldiers refused their orders and turned on their officers. The Tsar abdicated and a constitutional government was formed, eventually coming under the leadership of a young socialist lawyer, Alexander Kerensky.

Kerensky, in an effort to impress his western allies, mounted an assault upon the Austrians and gained some early successes, but the Germans, rallying to the Austrians' assistance, drove the Russians back. In less than three weeks, the Russian Army was in headlong retreat. At this, the Germans pressed home their attack, causing the Russian Army to disintegrate, followed by the collapse of the Kerensky government. The Bolsheviks, under Vladimir Lenin, then took over, governing through local workers' councils or 'Soviets'.

In late December 1917 the Bolsheviks agreed an armistice with the Germans and the other Central Powers but, through a series of disagreements among the Bolsheviks themselves, the Germans ignored the armistice and, in February the following year, captured Belarus, Ukraine, and the Baltic States. The Bolsheviks responded by signing the Brest-Litovsk Treaty on 3 March. The Russians were now out of the war, freeing a huge amount of manpower and equipment to be transferred to the Western Front.

When the Canadians and the British made their gains during the ill-fated Nivelle offensive in the spring of 1917, they had done so at the cost of almost 159,000 casualties. Inevitably, Lloyd George blamed Haig for the losses, but did nothing to stop the field marshal when he decided that he needed to attack the Germans in strength in order to take the pressure off the weakened French. In addition to aiding their ally, there was another possibility open to the British. If the front line could be pushed back far enough, the Channel ports of Ostend and Zeebrugge could be taken. These important outlets to the sea could not only be used as a means of supplying the army as it advanced but, once taken, would put a stop to their use by enemy submarines.

The battle began well when a number of mines were exploded beneath the German defences before Messines Ridge. The position was taken at a relatively small cost, but then the momentum was lost when Haig decided on a change of command, giving the Germans time to strengthen their positions. After only minor gains the British then faced almost a month of continuous rain, which, when combined with the heaviest artillery fire known since the beginning of the war, turned the ground over which they fought into an impassable quagmire. The construction of trenches and dugouts was impossible and the troops could do no more than attack or defend water-filled shell craters in a sea of mud.

Eventually, in November, an insignificant ridge just to the north of Passchendaele proved to be the limit of the advance. Despite enormous courage, endurance, and determination, barely a dozen miles had been gained. The pressure had been taken off the French but the Belgian ports still remained in German hands – and Lloyd George refused to allow fresh troops to be sent to Haig to replace the losses incurred in the battle.

By March 1918 the German general, Erich Ludendorff, had at his disposal 750,000 men and the largest assembly of heavy artillery ever seen on the

Western Front, which he was about to use against 300,000 British troops along a 50-mile front stretching from Arras to St Quentin. The blow fell on 21 March and the British, completely overwhelmed, were sent reeling back. In just over two weeks the Germans had advanced an astonishing 40 miles before their leading troops, by now well beyond the range of their much more slowly moving artillery, halted to consolidate their gains. Ludendorff then switched his attack to the south of Ypres, where the line had been left in the care of two poorly trained and unenthusiastic Portuguese divisions. Within three days all the ground captured at Messines and Passchendaele had been lost and Haig was forced to issue a desperate order to his troops: 'There is no other course open to us but to fight it out. Every position must be held to the last man: there must be no retirement. With our backs to the wall and believing in the justice of our cause each one of us must fight on to the end.'

Such, then, was the situation on the Western Front, and the news of the retreat was not long in reaching the British public – a people already worn down by recent waves of bad news. But it was not the worst that they heard.

The Royal Navy had not had a good war. In just over a century since Nelson and Trafalgar, British seamen had remained virtually unchallenged throughout the world. Even the occasional defeats at the hands of the Americans during the war of 1812 proved to have been American duplicity over the question of their ships' firepower. Once this had been realised, the American ships were either defeated or kept in harbour. The Royal Navy had broken the back of the slave trade, swept Chinese pirates from the sea, led exploration at the Poles, across Africa, and through the Middle East. It had fought Queen Victoria's wars and underpinned the empire. However, since August 1914 the demand 'What is the Navy doing?' was frequently heard both in the press and on the street:

What is the British Navy doing?
We have the right to ask,
In this mighty war that's being waged,
Do they fulfil their task?
Now tell me pray! What have they done?
Why don't they show some fight?
And fetch the German warships out
From Heligoland Bight?

The Navy, by early 1918 already under its fifth First Sea Lord since the beginning of the war, was apparently demonstrating that it was urgently in need of training in everything from operational coordination to basic gunnery. In the very first action against the enemy, the Battle of Heligoland Bight on 28 August 1914, the Admiralty agreed the plan – and then changed it without telling some of the senior officers involved. This very nearly resulted in the British ships opening fire on each other. Three weeks later, three British cruisers were off the Dutch coast when one of them was torpedoed by the German submarine *U9*. The captain of the submarine could hardly believe his eyes as the remaining two cruisers closed with the sinking ship to take off survivors. Within a very short time, all three cruisers were at the bottom of the sea, and the German people had received a very cheap boost to their morale.

In November of the same year, off the Chilean port of Coronel, a British squadron was outmanoeuvred by German ships to the extent that they were highlighted against a setting sun. Out of the four British ships, only one escaped being sunk. In the retaliatory battle off the Falkland Islands, which followed five weeks later, two British battle-cruisers had to fire 1,234 12in shells in order to sink two German armoured cruisers. In January 1915, at the Battle of the Dogger Bank, the flagship ordered each of the escorting battle-cruisers to open fire on a particular enemy ship. One of the battle-cruiser captains made the mistake of firing on the same ship as the flagship, leaving his actual target unmolested and free to attack the admiral. As if such an action was not bad enough, the battle-cruiser captain then assumed that the fall of shell from the flagship was his own and adjusted his range and direction accordingly – causing no damage to the enemy whatsoever.

There were other examples but none managed to combine blunders with brilliant seamanship, bad luck and good fortune in quite the same way as happened at the Battle of Jutland. In May 1916 the Admiralty ordered Admiral Sir John Jellicoe, the commander-in-chief of the Grand Fleet, out to sea. As he left Scapa Flow in the Orkney Islands, the Battle-Cruiser Fleet, under the command of Vice Admiral Sir David Beatty, in company with four battleships, sailed from Rosyth.

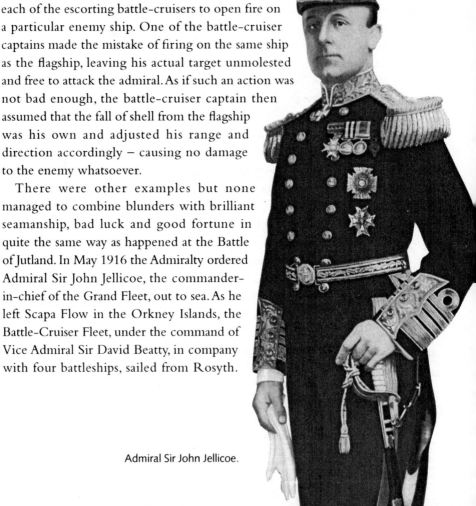

Admiral Sir John Jellicoe.

The battle-cruisers were to join Jellicoe's battleships some 90 miles west of the entrance to the Skagerrak – the strait running between Norway and Denmark. It was hoped that the appearance of the Grand Fleet in those waters would tempt the German High Seas Fleet out of harbour. What neither Jellicoe nor Beatty knew was that the High Seas Fleet was already out of its anchorage at Jade Bay (to the south of Wilhelmshaven) with the original intention of shelling the British coast. However, bad weather caused the plan to be cancelled and, instead, the Germans decided to visit the entrance to the Skagerrak in the hope of enticing the Grand Fleet out of Scapa Flow.

Having reached the assembly point, Beatty turned to the north in an attempt to locate Jellicoe, some 70 miles in that direction. As he did so, two of his light cruisers, acting with destroyers as a screen to the battle-cruisers, investigated smoke on the horizon. They discovered a number of German destroyers and opened fire in the belief that they were cruisers. In doing so, they alerted the German battle-cruisers long before there was any hope of Beatty joining up with Jellicoe. When he received news of the enemy, Beatty ordered his ships to turn south-east in an attempt to get between the Germans and the coast. The message failed to reach his battleships, which continued to sail northwards. Eventually the two opposing battle-cruiser squadrons met and opened fire. After seventeen minutes the British *Indefatigable* exploded, followed twenty minutes later by the *Queen Mary,* prompting Beatty's remark that 'there seems to be something wrong with our bloody ships today!' This was followed by an order to close with the enemy. The Germans, however, were frightened off by a torpedo attack and broke off the engagement only to meet up with the German battleships. Now it was Beatty's time to head northwards again in the hope that the enemy would follow him into the range of Jellicoe's guns, still some 50 miles away.

At last, having fended off the encroaching German battle-cruisers, Beatty found Jellicoe and placed himself at the front of the approaching battleships. As he did so, he ordered his four battleships to position themselves at the rear of Jellicoe's ships. In making her turn, the battleship *Warspite's* rudder jammed causing her to continuously circle at 25 knots.

On encountering the German fleet, Jellicoe demonstrated his skills by forming his ships into line of battle and twice crossing the enemy's 'T', thus being able to bring all his guns to bear on the foremost enemy ship, which could only reply with her forward guns. Nevertheless, the battle-cruiser *Invincible* was sunk in the general action. Eventually, under the cover of smokescreens, the German battle line turned away as their destroyers launched thirty-one torpedoes at the British fleet. Astonishingly, Jellicoe ordered his battleships to turn away from the attack. All the torpedoes missed their targets and passed harmlessly between the British ships. But had Jellicoe turned *towards* the torpedoes, there was every chance that the exact same result would have happened, and his ships could have pressed on immediately after the enemy. Instead, by the time he turned his ships around, the German fleet was nowhere to be seen.

With no clue as to the enemy's whereabouts, Jellicoe headed southwards with the battle-cruisers ahead of him and a force of cruisers and destroyers to his rear. At about midnight, these rearmost ships found themselves surrounded by a mass of large ships heading eastwards. Unsure of what was happening, they held their fire until they were illuminated by searchlights and hit by the fire of heavy guns. The German fleet was passing through the rearguard, about 6 miles astern of Jellicoe. He continued to the south in the belief that the searchlights and gunfire was nothing more than an isolated engagement between light forces. As it was, the Germans paid for their rash charge through the British lines when two torpedoes hit the battleship *Pommern*. She promptly exploded and sank – the only battleship casualty of the battle. Revenge came with the arrival of the armoured cruiser HMS *Black Prince*, whose captain mistook the Germans for the British fleet – and was blown out of the water for his mistake.

At 2.30 a.m., Jellicoe drew his fleet around him and turned northwards in the hope that the morning light would reveal the German fleet. But it was too late. An Admiralty signal told him that the enemy had almost reached the safety of Jade Bay. The battle was over.

The British battle casualties amounted to 6,097 killed and 510 wounded. The Germans had 2,551 killed with 507 wounded. Jellicoe's fleet lost three battle-cruisers, three cruisers, and eight destroyers. The enemy lost one battle-cruiser, one old battleship, four cruisers, and five destroyers.

But mere numbers do not give the true impression of the battle's outcome. The day following the engagement, Jellicoe was able to signal the Admiralty that the British fleet was ready to sail at four hours' notice. It took another six weeks before the Germans could send a similar signal, and fourteen months were to pass before the High Seas Fleet was to leave harbour. In September 1917 it steamed into the Baltic to aid the army in its operations against Russia, whilst a squadron of cruisers attacked a British convoy in the North Sea. In the Baltic operations, three battleships were damaged by mines. On its return, the High Seas Fleet was never to emerge again, except to surrender. Germany's naval war was otherwise to be left to her light forces and U-boats.

In February 1915 Germany had declared a blockade of British waters, which, due to the fear of losing the High Seas Fleet, would be carried out mainly by submarines. It was a reasonable decision but poorly executed. Less than a month after the blockade was imposed, an American tanker was torpedoed. In early May the Cunard liner *Lusitania* was sunk with a large loss of life, including several Americans. Later in the month the *Nebraskan* was torpedoed without warning. More American lives were lost when the British *Arabic* was sunk in August, followed by the US liner *Hesperian*. Repeated and growing threats from the United States were met by German complaints that allied merchantmen were being armed against submarines, that the *Lusitania* had been carrying munitions (thus making her a legitimate target), and that British 'Q' ships (naval-manned armed vessels disguised as merchantmen) were hunting the U-boats. The complaints failed to impress the US authorities and the Germans issued orders limiting the activities of their submarines. In truth, however, whilst the American complaints played a part in the German change of plan, the realities were that the submarine attacks were simply not working. In effect, the numbers of U-boats available were not enough. When the campaign began, only twenty-one submarines were available and, frequently, no more than four were on patrol at the same time. In March 1915 around 5,000 merchant ships left and entered British ports, yet only one out of every 238 ships came under attack.

By the beginning of 1917, the submarine arm of the German Navy had been considerably strengthened and, at the end of January, 120 U-boats were available. German strategic thinking had also changed. With a predicted loss of 600,000 tons of shipping per month, combined with the results of a poor harvest in 1916, the British could be starved into submission within five months. Even if the United States did enter the war, it could not be ready within that time, and with the loss of Great Britain and, inevitably, France, the Americans would be unlikely to continue with the prosecution of a war that had so little advantage to themselves. Accordingly, Germany declared a policy of unrestricted submarine warfare that began on 1 February 1917.

The results shocked the allies, most especially the British. In the first complete month of the new phase of unrestricted submarine warfare, over 520,000 tons of shipping was sunk. In March the figure rose to over 560,000 tons, and in April, with the Germans becoming ever more skilful in handling their U-boats, an unimagined 860,334 tons were sent to the bottom. Consternation raged throughout the government and the Admiralty. An American admiral asked Jellicoe – now the First Sea Lord – 'Is there no solution to the problem?' The reply, especially to an admiral who was just about to send thousands of his countrymen across the Atlantic Ocean, was appalling – 'Absolutely none that we can see now.'

But there was a solution, an answer that had already been in operation since at least October 1914 when troops from Canada were successfully escorted from the St Laurence to Plymouth (despite the Canadian press publishing the time of sailing). In 1916, coal being transported through the North Sea, and traffic between Britain and Holland had made tempting targets for U-boats and surface vessels based on the German and Belgian coasts. To protect this shipping, destroyers had been supplied to act as escorts, their presence proving a deterrent to both above- and below-water threats. Further evidence for convoying as a means of reducing the U-boat threat came after colliers taking coal across to France in convoy revealed that their losses to submarines amounted to less than 0.2 per cent. This compared to 25 per cent amongst the remainder of Britain's seaborne merchant traffic. Finally, the Royal Navy's own fleets travelled in convoys as a means of mutual protection, as did the ships of the Royal Naval Transport Service. However, despite such evidence, the Admiralty argued that to concentrate a large number of ships in one place would merely provide an excellent target for the U-boats, the ships would be tied to the speed of the slowest vessel, and that merchant ships were notoriously bad at station keeping. Furthermore, not only were ports and harbours unprepared for the sudden arrival of a large fleet of merchant ships, the Royal Navy would have to take destroyers and other escorts away from other duties.

The key to cracking the problem came in the form of a major of the Royal Marine Artillery. Maurice Hankey, after spending some time with Naval Intelligence, had been appointed as secretary to the cabinet by Lloyd George. He was also secretary to the Imperial War Cabinet. Well-connected, and with access to the cabinet papers, Hankey became convinced of the need for convoying. In a memorandum entitled 'Some suggestions for Anti-submarine Warfare' he argued that the introduction of convoys would mean that 'The enemy submarines, instead of attacking a defenceless prey, will know that a fight is inevitable in which he may be worsted.' Furthermore, 'The adoption of the convoy system would appear to offer great opportunities for mutual support by the merchant vessels themselves, apart from the defence provided by their escorts.' His arguments persuaded Lloyd George to put pressure on the Admiralty (later claiming that the whole idea was his).

A trial ocean-going convoy was tried between Gibraltar and Britain with all the ships arriving safely. Then Atlantic crossings were made with the same, or very similar, results. And the overall results were startling. From the 25 per cent losses in April, the end of May saw losses of 0.24 per cent. During the following months the total losses rose and fell but never again were the huge losses of the early part of 1917 repeated. Nevertheless, the U-boats continued to sink ships and the national food stocks continued to dwindle. Shop windows reminded their customers that 'England Expects Economies', whilst posters demanded 'Save the Wheat and Help the Fleet – Eat Less Bread'. Most pessimistic of all was Jellicoe. During a meeting of the Imperial War Cabinet in June 1917 he stunned the congregation into silence when, on hearing Haig's plans for his Flanders offensive, the admiral drew attention to the U-boat losses and said 'There is no good discussing plans for next spring – we cannot go on.'

By April 1918 the message had reached the people. Malnutrition had been reported amongst the poorer sections of society. Sugar had been rationed since December 1917. In February, meat and butter were also rationed. When added to the sombre tales of the German advances on the Western Front the cries went up yet again 'What is the Navy doing?' More to the point – what was the Navy doing about the U-boats? The Grand Fleet was still at anchor at Scapa Flow, and the U-boats were still sinking supply ships. Morale throughout the country was at a dangerously low ebb, and there was no hope on the horizon.

But someone was doing something. Something intended to jolt the people out of their despondency – something that would rock the Germans and show the allies that Great Britain could produce men from the same mould as Nelson, Hood, Rodney, Howe, and other great names from the Royal Navy's past.

All that was needed was to get the right men, in the right place, at the right time.

1

The Problem

Vice Admiral Sir Reginald Bacon, the son of a clergyman, may be said to have had an interesting, even successful, career – until, that is, 1909. Before that time he had shown himself to be a willing, competent, officer with an absorbing interest in engineering. As a commander serving in HMS *Theseus* during the 1897 punitive expedition against the West African state of Benin, he served as the expedition's intelligence officer. Ordered ashore on one occasion with a group

Vice Admiral Sir Reginald Bacon.

of his ship's seamen and marines and a party of Hausa natives, he earned himself a Distinguished Service Order by burning down a village – an event he later recorded as resulting 'in the capture of one parrot'.

Bacon's next appointment was to the Mediterranean Fleet, where he became a member of the 'Fishpool', a collection of promising officers that clustered around the station's commander-in-chief, Vice Admiral Sir John Fisher. The admiral encouraged these officers to write to him personally with any concerns, or ideas, they may have had regarding the personalities and activities with which they were involved. This caused outrage amongst senior officers who felt they were being spied upon by Fisher's acolytes. The admiral, however, ignored their indignation and Bacon continued to write to him for several years – eventually to his own cost.

Thanks in part to Fisher's influence but, at the same time, in recognition of Bacon's undoubted abilities, he was promoted captain and appointed as the first 'inspector of submarines'. It was an appointment seemingly made for his talents, and he was not long in making his mark on the fledgling Submarine Service. Unhappy with the American-designed 'Holland' boats with their inefficient periscopes and their poor sea-keeping design, he led teams that produced an effective 'attack' periscope and introduced the 'conning tower' into the design of the new 'A' boats. He went a step too far in 1902, however, when he attempted to give names to the submarines under his command. His suggestion of names such as *Ichthyosaurus*, *Pistosaurus*, *Nothosaurus* and *Plesiosaurus* was considered by the senior naval lord as 'rather formidable' (with which the First Lord concurred in a short note – 'I agree!').

When Fisher was appointed to the Admiralty as Senior Naval Lord (a title he promptly changed to the earlier style of 'First Sea Lord'), he took Bacon as his 'naval assistant' and also made him a member of his Committee on Designs. The committee oversaw the design and build of the new, all-big-gun battleship HMS *Dreadnaught*. Almost inevitably, the 43-year-old Bacon was appointed as her first captain, taking her into the Mediterranean for trials and 'work up'. There he observed at first hand the problems of design by committee. The officer's accommodation had – against all tradition – been placed forward in the ship, where they suffered the noise and vibration of the auxiliary machinery. Far worse was the positioning of the foremast behind the forward funnel. This meant that the men stationed in the foretop, used for spotting the fall of shells on and around a target, felt the full blast of the exhaust gases from the funnel.

Bacon also used his time on the Mediterranean Station to keep up his correspondence with Fisher, especially concerning the station's commander-in-chief, Vice Admiral Lord Charles Beresford – Fisher's greatest critic.

In 1907 Fisher had Bacon back at the Admiralty as 'director of naval ordnance and torpedoes' and, in July 1909, he was promoted to rear admiral. Almost immediately afterward, Fisher sent copies of the letters he had received from Bacon to other senior naval officers. Inevitably the contents became public knowledge. His criticisms of his superiors were of such magnitude that even Fisher could not protect him – Bacon had no other option but to resign.

At the same time as Bacon's resignation in November, the managing director of the Coventry Ordnance Works, a Mr H.H. Mulliner, who had frequent disagreements with the director of naval ordnance and torpedoes, and was also noted for supplying information to the parliamentary opposition parties, also resigned. This happy coincidence, which left an important vacancy at Coventry, was met by Rear Admiral Bacon's application for the post – one that was happily accepted. Under his management – and through contacts at the Admiralty and War Office – the Coventry works were soon supplying the Royal Navy with 5.5in guns and the army with 9.2in howitzers. The particular success of the latter weapon led (as a private enterprise of the Coventry works) to the design of a huge, 15in howitzer intended for the army. The first lord of the Admiralty, Winston Churchill, however, decided that the Royal Marine Artillery should have the new weapon and created the Royal Marine Howitzer Brigade.

Each of the new howitzers weighed just under 11 tons, and required a team of sixty men and three giant steam tractors to move them. In order to see that they were properly deployed, Bacon resigned as the managing director and took a temporary commission in the Royal Marine Artillery as a colonel. The guns themselves were not a spectacular success. Using 1,400lb shells, their range was shorter than expected and Churchill, busy with the failed naval attack on the Dardanelles and the approaching landings at Gallipoli, lost his enthusiasm and handed the howitzers over to the army (which considered them to be 'a waste of time'). This, in turn, left an unemployed rear admiral available for appointment.

Even before the outbreak of the war, it had been recognised that the greatest coastal threat Great Britain would face would be on the east coast. Accordingly, destroyer 'patrol flotillas', under the command of Rear Admiral George Ballard ('Admiral of Patrols'), were based at Dover, on the Humber, the Tyne, and the Forth. Local Defence Flotillas would protect the naval bases along the south coast, and the Scottish coast north of the Forth was protected by the Grand Fleet. A combined flotilla was based at Harwich, made up of two destroyer flotillas and a unit of light cruisers under the command of Commodore Reginald Tyrwhitt ('Commodore T'), and a flotilla of submarines under Commodore Roger Keyes ('Commodore S'). In addition, a Royal Naval Reserve Trawler Division was raised from fishermen and trained as an auxiliary minesweeping service. The trawlers were grouped into 'Trawler Stations' and deployed along the coast along with commandeered yachts and the vessels of the Motor-boat Reserve.

The situation facing the east coast patrols was made considerably worse when the right flank of the German Army pushed its way south, down the Belgian coast, capturing the ports of Zeebrugge and Ostend before being halted just north of Nieuport. The Royal Navy wanted to destroy the facilities at the Belgian ports before they were evacuated. Zeebrugge, in particular, with its canal link to the docks at Bruges, had great potential as a destroyer and submarine base. The army, on the other hand, confident that it would soon drive the Germans back, wanted to keep the ports as undamaged as possible in case they were needed to land troops to assist in the advance. In this, the army had the germ of an idea that could have altered the entire course of the war. Instead of the British Expeditionary Force going to the aid of the French, a decision that resulted in the 'race to the sea' and the Belgian ports ending up in German hands, it would have been better to have used those ports to land the British Army in force on the Belgian coast. If that had been done, the Germans would have found themselves with their enemy looking over their right shoulder and bearing down on an extended, and vulnerable, flank. Supported in the early stages by naval firepower, the British Army might well have knocked the German advance sideways.

However, in response, to the changing circumstances on the Belgian coast, it was decided to make the Dover Patrol a command of its own with its first commander being Rear Admiral the Honourable Horace Hood, a great-great-grandson of Admiral Samuel Hood who had gained fame in his battles against the French in the late eighteenth century.

The Dover Patrol's main tasks were to ensure a safe passage across the Straits of Dover for the troops on their way to, and returning from, France; to prevent enemy submarines from using the Channel as a passage to areas where they could attack shipping, and shelling enemy targets ashore. Hood's forces consisted of four light cruisers, twenty-four destroyers, thirteen 'B'- and 'C'-class submarines, many trawlers and other auxiliary patrol vessels, and the Downs Boarding Flotilla (to prevent breaches in the sea blockade against Germany). Three monitors – shallow draught vessels armed with three 6in guns and two 4.7in howitzers – were commandeered after they had arrived to take part in a cancelled operation. In addition, a number of French destroyers were available at Dunkirk along with aeroplanes of the Royal Naval Air Service.

It was hoped that success would be obtained by bombarding the enemy as he tried to make his way down the Belgian coast towards the French ports. This caused the Germans problems whilst they were on the march but, as they established fixed-gun positions, Hood's ships came up against the old naval problem – the near impossibility of successfully attacking fortifications from the sea.

The Germans were not long in coming to the conclusion that sending their U-boats through the Straits of Dover towards the Western Approaches was a much better arrangement than the alternative of submarines leaving Germany and making their way the extra 300 miles around the north of Scotland. At first, Hood could offer little more defence against the U-boats than drifters towing their drift-nets in the hope of entangling an enemy submarine. Failing that, it was hoped that the U-boats would be caught on the surface and be attacked by gunfire or by ramming. A possible answer arrived, however, in the shape of 'indicator nets'. Made of steel wire and held afloat by buoys, the presence of a U-boat trapped in the nets was given away by the action of the buoys. By April 1915 over 20 miles of netting had been strung across the Straits of Dover with a 'gate' off Folkestone, and another off Cap Gris Nez. On 4 March the nets claimed their first victim when *U8* was trapped and lost. The Germans were stunned by this turn of events and ordered their U-boat captains to stop using the Channel route.

However, the Admiralty was not convinced, and over the succeeding weeks, with rising losses to submarines, came to the view that Hood's measures against the U-boats were proving ineffective. Accordingly, in April 1915, he was pushed aside and sent to command a squadron of light cruisers off the coast of Ireland. Some time later the Admiralty, in the belief that they had made a mistake, sent Hood to join the Grand Fleet. In late May 1916 he was flying his flag in HMS *Invincible* as part of Beatty's battle-cruiser squadron, when a German shell penetrated 'Q' gun turret and exploded in the magazine, blowing the ship apart. Hood did not survive the explosion.

At the time when Hood left the Dover Patrol, Fisher was still First Sea Lord, but on the verge of resigning over his differences with Churchill concerning the Gallipoli landings. Nevertheless, he took the opportunity to recommend that the First Lord should offer the command of the Dover Patrol to Rear Admiral Bacon – an offer that was immediately accepted.

In some ways, Bacon seemed a perfect choice: his love of engineering, his feeling for science and his grasp of detail made him one of a growing band of senior naval officers who were rejecting tradition and the study of history as the way forward. Instead, they formed the 'materiel school', embracing design and technology at the expense of strategy and tactics.

Fisher was at the forefront of such thinking. He oversaw the introduction of the 'Dreadnaught' battleships, and the battle-cruisers, ignoring the danger that, by rendering all previous ships out-of-date at a stroke, he was allowing potential enemies to catch up with the British fleet. He introduced mechanical training for ratings at shore establishments, and championed the cause of fuel oil over coal, and the development of the submarine. He supported Henry Jackson, the Royal Navy's pioneer in the use of wireless communications, and Sir Percy Scott, who developed gunnery control and instruction, and who invented the loading tray, which enabled a gun to be loaded much more quickly. Arthur Wilson, a Victoria Cross winner, who had taken over from Fisher as First Sea Lord in 1909, invented the double-barrelled torpedo tube, and the 'net-mine'. He also introduced a modification to the searchlight, which allowed it to be used as a daylight signalling lamp. Jellicoe opposed the introduction of convoying merchantmen on the grounds that the answer must surely lie in a scientific advance to deal with the U-boats. All were very poor at delegation, preferring to keep even the smallest detail within their immediate control.

Bacon was so keen to advance the scientific side of his command that he appointed a New Zealand physicist, Lieutenant Eric Hercus, to his staff as the navy's first ever Scientific Flag-Lieutenant. The admiral's own engineering output in response to the needs of the war was phenomenal. He personally led each project whatever the scale, and the range of designs he produced can be illustrated by the two extremes.

With gunnery ranges of 20,000 yards, accurate shore bombardment proved very difficult to achieve as the fall of the shells could not be 'spotted'. Consequently, adjustments could not be made to improve the accuracy. The only solution that seemed to come close to addressing the problem was to anchor a ship between the firing vessel and the coast. This vessel would be on a known bearing from the target and burning a bright searchlight. The firing ship would take a bearing on the searchlight, transfer the bearing to the shore side and add the distance to the target in calculating the angle needed for accurate shooting. The system rarely worked to the degree where it could have been considered effective. Several attempts to use seaplanes as spotters also failed.

Bacon looked at the problem and, in a very short time, came up with the answer. Accurate spotting depended upon two positions, a suitable distance apart, measuring the angles to the target and to the fall of shot. Consequently, he designed two 44ft-tall 'portable islands' constructed out of railway lines ('of course, everyone laughed'). These structures could be taken close to the shore and lowered to the seabed. Once secured, a small platform at the top could be filled with two ranging instruments, two observing officers, and two signallers sending bearings back to the firing ship using oxyacetylene-powered signal lamps.

The islands were first used in an attack on Zeebrugge harbour. Three 12in gun monitors, *Sir John Moore, Lord Clive,* and *Prince Rupert*, protected from submarine attack by 16 miles of netting laid by drifters, took up their positions. The islands were taken closer to the shore by two coalyard vessels especially taken up for the purpose. The assault proved to be only a partial success as two of the monitors suffered defects that prevented their continuing to fire. Nevertheless, Bacon claimed that 'many of the enemy's works suffered considerably, two or more of their vessels were sunk, and they suffered severe casualties to personnel'. To the great disappointment of all, no German vessels came out to challenge the attackers.

The next trial for the portable islands came a few days later off Ostend. They were dropped in position, but a delay in firing caused a rising tide to cover them. When an attempt to pick them up was made, the lifting strops could not be

reached as they were still under water. They had to be abandoned with the result
that 'this method of observation of fire was given away to the enemy'.

In 1916 Bacon gave himself a challenge that might have daunted a lesser
man. He was concerned that the Germans might sue for peace whilst the coast
of Belgium remained in their hands. This carried with it the possibility that
negotiations might end the war leaving that coast still in German possession.
Such a situation would leave Great Britain at the mercy of the Germans in any
subsequent war. Having discussed the project with the First Sea Lord, Sir Henry
Jackson (who had taken over from Fisher), and confirmed matters with Jackson's
successor (Jellicoe), Bacon began work on his scheme. As he did so, he contacted
the military and arranged to see Field Marshal Haig. The army's commander-in-
chief was interested, but pointed out that that he would need to reach Roulers
(Roeselare) – some 20 miles south-east of Nieuport – and Thourout (Torhout),
8 or 9 miles further to the north, before any landing would be worthwhile.
Encouraged by Haig's modest enthusiasm, Bacon stepped up the planning.

For the idea to work, the army would need to be able to land an entire division
of troops (almost 14,000 soldiers), complete with their stores and transport, which
included three of the newly developed tanks. In addition, all the troops had to be
ashore within twenty minutes. The first landing at Gallipoli had been done in
open boats, resulting in very high casualties. The later, unopposed, landings at
Suvla Bay had used 'beetle' landing craft, which could never land a complete
division along with all their equipment within twenty minutes.

Bacon's answer was to build three enormous pontoons, each 550ft long, 30ft
wide and displacing 2,500 tons. As they were intended to be run ashore, the
draught at the stern needed to be 9ft, whilst at the bow, 18in was required. To
guard against problems likely to be encountered should a pontoon bow run
aground on a ridge just off the shore, a stout wooden 'raft' that could take the
weight of a tank was secured to the bow. With solid baulks of wood lowered
to the seabed to act as supports, the raft would enable the troops and all their
equipment to bridge any hollow on the bottom beyond the ridge.

Furthermore, as the pontoons had to be landed at high tide, an elderly 'C'-class
submarine, under the command of Lieutenant Wardell Yerburgh, was sent to lie on
the bottom off Nieuport for twenty-four hours, recording the tidal movements on
the depth gauge. The crew had to be reduced for the operation as the atmosphere
in the boat would tend to get stuffy. At the same time, Royal Naval Air Service
(RNAS) aircraft photographed the beaches to the east of Nieuport to record the
limits of high and low tides. In a rare delegation of detail, Lieutenant Hercus was
given the job of collating the tidal information.

In order to get each pontoon on to the beach, Bacon employed a pair of 12in
monitors. The shallow-draught vessels were secured alongside each other with
the pontoon's stern attached by chains between the monitors' bows. The two

ships would then proceed at 6 knots with the pontoon jutting out far ahead of them. On arrival at the intended target beach, the monitors would release their pontoon and secure its stern to the seabed by anchors. As this was being done, the soldiers would descend from the monitor's forecastles by ramps and ladders, ready to charge ashore.

The ships involved in the operation, along with their pontoons, were hidden from prying eyes in the Swin Channel at the entrance to the Thames. Fearing that 'a drink or two in the more jovial hours of the evening' might cause tongues to wag, Bacon cancelled all leave for the ships' companies. This inconvenience, however, was of little consequence when compared to the fact that 'You may congratulate yourselves … on the knowledge that your temporary seclusion is due to the privilege of taking part in operations that will go on to bring the war to a successful conclusion, and moreover, that will never be forgotten so long as the memory of the war exists.'

Unfortunately, despite showing immense courage against the enemy and the mud, the Third Battle of Ypres never got beyond Passchendaele Ridge and Bacon's plan to land on the Belgian coast was soon forgotten.

There was, nevertheless, still plenty of activities to keep all in the Dover Patrol busy. One of the key reasons for the Patrol's existence was the detection and destruction of U-boats.

Specific anti-submarine weaponry had become more sophisticated during the war but remained rudimentary. The earliest attempt to combat the U-boats had come in the shape of the 'modified sweep' fitted to some destroyers. This consisted of a 200ft-long loop of electric cable, the loop being held open by having one side kept afloat by wooden floats, the other pulled deep into the water by a flat, wooden, kite. It could only be deployed after a U-boat was seen on the surface, could only be operated at less than 10 knots, and took at least twenty minutes to run out. If the submarine was snagged, an electric charge, operated by hand from within the ship, fired explosive devices. During its operation life, it was credited with sinking two U-boats.

Another device was the 'Lance bomb' – an explosive charge on the end of a long wooden pole. This could only be used if the attacking vessel could come alongside the U-boat and jab at it with the pole. By this means, the unlucky *UB-13* was disabled by a drifter it was trying to capture.

Late 1915 saw the introduction of the 'high-speed submarine sweep'. This consisted of an explosive paravane on the end of a wire. The paravane was a torpedo-shaped device towed from the bows of the attacking vessel. As the ship passed through the water, the paravane steered itself away and, with luck, made contact with a submarine, blowing it up.

The Admiralty's Anti-Submarine Division (ASD) produced a passive, non-directional, hydrophone in late 1915. Its first victim was *UC-3*, sunk on

St George's Day, 23 April 1916. Later in the war, ASD claimed it was using a 'supersonic' means of attacking U-boats and attached the last two letters of 'supersonic' to 'ASD' to produce 'ASDic' as an identifier for all anti-submarine weapons. Over two decades later, the Admiralty was asked by a dictionary publisher for a definition of 'ASDic' and, to avoid any residue of secrecy left in the project, invented 'Anti-Submarine Detection Investigation Committee' as the answer. The acronym 'ASDIC' remained in use with the Royal Navy until the 1950s when it was replaced with the American 'SONAR' (SOund Navigation And Radar).

The most popular anti-submarine weapon to emerge during the war was the depth charge, first introduced in early 1916. Developed by the Royal Navy's Torpedo and Mine School at HMS *Vernon*, the cylindrical weapon was packed with explosive and intended to detonate at a pre-set depth. Designed originally to roll off the stern of a ship through a chute, the later introduction of rails provided a better system of delivery. Eventually, after military mortars had been tried, a specially designed depth-charge thrower was fitted to ships in 1918.

Mines were thought by many to be an answer to the U-boats, but the Admiralty's insistence upon mechanical contact mines brought many problems. Electrical contact mines were known about and favoured by some (including the admiral of the Dover Patrol and the Germans), but the Admiralty insisted that all evidence suggested that electricity and water did not mix. Nevertheless, the mechanical firing device on British mines frequently failed to work and,

U-boat shelters at Bruges.

eventually, in late 1917, the H2 mine was introduced – a variation on a German design. There was, however, one electrical contact mine that did find early favour with the Admiralty. This was the 'net-mine', invented by Admiral of the Fleet Sir Arthur Wilson VC. The mines were hung on submerged nets which, when torn away by a passing submarine, closed around the boat. When the mines made contact with the submarine, an electric charge supplied from a sealed battery-box detonated the mine.

Bacon's anti-U-boat campaign applied not merely to submarines attempting to pass through the Straits of Dover and the English Channel to await ships arriving at the Western Approaches, but also to mine-laying submarines intent on interrupting traffic down the east coast and across to France. In 1916 Bacon answered the latter problem by laying a barrier of mine-nets parallel to the Belgian coast. This caused a great reduction in the number of minefields laid by the enemy (Bacon claimed a complete stoppage) until the onset of winter weather prevented barrier patrols by destroyers and trawlers, allowing the nets to drift.

The resumption of unrestricted submarine warfare by the Germans had begun in February 1917; a turn of events that concentrated the minds of the entire Dover Patrol. With a fully active U-boat base at Bruges feeding submarines along the canals that connected that city with the ports of Zeebrugge and Ostend, the route to the Western Approaches through the Straits of Dover and the English Channel was too obvious to be ignored by either side. (There were many, both during and after the war, who believed that the Bruges to Ostend canal was never used for U-boats. After the war, however, Bacon had claimed confirmation from the Keeper of the Berlin Official Archives that the canal had been used for both submarines and destroyers.)

The net laid out by Rear Admiral Hood by early 1915 had proved impractical. The securing chains wore through with alarming regularity resulting in the nets becoming entangled, great baulks of timber used to help support the nets broke free and proved a hazard to shipping and, eventually, the whole system became such a danger to navigation that the First Sea Lord ordered it to be abandoned.

The submarine menace, nevertheless, still persisted and during one week in September 1916 the Channel defences were cruelly exposed. Three U-boats out of Zeebrugge sank enough vessels between Beachy Head and the Eddystone Light to cause the cancellation or diversion of traffic across the Channel. This blow had fallen despite the U-boats operating in an area patrolled by forty-nine destroyers, forty-eight torpedo boats, seven 'Q' ships, and 468 armed auxiliary vessels – a total of 572 ships employed specifically for anti-submarine operations. By the end of the month, almost 50,000 tons of allied shipping had been sunk in the Channel. Bacon, already at work finding a technical answer to the problem, had come up with the idea of combining indicator nets, net-mines, and electrical contact mines, which he had been assured would be ready the following year.

The nets, made of thin steel wire, would be kept upright by 'invisible' glass floats, and each 100ft section of the net – with its net-mines – would be secured to a wire rope frame by clips. As the enemy submarine hit the nets, the entire section would break free from its clips, and the net – carrying its net-mines – would wrap itself around the U-boat with the mines exploding on contact. Ideally, should the mines not work, an indicator buoy would burst into light, summoning any close-by destroyers who would finish the job off with depth charges. Unfortunately, such an indicator buoy, using a chemical compound to produce smoke and flame on exposure to sea water, proved to be beyond practical design.

Bacon decided that his net would have to stretch from the Goodwin Sands to the outer Ruytingen Shoals off the Continental coast, making it longer than Hood's Folkestone to Cap Gris Nez attempt. As a result the new net would have to be suspended over deeper waters, but design limitations prevented the nets from going deeper than 60ft in modest tides, and 40ft in strong tides. With the sea bottom at least 120ft deep along parts of the net route, this left a clear invitation for the U-boats to simply slip under the nets. To address this possibility, Bacon planned to have banks of electrical contact mines just to the east of the nets (whenever the mines became available). If the submarines tried to sail over

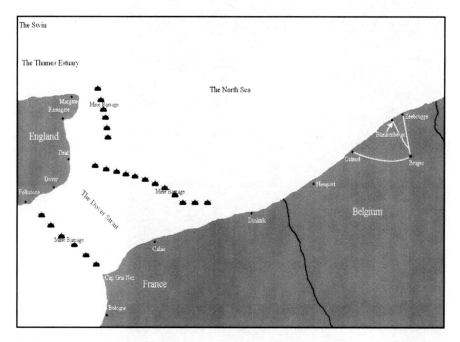

The Dover Strait defences.

the top of the net during the night, lightships and shore batteries would shine search lights along its length. Under the protection of one or more destroyers, the barrage was patrolled and maintained by drifters, each armed with a single rifle and a few rounds of ammunition. Further protection against surface vessels was known to be unnecessary as the enemy Flanders Flotilla, based at Bruges, was too weak to engage the British forces.

On the night of 26/27 October 1916, the destroyer *Flirt* was cruising through the barrier area looking after four divisions (twenty-eight vessels) of drifters. She was accompanied by a yacht and a trawler acting as wireless ships. In the darkness, the *Flirt* came across a number of vessels heading towards the English coast. The captain ordered a recognition signal to be sent, which was promptly answered by the same signal being repeated. Assuming the ships to be part of the Dunkirk force returning to Dover, the *Flirt* continued on her way. Shortly afterwards, gun flashes and the sound of firing could be detected ahead. The *Flirt*

Vice Admiral Sir
Roger Keyes.

had not gone far before her crew heard cries from men in the water. Turning her searchlights on, the destroyer lowered a boat, only to come under fire from German destroyers. Within minutes the *Flirt* was sunk, the only survivors being the men in the boat pulling other men from the water. Close by the Goodwin Sands, other German destroyers (possibly the same ones signalled by the *Flirt*) sank an empty transport.

The sound of gunfire had been heard in Dover, and Bacon dispatched six destroyers to investigate. At the same time he signalled the destroyers at Dunkirk to put to sea. The first of Bacon's Dover destroyers, the *Nubian*, fell in with the German destroyers as they were pulling back to Zeebrugge, but made the same mistake as the *Flirt* in assuming them to be British. The error cost the *Nubian* her bows and most of her forecastle as a torpedo struck her. The *Amazon*, closing in quickly, was almost immediately, knocked out by shells damaging her boiler room. In another part of the action the *Mohawk* was also badly knocked about, and the entire German forces escaped before the Dunkirk destroyers could arrive on the scene.

In all, the Germans, putting twenty-three destroyers into the battle, suffered one destroyer damaged, whilst the British lost one destroyer and six drifters sunk. Three destroyers, three drifters, and one trawler were damaged, and forty-five men were killed, four wounded, and ten taken prisoner.

Bacon took the whole affair as a 'compliment' by the Germans on the success of his net and mine barrage. In a memorandum to his men, he wrote:

> Anyone can run round a corner and throw a stone, and then make off. It is merely a question of whether the damage of a broken window is worth the risk of being caught by a policeman, especially if the window is open and the glass cannot be broken.

Then, with an eye on his superiors, he added, 'The extent of our area is large, the vessels necessarily comparatively few … It is pleasing to see that our defence against submarines has led the Germans into the far more risky method of attack by destroyers.'

Despite later raids by enemy destroyers, which Bacon continued to see as confirmation of his success with the barrage's progression, he turned his mind to the possibility of a direct assault on the Germans.

As early as 1915 Bacon had been considering an attack at Zeebrugge to destroy the canal lockgates that admitted U-boats and destroyers into the North Sea. The exit from the canal is guarded by a long concrete mole that curves to the west, then north, until its final extremity – guarded by a lighthouse – ends about a mile from the canal entrance. His first plan was to send in trawlers to lay a smokescreen around the inner and outer mole as monitors raced to the canal and opened fire on the lockgates. After discussions with the First Sea Lord and others, the plan was abandoned – mainly due to the poor qualities of the smokescreen then available.

Bacon returned to the idea in 1917, almost certainly as a result of others coming forward with proposals affecting areas that Bacon considered solely his preserve. Vice Admiral Sir Lewis Bayly, the commander-in-chief at the Western Approaches, based at Queenstown in Ireland, was concerned at the number of U-boat attacks in his command. He proposed a landing of troops to take Borkum (off the north Netherlands coast), Zeebrugge and Ostend. His idea, however, was considered impractical in economic terms and rejected.

Other ideas came from closer to the scene. Commodore Tyrwhitt, commanding the Harwich Flotilla, proposed a combined blockship assault with an attack on the lockgates at Zeebrugge. His idea was that, preceded by a cloud of poison gas, and hidden by smokescreens, a blockship would enter the canal, ram the lockgates, and then have its bottom blown out. The use of poison gas, however, did not find support amongst those reviewing the plan. What if the wind turned? What if the gas cloud drifted inland and caused heavy casualties amongst Belgian civilians?

Tyrwhitt looked at his proposal again and suggested a modified version in which the entire town of Zeebrugge, including the harbour, would be the target. When asked for his opinion, Bacon opposed the idea and fell back on the frequently tried – and frequently failed – idea of shore bombardment from monitors. Furthermore, such plans might interrupt his idea for the landing of an army division on the Belgian shore. Then ideas began to arrive from a most unwelcome source – from the Admiralty itself, via the First Sea Lord.

At the end of September 1917 a new post had been created at the Admiralty under the title of Director of Plans. The first man into the job was Rear Admiral Roger Keyes who, after just a few days, came to the conclusion that there was a desperate need to tackle the U-boats, which – according to Naval Intelligence – were making their way through the Straits of Dover into the English Channel. There were, according to Keyes, two ways in which this should be done. Firstly, Zeebrugge and Ostend must be rendered useless as transit ports for the submarines, and secondly, the effectiveness of the Dover Barrage must be examined. In order to carry out the latter, a Dover Barrage Committee was set up with Keyes as its chairman.

Bacon was furious. A committee was bad enough but the people on the committee made it even worse. Engineers, he later conceded, were just about acceptable, but attempting 'to run a mine-barrage from the Admiralty with naval officers who know nothing about the practical work at Dover, and the general patrol details from Nieuport to the Downs, was of course absurd'.

An early cause of conflict was the committee's suggestion that flares should be used to illuminate the barrage at night rather than lightships. Already, a million-candle-power flare was being talked about at the Admiralty Board of Inventions

Rear Admiral R.A. 'Blinker' Hall, Director of the Admiralty's Intelligence Division.

and Research and at the Royal Naval Experimental Station at Stratford. Bacon considered such 'meddling' and 'dabbling' to be 'irresponsible' and 'such foolery'. The committee, he believed, were nothing more than a 'fifth wheel'.

In an effort to demonstrate to the Admiralty that he did not need a Dover Barrage Committee, or instructions from the Director of Plans, Bacon put together his own proposal for an assault on the Zeebrugge canal. As in his plan of 1915, he intended to use a smokescreen but this time laid down by fast motor launches rather than trawlers. A monitor would then approach the outer mole wall (i.e. the wall facing the sea rather than the inner harbour) and bombard the canal lockgates over the mole wall using reduced charge shells. Destroyers would keep the mole's artillery defences busy and a landing party of seamen and marines would land on the mole from another monitor to attack the remaining defences and to act as a distraction.

It was the landing of the assault parties that required the most novel and inventive aspect of the raid. Bacon decided that the monitor from which they would land would require a rather startling addition to its design. As there were no bollards to help secure a vessel alongside the outer mole, he was convinced that the only way to secure the ship and get men ashore quickly was to ram the wall head-on. As the vessel crashed into the concrete structure, a giant brow (gangway), 80ft long and 10ft wide would unfold from the forecastle, its first section reaching to the top of the wall with an angle of 30 degrees. A hinge would then allow the second, stepped, section to reach beyond a 4ft walkway and project far enough to be lowered an extra 16ft onto the floor of the mole. This would then allow the attacking parties to charge up the ramp and race down the 40-degree slope onto the mole whilst the Germans were still wondering what had hit them – a tactic named by Bacon as 'One great rush and one great cheer.' The shock of the collision with the wall would be much reduced by building a 20ft false bow onto the monitor to absorb the impact.

When he submitted this plan to the First Sea Lord, Bacon was somewhat disappointed to be told that Jellicoe had suggested that blockships should be added to the plan. He had always argued strongly against using blockships, as the tide at Zeebrugge rose and fell 13ft and, once a blockship was sunk in the channel, there was every chance that the depth of water at high tide would allow the passage of vessels over her. Even if that was not the case, and the superstructure remained above water, the upper works could be cut away or a channel dredged around the ship. Jellicoe, however, whilst agreeing that no blocking operation could be considered as permanent, took the view that 'a temporary block would be of use, and that *the moral effect alone of such an operation would be of great value*' (Jellicoe's italics). To make matters worse, as far as Bacon was concerned, the blockship suggestion had come from Keyes, the director of plans.

Bacon, regarding such an idea as 'a farce', returned reluctantly to his plan. The biggest problem he faced under the new proposals was the destroyers that were likely to be tied up on the inside of the mole. If they remained unmolested, the blockships, making a dash for the canal entrance, would be unlikely to survive the destroyers' guns or, more particularly, their torpedoes. Bacon decided that they would be attacked by the assault parties or, if they had already moved away from the mole, by howitzers mounted on the turret and forecastle of a monitor.

On Tuesday, 18 December, Bacon arrived at the Admiralty to present his plans to a group consisting of: Jellicoe; his chief of staff, Admiral Sir Henry Oliver; Vice Admiral Sir Rosslyn Wemyss; and the members of the Operations Committee (a sub-committee of the Directorate of Plans) under their chairman, Roger Keyes. All went well and Jellicoe granted his approval for Bacon's proposals. Keyes, having argued away Bacon's plan to use an infantry battalion to storm the mole, persuaded the meeting that it should be an entirely Royal Navy affair. Consequently, Jellicoe sent Keyes to Scapa Flow to discuss with Beatty the question of raising volunteers. The First Sea Lord also invited Bacon back to the Admiralty on 29 December to explain his plans to the Admiralty Board. But in

Room 40, not far from where the meeting had taken place, another group of naval officers under the direction of Rear Admiral William 'Blinker' Hall, were looking very closely at some documents recovered from a U-boat four-and-a-half months earlier.

During the first few days of August 1917 *Kapitanleutnant* Kurt Tebbenjohans would have been on the verge of being considered as a U-boat 'ace'. He had sunk one Royal Navy ship and damaged two others. In all, he had sunk twenty-eight ships totalling 25,709 tons, and taken another vessel as a prize but, as he was about to learn, the gods of war are fickle.

Tebbenjohans was commanding *UC-44*, a mine-laying submarine, off the coast of Ireland when the unthinkable happened — he ran afoul of one of his own mines. The mines, which were discharged from the bows of the submarine, would normally sink to the seabed. After a period of time, a soluble plug would dissolve, allowing the mine to separate from its heavy sinker and rise towards the surface, its final depth being controlled by a pre-determined length of wire. Unfortunately for the submarine's crew, the soluble plug occasionally dissolved immediately, allowing the mine to float free before the boat was clear. Tebbenjohans survived the explosion but *UC-44* sank in the shallow waters off Waterford. Two months later, the U-boat was raised and the recovered code books and log were sent to Room 40, where Hall and his team went to work on them.

Most of the information revealed by *UC-44*'s documents was of great value — albeit the sort of bread-and-butter details that would have been expected. What were of great concern, however, were Tebbenjohans' instructions. He had been told that the best way to reach the Atlantic was through the Straits of Dover. He should travel at night and on the surface. At all events, he should try to avoid being spotted, thus keeping the British unaware that the English Channel route was being used by the U-boats. The instructions continued, 'on the other hand, those boats, which in exceptional cases pass around Scotland, are to let themselves be seen as freely as possible, in order to mislead the English'.

Contradicting any claims by Bacon that he was dealing with the U-boat problem, up to thirty U-boats a month were passing through the straits undetected and unchallenged. Even worse, from Bacon's point of view, was that he had been ordered to put in to practise the suggestions by Keyes' Dover Channel Committee. With the patrolling drifters being supplied with the new powerful flares, on the night of 19 December — the day after the Admiralty meeting — a submarine was spotted on the surface and forced to dive. The U-boat struck a mine, underlining the weakness of both Bacon's system and his claims.

When, on 29 December, Bacon arrived at the Admiralty, he may have had a feeling of foreboding. Only a few days earlier he had heard the appalling news that Jellicoe, his friend and supporter, had been removed from office. A loyal friend, Bacon had the unfortunate knack of polarising opinion amongst those with whom he worked. Fisher described him as 'the cleverest officer in the Navy'. To Sir Henry Oliver he was 'most energetic and tireless', but Tyrwhitt dismissed him as 'the streaky one' (a pun on his name) and commented, 'You will understand me when I say he is not a white man [i.e. not upright and honest].' With all of his supporters gone, all power lay in the hands of his detractors.

There was no Board of Admiralty waiting for him, just the first lord, Sir Eric Geddes, who had no wish to hear any of his plans. Bacon would no longer be involved with any events concerning the Dover Patrol – he was dispatched without ceremony to the post of Controller of the Inventions Department at the Ministry of Munitions. His place at Dover was to be taken by a man of a quite different stamp.

2

The Answer

Admiral Bacon's successor as commander of the Dover Patrol was as different from his predecessor as he could possibly be. Whereas the bluff, solidly built, Bacon could be guaranteed stubbornly to hold his ground when the occasion arose, his church-going, shy-looking, slightly built, replacement did not merely insist on being at the centre of the action, but demanded to be in the front line – better still, *ahead* of the front line.

In August 1900 British forces in China were attempting to break through Peking's Shawo-men Gate when a young naval officer galloped up on a Chinese pony he had named 'Torpedo'. Ignoring the bullets fired by Boxer rebels, he climbed the 30ft city wall with a Union Flag gripped between his teeth. On reaching the top he waved the flag before draping it over the wall as a signal to the artillery, still firing into the city from behind the advancing British troops.

Clambering down the inside of the wall, the young man rallied the troops around him as they entered the city. A 2½-mile advance through the streets was made under his leadership before he raced ahead across the Peking-Tung-chau canal and reached the south-east corner of the besieged Foreign Legation Quarter. Running along its southern wall he found a slight gap close by the Legation watergate. He just managed to squeeze through the opening and stood, panting and dishevelled, before a sight that utterly baffled him. On the Legation lawns, a tea party was in progress with ladies in elegant, light-coloured, dresses attended by men dressed appropriately for a garden party. As they chatted and sipped from their teacups, the air was filled with bullets striking the surrounding walls, roofs, and the tops of the trees under which they were shading. As more soldiers stumbled onto the lawn through the gate, the young man and another officer approached the British ambassador's wife, who stood up, extended her hand and told them that 'she didn't know who we were' but that she 'was simply delighted to see us'.

The courage and enterprising initiative shown by the naval officer was not restricted to action against an enemy. As the captain of the destroyer, HMS *Fame*, he had, without official sanction, left his ship in the hands of his first lieutenant to get involved in the relief of the Legation. On his return, a month later, he was mortified to learn that the commander-in-chief – Admiral Sir Edward Seymour – had ordered his dismissal as captain and a replacement was on the way. Despite being advised against it by the admiral of his squadron, he took a boat to the commander-in-chief's flagship and found the admiral on the poop-deck. There he immediately challenged him by saying 'I think you have treated me very badly, Sir.' Regardless of the frosty reception earned from such an opening remark, the junior officer pressed home his complaint to the extent that the admiral not only restored his command of the *Fame* but, two months later saw him, at the age of 28, promoted to the rank of commander. The reason for Seymour's retreat in the face of a junior officer may have been his admiration for the stand taken by the younger man. The admiral later wrote that, as a general rule, 'I never could understand why anyone minds taking responsibility. You have only to do what seems proper, and if it turns out badly it is the fault of Nature for not having made you cleverer.'

Such then, was the manner and bearing of the newly promoted Vice Admiral Roger John Brownlow Keyes, who took command of the Dover Patrol on 1 January 1918. Descended from generations of soldiers, Keyes had decided at an early age that he would seek a career in the Royal Navy. There had been setbacks. When he was young he had broken his left arm, only to have it set incorrectly, leaving him with a weakness in the limb. Furthermore, he could claim no ability as a scholar, frequently only just scraping through his examinations. Nevertheless, he refused to allow physical imperfection and scholastic failing to bar his progress and, in late 1884, he entered the training ship HMS *Britannia* as a 12-year-old cadet. Six years later Keyes was serving off the coast of East Africa as a midshipman battling Arab slave traders. On his return to England, he was sent to serve on the South America Station before returning to become an instructor training boy seamen. Some time was spent with the Channel Fleet, along with a period serving in the Royal Yacht *Victoria and Albert* – during which service he became good friends with the future King George V.

In January 1898, at the age of 26, Keyes was appointed to his first command, the destroyer HMS *Opossum*. Shortly afterwards he was transferred to the China Station, where he took command of another destroyer, HMS *Hart*. Just two months later he was transferred yet again, this time to the newly built destroyer, *Fame*. Once the ship had been 'worked up' to his satisfaction, with her gleaming white hull, yellow funnels and glittering 'bright work', Keyes set off with the intention of making her worthy of her name.

Always at the forefront with suggestions for taking the fight to the enemy, Keyes used the Boxer Rebellion to demonstrate his worth in naval warfare. He captured enemy destroyers, attacked and destroyed forts and, on one occasion, commandeered a railway train in order to get a message through to his squadron's admiral. When the train driver refused to proceed through a station packed with Chinese troops, Keyes took out a pistol and pointed it at the man's head. The train, the message – and the driver – arrived safely.

On his return home from the China Station, Keyes was appointed second-in-command of the Devonport Destroyer Flotilla. He had two happy years practising and perfecting destroyer manoeuvres before being sent to work in the Naval Intelligence Department under Captain Prince Louis Battenberg. He did not, however, take easily to office life and kept fit by running around the park at Windsor, where he was living with his mother. He also took up polo, which allowed him to meet a young Member of Parliament named Winston Churchill, and a young subaltern in the Blues cavalry regiment whose sister, Eva, was later to become his wife.

Tiring of the office inactivity, Keyes twice tried to persuade Battenberg to send him to Russia as an extra naval attaché. On the first occasion, another officer was sent in his place and, on the second, he almost found a place with the Russian Baltic Fleet as it headed for the Far East. At first Battenberg agreed but, fortunately, then changed his mind – the fleet was almost totally destroyed by the Japanese at the Battle of Tsushima.

However, some months before the battle, the 32-year-old Keyes did receive a new appointment. He was sent as a naval attaché to Rome, Constantinople, Vienna and Athens, with his office in the Italian capital – an appointment usually reserved for captains. Sure enough, after six months in the job, Keyes was promoted, becoming the youngest captain in the navy. He also took his promotion as a sign that it was time to be married and took Eva Bowlby as his wife.

On his return to sea in January 1908, Keyes was given the second-class cruiser HMS *Venus*. For most of the next two years he was attached to the Atlantic Fleet, at the same time gaining the respect and popular acclaim of his ship's company. Finally, after the fleet manoeuvres of 1910, he was summoned to the Admiralty, where he was told of his new appointment – he was to become the new inspecting captain of submarines.

At first, the idea of such an appointment did not sit comfortably with Keyes. His knowledge of submarines was minimal, and he could claim no mechanical (or any other specialist) knowledge that he could bring to the position. He, nevertheless, accepted the appointment with the intention of gathering around himself a staff of engineers and others who could provide the sort of detailed knowledge required. His flair for selecting the right men demonstrated itself in his choice of officers to help him. Of the six chosen, one was awarded the Victoria Cross and became the youngest admiral of his generation; another had served with Captain Scott in the Antarctic and later became engineer-in-chief of the Royal Navy. One of them became a lord commissioner of the Admiralty and deputy chief of the Naval

Staff, whilst another rose to become head of the Submarine Service. Of the two remaining, one left the navy after a distinguished career in submarines to work for the major British arms manufacturer Vickers Ltd, ending up as managing director; the other was appointed as the commander-in-chief of the Royal Australian Navy before becoming the Admiralty's director of dockyards.

With such men to advise him, Keyes could concentrate on the operational training of the submariners and the development of the Submarine Service as a whole. It was not long before he had made such an impression upon his command that, when he requested an appointment to a ship in the Battle-Cruiser Squadron, he was turned down. Instead, he was promoted to Commodore 2nd Class (a temporary appointment, usually granted to the senior captain of a flotilla), and his role with the Submarine Service was changed to an operational seagoing command. This change from administrative to operational duties allowed Keyes to instigate tactical planning of his own and, with the outbreak of war, he approached his fellow commodore at Harwich, Reginald Tyrwhitt, with such a plan.

Keyes had already outlined his basic idea to the Admiralty's director of operations. In his letter, he described how he wished to create 'the correct atmosphere on both sides' (i.e. the British and the German sides). For the British, he wanted them to be confident in the belief that 'when the enemy come out we will fall on them and smash them'. For the Germans, he wanted them to be equally confident that 'when we go out those damned Englanders will fall on us and smash us.'

The way to do this, Keyes informed his fellow commodore, was for Tyrwhitt's destroyers to attack the German destroyers patrolling the Heligoland Bight and drive them on to his submarines. This would tempt out German cruisers to come to the aid of the destroyers, only for themselves to come under attack by the submarines.

During a conference at the Admiralty where Keyes put forward his plan, he pushed for a supply of light cruisers from the Grand Fleet along with Rear Admiral Beatty's battle-cruisers. This request was rejected outright; the only cruisers available would be the two light cruisers already under Tyrwhitt's command. Jellicoe, however, commanding the Grand Fleet, heard about the plan and offered exactly the vessels that Keyes had requested. The Admiralty accepted the offer and ordered the ships to join Keyes. Unfortunately, both he and Tyrwhitt had already sailed. In consequence, both had a shock and narrowly escaped a disaster as the solid shapes of battle-cruisers and cruisers appeared out of the mist. At the end of that day, 28 August, every British ship returned to base. The Germans, on the other hand, lost three cruisers and one destroyer sunk, along with three cruisers badly damaged, and 381 seamen taken prisoner. Astonishingly, the Admiralty response was to ban Keyes from proceeding to sea as they considered he would be taking 'quite unjustifiable risks'.

Undeterred, Keyes went even further and pestered the Admiralty over – what he called – the 'live-bait' squadron. These were five ancient Bacchante-class cruisers serving in the North Sea and manned by reservists, pensioners, and young officer cadets. Eventually, after a direct appeal, Keyes managed to persuade the first lord – Winston Churchill – not only to allow him to substitute some of his own trained men for some of the more poorly trained men in the cruisers, but to replace the ships with more modern vessels. The morning after he had heard the welcome news, he was awoken to be told that three of the five cruisers, the *Cressy, Hogue,* and *Aboukir,* had been sunk by a single U-boat. Keyes, 'simply boiling with rage', learned that his failure to persuade the Admiralty to remove the ships earlier had cost 1,400 lives.

Intent on revenge and disregarding his orders to stay ashore, Keyes put to sea in Tyrwhitt's light cruiser *Fearless* in company with seventeen destroyers. He ordered his two submarine flotilla destroyers to join him, and even managed to convince Jellicoe that the Grand Fleet should contribute two cruisers. But it was to no avail. The Admiralty, listening in on the signals, ordered not merely his return to Harwich, but that Keyes should report immediately to the Admiralty.

The reception awaiting Keyes at the Admiralty was frosty but not overtly hostile. He had disobeyed orders, but in a manner that many senior officers actually approved. Nevertheless, a point had to be made, and the point was made, leaving Keyes to return to his command unbowed and unchastened.

Two weeks later, Keyes was off to sea again, this time legitimately. Two of his submarines were covering the landing of an army division at the port of Zeebrugge, thus giving him an excuse to have a close look at the place. He walked along its huge curving mole, mounted its outer parapet, crossed the linking viaduct, and made his way to the canal entrance with its swing bridge and lockgates. He was highly unlikely to have been thinking of anything more than the port's advantages as a supply point for the army, but his walk around the site was, subsequently, to prove of great value.

If a chance visit to Zeebrugge was later to bear fruit, Keyes, in fact, was apparently in danger of having badly depleted his store of fortune. On 15 December he was ordered by the Admiralty to take his two destroyers and eight submarines to sea and form a 30-mile line north–north-west off the Dutch island of Terschelling. Apparently modest enemy forces were at sea and the lines would be a trap 'through which it is thought these enemy ships may pass'. If the enemy failed to materialise, the submarines were to return to Harwich on the evening of 16 December. No other details were given and, after a night of very poor weather conditions in which the submarines became scattered, Keyes remained unaware that German battle-cruisers had begun the day by bombarding Whitby, Scarborough and Hartlepool.

Mid-way through the morning, a faint wireless signal was picked up, informing Keyes that the enemy was off Scarborough. Realising that his line of submarines would be of little use in their current position, he sent his accompanying destroyer to Yarmouth for instructions whilst he remained on station trying to find his boats on their invisible 30-mile line. This was to prove a doubly difficult task as, not only was the surface visibility very poor, the submarines had been ordered to dive at the sight of any approaching warship. By the time the *Firedrake* had returned from her errand in mid-afternoon, Keyes had only located four of his charges.

The instructions from the Admiralty informed him that the High Seas Fleet was at sea, and that his submarines should proceed to Heligoland and try to intercept. After spending a further, fruitless, three hours searching for the remaining submarines, Keyes knew he had to make a far-reaching decision. He knew that, by now, the missing submarines would be on their way to Harwich in accordance with their orders. Should he take the four he was left with to Heligoland and risk running into the High Seas Fleet? Such an event would inevitably mean the destruction of his two destroyers, but it could mean that German battleships and battle-cruisers might come within torpedo range of the submarines. On the other hand, if he raced south-westwards, he could catch his returning submarines and send them to the Heligoland Bight to extend the ambush line. Having already had a bruising encounter with the Admiralty over what the chief of staff referred to as his tendency to 'barge about in the Bight on his own', Keyes went against his own instinct and ordered the four submarines he had with him to proceed to the Bight at best speed with the intention of being on station by 0300hrs the following morning, whilst he and the other destroyer tried to catch up with the returning four.

At 0120hrs on the morning of the 17th, Keyes received a signal from the Admiralty informing him that the enemy was likely to pass Heligoland at 0200hrs. He was now 200 miles from the area, and the submarines he had sent had been delayed for, at least, three hours whilst he had searched for the remainder. If he had acted on his instincts, he could have been on station with a deadly 12-mile line of submarines aching for an opportunity to launch their torpedoes.

Then, just a few weeks later, at the moment when his submarines could have played an important part in the Dogger Bank battle, a delay in Keyes' orders meant that his boats could not get on station in time. A despondent commodore of submarines requested an interview with the First Sea Lord. Admiral Lord Fisher, who had been brought back into the post to take over from Battenberg some three months earlier, viewed Keyes with a belligerent eye. Just before the outbreak of war, Fisher had bluntly, and publicly, demanded of Keyes an explanation why there were so few deep-sea (or 'fleet') submarines in the Royal Navy. Keyes had responded in like manner by brusquely pointing out that it was all Fisher's fault in awarding the building contracts to a single manufacturer when he was First Sea Lord. The admiral, on the point of exploding, abruptly turned on his heel and left the building. In fact, Keyes was being somewhat disingenuous. He had arranged for a severe reduction in the production of the shorter range patrol submarines, and ordered the construction of an Italian submarine with better sea-keeping qualities and a superior, French-designed, diesel engine. The British monopoly contract was terminated and the manufacturer started building submarines for foreign navies. Even worse, the Italian submarines proved to be inadequate and, on the outbreak of war, the Royal Navy found itself to be short of both patrol and fleet submarines. The incident with Fisher, nevertheless, is a prime example of Keyes' belief in taking the fight to the enemy.

At the interview with the glowering Fisher, Keyes put forward the case that, having held the appointment as head of the Submarine Service for over four years, the time might be right to hand the position on to a new man. In reality, however, Keyes felt that he was living in the shade of a volcano that might erupt at any moment, both to his own, and the Submarine Service's disadvantage. At the end of the meeting, Fisher was non-committal but, a few days later, Keyes was summoned to the office of the first lord. There, Churchill told him that he was to be ready to leave for the Mediterranean the following morning. With no time to say goodbye to his family, or his submarine command, he was to become chief of staff to Rear Admiral Sackville Carden, who had been given the task of forcing the Dardanelles – the straits dividing the Gallipoli Peninsula from eastern Turkey.

In the time Keyes had spent with the Submarine Service he had brought it from a peacetime organisation, looked upon with both suspicion and disinterest, into a devastating wartime weapon whose real potential had yet to be realised. Although the submariners that had served under his command had no time to show their appreciation of the efforts he had made on their behalf, they did introduce one enduring custom in honour of his name. Lieutenant Commander Max Horton, the captain of submarine *E9* of the Harwich Flotilla, had sunk a German warship in September 1914. When he returned to harbour, the *E9* was flying a 'Jolly Roger' in celebration of his victory and as a salute to his commodore. The incident started a tradition that still continues.

Keyes arrived in Malta in mid-February and by the 18th was with Vice Admiral Carden onboard the flagship HMS *Albion* as she approached the entrance to the Dardanelles. For most of the day, the guarding forts came under a savage bombardment from the British and French ships. When the light began to fade, Carden ordered a withdrawal against the protestations of his second-in-command, Rear Admiral John de Robeck – a friend of Keyes.

Further probes into the straits, attempting to reduce other forts by gunfire, and landing demolition parties of Royal Marines ashore, went well. There had, however, been return fire from the Turks using mobile howitzers that were difficult to locate. In particular, these had caused concern to the trawler crews, forging ahead of the warships as minesweepers. The trawlermen were quite happy to take on the mining hazards, but the fall of shot around their frail craft was something for which they were wholly unprepared.

On 17 March Carden was replaced by de Robeck and returned home worn down by the stress. Keyes remained as de Robeck's chief of staff, eager to race through the straits and burst into the Sea of Marmara, there to put Constantinople under the guns of the British fleet.

The following day, a combined Franco-British fleet steamed into the Dardanelles. Seventeen battleships and one battle-cruiser, led by the trawlers, opened fire on the Turkish positions. By 1400hrs the entrance forts had been silenced and a French battleship had been forced to retire. The Turks had suffered greatly. Many of their guns had been put out of action, and communications between the forts and gun emplacements had been destroyed. Just at this moment, the trawler crews decided that they had had enough. As they retired, the French battleship *Bouvet* hit a mine, heeled over and sank with enormous loss of life. This was followed a few minutes later by HMS *Inflexible,* and then HMS *Irresistible* running afoul of mines. *HMS Ocean* rushed to assist the stricken vessels, only to strike a mine of her own. Faced by an obvious disaster, de Robeck ordered the fleet to withdraw. The *Inflexible* managed to limp out of the straits under her own steam, but as darkness fell there was no sight of the *Irresistible* or the *Ocean.*

Keyes, well aware that the damaged ships could fall into enemy hands, asked de Robeck's permission to return to the straits to see if the two ships could be found. There might just be a chance of hauling them clear, failing which they should be torpedoed. De Robeck agreed and Keyes set off. But the ships could not be found – both had sunk. It later transpired that it had not been the trawlers leaving the minefield that had been the problem, but a line of mines of which no one had been aware, and which no one suspected.

For the next few months, Keyes became involved in every area he was permitted. He took charge of the mine-sweeping trawler problems, stiffening the crews with Royal Navy seamen and even proposing that he personally led the sweeping by being in the lead trawler – an idea rejected out of hand by the admiral. He had been involved with the planning of the initial landings at Cape Hellas and Anzac Cove, and with the later landing at Suvla Bay. He had seen the land battles surging forward, only to be driven back by the entrenched, German-supported, enemy. He also recognised the growing war-weariness that hung over the British and Empire forces, their lack of support, and the absence beyond the divisional level of any vigorous leadership. The answer, he believed, was to fire up the campaign by the Royal Navy, once again, attempting to break through the Dardanelles. With de Robeck's deputy, Rear Admiral Rosslyn Wemyss, and the whole of the naval staff in favour, Keyes put his proposals to the admiral. In

concert with a thrust by the army towards the Narrows forts, the fleet would
bombard its way into the straits. A reduction in the numbers of the Turkish
mobile howitzers meant that the mine-sweeping trawlers would be less affected
by the shelling that had prompted their initial withdrawal; and newly arrived,
heavy-gun, shallow-draft, monitors could add their fearsome firepower to that of
the battleships, battle-cruisers, and destroyers. Overhead, the aircraft of the Royal
Naval Air Service would do valuable work in spotting fall of shot, and reporting
enemy movements. Once past the mile-wide Narrows, half way up the straits,
all that remained would be a dash into the Sea of Marmara and the unprotected
supply lines that fed the Turko-German troops at Gallipoli. That alone would give
the enemy no choice but to retreat or starve. Even better, just 60 miles from the
northern mouth of the straits, lay the greatest prize of all – Constantinople. No
one doubted for a second that a few well-directed battleship shells into the city
would cause the collapse of the government and knock Turkey out of the war. De
Robeck, with his customary courtesy, listened politely to Keyes' plan before flatly
rejecting it.

Just a few days later, Keyes resubmitted the plan, only to have it rejected once
again. Then it seemed as if fate, in the shape of the Admiralty, was about to back
him. De Robeck received a signal from the First Sea Lord, Sir Henry Jackson. It
read:

> If you think that your old battleships could make any really decisive or
> important contribution to success of land operations you will be supported in
> any use to which you may think it desirable to put them.

But de Robeck, still apparently shocked by the heavy loss of capital ships on
18 March, once again refused to lead – or even sanction – any attempt on the
Dardanelles.

Keyes fumed in frustration. He even considered resigning, but his sense of
responsibility to his wife and children stayed his hand. When he wrote to his
wife, telling her of his quandary, she replied - 'Your first duty is to the country.
Remember you belong to England, not to me, and until the war is over you must
not think of us.' With the knowledge of such unfailing support, Keyes then did
something utterly astonishing – he persuaded de Robeck to allow him to return
to England and put his plan before the Admiralty in person.

As Keyes arrived in England at the end of October, momentous changes were
taking place in the command of the Dardanelles operations. The secretary of
war, Lord Kitchener, had sent a message to General Hamilton, the kindly, artistic,
but wholly unenterprising commander-in-chief at Gallipoli, asking him the
number of casualties he could expect if he was asked to evacuate the peninsula.
Hamilton's reply that it could cost up to 50 per cent of his troops caused shock

and consternation. With no progress having been made beyond a few miles from the initial landings, and with casualties already heavy enough to promote vocal disquiet throughout the land, it was easy enough for Kitchener to take decisive action. He promptly discharged Hamilton from his responsibilities and replaced him with General Sir Charles Monro, a soldier whose experiences on the Western Front had made him a convinced 'Westerner' and who had no time for irrelevant 'side shows' such as Gallipoli.

It was not long after Monro's arrival that the senior military officers in his new command got the message that he was eager to evacuate the peninsula. His chief of the general staff, Major General Lyndon Bell even stated baldly 'that's what we have come to do'. With just three days in his new appointment, Monro received a message from Kitchener urging some decision on the question – 'leaving or staying'. Thus prompted, the new commander-in-chief was transported by a destroyer to the three established fronts. Each visit was limited to the shortest possible time with divisional commanders being allocated just minutes to put their case. That evening Monro returned to his headquarters on the isle of Imbros from the only visit he ever made to the peninsula. With no consultation with his staff, he telegraphed Kitchener to advise in favour of evacuation. The secretary of state for war responded immediately asking for the numbers of casualties Monro expected. When the answer came, Kitchener was appalled. Monro was expecting casualties somewhere in the region of 30 to 40 per cent – less than Hamilton's expectations, but horrifying nevertheless. Then Kitchener heard of Keyes' plan for an assault on the Dardanelles.

When he first explained his plans to the Sea Lords, Keyes' proposal was met with little more than polite disinterest. His heavy disappointment was lifted considerably, however, when he was invited to explain his ideas to the First Lord, Arthur Balfour – Winston Churchill's successor. Balfour listened, asked probing questions, and even ripped naval protocol apart by asking Keyes who should replace de Robeck if it was decided that the admiral had to go. Keyes immediately suggested that there was no better candidate than Wemyss for overall command, but that he, himself, should be given command of the fleet assaulting the Dardanelles. The first lord, suggesting that nothing could be done until Monro's report arrived, sent Keyes to his family home in Fareham for a few days with the words, 'It's good to play with children, and it is good also to sleep, and you evidently need it.'

After a delightful, relaxing time with his family, Keyes received a message from Balfour asking him to report to Kitchener. On his arrival at the War Office, he found the secretary of state for war in an angry and aggressive mood. The telegram from Monro giving the probable casualties to be expected in the case of evacuation (which Monro still favoured) had arrived. Kitchener, having leaned towards support for evacuation, now adamantly opposed such an operation. If, on the other hand, the Admiralty could show support for Keyes' plan, there was every chance of a successful outcome.

Keyes was sent by Kitchener to put his case once again before the First Sea Lord. If Jackson would agree to the plan, not only would Turkey be forced out of the war, but the troops on Gallipoli would not suffer an ignominious, and costly, retreat. Yet again, however, the First Sea Lord, proved less than encouraging. Jackson, lacklustre as usual, refused any idea of a solely naval operation but was willing to put on standby a few extra ships that might be needed if the army agreed to cooperate.

Consequently, a situation existed where the Admiralty, under certain circumstances, would approve an attack on the Dardanelles, but the admiral on the spot was adamantly against it, and the War Office was wholly in favour of staying in the field, but the local commander-in-chief was unalterably demanding evacuation. Someone had to make a decision, and Kitchener knew exactly who that would be – he would go to Gallipoli and sort things out himself.

In a telegram to General William Birdwood, temporarily in command with Monro in Cairo, Kitchener reiterated his views on any withdrawal from the peninsula: 'I absolutely refuse to sign order for evacuation, which I think would be greatest disaster and would condemn a large percentage of our men to death or imprisonment.' Then, however, he heard that the Admiralty had made great play of their insistence that only army cooperation in capturing the Narrows forts would persuade them to authorise an attack on the Dardanelles. Kitchener wavered in his determination and telegraphed Birdwood that he should 'very quietly and very secretly work out any scheme for getting the troops off'.

Despite his uncertainty, Kitchener ordered Keyes to remain behind and keep up the pressure on the Admiralty as he set off for Gallipoli. Calling at Paris he was genuinely surprised at the French attitude to the current circumstances. They had no great desire to evacuate Gallipoli and might even be persuaded to replace the exhausted French troops on the peninsula with fresh divisions. Yet again he telegraphed Birdwood telling him that any evacuation would be a 'frightful disaster to be avoided at all costs' and that Birdwood should consider plans to 'enable us to improve our positions and render them secure against increasing artillery fire'. He then sent a message to Keyes, telling the commodore to join him at Marseilles so that the naval plans could be discussed in depth on the way to the eastern Mediterranean. But something strange happened. A minor incident (among others) was to lead to an event that if committed to paper as fiction would be dismissed as being ludicrous. Somehow, Kitchener's message failed to reach Keyes. With his non-appearance at Marseilles, Kitchener sailed without him under the impression that Keyes' plans had come to naught and the navy was not about to help any intended advance by the army – an attitude reinforced on his arrival at Mudros by de Robeck's continued insistence that no benefit would be obtained by an attack on the straits. Birdwood's estimate that up to 25,000 casualties could be incurred was accepted as the price that needed to be paid, and 12,000 hospital beds were prepared in Egypt and Malta. The War Office was expecting 50,000 casualties. Like Keyes himself, Birdwood's plans and the opportunities they would have provided, had missed the boat.

Also at Mudros, waiting to meet Kitchener, were the British high commissioner to Egypt, Sir Henry MacMahon, and the commander of British troops in Egypt, General Sir John Maxwell. They were ostensibly there to put the case for the defence of the Suez Canal and for a landing of troops at Alexandretta, tucked away in the north-east corner of the Mediterranean. Furthermore, MacMahon, an experienced and well-connected Middle East diplomat, was deep into negotiations with the Arabs in an attempt to persuade them to revolt against their Turkish overlords.

When Keyes eventually arrived from England, Kitchener behaved very curtly towards him and would not consider any further discussion on a naval attack. It seemed as if a slight chance appeared when de Robeck returned home on leave, but when he and Wemyss discussed the matter with Birdwood, Monro (now in Salonika) heard about the discussion and Birdwood found himself forbidden to talk to naval officers on any subject other than the evacuation.

Eventually, the British Cabinet, urged on by French and Russian demands that the presence of troops in Salonika was more important than staying on Gallipoli, and impending Turkish successes in Mesopotamia, gave the orders to evacuate. Only one person seemed prepared to ignore the dire warnings of high casualties. Just as he was about to depart for England, Kitchener was told by Birdwood's staff officer that it was hoped that the cabinet would not delay in coming to a decision over evacuation. The field marshal replied in a light-hearted manner:

> I don't believe a word about those 25,000 casualties. Carry on just as you are doing; and when the order does arrive, as it will, you'll just slip off without losing a man, and without the Turks knowing anything at all about it!

And so it was. Suvla and Anzac were evacuated by the morning of 20 December, and Helles by the early morning of 9 January. In all, 134,000 men, 14,000 animals, and 400 guns were stolen away from directly under the eyes of the Turks – and not a man had been lost.

How had such an astonishing act been carried out? It was not only Turks who were defending the peninsula, but Germans as well. They would not have been keen to allow an enemy to quietly slip away, only to reappear in another theatre of the war in opposition to their soldier-comrades. There was, however, one thing in which the Turks, the Germans, and the British were united – none of them wanted the Russians to take over Constantinople. But it was not that simple.

On 18 March 1915 Great Britain had signed a secret treaty with Russia that gave the Russians Constantinople and lands on both sides of the Dardanelles. If the Anglo-French forces on Gallipoli had defeated the Turks, Russia would have gained a prize for which it had been seeking for centuries. The idea was not unreasonable (although the Turks would certainly not have thought so) whilst Russia remained a monarchy with prospects of becoming a democratic one. The idea was not so good, however, when there were clear signs that Russia was beginning to descend into chaos.

After the war, Brigadier General Cecil Aspinall-Oglander, Keyes' biographer and a senior staff officer at Gallipoli, was told by a senior Turkish officer that 'British diplomats are the astutest men in the world.' He then added, as an explanation, why de Robeck had failed to persevere in his attempt on the Dardanelles:

> Your Government had just signed an agreement that, if Constantinople fell, Russia should have it. But they didn't want Russia to have it. So they telegraphed to your Admiral, forbidding him to go through the Straits. And see how clever they were. How much better for you to have us here instead of the Bolsheviks.

Aspinall-Oglander considered the idea to be 'absurd'. It is certainly extremely unlikely, but the Turkish officer may have got the story slightly wrong. De Robeck, despite agitation by Keyes, Wemyss, and the rest of his staff, always rigidly opposed the idea of a further attempt at the Dardanelles. Indeed, had he deliberately allowed Keyes to put his plan before the Sea Lords in the full knowledge that any proposal for a further attack on the straits would be rejected? Was the meeting between the High Commissioner, Sir Henry MacMahon, and Kitchener really about an assault on Alexandretta – which never happened? And why was the field marshal so certain that over 100,000 men would be able to 'just slip off without losing a man'? The only attack on the withdrawing troops took place as they fell back at Helles, but that was probably in retaliation for a mine that had been exploded under the Turkish trenches during the evacuation at Suvla. As it was, many of the Turkish soldiers refused to leave their trenches during the attack, which quickly fizzled out. Were they aware that the enemy was leaving, and not prepared to risk their lives in a pointless attack? In their report, the Dardanelles Commission – set up to investigate the campaign – noted:

> We think that after the advice of Sir Charles Monro had been confirmed by Lord Kitchener the decision to evacuate should have been taken at once. *We recognise, however, that the question of evacuation was connected with other questions of high policy which do not appear to come within the scope of our enquiry* [Author's italics].

As a result of Keyes' failure to obtain permission for another attack, Russia failed to gain Constantinople and the straits, and Turkey came under the rule of an old Gallipoli adversary, Kemal Ataturk, who, after over thirteen centuries of Islamic domination, ejected – and effectively destroyed – the Caliphate. This, then, was probably the result of the 'high policy' and diplomacy threatened by Keyes' eager desire to get at the enemy.

Although, as a devout Christian, he may have had his own views on the effect on Islam, the first time Keyes sailed through the Dardanelles after the war, he noted, 'it would have been even easier than I thought; we simply couldn't have failed … And because we didn't try, another million lives were thrown away and the war went on for another three years.' On the question of the evacuation, Keyes dismissed it as 'one of the most disastrous and cowardly surrenders in the history of our country'.

In June 1916 Keyes, disappointed at missing the Battle of Jutland, was appointed to the Grand Fleet in command of HMS *Centurion*, a five-year-old battleship, carrying ten 13.5in guns. Now back in the rank of captain, and joined by his family, he settled down to the life he knew and enjoyed above all. It was a straightforward life of evolutions, preparing for action, coaling ship, studying naval history, and praying that the German High Seas Fleet would put to sea. An even higher gloss was added, however, when over the succeeding months, he rose to the top of the Captain's List.

Keyes was promoted to rear admiral in April 1917, but voluntarily remained as a captain for a further two months until a suitable appointment became available. When the appointment arrived, the ship's company of the *Centurion* presented him with a teak casket containing a large silk rear admiral's flag along with the instructions that it was 'to be worn in battle'.

Remaining with the Grand Fleet, Keyes' first flagship was the battleship *Colossus*. His flag-captain was Captain Dudley Pound who had been his first lieutenant in HMS *Opossum*, nearly twenty years earlier. Pound, however, was shortly afterwards appointed to the Admiralty, his place being taken by another long-standing friend, Captain Wilfred Tomkinson.

At about this time, Keyes became aware of rumours that he was about to be sent to replace Vice Admiral Bacon, currently in command of the Dover Patrol. He quashed such suggestions whenever he came across them. It was far better to be serving in the Grand Fleet under Admiral Sir David Beatty (Jellicoe was now First Sea Lord) where there was every chance of coming up against the Germans. The only possible attraction for him in Dover was the chance 'to have a go at Zeebrugge'. But even that opportunity seemed to be further withdrawn when he was visited by the newly promoted Admiral Sir Rosslyn Wemyss in his capacity as an additional Admiralty Board member with the title of Deputy First Sea Lord.

The keenest supporter of Keyes' plan to attack the Dardanelles was highly concerned about the lack of energy being shown at the Admiralty. It seemed to Wemyss that everyone was quite happy to fight a defensive war, rather than taking the fight to the enemy. In an effort to change this attitude, Wemyss had created a Plans Directorate responsible for both the provision of operational plans, and for the resources required to carry them out. Wemyss knew exactly who he wanted to be the director – Rear Admiral Roger Keyes.

Saddened by the loss of his appointment with the Grand Fleet, but also excited at the possibilities of effecting the direction of the war at sea, Keyes moved in to his new appointment at the end of September 1917. What he found, however, was not so much exciting, as alarming.

There were two key elements in the war at sea that immediately caused him concern. Firstly, the numbers of vessels lost to U-boats was far higher than could be expected from the number of submarines believed to be passing through the North Sea and around the top of Scotland, and yet the commander of the Dover Patrol, Vice Admiral Sir Reginald Bacon, repeatedly claimed that only a tiny proportion of U-boats were passing though the straits. Secondly, that Bacon's idea of lighting the Dover Barrage at night by use of specially protected stationary lightships shining searchlights along its length, in company with other searchlights sited ashore, would be ineffectual.

To examine the latter problem, Keyes created the Dover Barrage Committee, with himself as chairman. It was an action that outraged Bacon – especially when the committee recommended that his fixed searchlights should be replaced by searchlight-bearing ships cruising along the barriers' length. They, in turn, he was told, should augmented by extremely powerful flares.

In the conundrum caused by the number of successful U-boat attacks, Keyes had a powerful, and highly respected ally. Rear Admiral William Reginald Hall's father had been the first director of naval intelligence, a position his son now held from Room 40 with competence and flair. Although known as 'Reggie' to his family and close friends, he was known to the wider navy as 'Blinker', from a persistent facial twitch (caused, according to family tradition, by public school starvation leading to a supplementary diet of raw turnips stolen from a neighbouring field), Hall had a distinguished seagoing career that included the novel introduction of chapels, cinemas, and washing machines in his ships. He had also served as 'inspecting captain of mechanical training establishments', a role in which he had served with Bacon on a submarine manning committee. Included in his intelligence successes since his appointment in 1914 were the detentions of the gun-running ship *Aud*, taking German arms to Ireland, and the capture of the Irish nationalist leader Sir Roger Casement. When he learned that support was being expressed in America, and even in the British Cabinet, for Casement, Hall simply arranged for copies of extracts from Casement's diary to fall into the hands of the American ambassador and members of parliament. These extracts revealed Casement's 'addiction to unnatural vices'. All support immediately fell away. Hall had also established contact with the Turks after their entry into the war and attempted to bribe them into changing sides. His plan nearly came to fruition, but he was instructed to break off negotiations by Fisher. Hall's greatest coup, however, was the way he skilfully managed the exposure of the Zimmermann telegram, revealing that Germany was coaxing Mexico into an invasion of the USA – his action bringing a reluctant America into the war.

Hall's most pressing problem in October 1917 was the questions of the U-boat penetration of the Straits of Dover. No matter what conclusion Hall deduced from the scanty evidence available, Bacon always denied that the enemy submarines were getting past his barrage. Then the documents from *Kapitanleutnant* Kurt Tebbenjohans' *UC-44* arrived at Room 40.

Once the paperwork from the sunken submarine had been decoded, Hall invented a story of *UC-44* striking a mine that the British had failed to sweep. This was then passed on to the Germans through known enemy agents. To confuse the Germans even further, a fake chart purporting to show swept channels off Waterford was sold to the enemy through an agent which, in due course, was to cause the loss of a number of U-boats. Hall also presented the revelations to his old friend, the new director of plans. With such information available to him, there could be no doubt, as far as Keyes was concerned, that the enemy submarines were transiting the straits by night on the surface, often as many as thirty a month. The only answer, it seemed, was massively to strengthen the barrage, but this would take time. There was, for example, a shortage of mines available and supplies would have to be brought over from America.

Keyes and Pound looked at the problem and decided that the best answer lay in an assault upon the canal entrances at Zeebrugge and Ostend. They studied Admiral Bayly's and Commodore Tyrwhitt's earlier proposals (both rejected by Bacon), and Bacon's own suggestion that the outer mole wall should be rammed by a monitor and a suspended ramp dropped to allow access to the mole floor. They came to the conclusion that the only practical solution lay in sending in blockships to close off the canals to traffic. At both Zeebrugge and Ostend, three old warships could be steamed into the canal entrances and sunk under the cover of a heavy smokescreen. It would clearly be a hazardous operation, but in his covering memorandum to Jellicoe, Keyes noted that those involved would not be at 'any greater risk than the infantry and tank personnel are subjected to on every occasion on which an attack is delivered on shore'.

Unfortunately, the outline plan and the memorandum intended for the First Sea Lord were dispatched instead to Bacon at Dover. To try and calm any expected show of resentment, Jellicoe telephoned Bacon to ask for the return of the papers and was promised that Bacon would deliver them in person to the

Admiralty in a day or two. When nothing happened after a week, an officer was sent to Dover only to be told that Bacon would bring proposals of his own to the Admiralty on 18 December.

On that day, Bacon, still opposing the idea of blockships but forced to include them because of Jellicoe's support, proposed the addition of two monitors, one arriving at the inside of the mole to bombard the lockgates as the other discharged a battalion of infantry over the outer wall. Keyes supported the idea of an attack from the outer mole wall but insisted that it should be made by seamen and Royal Marines. Again Jellicoe gave his support and sent Keyes north to the Grand Fleet to get the views of Beatty on the supply of men from that source.

The director of plans was away for just a few days but returned to a changed and shaken Admiralty. The first lord, Sir Eric Geddes (a former railway manager who, most unusually, had been given the honorary rank of vice admiral to go with the rank of major general he had been given by the army when he ran the military rail system in France earlier in the war) called a meeting of Jellicoe and Wemyss. At the meeting, Wemyss, best known to the seamen of the fleet for his skill at catching his monocle in his right eye, argued strongly that Bacon should be relieved of his command at Dover and replaced by Keyes. Jellicoe, equally strongly, disagreed. Geddes could not come down on either side in what was clearly a professional disagreement, but he *was* a politician. After discussing the matter with the king, Geddes immediately invited Jellicoe's resignation on the grounds that he should not be subjected to yet more stress in the service of his country. By the end of the day Jellicoe had gone and Wemyss had been installed as his replacement.

On his return to the Admiralty after his visit to the Grand Fleet, Keyes was promptly summoned by the new First Sea Lord. Before he had even sat down, Wemyss said to him, 'Well, Roger, you have talked a hell of a lot about what ought to be done in the Dover area. Now you must go down and do it all yourself.'

The men of the Dover Patrol were about to find themselves under a new style of leadership.

3

The Challenge

Keyes' assumption of command at Dover was not to be as uneventful as he had hoped. On the surface, Bacon appeared unperturbed at his re-assignment but, in reality, considered his move to be the equivalent of being 'abused in public without cause, and without check or protest from those in authority'. He considered that he had been 'summarily dismissed' and his parting words to his replacement were that he considered Keyes to be not only 'all wrong' but would soon find out his 'mistake' in taking over from him. Some of Bacon's supporters loudly claimed that Keyes was going against a naval tradition that stated no officer should benefit from his part in the removal of another officer. Not only does such a tradition not exist, but the Royal Navy – as in all armed services – has to be pragmatic rather than precious. Long experience had shown that putting the wrong man into a vital job can be tantamount to aiding the enemy. Keyes had a reputation as an aggressive fighter who was, almost certainly, the best man to take over from his well-meaning, but plodding predecessor. One of Bacon's friends and supporters, Admiral Sir Henry Oliver, said to Keyes when he left the Admiralty for Dover, 'Well, now it is up to you to deliver the goods.' And Keyes meant to do exactly that.

In purely naval terms, one considerable obstacle existed on the route to Keyes' taking over at Dover. The second-in-command to Bacon was Rear Admiral Cecil Dampier, the admiral superintendent of Dover Dockyard with responsibility for all naval shore establishments at the port. Many years earlier, Dampier had been a lieutenant serving in the same ship as a nervous, but eager, Midshipman Keyes. On Keyes' appointment to Dover, Dampier had over two year's seniority to Keyes as a rear admiral. Wemyss, unwilling to have his plans for Keyes placed in jeopardy, circumvented service niceties and used his authority as First Sea Lord to immediately promote Keyes to acting vice admiral.

Keyes was also surprised to find that, on gathering his senior officers together, there was a clear element of hostility to his arrival. Having been assured for so long that the U-boats had failed to breach the Dover barrage, they were unwilling to accept any change in the, apparently, successful defences. There was, furthermore, a marked resentment at Bacon's abrupt departure. Keyes' response was to shock them rigid. He showed his officers the intelligence file that not only informed them that at least one enemy submarine was passing through the straits every night, but that the much-vaunted barrage was, in effect, useless.

This news had a particularly serious effect upon Keyes' chief of staff, Captain Edward Evans (who had also held that position under Bacon). Evans had all the heroic qualities admired by Keyes. He had been second-in-command to Captain Scott on the *Terra Nova* expedition, and had earned widespread fame as 'Evans of the *Broke*' when, commanding the destroyer of that name, he rammed a German destroyer. When the Germans began to clamber onto the *Broke*'s forecastle, his petty officers and men attacked them with bayonets and cutlasses, as the first and second lieutenants, firing from the bridge wing, emptied their pistols into enemy seamen trying to emerge onto the upper deck of their sinking ship. As this was going on, the *Broke*'s torpedo-layers brought their tubes to bear on another German destroyer, sending her to the bottom. Unfortunately, Evans was not made of the right material to be a successful chief of staff. Under Bacon he had been given no responsibilities and, as demonstrated by Keyes and the intelligence file, he had been denied access to vital information. This blow to Evans' morale came on top of an admission of feeling 'seedy', possibly as a result of the scurvy he had suffered in the Antarctic. With his eyesight in poor condition, probably as a result of snow-blindness, and with firm medical advice that he should take a rest, Evans turned down the chance of an alternative appointment with the Dover Patrol and asked to be relieved. He was replaced by an old Gallipoli friend of Keyes, Commodore the Honourable Algernon Boyle, who had commanded a battleship at Jutland.

Keyes retained Bacon's flag-lieutenant, Lieutenant Llewellyn Morgan – a signals specialist – but turned, once again, to his Gallipoli associates to fill other roles. To look after his accommodation and offices on Dover's Marine Parade, he appointed Staff Paymaster Alec Haine, whilst at sea the secretarial duties were undertaken by Assistant Paymaster Woolley. The latter had come to Keyes' attention after he had smuggled himself ashore in a ship's boat, landing seamen to destroy guns in a Turkish fort. His flimsy excuse – which no one believed – was that he wanted to make a scribbled record for the officer in charge. Searching even further back in his career, Keyes appointed his old friend and first lieutenant from his time in HMS *Fame*, Captain Wilfred Tomkinson, as captain of the Dover destroyers.

With his immediate team in place, Keyes could look around the vast command of which he was the head. Although actually living ashore, Keyes flew his flag in the old cruiser HMS *Arrogant*. She acted as depot ship for the command's submarines and motor launches (MLs) – the latter being under the command of Captain Graham Edwards. The senior motor launch officer at Dunkirk was

Captain Ion Hamilton Benn MP, who had served as the mayor of Greenwich until elected as the borough's Member of Parliament in 1910.

The command's coastal motor boats (CMBs) were tied alongside the dockyard wall close to the workshops that oversaw their maintenance. They were under the command of the 24-year-old Lieutenant Arthur Welman.

Captain Vansittart Howard was in charge of the command's trawlers, and the drifters were led by Captain Frederic Bird. Both were 'dug out' (retired) officers who had been called back into service on the outbreak of war.

In all, Keyes had at his disposal over 300 vessels including light cruisers, monitors, destroyers, minelayers, submarines, P-boats (light, fast patrol boats designed to attack submarines), motor launches, coastal motor boats, yachts, trawlers, drifters and, operating out of Dunkirk, a division of French destroyers.

Also at Dover, Keyes had a seaplane base, a RNAS station, and a squadron of dirigible airships known as 'Blimps' (said to have been named from the sound they made when being flicked with a finger). All the Dover Command RNAS men and equipment came under the control of Commodore Charles Lambe, with Wing Commander Frederick Halahan serving as Keyes' Air Staff Officer. Across the Channel at Dunkirk, Lambe was also responsible for a further ninety aircraft of the Dover Command comprising five RNAS squadrons of every aircraft type from night-bombers to fighters. Keyes was a great supporter of the RNAS and vociferously opposed the developing plan to merge the service with the Royal Flying Corps to form a completely separate independent service.

Along with the aircraft at Dunkirk, Keyes' command also covered an advanced base under the supervision of the highly experienced Commodore Hubert Lynes, an internationally known and highly regarded ornithologist. Lynes had a particular reason to dislike the Germans. At the end of October 1914, as captain of the seaplane tender HMS *Hermes*, he had just delivered a number of aircraft to Dunkirk. As she began her return journey, *Hermes* was struck by a torpedo launched from the submarine *U27*. She sank immediately with the loss of twenty-two of her ship's company.

An unusual element of Keyes' command was the Royal Marine Artillery Heavy Siege Train consisting of four 12in and four 9.2in guns. Even more unusual were the Royal Naval Siege Guns, more heavy-calibre weapons employed by seamen and marines against the powerful German shore batteries north of Ostend. The latter guns came under the command of Captain Henry Halahan, the older brother of Keyes' Air Staff Officer.

Although such resources could have been deployed in a number of ways, particularly in ensuring the safety of ships supplying the army fighting in France and Belgium, Keyes knew that his first priority was to stem the flow of U-boats through the straits. Acting with characteristic resolve, he ordered the nets of the barrage to be abandoned and demanded vast quantities of mines from every source he could pester. Instead of the complex system of nets, clips, floats, weights, and buoys, he pared the problem down to its basic components. Submarines were passing down the straits at night on the surface to avoid the barrage. If they could be forced to dive, there was every chance that they would strike one of the newly sown mines – and submarines rarely survived the blast from almost 200lb of the highly explosive amatol.

There was nothing to be gained from trying to hide the minefield. The chief aim of Keyes' strategy was to convince the U-boat captains that the risks involved in attempting to pass through the straits were too high to be considered, causing them to take the long route around the top of Scotland. As a result, at night, the limits of the minefield were marked by light-buoys. With darkness settling over the straits, sixty or more armed drifters searched the minefield as four destroyers or P-boats, and two paddle minesweepers, probed the area with powerful carbon-arc searchlights. At the same time, fourteen trawlers would fire million-candle-power flares (designed by the pyrotechnic expert Wing Commander Brock) into the night sky. If an enemy submarine was seen, red-and-white flares alerted patrolling motor launches, which swooped in to drop depth charges. If the U-boat refused to dive and tried to dash for the safety of the darkness, they would soon find themselves pinned down by the destroyer's or P-boat's searchlights and subjected to the fire of 4in guns, 2pdr pom-poms (rapid-firing guns originally designed for use against aircraft) or torpedoes. The new system became known as the 'light barrage'. Only if a green flare arced into the sky were the searchlights switched off and the flares stopped. A green flare meant that enemy surface warships had been sighted.

At first, it seemed as if there was a disappointing lack of success at the barrage. U-boats were spotted but then disappeared beneath the waters. In time, however, evidence of sinkings began to appear in the shape of observed underwater explosions and with oil and debris floating to the surface. In late January, divers found a U-boat on the bottom of the straits. She was *U109*, which had been

A Coastal Motor Boat (CMB) undergoing builder's trials.

Captain I. Hamilton
Benn RNVR.

spotted and fired on by the drifter *Beryl II* on the 26th. The submarine had been
based at Heligoland Bight and when the Germans realised that it was not going
to return to harbour, they ordered that no more U-boats from Heligoland were
to attempt the straits. For them, the only route to the Atlantic was to be the long
passage around Scotland. Only for the Flanders Flotilla with their smaller, coastal
submarines issuing from Zeebrugge and Ostend, was the light barrage still a risk
worth taking.

There was, nevertheless, still the risk of retaliation. For several months the two
sides of the North Sea had kept an uneasy distance. The RNAS bomber squadrons
had been forced to keep their operations to a minimum for fear of provoking
retaliatory attacks on civilian targets on the east coast, and the many gun batteries
on the Belgian coast had been left unmolested by the monitors in case the ships
fell victim to the enemy's greater range. As if by unstated agreement, the Germans

had not attacked the obvious and relatively easy target of the net barrage, nor had their surface vessels or submarines carried out any attacks on the Dover Patrol. Keyes' arrival at Dover, however, had altered the balance of this arrangement, as he was to find out to his fury.

On 14 February, after a telephone call from Rear Admiral Hall, Keyes was able to inform the patrolling vessels that a German submarine was likely to attempt a surface passage that night. Keen to see if the intelligence was correct, Keyes waited up that night and at 2345hrs was delighted to see the slow rise of red-and-white flares followed by the sound of gunfire. His delight, however, gradually turned to concern as not only was the gunfire still continuing an hour and a half later, but no reports had been received from any of the patrolling ships. Captain Tomkinson had boarded the duty destroyer and was on his way to see what was going on. In the meantime, Keyes signalled the monitor *M26*. Her position in the centre of the barrage should have kept her informed of the situation. After a delay, the monitor replied that she was on the way to investigate. After further prompting by Keyes the monitor replied, informing him that a drifter had reported a green flare but everything was 'All quiet now'. This made no sense. A green flare should have sent the drifters and trawlers running for safety as the searchlights were switched off and the firing of Brock's flares halted. Half an hour after the monitor's signal, Keyes received another message, this time form the destroyer *Syren*. She had come across the burning hulk of a drifter.

With the approach of dawn came the gradual realisation that something had gone terribly wrong. With all the reports in, Keyes was shocked at what had happened. German destroyers had pounced on the light-barrage with the result that seven drifters and a trawler had been sunk. Another three drifters and a paddle minesweeper had been damaged. Altogether, seventy-six officers and men had lost their lives, and thirteen had been wounded. It was not the German retaliation that fuelled Keyes' anger; he had been expecting such an attack and viewed it as an opportunity to get to grips with the enemy. What had particularly raised his ire was that the trawlermen and drifter crews looked upon the incident as an example of being let down by the Royal Navy. Where there should have been protection, there was chaos and incompetence. Even worse, the German Navy was soon boasting about a great victory over the Dover Patrol. Elated by the success of the attack, the following night saw a U-boat surface off Dover and fire twelve shells into the town, killing a child and injuring five people. This was followed by an attack by German aircraft dropping bombs on Dover – fortunately without causing casualties.

The fault was soon revealed to be a combination of poor tactical understanding and lack of aggression. The monitor *M26*, for example, had steamed off in the direction of the gunfire but had reported the incident to no one, nor had she responded in adequate time to Keyes' urgent signals. It further turned out that she had sighted a green flare at about 0100hrs but had taken no action to extinguish the searchlights and flares. Her captain was dismissed from his ship. Even worse, one of the patrol's destroyers, HMS *Amazon*, watched as three unidentified destroyers steamed eastwards in the darkness. She signalled a challenge but instead of receiving the correct reply saw her own signal being repeated back to her. At this she assumed that the other vessels were Royal Navy destroyers out on a patrol of which she was unaware. She may well also have been affected by Bacon's orders to the Patrol, orders which Keyes had left unamended. Bacon had written that 'It is not the function of the large destroyers in the first instance to force an unequal fight, as our boats will be spread. It is far more important to hang on and keep in touch with the enemy ...' Keyes changed this to 'if the challenge is made and not immediately answered, offensive action is to be taken without further delay'.

The captain of the *Amazon* was relieved of his command, as was the captain of the destroyer-leader who, on learning of the *Amazon*'s sighting of the unrecognised destroyers, wasted time interrogating the *Amazon* by signal instead of setting off in pursuit of the enemy.

As for the discouraged and dazed crews of the trawlers and drifters, Keyes was heartened to learn that Captain Bird had told his drifter men, 'Don't you make any mistake about it, the Admiral will take tea with those blighters before long, and make them pay for last night's raid.'

Keyes had intended to 'take tea' with the Germans for some time. On assuming command at Dover, his work on the restructuring of the barrage, the day-to-day ferrying of troops and supplies across the Channel and, since the Destroyer attack in February, the strengthening of his naval forces, had all been done to a background of a pressing need to tackle the problem of Zeebrugge and Ostend. The problem was not merely one of fearsome complexity, but one that required actions that had only once been successfully carried out in the entire history of the Royal Navy, and, so far as was known, never achieved by any other navy.

The 26-mile-long North Sea coast between Nieuport and the Dutch border consisted mainly of sand dune beaches. Offshore, the shoaling waters of the Flanders Banks provided a shifting hazard for all but the most shallow-drafted vessels. If the 12-mile section of the coast between Ostend and Zeebrugge was considered to be the base of a triangle, the apex was the city of Bruges, some 6 miles inland.

Until the late Middle Ages, Bruges had its own, natural, access to the North Sea but this had silted up, leaving Antwerp as the key inland port. In 1895, work had begun on constructing a canal between Bruges and Zeebrugge, which opened to shipping ten years later. The depth of the canal was 24ft, allowing modestly sized vessels and stout barges passage all the way between the sea and the newly built docks at Bruges. At Zeebrugge, lockgates maintained the canal's water whilst a swing-bridge allowed the passage of a road to cross alongside the lockgates.

The third side of the triangle was completed by a 12-mile canal between Bruges and Ostend that could only allow the passage of smaller vessels. As this canal met the North Sea it was protected against silting by a pair of outward-curving piers. Just offshore, the Stroom, Middlekirk, and Boone Land banks provided considerable hazards to the navigation of vessels with passage between the banks limited to about thirty feet in depth. The chief aid to navigation was the Stroom Bank buoy which, once located, served to indicate the canal's entrance. The difference between high and low tide could be in the region of 14ft.

As at Ostend, the Zeebrugge canal exit, about half-a-mile beyond the lockgates, was guarded by a pair of curved piers. In addition a huge, solid, harbour wall or 'mole' curved for over a mile out to sea in a massive northeasterly hook. Extending the landward end of the mole towards shore was a 300yrd viaduct held above the seabed on substantial steel piles. The viaduct was deliberately so designed to act as an exit for the tide, thus assisting the area inside the mole to be scoured of silt. The final link with the land was provided by a 300yrd stone pier connecting the viaduct to the shore some half-a-mile west of the canal. At the seaward end of the mole, a narrow extension of over 300 yards ended in a lighthouse.

The main part of the mole, between the seaward end of the viaduct and the start of the lighthouse extension, had a granite-paved floor 80 yards wide and high enough to cater for a tidal range of about 13ft. This allowed for its inner (harbour) edge to be used as a safe mooring for vessels up to the size of large cargo carriers. Its outer (seaward) side was dominated by a 16ft high concrete wall that carried a 9ft-wide pathway. At the outer edge of this pathway, a further 1ft thick and 4ft-high wall or parapet provided protection against a, frequently wild, sea. The inner edge of the pathway was guarded by an iron handrail. The wall and parapet extended the entire length of the mole, whilst the handrail was interrupted by a small number of iron stairs leading down to the mole floor.

The tall outer mole wall was continued across the viaduct by a steel screen of the same height bearing a iron walkway that connected with the upper mole pathway. At the far end of the mole, the outer wall, complete with its parapet and pathway, continued along the entire lighthouse extension above a floor reduced to a width of about 15ft. The floor of the mole itself carried a railway line, including sidings, a railway station, warehouses, cranes, and the usual paraphernalia of docks, wharves, and port administration.

By 1914 Ostend had become a popular seaside resort whilst Zeebrugge grew into a bustling port. The local people and tourists strolled along the mole wall for exercise and the bracing North Sea air, they watched the lockgate opening and closing to allow the transit of the canal traffic, or took rides to nearby Blankenberg on the electric tram. Belgium and the Belgians were quietly proud of their short, sandy, stretch of coast. Then came the Germans.

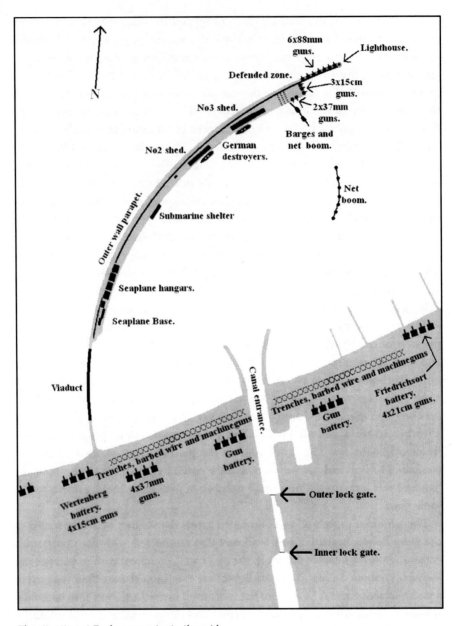

The situation at Zeebrugge prior to the raid.

The German Navy, in the shape of the Flanders Flotilla, under the command of Admiral Ludwig von Schroeder, had two particularly important tasks to fulfil: first, to mount aggressive actions against British commercial shipping, against the Royal Navy, and against cross-Channel transports; second, to protect the German Army's right flank, currently anchored just north of Nieuport.

To prosecute the war at sea, Ostend docks and harbour were turned into a safe haven for submarines and other small vessels to use during operations in the Channel. At Blankenberge – less than 3 miles west of Zeebrugge – the fishing harbour accommodated thirty torpedo boats. The Zeebrugge mole provided protection and maintenance facilities for destroyers as they prepared to go out on patrol, or for U-boats waiting to pass through the Bruges canal. Many of the U-boats were manufactured in Germany, assembled at Antwerp and taken through the inland canals to Bruges. In all, the Bruges docks provided berthing facilities for about thirty-five torpedo boats and thirty submarines. The U-boat officers had commandeered the nearby house of M. Catulle as a mess and had converted the vaulted cellars into a bar. The walls were painted with frescoes showing mines dancing with torpedoes, John Bull drinking champagne with monkeys, and memorial portraits of U-boat officers lost at sea. The images were accompanied by mottoes such as 'Life is short, and you'll be a long time dead' and 'Drink, for tomorrow you may die.'

Coastal defences were provided by twenty-six gun batteries, deploying a total of 229 naval guns mounted on land carriages, sited between Nieuport and Knokke. The calibre of the guns ranged from 3.5in to 15in, the latter capable of firing a ¾-ton shell almost 30 miles. Four of the 15in guns were sited in the Deutschland Battery at Bredene, just to the east of Ostend. Two more were sited well inland, south of Ostend, where they could be used to fire at Nieuport and the RNAS aerodromes at Dunkirk. In all, Ostend was protected by thirteen heavy gun batteries and heavy machine guns mounted on the piers guarded the entrance to the Ostend canal. Sited between these batteries, and in other positions all along the coast, were entrenched machine-gun positions protected by barbed wire. At Blankenberge, the harbour was covered by one battery mounting four 3.5in guns, and another with four 8in.

Zeebrugge was protected by the four 6in guns of the Wurtemberg Battery situated just to the west of the point where the mole pier met the shore. Alongside them lay two 4.2in guns and the 5.9in guns of the Lubeck Battery. Just to the east of the pier lay a battery of four 37mm anti-aircraft guns, whilst further to the east, aiming directly at any vessels rounding the lighthouse end of the mole less than a mile to their front, were the four 8.2in guns of the Friedrichsort (or Goeben) Battery.

The mole itself had been changed dramatically by von Schroeder. The railway station had gone, to be replaced by a seaplane base, its main building being known as No. 1 Shed. The base staff were accommodated in adjacent buildings and onboard the Great Eastern Railway steamer SS *Brussels*, tied up alongside. The *Brussels* had been commanded by a Southampton-born Captain Charles Fryatt, who had been executed by the Germans for escaping from one U-boat and attempting to ram another. The death of Captain Fryatt had been widely considered as a crime equal to the execution of Nurse Edith Cavell.

Further along the mole, a submarine shelter had been built to protect U-boats from air attacks. This was followed by Nos. 2 and 3 Sheds, several more buildings, including workshop facilities, stores and accommodation, all interspersed with machine-gun emplacements.

A little beyond No. 3 Shed, behind several deep barbed wire barriers guarding trenchworks, lay a heavily fortified zone. The reasons for this zone could be seen to the rear of the trenches. At the far extremity of the mole, where the lighthouse extension began, three 5.9in guns lay in wait for any unwelcome vessel passing the lighthouse just over 300 yards away. Above them, spread along the lighthouse extension wall, were six 3.5in guns, capable of operating through almost 360 degrees.

At the point where the mole proper met the lighthouse extension, and built high enough to see over the top of the outer parapet, a fire control position linked to the Friedrichsort Battery had been constructed. The guns of the battery were masked for much of their firing arc by the mole, and the fire control position was needed to spot the fall of shot and to relay the information back to the guns. In case of attack, the occupants of the fire control position could leave in the direction of the extension, descend a flight of stone-built steps, and take cover in a passageway that extended through the whole length of the extension. It had originally been built to provide shelter for the lighthouse keepers as they made their way to work in inclement weather.

The Germans were assisted by the build-up of silt within the arc of the mole. Although the gap beneath the viaduct had helped, the Germans' failure to regularly dredge the area had led to the build-up of sandbanks just beyond the exit from the canal. The shore line was rendered unusable by the accumulation of silt which even penetrated the canal beyond the piers and was clearly visible at low tide. This meant that the narrow dredged channel through which any vessel navigating between the lighthouse and the canal had to pass was difficult to find without buoys or pilotage. To make matters even more difficult, the Germans had erected two booms level with the fortified zone. The boom closest to the inner wall consisted of a string of barges. A suspended net then extended the boom further across the dredged channel. The boom was defended by two 37mm anti-aircraft guns sited on the mole within the fortified zone.

The manning of the mole defences, including the seaplane base, was believed to require a minimum of a thousand men. Hundreds manned the guns at the shore end of the mole, and many more waited in reserve ready to reinforce the mole garrison. Any destroyers moored alongside the mole would also have been available to assist with their guns, torpedoes and men.

Such then were the obstacles, firepower and trained fighting men that lay in wait for any attempt to attack the harbour and facilities at Zeebrugge. All that was needed was a plan to defeat them.

4

The Plan

Schemes for seaborne attacks on Zeebrugge and Ostend had frequently found their way onto the Admiralty's desks. In 1916, Vice Admiral Sir Lewis Bayly, the commander-in-chief of the Western Approaches, desperate to reduce the number of U-boat attacks in his area, had put forward a plan to 'neutralise' the Belgian ports. In his plan, he advocated a combined naval and military operation. The idea never got further than the initial paperwork.

Shortly afterwards, Commodore Reginald Tyrwhitt proposed a more innovative plan. Aided by a heavy bombardment, smokescreens and poisoned gas, a blockship would be steamed into the canal entrance and sunk, sealing off the waterway. This was opposed by Vice Admiral Bacon, who proposed instead an attempt by coastal motor boats to torpedo the lockgates. This, in turn, was countered by Tyrwhitt, who, expanding upon his original idea, suggested capturing both the mole and the town of Zeebrugge. Bacon, by now desperate to fend off any more attempts to impose suggestions on his domain, returned once again to his favourite means of attack – a heavy bombardment.

At first glance, the idea of simply shelling the lockgates at Zeebrugge and the harbour at Ostend seemed the most obvious answer but despite Bacon's wealth of gunnery experience, and the improvements in naval shore bombardment, he had failed to achieve anything worthwhile. The difficulties with a shore bombardment lay in the trouble of accurately spotting the 'fall of shot', the inadequacy of communications between spotter and gunner, and the tendency of the enemy to hide the target behind a smokescreen. Furthermore, the position of the firing ship was fixed by dropping a buoy from a destroyer, only to find on many occasions that the buoy was subject to considerable drift from its original position. Bacon, nevertheless – in the absence of his 'portable islands' – was happy with the 'By guess and by God' method in the belief that at least a proportion of his shells would land on target. Unfortunately, they rarely did.

Somewhat surprisingly in view of his own interest in scientific improvement, Bacon failed to take advantage of a technical advance offered from within his own command. Commander Edward Altham, the captain of the monitor

HMS *General Craufurd*, had devised a gyroscopic director, which, once the range and bearing had been calculated, would keep a gun's bearing and elevation fixed firmly on the target. Altham sent the details on to Bacon, who simply filed them away.

When forced to come up with a viable scheme that did not depend solely upon the firepower of his heavy guns, Bacon came up with his idea of bombarding the lockgates at Zeebrugge with one monitor, whilst another was rammed against the mole wall. The second monitor would then flip a huge ramp over the mole parapet and wall to land with its foremost edge on the mole floor. With this in place, 900 soldiers would rush over the ramp and capture the mole. Shortly after this proposal, he was replaced by Keyes.

For Keyes himself, the first task was to sort through the proposals and counter-proposals in an effort to come up with a practical plan of action. Basing much upon the 'Staff Appreciation' he had worked at when he was the director of plans at the Admiralty, he retained Tyrwhitt's idea of blockships and smokescreens, but rejected the idea of poisoned gas.

Previous history provided very little in the way of example in the use of blockships, and most of what there was proved hardly encouraging. In 1898 Lieutenant Richard Hobson of the United States Navy attempted to sink the *Merrimac*, a large collier, beneath the walls of Morro Castle, in an effort to block the entrance to Santiago harbour. All went well until the last moment, when the ship's steering gear was shot away, the *Merrimac* struck a mine and several of the 'torpedoes' (mines) secured along the ship's side to blow her side out, failed to explode. Finally, a strong tide swept the collier through the channel until she was sunk in a harmless position by Spanish torpedo boats.

Six years later, the Japanese expended eight ships in three attempts to block Port Arthur. All ended up in the wrong position and the attacks failed – despite the Russians having run one of their own battleships aground in the channel.

There was, however, one incident that lent encouragement to any proposal to use blockships. In August 1914, whilst hunting the German light cruiser *Königsberg* off the coast of German East Africa, the cruiser HMS *Astraea* opened fire on the *Königsberg*'s local base port, Dar-es-Salaam. The early morning raid so shocked the harbour master that he ordered the sinking of a floating-dock across the harbour entrance. This certainly prevented the *Astraea* from entering but also prevented the *Königsberg* from leaving. Consequently the German cruiser took refuge in the delta of the Rufigi River where, once she had been located, the restricted channels, combined with shore artillery, proved a difficult place to attack. Captain Drury-Lowe of the cruiser HMS *Chatham* was the senior officer on the station and, guided by the example of the Dar-es-Salaam harbour master, he converted a Sunderland-built collier, the *Newbridge*, into a blockship and sent her into the delta under the *Chatham*'s second-in-command,

Commander Raymond Fitzmaurice. Escorted by steam cutters and under heavy fire from shore batteries, Fitzmaurice steered the *Newbridge* until she was placed squarely across the channel. Explosive charges sent the ship to the bottom as Fitzmaurice and his volunteer crew escaped to the sea in one of the *Chatham's* cutters. Although there were other possible exits from the delta, the incident caused the *Königsberg* to retreat upriver where she was eventually destroyed by the monitors *Severn* and *Mersey*. Fitzmaurice earned the Distinguished Service Order for his exploit and went on to achieve a knighthood and promotion to vice admiral, serving as a notable convoy commodore during the Second World War.

From Bacon, Keyes took the suggestion of attacking the mole by landing men from the seaward side. Their role would be to descend upon the end of the mole, capture and disable the guns, and sink any destroyers found alongside. The most important aspect of the mole landing, however, would be to act as a distraction to the defenders as the blockships made their way behind their backs to the canal entrance. Keyes emphatically disagreed with one feature of Bacon's plan. His predecessor had intended to ask the army for the loan of a battalion of infantry to carry out the attack. This, Keyes felt, was tantamount to 'an insult to the Navy'. In the Grand Fleet and elsewhere there were thousands of seamen of every rank and rate who were thoroughly disenchanted with the idea that their soldier brothers-in-arms were daily facing the enemy, whilst they remained in the relative safety of Scapa Flow, Portsmouth, Dover, Harwich, and elsewhere. All of them were 'splendid people' who deserved their chance to have a go at the enemy.

Then there was the question of the main ships involved in the operation. The blockships would have to be substantial vessels, almost certainly of cruiser size. They would have to be fully operative with engines in good condition and with enough armament to give a good account of themselves as they closed with the enemy. It was anticipated at the early stages of planning that three would be required for Zeebrugge and a similar number at Ostend. To land the storming parties on the mole, another well-armoured and well-armed cruiser would have to be found. Bacon's idea of using a monitor would not work as even the large ones would be too small when placed against the towering mole wall.

The height of the wall would also dictate the time of arrival alongside. Only a high tide would work – and it had to be during a period of darkness. A high tide was also necessary for the blockships to penetrate the entrance to the canal, and to reduce the risk from the hidden, shifting, sandbanks.

There was also the question of the smaller vessels. Monitors, destroyers, coastal motor boats, motor launches, and even submarines, all had vital roles to play. An accommodation ship had to be found for the volunteers from the fleet, along with training facilities for the landing parties. One major irritant for Keyes was the fact that he was shortly to lose control of his aircraft. From 1 April 1918 all

Captain A. Carpenter
VC, captain of the
Vindictive.

RNAS squadrons, including those at Dunkirk, were to be subsumed, along with the Army's Royal Flying Corps, into a new, independent, Royal Air Force. No longer would sailors fly for the navy and soldiers fly for the army. Instead, the new organisation, an unwelcome offspring of political manoeuvring, would decide upon its own operations. Cooperation would depend upon agreement – and it was suspected that there would be some striking of attitudes to establish the new status. All of this had to be done against a background of total secrecy.

From its overarching design down to the minutest operational adjustment, the plan required the skilled hand of someone prepared to pay attention to everything from cruiser armament to the seamen's rum ration. There was no aspect too small to be overlooked, no problem too difficult to be answered. Keyes originally wanted the plan to be placed under the supervision of Major William

Wellington Godfrey, a Royal Marine with whom he had worked at Gallipoli, but Godfrey was not available. Instead, Keyes turned to the officer who had been his navigator in HMS *Venus* before the war. The 36-year-old London-born Commander Alfred Carpenter had a flair for detail. He had served as a staff officer under Jellicoe and could spot gaps in reasoning, flaws in logic, and deviations from common sense. He was a popular officer who could be depended upon, and he had also worked under Captain Pound on the Staff Appreciation at the Admiralty Plans Division. Keyes had no hesitation in giving him a free hand in the organisation of the enterprise.

Tyrwhitt also proved to be the inspiration behind another feature of Keyes' initial planning. He had decided that smokescreens would play an important part in his scheme of attack. There was, however, a problem. The smoke-making apparatus available emitted a bright orange flame that could be seen by the enemy at night glowing through the smokescreen. Tyrwhitt had discussed the matter with Flight Commander Frank Brock of the Royal Naval Air Service. Now, Brock – since promoted to Wing Commander and made an Officer of the Most Excellent Order of the British Empire – received a summons from Keyes. A member of a family of firework makers, the 34-year-old Brock possessed a mind of insatiable enquiry. Fascinated by old prints, stamps and books, he was also a man of action. He played for Richmond Rugby Club, was a superb shot, a boxer, and a first-rate pilot. Like Keyes, he was a deeply committed Christian and always carried a copy of the New Testament wherever he went. Before the outbreak of war he had visited Germany in the guise of an American tourist to collect data on

Pyrotechnic expert Wing Commander F. Brock of the Royal Naval Air Service.

Zeppelin airships. When war was declared he entered the Royal Naval Volunteer Reserve and obtained a commission in the Royal Naval Division – a unit fighting ashore as infantry battalions. By early 1915, however, he was seduced by the idea of flying. Consequently he learned to fly and (although there is no evidence of a qualifying Royal Aero Club certificate) transferred to the Royal Naval Air Service as a flight lieutenant. He was not, however, destined to stay long in his new appointment as it soon became clear that the skills he had developed whilst rising to be a director at his family's firm were both rare and valuable. Accordingly, he was appointed to set up and command the Royal Naval Experimental Establishment at Stratford, London.

Given a free hand and access to a wide range of materials, Brock and his team of officers and ratings produced numerous items destined to play an important part in the war. They designed entirely new cartridge flares for Very pistols, including flares that divided into different colours, smoke flares, and parachute flares that would light up a battlefield. The million-candle-power 'Dover Flare' was invented at Stratford, as was a smoke float designed to help merchant ships under attack by U-boats. Once thrown overboard, the float automatically produced great clouds of impenetrable smoke that – in theory – could allow the ship to escape. Over 200,000 of the floats were manufactured and supplied to merchant vessels. Brock also developed the incendiary bomb by adapting the hotly burning aluminium compound used in some fireworks. One of his greatest inventions, however, was the Brock explosive bullet designed for use in aircraft attacking Zeppelins. Ordinary bullets passed straight through the thin airship envelope merely causing the inconvenience of a minor leak. The 'Buckingham bullet' depended upon its tracer qualities to ignite the hydrogen gas inside the Zeppelin but never worked as the tracer element was depleted before it reached the airship. The 'Pomeroy bullet', which contained nitro-glycerine, exploded only after it had passed through the airship. Brock's bullet, on the other hand, was so sensitive that it exploded immediately on making contact with the Zeppelin's skin. In September 1916 Lieutenant Leefe-Robinson of the Royal Flying Corps, shot down Zeppelin *SL11* over Cuffley in Hertfordshire, the first airship to be destroyed over England. His successful use of an alternate mixture of Brock and Pomeroy bullets earned him the Victoria Cross.

When Keyes explained his ideas for an assault on the Belgian ports, Brock jumped at the chance to develop an 'artificial fog' that would not expose a bright flame identifying its source. Carpenter also came up with further requests. There was always the risk of the Germans attacking the ship in force once it was alongside the mole. A crude but effective means of repulsing such an attack would be the use of powerful, fixed, flamethrowers. Brock not only agreed, but offered to produce a portable version for men landing on the mole. Carpenter also asked Brock to look at one of the key navigational problems. As the attack would be carried out at night, it would be very difficult for the ships involved to cross the North Sea and approach the Zeebrugge mole with the accurate positioning and timing needed. Within twenty-four hours of the request, Brock had invented and produced a working model of a 'light-buoy' that burst into light when dropped into the sea. With a single ship navigating the course, a string of light-buoys could be dropped, leading directly to the target area.

There was just one further problem affecting both Keyes and Brock. Although it was hoped to make the attack as soon as possible, if the conditions were not right, the night of the assault could extend well into April. From 1 April, Keyes knew he would lose control over his Royal Naval Air Service units – including Brock and the other RNAS officers and ratings at Stratford – to the newly created Royal Air Force. For Brock, it was more personal. His substantive naval rank was that of lieutenant RNVR – a rank relative to, but not necessarily equivalent to, the Army and RAF's Captain. That rank had 'marked time' when he was transferred to the RNAS. As his current rank of Wing Commander was only in a 'temporary acting' capacity, his substantive rank in the RNAS was flight commander – a rank also relative to the army and RAF's captain. As the new RAF tended only to take

The second-class cruiser HMS *Vindictive* in her prime. Launched in 1897, she is pictured in 1903 off Gibraltar about to take in tow the whaling ship *Terra Nova* on her way to assist Captain Scott's Antarctic Expedition.

HMS *Sirius*, a second-class cruiser. Launched in 1890.

The second-class cruiser HMS *Brilliant*. Launched in 1891.

officers at their substantive ranks, Brock, instead of transferring as a lieutenant colonel to match his current rank, could find himself, in effect, reduced to captain. There was, of course, the option of reverting to his RNVR rank of lieutenant, which would make him not only junior in rank to some of his own Stratford officers, but also many other officers in the Dover command.

Keyes dealt with the problem with his customary vigour. Brock and three other officers, and eighty-seven of his men under the command of Lieutenant Graham Hewett, would be transferred from Stratford to laboratories and workshops at Dover. From that moment until the completion of the attack the RNAS men

The second-class cruiser HMS *Thetis*. Launched in 1890, she was converted to a minelayer in 1907.

HMS *Intrepid*, a second-class cruiser. Launched in 1891.

The second-class cruiser HMS *Iphigenia*. Launched in 1891, she was converted to a minelayer in 1910.

came under the same security conditions as everyone else involved. Furthermore, all the Stratford RNAS personnel had their service documents and pay records retained at the naval accounting base, HMS *President*. That meant no transfer to the RAF and the retention of naval rank and rates. The final outcome, however, was only partly as Brock feared. When the first Air Force List appeared, Brock was listed as a 'Major (Acting Lieutenant Colonel)' in the RAF's Administrative Branch. That of course meant the loss of the pilot's 'wings' proudly worn on the cuff of his naval uniform. As a result, any moves to transfer Brock to the RAF were ignored.

When Keyes was still at the Admiralty undertaking the Staff Appreciation of a prospective raid on the Belgian ports, he had decided that eight old cruisers would be ideal for blocking ships. Dockyard officials were told that the ships were needed to block much of the channel entering Scapa Flow. All were capable of steaming at 8 knots, and two were planned to undergo dockyard refits. Eventually six ships were chosen. Those intended to block the canal at Ostend were the *Brilliant,* the *Sirius* and the *Vindictive.* The *Thetis, Intrepid,* and *Iphigenia* would play their part at Zeebrugge. Now, with the planning firmly under way, the First Sea Lord, Admiral Wemyss, approved the use of the cruisers.

One large gap in the proposal was the vessel that would be used to attack the seaward side of the mole. Ideally, the ship would sit high enough out of the water to enable the mole wall to be crossed by the disembarking attackers, yet have a shallow draft to pass over the top of any minefields. It had to be sturdy enough to hold its own when being pounded by shore-mounted guns, and be capable of carrying enough men for the task. To find such a vessel (almost invariably a merchant ship) Keyes sent Captain Herbert Grant. A friend of Bacon, now reluctantly serving as the intelligence officer on Keyes' staff, Grant later admitting spending much of his time compiling a dossier that he hoped to use against Keyes when the attack failed. He also despised Wemyss and Beatty, whom he considered to be 'Keyes cronies'. After a few days search, Grant returned to inform Keyes that he had been unable to locate any available ship that matched his requirements.

Faced with such news, Keyes decided upon a realignment of resources. Of the chosen blockships, the one with which he was most familiar was the *Vindictive*, a vessel of the same class as his flagship, HMS *Arrogant*, serving at Dover as a depot ship. The *Vindictive*, a second-class cruiser launched at Chatham in 1897, was a coal-burner displacing 5,750 tons and designed with a heavy, pronounced ram. With six Belleville water-tube boilers in each of her three boiler rooms supplying two triple-expansion steam engines, her twin screws gave her a maximum speed of 19 knots. She was 320ft in length with a beam of 54ft. From her upper deck, three tall funnels rose out of a forest of broad ventilation shafts, their tops curved over to face the bows. The ship was controlled from a conning tower with an open bridge above an enclosed steering position. The conning tower was protected by 9in armour. She carried two spindly masts with a control platform (or 'foretop') carried on the foremast. The masts had been of particular use during her time in the South Atlantic when they carried the ship's newly fitted wireless aerials. Her armament had originally been four 6in and six 4.7in guns but in 1904 she had been refitted to carry ten 6in with a secondary armament of nine 12pdrs. Despite being generally considered as obsolete, the *Vindictive* had given good service during the war, seeing action off Portugal, in the South Atlantic, and in the White Sea.

Commander Carpenter had constantly pestered Keyes for the opportunity to take part in the attack. The admiral finally gave in and obtained permission from the Admiralty to appoint Carpenter as his flag-captain. This meant that Carpenter had command of the *Vindictive*, with the rank of acting captain, as Keyes intended to use the cruiser as his flagship. However, it was soon pointed out that Keyes would be better deployed on a destroyer, giving him the mobility and flexibility to race around the scene of battle directing events as they occurred. Carpenter, nevertheless, remained as the cruiser's captain.

With the *Vindictive*'s new captain still occupied with formulating the overall plan, Keyes needed an officer to take over as the ship's first lieutenant with

The Liverpool ferry *Iris* undergoing smoke generator trials during refitting.

the onerous responsibility for preparing her for the forthcoming action. Just at the right time, Lieutenant Commander Robert Rosoman arrived with an appointment as first lieutenant of the *Arrogant*. After an interview, Keyes decided that Rosoman was 'a stout fellow, a good seaman, and a good organiser' and, much to Rosoman's delight, redirected him towards the *Vindictive*. To assist the new first lieutenant, Keyes also sent an experienced gunnery officer, Commander Seymour Osborne, and Lieutenant Commander Frank Bramble to propose and install changes to the ship's armament, whilst Engineer Lieutenant Commander William Bury attended to the ship's machinery.

As the cruiser would not be able to take all the storming parties of seamen and Royal Marines, Keyes knew that he would have to find other vessels to take some of the parties, mainly the Royal Marines, across the North Sea. Captain Grant, sent once again by Keyes to find suitable vessels, finally came across two Mersey ferries – the *Iris* and the *Daffodil*. Launched in 1904, the ferries were fitted with three-cylinder, triple-expansion engines and could reach a speed of 12.5 knots (just over 14mph). Of shallow draft, and double-hulled, the ferries had already shown their qualities when, some time before, one of them had a collision whilst carrying about a thousand passengers. A huge rip in her side extending to the waterline had failed to sink her, and all the passengers were disembarked safely. There were loud complaints from many ferry users when Keyes arranged for the boats to be commandeered, but these quietened down when it was learned through carefully planted rumours that the fixing of armour plate to the ferries was being done to bring American troops safely across the Atlantic. Such rumours were unchallenged by the ferries' manager, William Henry Fry – who just happened to be a commander in the Royal Naval Reserve.

Whilst the final alterations to the Liverpool ferries were being carried out at Portsmouth dockyard, the blockships were undergoing significant alterations for their final roles. Of the five vessels, only two – *Brilliant* and *Sirius* – had been retained in their role as second-class cruisers. The remaining three had been converted to minesweepers before the outbreak of war and none had seen service of any significance during the conflict. For the raid, the main control position was situated at the base of the conning tower, with all controls duplicated in additional control positions further aft. The main conning tower and the reserve position were draped with dense splinter mats designed to protect against machine-gun and small-arms fire. As many compartments as possible within the hull above the engine and boiler rooms were filled with concrete, rubble and bags of cement, while (on the advice of experts from the Liverpool Salvage Company) cement blocks were placed in strategic positions. In all, 1,500 tons of extra weight was added with the dual purpose of taking the ships to the bottom, and in order to make life as difficult as possible for any subsequent salvage operation. To act as a counter-weight to this increased load, the ships' double-bottoms were flooded. A series of explosive charges was spread throughout the lower part of the ships, and holes drilled to allow the air in the lower compartments to escape. The charges could be exploded from firing keys situated in each of the control positions. In order to reduce the risk of the ships being seen before they could complete their task, the masts were removed. The forward 6in gun and two 4.7in guns were retained so that shore batteries could be engaged. Each gun was to be rationed to twenty shells.

The *Vindictive* had undergone equally dramatic changes, both in appearance and in capability. Supported on skid-beams normally used to hold the ship's boats, a false deck had been constructed along almost the entire port side. This deck was reached by three broad, sloping ramps leading up from the starboard side of the upper deck and passing over the ship's centre line before reaching the false deck. It was calculated that, at times of high tide, the false deck would bring the storming parties to within 7ft of the top of the outer parapet. To reach the top of the wall from the false deck, eighteen 27in-wide 'brows' (gangways) were hinged ready to be swung up and dropped on to the parapet. On the port side, just abreast of the conning tower two 6ft-tall, double-barbed grapnels hung from derricks. At the after end of the false deck, a third similar grapnel hung suspended from its derrick. These were to act as parapet anchors and, once secured, would hold the vessels alongside the outer wall. As a precaution against damage from a projecting foundation step at the lower part of the wall, the ship's mainmast had been removed and laid athwartships (from side to side) across the quarterdeck. Projecting for several feet over the ship's side, the mast would protect the ship's port propeller – the actual ship's side port side, especially along the forecastle, taking protection from several huge fenders. The foremast had been reduced in size to the level of the foretop, the only part of the ship that would be seen above the parapet. To take advantage of this situation, the foretop was given a protective roof, draped with splinter mats, and was armed with three pom-poms and six Lewis guns that would engage the enemy and cover the storming parties. With the exception of the ship's four 6in guns – two to port and two to starboard – all the guns were removed and replaced by an 11in anti-submarine howitzer mounted on the quarterdeck, and two 7.5in howitzers, one on the boat deck with the other on the forecastle. The job of the howitzer crews was to engage the gun batteries at the shore end of the mole, the canal lockgates and the seaplane base. Finally, ten Lewis guns, three pom-poms, and sixteen 3in Stokes' mortars were positioned in batteries at either end of the false deck. The latter weapons were capable of firing twenty-five rounds a minute at targets up to 800 yards away and were intended to cause damage to any enemy destroyers tied up to the inner mole.

One novel feature in the *Vindictive's* armament was supplied by the indefatigable Wing Commander Brock. Two steel cabins were built on the ship's port side, one

Lieutenant Richard Sandford, captain
of HM Submarine *C3*.

abreast of the conning tower, just by the forward parapet anchor, the other at the after end of the false deck. Inside each cabin, Brock had constructed a powerful oil-fed flamethrower to be manned by his own RNAS men.

Brock had also successfully devised a smokescreen system that was vastly superior in operation to its predecessor. Using chlorosulphonic acid – a substance obtained from the reaction of hydrogen chloride gas with sulphur trioxide – Brock had produced a compound that, when fed into hot funnels of destroyers and the exhausts of motor launches and coastal motor boats, resulted in an extremely effective dense smoke cloud. In an earlier assault plan, Bacon had proposed the laying down of a smokescreen some 5 miles from the target in a wind speed of 5 or 6mph. Brock believed this to be far too slow, and proposed that, as the *Vindictive* closed with the mole, the MLs and CMBs should dash backwards and forwards in front of the ship, laying down a continuous smokescreen until the cruiser was right on top of the enemy. With the wind in the right direction, a similar screen could be produced in front of the blockships as they approached the lighthouse end of the mole, and as they passed within the arm of the mole itself. Keyes fully agreed, and gave orders that the vessels involved should be equipped with Brock's smoke-making apparatus. Then, quite unexpectedly, a problem arose. Keyes learned that the amount of chlorosulphonic acid available from the manufacturers would not be sufficient for a March, or even possibly an April, attack. Somewhat surprisingly,

Lieutenant J. Howell-Price, the first lieutenant of HM Submarine *C3* as a sub lieutenant in the Royal Naval Reserve.

Keyes reacted badly to the news. Instead of promptly lending his weight in support of Brock, he seems to have viewed the fiercely loyal wing commander as yet another scientifically driven officer in the mould of Bacon. He told Admiral Beatty, 'Brock means well, I believe, and has been invaluable in providing the latest trench warfare devices and special rockets and flares – but I am afraid he is unreliable and he has certainly let me down in the matter of smoke.' In fact, the problem arose from a quite unexpected combination of food controllers, the Ministry of Munitions, and the director of government contractors.

Brock had already begun trials with a new compound which, although effective, fell far short of the level achieved with chlorosulphonic acid. The matter was reported to the Admiralty by Keyes and, within a short time the source of the difficulty was revealed. Chlorosulphonic acid was a key ingredient in a number of synthetic products – one of which was saccharin, a sugar substitute. This was mainly produced by the firm of Burroughs, Wellcome and Co. under the commercial name of 'Saxin', which, although popular, was causing concern in some quarters regarding its effect upon the user. By sheer good fortune, the question of the side effects of saccharin use had recently been raised in the House of Lords. In the previous November, the Earl of Meath had asked the parliamentary secretary to the Board of Agriculture why saccharin was freely available in Britain when it was prohibited in the United States, and also banned in many French food products. He had received a soothing reply assuring him that there was no danger in saccharine. However, when the question of supplies for Brock reached the War Cabinet, it was not difficult for them to redirect the entire production of chlorosulphonic acid to Dover.

There remained one significant detail in the formulation of a plan to send blockships into Zeebrugge. With the launch of *Vindictive*'s distraction attack, it would not be long before the Germans sent reinforcements on to the mole from support troops based on the shore. Keyes had formulated an idea in which rafts bearing high explosives would be towed towards the viaduct. When within range of the structure, the rafts would be set free to drift with the current to become trapped by the viaduct's piles. Preset timers would then trigger the explosion, destroying the viaduct and preventing reinforcements reaching the mole defenders. Then, just as trials were being carried out, Keyes was approached by someone with a different idea.

When first appointed to Dover, Keyes had secured the services of Lieutenant Commander Francis Sandford, whom he had found toiling at the Admiralty. Sandford had been serving on de Robeck's staff at Gallipoli and was highly regarded by those with whom he had served. Unfortunately, he was badly injured by shrapnel during a mining operation and lost the sight in one eye. After a fight to avoid being forcibly retired due to his injuries, Sandford obtained an appointment at the Admiralty – a position in which he would have agreed with Commodore Tyrwhitt's generally low opinion of the place. A man of great conviction (he was a son of the Archdeacon of Exeter) who allowed little to stand in his way, Sandford soon gained a reputation as someone who bulldozed his way through bureaucracy, ignored inconvenient orders from his superiors, and always believed that the end was worth the means. Keyes noted that 'it was a long time before my office was free of correspondence connected with his activities'. Initially acting as a liaison officer between Brock and Keyes on the question of the smokescreen, Sandford was now proposing that, instead of using rafts, why not use an obsolete submarine?

With the backing of Commodore (Submarines) and the First Sea Lord, Keyes put the matter directly into Sandford's hands with full authority to set the scheme up. Within a few days Sandford was at Portsmouth obtaining the use of two obsolete C-class submarines – *C1* and *C3*. With an overall length of 143ft and a 13.5ft beam, the submarines were powered on the surface by a 600hp petrol engine capable of giving the boat a surface speed of 13 knots – about 14mph. *C1* was under the command of Lieutenant Aubrey Newbold, who was more than happy to be involved. *C3*, on the other hand, was commanded by an officer who, in Sandford's view (supported by Keyes), suffered from a serious impediment in that he was a married man. With the officer gently reappointed, Sandford looked around for a replacement. He did not have to look very far before appointing Lieutenant Richard Sandford – his younger brother. The normal complement of a C class consisted of two officers and fourteen ratings. Such numbers were unnecessary for the attack against the viaduct and, consequently, were reduced to the commanding officer, the first lieutenant, a petty officer coxswain, a leading seaman, an engine-room artificer and a stoker. To rescue the crews once the submarines had been forced under the viaduct, the elder Sandford required a reliable boat. His covetous eyes fell upon a brand-new picket boat on its way from Chatham to Portsmouth, where it would have undertaken the usual unremarkable harbour picket-boat duties, carrying stores, mail and liberty-men to and from warships. Having called in at Dover, the picket boat found itself commandeered by Sandford, who telegraphed the authorities at both ports to tell them that Vice Admiral Keyes needed to borrow their shiny new boat for just a couple of weeks or so.

Other vessels required to take part in the attack arrived in the more formal way. The squat, shallow-drafted monitors with their heavy firepower were already part of Keyes' command. They would be needed to take on the German defences at long range and especially to keep them occupied during the lead-up to the attack.

Numerous motor launches were to be involved. The 'movies' or MLs as they were known, had probably stemmed from an idea of Lieutenant Oscar Freyberg, a New Zealander serving with the Royal Naval Division (his brother, Bernard, was a famous Victoria Cross holder in the same division). Freyberg had hunted whales

A 40ft CMB. The single torpedo can be seen in its stern trough, ready to be launched backwards over the transom.

CMBs at speed. In calm weather, 40 knots could be achieved.

using a fast boat armed with a harpoon and was of the view that if 'speed and one reliable weapon accounted for the whale, why not a submarine?' To the annoyance of many people, the Admiralty approached the Electric Launch Company ('Elco') based at Bayonne, New Jersey. They produced a design for 75–80ft-long launches, powered by petrol engines capable of producing 19 knots. They were to be armed with quick-firing guns, usually 3pdrs, and depth charges. Initially manufactured at Bayonne, after the first had been despatched, factories at Quebec and Montreal were organised to assemble the remainder using ship's fittings manufactured by

Tiffany Studios, based in New York. Once assembled in Canada, the launches were transported to Britain as deck cargo. Although popular with their crews (and frequently demonstrating their worth against U-boats) the MLs had their detractors, who were eager to point out that the quality of their construction was not as expected. A fake newspaper report doing the rounds at the time told of an ML officer who had his gold watch stolen as he slept in his bunk. Apparently a thief had put his hand and arm through a gap in the side planking and stolen it. As an aid to recognition, and to reduce the risk of being fired on by their own side as they weaved in and out of the expected smokescreens, each ML's bridge house had a canvas cover draped over it bearing a large red-white-and-blue roundel.

The crews of the MLs were usually made up of Royal Naval Volunteer Reserve men with a sprinkling of Royal Naval Reservists. Each ML carried two officers and eight ratings. The latter were often recruited through advertisements in yachting magazines such as *Motor Ship and Motor Boat*, which announced that 'there is at the moment a special need for a number of men who have been accustomed to marine motors, preferably of the large size and of the paraffin type, for service in a special branch of the Forces. These men must have had mechanical experience, and good pay will be given.' There was no mention of reckless courage and the ability to deploy Brock's smokescreen.

The Dover Patrol's Coastal Motor Boats (CMBs) had earned the name 'Scooters' from their high speed. Some 40–55ft long with 350–375hp engines, they were capable of speeds of over 40 knots. Their armament was a combination of torpedoes, Lewis guns and depth charges. Although some were designed to drop torpedoes over the boat's side, the majority carried one or two torpedoes in a stern trough. To deploy the latter, the CMB itself had to be aimed at the target ship until, when in range, the torpedo could be set running and let free. Once that had happened the CMB had to put on a spurt of speed to outrun its own torpedo and get out of its way as it shot off on its way towards the target. They were also to be issued with Brock's smoke-making apparatus.

In all, the fleet that had to be assembled at Dover and Dunkirk to attack Zeebrugge and Ostend numbered sixty-two motor launches, forty-five destroyers, twenty-four coastal motor boats, eight monitors, eight light cruisers, seven flotilla leaders (large destroyers for senior officers), five blockships, two submarines, two auxiliary craft (*Iris* and *Daffodil*), one minesweeper, and one picket boat.

It was now time for Keyes to seek Admiralty permission to go ahead with the attack. Given the surprisingly obvious code name 'Operation Z.O.' ('Zebra. Orange.' in the contemporary phonetic alphabet), Keyes' plan was proposed under the heading 'Our object. To deny the use of Zeebrugge and Ostend to the enemy as bases for submarines and torpedo craft.'

Five blockships were to be deployed to block the two canal entrances. The blockships were filled with concrete to a height that would make any attempt to cut them down by the enemy – and thus allow passage over the top at high tide – extremely difficult. Three blockships, *Thetis, Intrepid,* and *Iphigenia* would be taken to Zeebrugge, and two, *Brilliant* and *Sirius,* would be used at Ostend.

At Zeebrugge it would be necessary to create a diversion from the blockships and to capture the guns at the end of the mole – including those on the lighthouse extension – in order to prevent their being used at very close range against the blockships. This diversion would consist of an attack by storming parties landing from the *Vindictive,* the *Iris* and the *Daffodil* over the outer wall of the mole at a point level with the end of the mole and the start of the lighthouse extension. The *Iris* would be secured alongside the wall just to the west (i.e. ahead) of the *Vindictive,* whilst the *Daffodil* would assist the *Vindictive* as a tug until she was secured alongside. When this was achieved, the *Daffodil* would discharge her storming parties.

Both the arrival of the blockships and the landing vessels would be obscured until the last moment by smoke laid down by motor launches and coastal motor boats. Smoke would also be deployed by the blockships and accompanying destroyers whenever the need arose.

In addition to the naval storming parties intent on capturing the guns, another naval storming party would be landed to destroy as much of the enemy's facilities as possible. This may include attacking any enemy vessels found berthed alongside the inner wall.

To coincide with the arrival of the storming parties two submarines, *C1* and *C3*, were to be steered to force their bows beneath the viaduct connecting the mole to the concrete pier. Both submarines would be packed with explosives, and the final few yards of the voyage would be under the control of a self-steering gyroscopic system to allow the crews to escape. They would board a motor skiff that would take them clear of the explosion and to a rendezvous with an escorting picket boat.

On attaining the entrance to the canal, the leading blockship would endeavour to continue directly ahead in order to ram the lockgates or, if the lockgates were open, to sink herself in the lock. The following blockships would then aim to sink themselves across the canal taking advantage of the large accumulation of silt on either side. On completion of their task, the blockship crews would take to the ships' boats and be picked up by motor launches at the entrance to the canal and be taken out of the harbour.

At Ostend, the blockships *Brilliant* and *Sirius* would use the Direct Pass – a channel connecting the Outer Roads with the entrance to the canal. On arrival between the canal piers, they would place themselves across the canal before blowing out the ships' bottoms. As at Zeebrugge, the rescue of the ships' crews would be achieved by a combination of boats and motor launches.

As it was intended to arrive at the Zeebrugge mole in darkness, part of the crossing of the North Sea would have to be done in daylight with a clear risk of being discovered by the enemy. To assist in this, aircraft from Dunkirk would patrol ahead of the fleet. Furthermore, aircraft would bomb the mole at Zeebrugge prior to the arrival of the blockships.

Minesweeping activity would risk attracting the attention of the enemy. Therefore, risks posed by enemy minefields and uncharted shoals would have to be accepted.

Navigation of the 72 miles to Zeebrugge would be aided by light-buoys. At Ostend, the Stroom Bank Buoy and a Bell buoy had been accurately located by officers from the Admiralty Hydrographic Department and would be used to locate the entrance to the canal. Smokescreens would be laid down on both sides of the entrance channel, the blockships passing inbetween.

The attack at Zeebrugge would have to be carried out both at a time of high tide and of darkness. This would limit the timing of the attack to three hours centred around midnight, and then only on four, possibly five, nights in a lunar month. In addition, it was necessary to have a light breeze blowing offshore to allow the smoke to float towards the guns on the mole.

Such then was the gist of the formal application made by Keyes to the Admiralty. The replies he received were somewhat less than enthusiastic. The deputy chief of naval staff thought that, even if successful, the canal blockage would not stop the U-boats at Bruges being sent back to Antwerp. Also, the Dover Patrol destroyers would have to remain on station to defend against attacks from the German ports. Moreover, securing the *Vindictive* alongside the wall would be 'the most probable source of failure'. Nevertheless, he thought 'the objects to be achieved are considered to be worth the risk' – but suggested that the attack should be carried out in the 'morning twilight'. The Second Sea Lord agreed with the difficulty of getting the *Vindictive* alongside, and thought that more smoke would be required further out from the shore. He did, however, think that the proposal was of 'great value'. The assistant chief of naval staff also commented on the supposed difficulty of securing the *Vindictive*. He thought it 'likely to prove one of the most difficult and uncertain factors in the Enterprise'. However, 'Assuming the information on which it is based to be correct', the plan could work. The Deputy First Sea Lord agreed with the ACNS but, at least, thought that 'if successful' the attack might have a 'far-reaching political & moral effect'. The Fourth Sea Lord had nothing original to say, and so concurred with the ACNS and the Second Sea Lord. The Third Sea Lord agreed with everyone else.

What Keyes thought of such muted enthusiasm was not recorded. In all likelihood he gathered his senior officers together, told them that he had permission to proceed, and let them get on with it. He, in the meantime, had to entertain the First Sea Lord, who had decided to visit Dover to see things for himself.

5

The Muster

In order to man the 154 ships of the Dover Command involved in Operation Z.O. Keyes required around 8,250 officers and ratings. An extra 1,780 officers and men would be needed to man three boarding ships (including two auxiliaries), five block ships, two submarines, a picket boat, and to provide sufficient numbers for the storming parties.

When Admiral Bacon had submitted his proposal to the Admiralty, he had suggested that the War Office be approached for the loan of an army infantry battalion. Keyes, however, would entertain no such suggestion. For him, the entire affair was to be wholly naval. Consequently, he sought the advice of General Sir David Mercer, the adjutant-general of the Royal Marines. Mercer had commanded one of the Royal Naval Division brigades at Gallipoli and not only knew the type of men that Keyes would be looking for, but had himself experienced the grim trench fighting that could be expected on the mole at Zeebrugge. He also knew where to obtain such men.

The 4th Battalion of the Royal Marine Light Infantry had initially been raised to meet the threat posed by Irish nationalists in 1916. They had never been used in that capacity, however, and the companies raised had been returned to their divisional bases. The headquarters staff, nevertheless, remained in existence, acting as the administrative centre for the

Captain H. Halahan, commander of the naval landing parties.

Lieutenant Colonel B.N. Elliot, commander of the Royal Marine contingent at Zeebrugge.

battalion's new role – that of a manpower reserve for the Royal Marine battalions of the RND, now fighting in France. Having obtained permission from the First Sea Lord, Mercer stopped the flow of men to the Western Front and transferred one company from each of the three Marine divisions (Portsmouth, Chatham, and Plymouth) to the Royal Marine Depot at Deal. A further company, made up of machine-gunners and Royal Marine Artillery officers and gunners, was provided by the Grand Fleet. Shortages were made up from men at the Deal Depot, including several buglers – the oldest being aged 38.

The battalion was originally placed under the command of Lieutenant Colonel Frank Chichester, but his clearly deteriorating health gave Keyes strong grounds for concern and eventually Mercer had him removed. The adjutant-general then asked Keyes to interview Major Bertram Elliot for the job.

Elliot had taken a prominent part in one of the almost forgotten sectors of the front. In 1915, with the approach of the Gallipoli landings, a British naval mission was sent to Serbia under the command of Rear Admiral Ernest Troubridge. Armed with eight 4.7in naval guns and a torpedo-armed picket boat, their task was to prevent Austro-Hungarian naval forces, which included monitors and patrol vessels, from using the River Danube to reach the Black Sea and provide supplies to the Turks. Elliot, whose forebears had served with the Royal Marines continuously since 1755, was placed in command of the Royal Marine detachment. The mission had performed its task well but was forced to withdraw when the Serbian forces collapsed on the entry of Bulgaria into the war. Troubridge, with his seamen and marines, fell back to the Adriatic port of San Giovanni di Medua. There they supervised the evacuation of the Serbian Army and thousands of civilians. For his work with the mission, Elliot was awarded the Distinguished Service Order, the Serbian Order of the White Eagle with crossed swords, and the Serbian Order of St Sava.

It did not take Keyes long to come to the opinion that Elliot was just the man needed to command the Royal Marine storming parties. With a promotion to lieutenant colonel, Elliot took over the 4th Battalion at Deal. His second-in-command was Major Alexander Cordner, and Captain Arthur Chater was appointed as the battalion adjutant. Chater had served with the Chatham Battalion of the Royal Naval Division at Antwerp and at Gallipoli, where he had been mentioned in dispatches and awarded the French *Croix de Guerre*.

The battalion was divided into four companies, three of whom were named after their base division. The Chatham Company was led by Major Charles Eagles, the Portsmouth Company by Captain Edward Bamford, and the Plymouth Company by Major Bernard Weller. The Machine-gun Company was under the command of Captain Charles Conybeare, and included gunners of the Royal Marine Artillery led by Lieutenant Reginald Dallas Brooks, the son of a naval chaplain. A Gallipoli veteran, Dallas Brooks had also been awarded a *Croix de Guerre* by the French as a result of his leadership on the battlefield. On one occasion, standing with Captain Chater at a rest camp, a Turkish shrapnel shell exploded above them. Chater was knocked to the ground by a shrapnel ball but was only bruised. Dallas Brooks, on the other hand, had been hit by a ball that penetrated his back. The missile had lodged so close to his spine that the surgeons decided to leave it where it was rather than risk further damage in attempting to remove it. The ball was still in his back when he was sent from the Grand Fleet to join the 4th Battalion.

Keyes was very keen that the remainder of the Royal Navy involved in the diversionary attack were not to be seen simply as a ferry service for the Royal Marines. It was true that the blockships were solely in the hands of sailors, but he knew that they would also want to be involved in the actual attack on the mole. Furthermore, it would be a task of seamanship to secure the *Vindictive* and the ferries alongside the wall using the parapet anchors. Keyes decided that the first men to land on the wall would be the seamen storming parties. Once the grapnels had been secured they would then rush the guns on the lighthouse extension and inflict as much damage as they could on the mole itself.

To set an example, Keyes set about finding the first of his seamen storming parties from his own command. He arranged for the naval siege gun crews stationed near Dunkirk to be replaced by gunners from the Royal Marine Artillery. When he informed the commanding officer of the siege guns, Captain Henry Halahan, of these arrangements whilst asking for volunteers, Halahan replied with a note containing the following:

> May I say that if the operation for which you said you might want these men is eventually undertaken, I should very much like to take part in it. I would willingly accept the same conditions, viz., that I should not expect to come back.

I have lived for 3 years inside field gun range and I can say (quite impersonally) that I do not suffer from physical fear. It may be thought that it is bad business to lose an officer whose training has cost the country so much on what may for all I know be a comparatively small operation, but on the other hand if the experience, resource & adaptability such an officer is bound to have as the result of his longer training is sufficient, at the crucial moment, to make the difference between success and failure, the question rather falls into the same category as risking an expensive monitor on an important but isolated coast bombardment.

It was the kind of plea that might be expected from a very junior officer fearful of being left behind during an attack upon the enemy. Halahan, however, had begun the war commanding a ship off the Belgian coast before being sent to trade heavy shells with the enemy. He was experienced, enthusiastic and fearless. Keyes had found the man to lead the naval storming parties. There was, however, a problem. Keyes had appointed Carpenter to the command of the *Vindictive* with the intention that the old cruiser would be his flagship. General opinion, nevertheless, had prevailed upon Keyes to shift his flag to one of the destroyers in order to keep better control of the action. This meant that Halahan, although only very recently promoted to captain, would, in effect, be under the command of Carpenter – the more junior officer. Although Halahan had raised no objections (in fact he had offered to waive his rank), having already told Carpenter that he was no longer to have command of the ship, Keyes 'rather weakly gave in' when Carpenter pleaded with him. He then decided to deal with the 'somewhat irregular' situation by informing both captains that the naval storming party was to be considered as an entirely separate command over which Carpenter was to have no authority. In any case, Carpenter would not 'ship' his fourth (captain's) stripe until he actually took command of the *Vindictive* sometime in late March or early April. As a gesture, both of compensation and of personal support for Carpenter, Keyes presented him with a 'lucky' horseshoe. Carpenter had it bolted to one of the *Vindictive*'s funnels.

The officer appointed as Halahan's deputy appeared to have all the qualities required to be at the forefront of the storming party. Square-jawed and very powerfully built, Lieutenant Commander Arthur Harrison was well over 6ft tall. The son of a lieutenant colonel of the Royal Fusiliers, Harrison entered the Royal Navy at the age of 16 and soon established a reputation on the rugby field, playing as a forward for the Royal Navy, the Combined Services and for Hampshire. In February 1914 he was selected for the England side against Ireland, the first ever international rugby match attended by a reigning monarch. England won the match and Harrison – along with the rest of the team – was introduced to the king. Two months later Harrison was selected for the national side once again, this time taking part in a victory over the French. Since the outbreak of

Lieutenant Commander F. Harrison, leader of the *Vindictive* naval landing parties.

war Harrison had taken part in the battles at Heligoland Bight, Dogger Bank, and off Jutland, where he was mentioned in dispatches. He was serving with the Grand Fleet in the battlecruiser HMS *Lion* when he was made aware of the need for volunteers to take part in an undefined, but certainly risky, venture. He put his name forward immediately.

The naval storming party was to be formed up into three companies. 'A' Company was to be led by Lieutenant Commander Bryan Adams, 'B' Company by Lieutenant Arthur Chamberlain, with Lieutenant Harold Walker as his second-in-command, and 'D' Company by Lieutenant Commander George Bradford, assisted by Lieutenant Claude Hawkings. A smaller group – 'C' Company – was to act as a demolition party under the command of Lieutenant Cecil Dickinson with 20-year-old Sub Lieutenant Felix Chevallier as his deputy. Dickinson and his teams were to be based in the *Vindictive*, whilst Chevallier and his men were to land from the *Iris*.

George Bradford was one of four brothers, three of whom had already distinguished themselves during the war. Thomas had been awarded a Distinguished Service Order before being badly wounded at Ypres. James had earned a Military Cross, only to be killed in France. Roland, the most astonishing of all, had started the war as a second lieutenant. By 1917, not only was he the youngest general in the British Army at the age of 25, he had also earned a Victoria Cross, holding his men together by his example whilst leading an assault on the enemy. Despite initial ridicule, Roland had become well-known for leading his brigade in singing 'Abide with me' before a battle. He was killed in November 1917. Thirty-year-old George Bradford, tired of inactivity with the Grand Fleet at Scapa Flow, leapt at the chance to be involved with an, as yet unknown, operation starting out from Dover.

There remained one further important appointment to the naval storming parties. Word reached Keyes that, without any idea of what was intended to take place, the bearded and piratical Lieutenant Commander Patrick Harrington Edwards was keen to be involved. Harrington Edwards had served in Gallipoli and on the Western Front with the Royal Naval Division. Badly wounded on both fronts, during the trench fighting on the Somme, he had lost the sight in an eye and had been sent home to recuperate. Rapidly tiring of such inactivity, he managed to obtain an appointment to the Dover Balloon Station. There he picked up word that something exciting was about to happen and promptly began to sound out all contacts who might be able to get him involved. After interviewing Harrington Edwards, Keyes had no doubt that he was just the man to train the naval landing parties and offered him the job. Harrington Edwards was not only delighted but almost overcome with joy when Keyes gave him permission to join the naval companies onboard the *Vindictive*. He later noted that 'I thought it (the raid) was quite hopeless, but, oh my goodness, it was quite gloriously hopeless … I went off to my cabin that night, but I could not sleep. How lucky I was to be in it.'

With Carpenter confirmed as captain of the *Vindictive*, Rosoman as his first lieutenant, Osborne and Bramble looking after the fitting and operations of

Lieutenant Commander G. Bradford, in charge of the naval landing parties from the *Iris*.

The V/W Class destroyer HMS *Warwick*. Vice Admiral Keyes' flagship during the raids, the newly built *Warwick* survived her mining off Ostend. She was sunk off north Cornwall by a U-boat in 1944.

the ship's guns, and Bury in charge of the engineering, it was time to add a couple of junior officers to the ship's company. One was a surprise, the other an officer whose life appeared to be one of gilded achievement and distinguished enterprise.

Lieutenant Adam Ferguson had been the captain of HMS *Amazon* during the Dover raid and his inactivity on that night had earned him the full force of Keyes' anger. Having seen that Ferguson was court-martialled, Keyes then considered that the court had been too lenient and had the lieutenant dismissed from his ship. Such a damning action would, under normal circumstances, have meant an abrupt end to an officer's career. However, Ferguson had acted well in the face of such adversity and had not complained, sulked or even asked for a transfer from the Dover Patrol. Keyes was impressed by his attitude and now decided that his actions during the German destroyer raid had been more the result of a 'lack of experience rather than want of courage' and offered him an appointment in the *Vindictive*. Ferguson needed no second prompting and 'gladly accepted'.

Lieutenant Edward Hilton Young was the youngest son of a Baronet and grew up on an estate on the banks of the Thames and at a town house on Sloan Square. At his preparatory school he befriended future prime minister Clement Attlee before moving to be educated at Eton. After studying at University College, London and at Trinity College, Cambridge he left with a first-class degree in

Commander V. Gibbs, captain of the *Iris*.

Natural Sciences, and with experience as the president of the union. He then studied Law, being called to the bar in 1904. Hilton Young then turned his talents towards a career in financial journalism becoming assistant editor of the *Economist*, followed by an appointment as city editor of the *Morning Post*. Through a Cambridge friendship with Thoby Stephen he met Stephen's sisters (later to become well-known as the artist Vanessa Bell and the author Virginia Woolf) who gained him entry into the influential Bloomsbury Group. He was also closely associated with the writers G.M. Trevelyan and Lytton Strachey, and proved to be an accomplished poet in his own right. With the outbreak of war, Hilton Young applied for, and was granted, a commission in the RNVR and was appointed to HMS *Iron Duke*, serving with the Grand Fleet at Scapa Flow. In February 1915 he stood as the sole candidate for the parliamentary seat at Norwich, remaining on active service with the fleet. Service with the British naval mission to Serbia (where he served alongside Colonel Elliot) was followed by time with the Harwich Force before he was appointed to the Naval Siege Guns in France under the command of Captain Halahan. When he entered the *Vindictive*, Hilton Young had already been awarded a Distinguished Service Cross, the Serbian Silver Medal, and a French *Croix de Guerre*.

The Mersey ferry *Iris* was given the official title of HMS *Iris II* to avoid administrative confusion with an Acacia-class sloop of the same name – but was known to all simply as the *Iris*. Her command went to Commander Valentine Gibbs, who had first come to Keyes' notice as a midshipman, and was currently serving as the gunnery officer in the Grand Fleet's 'Gin Palace', HMS *Agincourt* – originally built for the Brazilians as *Rio de Janeiro*, then obtained by the Turks as *Sultan Osman I*, only to be commandeered by the Royal Navy at the outbreak of war. Gibbs was better known, however, for his determined retention of the Cresta Run bobsleigh championship. His first lieutenant was Lieutenant Oscar Henderson, who had put the Royal Marines ashore at Morto Bay during the

Gallipoli landings. Instead of remaining by the boats, he had earned recognition by advancing in support of the marines. The *Iris'* navigation officer was Lieutenant George Spencer, who had earned a Distinguished Service Cross onboard a 'Q' Ship whilst attacking a U-boat.

The *Daffodil* (officially *Daffodil IV*) went to Lieutenant Harold Campbell, who had served as the first lieutenant in HMS *Lurcher* – Keyes' command ship during the Battle of the Heligoland Bight. Lieutenant Harold Rogers was appointed as her navigating officer. Whilst the *Iris* was to proceed directly alongside the mole wall to land 'D' Company of the Royal Marines, the *Daffodil's* first task was to hold the *Vindictive* against the wall until she was secured by her parapet anchors. When that had been achieved, she was then to land the Royal Marine's 'C' Company on the mole over the decks of the cruiser.

The coastal motor boats (CMBs) at Zeebrugge were to be under the command of Lieutenant Arthur Welman, who had already earned a Distinguished Service Cross for his work off the Belgian coast. Captain Ralph Collins commanded the Zeebrugge motor launches whilst the Dunkirk motor launch flotilla – intended for the attack on Ostend – was commanded by the 55-year-old Member of Parliament for Greenwich, Commander Ion Hamilton Benn. The destroyers were led by Keyes' old friend, Captain Wilfred Tomkinson. HMS *Warwick,* under Tomkinson's command, would be Keyes' flagship.

The medical services for the Zeebrugge raid were led by Staff Surgeon James McCutcheon with his particular responsibility being the *Vindictive's* wounded. Surgeon Henry Colson would land with the *Vindictive* and the *Daffodil's* marines, as Surgeon William Clegg organised stretcher bearers operating between the mole and the ship. Surgeon 'Jack' Payne, an Australian from Tasmania, would establish a main first-aid post just below *Vindictive's* conning tower. Surgeon Frank Pocock was responsible for the wounded onboard the *Iris.* Pocock had already earned a Military Cross whilst serving with the Drake Battalion of the Royal Naval Division in France. His MC was awarded after he had tended to the wounded whilst under three days of continuous bombardment. When serving in the front line in November 1917 he was wounded and invalided home. A medical examination declared that he was 'unfit for general service' but within days he was pestering anyone he could to get back into the war. On New Year's Eve he turned up at the Admiralty requesting to be re-examined only to be found 'unfit for active service'. He was, however, appointed to Chatham Naval Barracks where, no doubt, he met Royal Marine officers from the Royal Naval Division, now serving as part of the 4th Battalion. A further application to the Admiralty on 1 February 1918 resulted in his being found 'fit for duty'. Almost immediately, and without a single mention on his service record, he reappeared as one of the two medical officers serving with the 4th Battalion of the Royal Marines. It was almost as if he had smuggled himself into his new appointment behind the

Commander A. Godsal, standing second from right with his pet dog on his shoulder. Seated second from left is Sub Lieutenant V. Crutchley, shortly before his promotion to lieutenant.

Admiralty's back. It is not known if Keyes was aware of such an arrangement – but, if he had known, he would have approved.

One officer that Keyes was not keen to take was Wing Commander Brock. When Brock approached him for permission to sail with the *Vindictive*, Keyes 'preferred to refuse' on the grounds that Brock's 'genius for inventions was so invaluable'. However, Keyes claimed that Brock's plea to go, complete with additional approval to land on the mole, was based on the idea that the Germans' gunnery accuracy stemmed from a newly introduced sound ranging system – and it was believed that such a system had been installed near the end of the mole. It was, apparently, with an eye to getting hold of this equipment that had led to Brock's urgent desire to take part in the attack. Whether or not Keyes actually believed this is not certain but his final decision meant that, much to his delight, Brock was allowed to go. He was not to be alone: thirty-four men from his Admiralty Experimental Station had volunteered to take part in the attack as the 'pyrotechnic party'. Lieutenant Graham Hewett and Lieutenant A.L. Eastlake of the Royal Engineers were to lead them in operating the large flamethrowers mounted in two specially constructed steel cabins built on the port side of the *Vindictive*. Arthur Lloyd Eastlake was an engineer employed by the Ministry of

Munitions with a particular interest in flamethrowers. To make life easier for him when dealing with naval and military matters he was gazetted as a temporary second lieutenant in July 1916 and loaned to Brock's Experimental Station. He became, therefore, the only exception to Keyes' insistence that the attack would be an entirely naval affair. In addition to operating the flamethrowers in the *Vindictive*, the men of the Pyrotechnic Party would also land on the mole with portable flamethrowers and phosphorous grenades, operate smoke apparatus, and fire rocket flares from the *Vindictive* to light up the lighthouse at the end of the mole for the benefit of the blockships.

Keyes needed an accommodation ship for the officers and men coming down from the Grand Fleet and elsewhere. HMS *Hindustan* was available at Chatham and Keyes put her under the command of Captain A.P. Davidson, the former captain of the Gallipoli veteran HMS *Cornwallis*. Davidson recommended his chaplain from the *Cornwallis*, the Reverend Charles Peshall, for the same appointment onboard the *Vindictive* – 'He would be a spiritual force, and a fighting force, too, if you will let him.' Peshall had been ordained in 1904 and had entered the Royal Navy four years later. A tall, strongly built man, he had earned a well-deserved reputation as a fearless player on the rugby field. He also had considerable experience of the grisly side of war during his time in *Cornwallis*. Shortly after the landings, he was asked to carry out a funeral service over a mass grave:

Commander Sneyd with the blocking crew of HMS *Thetis*. To his left is Engineer Lieutenant Commander Boddie. Lieutenant Lambert is to his right.

It was a gruesome business, and the stench was awful, as all the bodies had lain in the sun for two days, and some had been in water. In one grave two hundred and four men were buried, and in a smaller, quite close by, five officers.

Finally, Keyes had to select the officers who were to take command of the blockships. As usual, he was never afraid to turn to those who he knew by their past endeavours would not be turned aside by the magnitude of their task, or whose deeds and actions brought them recommendations from other officers he trusted. His firm rule, however, for the blockships was that no one should be appointed or drafted to them who was married.

To take command of HMS *Brilliant*, Keyes sent for Commander Alfred Godsal, who had served as the first lieutenant of his first flagship, HMS *Centurion*. Godsal was the son of a soldier, historian and rifle designer who was not afraid to challenge orthodoxy. His father had come to the conclusion that the English had chosen Saint George as their patron saint as the old Saxon word for fond memories of former heroic times was 'Geogeara'. With the defeat by the Normans at Hasting, the Saxons, he argued, adopted the word and gradually transformed it into 'Saint George' to conform to the practice of Roman Catholicism. Whether Alfred Godsal agreed with his father's theory is not known but Keyes recognised the former's leadership abilities and intended to put them to good use. There was certainly a large degree of courage in the family. Alfred's brother, Walter, had been awarded a DSO and a Military Cross before being killed and, during the Second World War, his nephew Phillip won another Military Cross and made a home run from a German prisoner-of-war camp. Godsal also brought with him Lieutenant Victor Crutchley, another *Centurion* officer known and welcomed by Keyes.

HMS *Sirius* went to Lieutenant Commander Henry Hardy. He had come to Keyes' attention during the Gallipoli campaign when, whilst commanding trawlers collecting the wounded from the shore, he was suddenly surrounded by French colonial troops fleeing from a heavy Turkish assault. Grabbing a passing Senegalese bugler, he ordered him to sound 'Charge', rallied the troops, and stormed the position they had just vacated. Once he had secured the trenches, Hardy handed them over to the French military authorities before returning to his duties on the beach.

The senior officer of the Zeebrugge blockships was recommended by Captain Cyril Fuller, Keyes' liaison officer with his old Planning Directorate. As a lieutenant commander under Fuller's command, Ralph Sneyd had distinguished himself in September 1914 when, leading a force attacking the Germans in their West African Cameroons colony, he sank an enemy vessel, drove the Germans out of their fort at Piti, and captured plans of the enemy defences. For his achievements during the campaign, Sneyd was made a member of the Distinguished Service

Order and promoted to commander. Keyes appointed him to command the cruiser, *Thetis.*

Lieutenant Ivan Franks came with no less than a recommendation from Admiral Beatty. A submarine captain, Franks had also served with Keyes' brother, Adrian, in a 'Q' ship. He brought with him another submariner, Lieutenant Edward Billyard-Leake, with the comment that he was 'one in a thousand'. After interviewing Franks (leaving him 'bubbling over with joy') Keyes appointed him as captain of the *Iphigenia* with Billyard-Leake – despite having barely a year's seniority as a lieutenant – as his first lieutenant.

The final blockship, HMS *Intrepid,* went to Lieutenant Stuart Bonham Carter on the recommendation of Captain Carpenter. Coming from a family with a long history in brewing and politics, Bonham Carter had spent the war with the Grand Fleet at Scapa Flow where, like many of his fellow officers, he was forced to watch the war from a distance. Now given the opportunity to volunteer for some action, he jumped at the chance.

With a single exception, all the officers interviewed were bursting with enthusiasm at the prospect of being involved in the action. Not for them the detailed enquiry of means, method, objective, or risk – just the absolute delight at being chosen to take part. Commander Sneyd, on the other hand, *did* want to know, and to know in detail. Unused to being questioned, Keyes sharply reminded Sneyd that if he had any doubts there were plenty of other officers eager to take his place. Sneyd, however, refused to be overawed at being on the edge of dismissal and replied that he had no intention of giving his place to anyone. If he was to be expected to lead men in a situation of extreme danger, he wanted to know why. Keyes, possibly recognising an officer with a determined attitude not too far removed from his own, controlled the impatience welling up inside him and answered Sneyd's questions. By the end of the interview he had decided that Sneyd was, indeed, the man for the job – 'and I had every reason to be thankful for the choice'.

As the leaders were being selected, other officers and ratings from the Grand Fleet and the naval bases began to muster onboard the *Hindustan* at Chatham. Keyes had stipulated that he did not want volunteers, he much preferred men specially chosen by their officers because of their service background and history. To have merely asked for volunteers would have seen a rush resulting in huge numbers accompanied by an administrative nightmare. The men selected had, however, been told that they had been chosen for a special service. The majority came from the British Isles but others had come a great deal further. HMAS *Australia* supplied a warrant officer artificer engineer, five stokers and five seamen. Although New Zealand was already well represented amongst the Dunkirk coastal motorboats, HMNZS *New Zealand* sent a further party. Wearing 'grass' skirts made of yarn, with skins stained a mahogany brown, and led by Able Seaman

Harold Eaves, the New Zealanders produced a fearful, tongue-poking, wild-eyed, 'Haka' to entertain their new shipmates onboard the *Hindustan*. Canada was represented by Lieutenant Roland Bourke. Born in England he had emigrated with his parents when he was aged 17 and took up farming. With the outbreak of war he tried to enlist in the Canadian armed services but was rejected because of his poor eyesight. Unwilling to let the matter rest he returned to England, where he managed to obtain a commission with the Royal Naval Volunteer Reserve, ending up serving in command of a coastal motorboat at Dunkirk.

    With the United States of America now in the war, when word got out that a 'stunt' was about to take place, and that men were being selected from the Grand Fleet, the US Sixth Battle Squadron began to show a strong interest in being involved. Discussions took place between the American senior officer, Rear Admiral Hugh Rodman, and Admiral Beatty, but it was decided that the arrival of US seamen and ships at Dover or Chatham would cause too much of a stir and prove a threat to security. Nevertheless, one post-war account of the action, aimed at the American market, included three US destroyers, and a rumour lasted for many years after the war (until finally quashed by Carpenter) that a US officer had smuggled himself on to the *Vindictive* and taken part in the fight.

    The Royal Marine Light Infantry training for the attack was placed directly in the hands of Lieutenant Colonel Elliot. For the most part this consisted of rehearsing attacks against lines of tape – believed by most to represent trenches – and sharpening up the already high standards of infantry fighting reached by the marines. Members of the Royal Marine Artillery who were involved concentrated on the use of the 11in howitzer sited on *Vindictive*'s quarterdeck, and the two 7.5in versions on the forecastle and the false deck. In fact both branches of the Royal Marines were undergoing training that varied little from that they had received throughout most of their careers. The most peculiar variations were the order to remove all hob-nails and steel heel-plates from their boots, whilst the officers had a white band painted around their steel helmets. In the case of the seaman storming parties, however, matters were entirely different.

    Seamen on ships such as those in the Grand Fleet could always expect to be deployed ashore in a fighting capacity. For several decades, certainly throughout the Victorian period, Royal Naval seamen – not infrequently accompanied by stokers – defended the empire in naval brigades or smaller detachments when extra firepower or manpower was required, either in isolation or in company with the army. The training for these enterprises was, however, rudimentary, and consisted of little more than learning to 'Form square' or 'Stand by to repel cavalry'. Such limited evolutions were bound to be of little use in storming a German strongpoint or countering an enemy bayonet charge. With this in mind, Keyes had approached the adjutant-general of the Royal Marines, asking him to suggest a training regime more suited to the task at hand. From his experiences with the Royal Naval Division on the Western Front, General Sir David Mercer understood clearly that seamen were not Royal Marines. They did not need, nor did they have the time for, the full rigours of an intense infantry course. Accordingly his advice was tempered with a broad swathe of common sense. He wrote:

> The object of the training is to get the men physically fit, full of dash, and accustomed to short sharp raids by night, equipped in the lightest order.

> The Company must therefore be worked up in bayonet, bombing, Rapid Shooting at short range, Snap Shooting (especially at short range), and Trench Fighting.

> Heavy marching is not required. Marches should be from 5 to 10 miles without packs, to get men in condition only. Wrestling, football, running, boxing (when gloves are available) and such games prisoners have, can be easily carried out during instruction hours. (These sort of games now form a great feature of Army instruction.)

> Practice in Trench fighting is essential. Lewis Gunners and Bombers must be thoroughly trained. They must be exercised respectively with Ball Ammunition, and Live Bombs at night.

> Lewis Gunners are not required to be mechanical experts, but men who can get in to action quickly, keep their guns going and instinctively remedy stoppages. Similarly Bombers are required to be skilful throwers of the Mills Grenade, and not to know the details of construction of a variety of Grenades.

> All the Company should be put through a Musketry Course with Mark VII Ammunition, the practices being formed to develop rapid shooting at short ranges, and snap shooting.

> Practice in Night firing is essential.

> It is suggested that in the daily programme should be included:-

> 1 hour, Bayonet and Trench fighting (not necessarily continuous).
> ½ hour Swedish.
> ½ hour Games at odd times, and running.
> 1 hour Section, Platoon, or Company training.

½ hour Musketry Instruction, chiefly rapid snapping, with marches of from 5 to 10 miles without packs.

Practice at night work, even if this can only be carried out in a very elementary way, is essential.

Digging is not required, but men should be practiced in quickly passing up filled sandbags.

Open warfare tactics are not required, and should only be occasionally carried out as a change.

Officers should practice with the revolver.

With such guidance, and under the practised (and sole) eye of Lieutenant Commander Harrington Edwards, Captain Halahan and his officers led their men against yet more rows of tapes, convinced that they were on their way to France in support of the army. If that was the case, it was argued, the Royal Marines and seamen storming parties should be supplied with 'ash plants' – loaded canes used as bludgeons in trench warfare; 300 were ordered and issued. The seamen were not averse to adding even further to their personal weaponry. In their case, the favourite was the old naval cutlass with its heavy, broad blade and its black grip and knuckleguard.

Lieutenant Dickinson and his fifty-strong Demolition Company, supported by a 'bodyguard' of twenty Royal Marines, practised blowing up apparently random squares of tape unaware that they represented buildings, cranes, gun sites, etc. taken from Belgian plans of the Zeebrugge mole. To help them transport their explosives, Lieutenant Commander Francis Sandford had, somehow, managed to obtain large, wheeled wicker baskets from the General Post Office.

Towards the end of March, much to their surprise, instead of marching to St Mary's Island for further training, all the naval officers and ratings were marched to the Chatham Royal Marine Barracks. There they were kitted out with khaki uniforms and introduced to the mysteries of having the lower legs wrapped in seemingly endless 'puttees'. Like the marines, their boots were to have no metal nails or plates.

Secrecy remained vital to success. Nevertheless, there was the occasional mention of Zeebrugge emerging from the messdecks and barracks, so Keyes decided to steer dangerously close to reality in an effort to counter any increase in accurate 'buzzes'.

Largely through the energetic efforts of his Chief of Staff, Commodore Algernon Boyle, Keyes continued to keep the Dover Patrol at full pitch. Life had not been made easy by the creation of the Royal Air Force on 1 April, thus depriving Keyes of control over his own aircraft. When Rear Admiral Hall heard that the newly fledged RAF intended to take over direction-finding stations on the French coast to help create their own intelligence and communications department, he asked Keyes to 'grab' them for the Royal Navy. Keyes was happy to oblige but there was a heightened possibility there might soon be no stations left to grab.

In March 1917 a revolution in Russia had led to the overthrow of the Tsar and the formation of a provisional government. Inevitably this caused consternation amongst the rest of the Allies. If the new government pulled Russia out of the war it would allow the battle-hardened German divisions on the Eastern Front to be transferred to the West. If these troops were used to mount an attack on the western sector of the front line there was every chance that the French ports, particularly Dunkirk and Calais, would fall into enemy hands. If such a risk appeared imminent, a plan authorised by the Second Sea Lord would be put into operation. This consisted of landing naval parties at the ports – possibly as far south as Le Havre – with the aim destroying as much of the facilities as possible in the hope of rendering them useless to the enemy. As early as June 1917 Captain Dudley Pound had written to Keyes saying, 'it has not been considered desirable to inform the French Authorities of the arrangements which have been made for demolishing the various ports.' By March 1918 the fears of the Allies were about to be realised. The Bolsheviks had taken over in Russia and were seeking a peace treaty with the Central Powers, and the French, working against British interests, were demanding that the front line be maintained in the face of an enemy assault at the cost of the ports. Keyes asked the First Sea Lord to write him a letter setting out the proposed response to a German advance in the West. Wemyss agreed and sent the following:

> In view of the possibility of the enemy breaking through the line on the North Coast of France, and attacking Calais and Dunkirk, a special battalion of Marines and a company of bluejackets will be placed at your disposal for reinforcements, and to act as demolition parties, etc., to destroy guns and stores. You are to make every preparation for blocking Calais and Dunkirk harbours at the last possible moment, with the ships whose names have been given to you verbally, so as to deny the use of these ports to the enemy if necessary.

Keyes then sent copies of the letter to all the other commanders-in-chief, deliberately forgetting to attach the high security status such a letter would normally attract. This would inevitably result in the letter going through normal, open, channels and setting rumours spinning off in all directions. As for the risk, there was every chance that the French, having already demanded that their

Channel ports be sacrificed rather than see the possibility of a German strike separating the Allied armies, were fully aware that the port facilities would be demolished. With regard to the security within the ships taking part in the attack, Keyes had agreed to an almost watertight proposal. Once the shore training was complete, the entire fleet would sail to an anchorage in the Swin Deep, out of sight of land in the wide Thames Estuary.

Much to Keyes' disappointment, delays caused by Brock's need for chlorosulphonic acid, a late arrival of the blockships, and the less than enthusiastic efforts by Captain Grant to obtain civilian transports for the Royal Marine companies, meant that his hopes for a March attack were dashed. This, in turn, meant that the aircraft under his command would be transferred to the Royal Air Force on 1 April. All was not entirely lost, however, whilst Commodore (soon to be Brigadier General) Lambe remained in command of the Dunkirk squadrons – themselves about to become the 61st and 65th Wings of the Royal Air Force. Lambe was unlikely to let his former naval colleagues down unless events – or superior orders – dictated otherwise.

Of even greater concern was the complicated combination of timing and weather conditions that was needed for the attack to be successful. It was generally agreed that, for the attacks on both Zeebrugge and Ostend, the approach, the actual assault, and the withdrawal, would have to take place in the dark – and the darker the better. For the blockships to penetrate the canals successfully it was necessary to carry out the attack at high water. That meant the high water would have to occur around the middle of the dark period in order that long enough durations of darkness would exist on either side of the attack to cover the approach and the withdrawal. To expose the fleet to the large, powerful guns guarding the ports would be to invite disaster.

Both the moon's cycles and the tides were relatively easy matters to calculate but the imponderable variation of the weather was a different matter. A cloudy sky might be of help in hiding the moon but could also prevent aircraft from taking off, especially when accompanied by rain. Fog could be useful in hiding the approaching ships but the same fog could hide the target. The most important weather condition of all, however, was the wind and its direction. To take advantage of the smokescreen, a wind had to blow steadily towards the Belgian coast, but not so strongly that it blew the smokescreen away – and certainly not strongly enough to prevent the small vessels from being at sea.

Keyes' experts looked at the matter and decided that the next suitable period would be between the 9 and 13 April. It was time bring the ships together at the Swin.

On the 3rd, a procession of light cruisers made their way down the Medway and out into the North Sea. One, the *Hindustan*, looked perfectly normal. Five of them, with their masts removed, simply moved sluggishly through the water as the sixth, with only the stump of a foremast reaching as high as the foretop, and the mainmast missing altogether, appeared to be breaking a very basic rule of smart seamanship by sailing with huge fenders hanging from her port side. She also had an additional deck running fore and aft along the port side with a large steel box at either end. To complete the ship's bizarre appearance, large splinter mattresses were fixed to the conning tower and around the foretop and funnels, whilst two giant double grapnels were secured to fore and aft, port side davits. Overall, with her unscrubbed decks, and with a lack of polish to her 'brightwork', her new captain considered that she looked like 'a home for lost coal-tips'.

On the evening of the 6th, the Royal Marines arrived onboard the transport *Royal Edward*. They had travelled by train from Chatham to Dover, where they had boarded the former Clyde ferry under the impression (given by baggage labels) that they were headed to France. Once clear of the shore, however, a change of course prompted a greater interest in their destination. Before long, the situation became even more confusing as the *Iris* and the *Daffodil* appeared out of the North Sea rain and the marines transferred into the Mersey ferries. Then, with the rain continuing to restrict their view, they found themselves boarding the *Hindustan* and the strange-looking *Vindictive*. On the following evening, Carpenter had the marines and his ship's company mustered on the quarterdeck. There he explained the scheme to them, concentrating on their particular roles, but briefly mentioning the other activities that would be going on at the same time. Without going into detail concerning the role of the two submarines, he told them that, if they heard the sound of a huge explosion in the vicinity, they should not be concerned as it was a vital part of their own operation.

The same day, Keyes arrived in the destroyer *Phoebe* to speak to the ships' companies of the blockships and the seaman landing parties. There was a clear distinction between those men and the other ships' companies, the boats crews, and the Royal Marines. The latter groups were, in effect, carrying out the duties they could normally expect to perform in wartime – the former, however, had been selected without knowing the high degree of hazard to which they were about to be subjected. When he addressed the men, Keyes explained the need for secrecy up until that time, but now, having explained the formidable task ahead of them, he invited anyone who was married or had any other reason to withdraw, to do so 'and no one would think any the worse of them'. The only reply he got was a burst of sustained cheering – not a single man withdrew.

There was one aspect of Keyes' speech, nevertheless, that did cause considerable disquiet in some quarters. The plans for the deployment of the blockships required fifty-three men to take them into the canals, but only thirty-four to take them on passage to within sight of their destination. Consequently it was intended that the passage crews would steam the ships to the area of operations whilst the blocking crews rested. When the time came for the blocking crews to take over, the passage crews would disembark on to the minesweeper HMS *Lingfield* and be returned to Dover. That was exactly what the passage crews did not want to happen. They had understood that there was to be some action, and they wanted to be part of it. Some of them – such as the Australians in the *Thetis* – became so vocal that their behaviour verged on the insolent; others decided that they would simply ignore the order to disembark. The passage crew in the *Intrepid* tried a different tack – they requested to see the captain. When Bonham Carter agreed to meet them, he listened to their complaint before explaining the problem. After the blocking crews had sunk the ships in position, they were to be picked up by CMBs, which were not designed to carry large numbers of passengers. Even then, there was always the possibility they might not be able to get directly alongside. In that case, the escapers would have to depend on small craft such as the ship's boats or Carley floats to reach the CMBs or, in dire circumstances, attempt to get out of the harbour on the same small vessels. When this reasoned appeal fell on deaf ears, Bonham Carter tried something different. He offered to take enough extra men to form a spare gun crew, provided the passage crew held a ballot. This was agreed and six men were selected, the unlucky remainder quietly making their own arrangements.

To fill the few remaining days until the start of the dark period, practice landings were made by storming onto the *Hindustan*. At other times, groups of seamen and marines, yelling at the top of their voices, made bayonet charges along the upper deck or along the ship's 'flats' and passageways. Whilst this was going on, the *Vindictive*'s first lieutenant, Rosoman, supervised the construction of the port landing brows. These had not been erected during the time at Chatham as such strange additions would have inevitably caused comment and conjecture. In the evenings, concert parties and boxing matches were organised for the men whilst the officers depleted the ship's supplies of gin and angostura bitters ('pink gin').

The start of the dark period arrived with the 9th, but the weather proved to be entirely unsuitable, the 10th arrived in the same fashion but, on the 11th, conditions improved dramatically. Keyes, already alert to outside events urging him to act, had to make a decision.

6

The Trial by Patience

At 0440hrs on the morning of 21 March 1918 British troops defending Amiens, some 40 miles to their rear, found themselves under the heaviest artillery bombardment the world had ever seen. With a combination of high explosive, shrapnel and gas shells around 6,500 heavy guns and 3,500 trench mortars attacked artillery emplacements, divisional headquarters, communication trenches and rear supports. After five hours of constant shelling, the guns changed their aim to the British front line as specially trained infantry 'stormtroopers' passed through the line to attack the British rear positions. Entire sections of the line were destroyed along with their defenders before retreat in the face of overwhelming force became the only option.

The moment the British and French had feared had arrived. German troops, fresh from the Eastern Front, had provided huge reinforcements in the West. Now fifty-eight German divisions faced eighteen British along a 46-mile front – most of which had only just been taken over from the French, and all in a poor defensive condition.

The Germans, led by General Ludendorff, knew that, to win the war, they had to strike hard before the Americans arrived in sufficient numbers to alter the balance on the Western Front. The British were exhausted by the 1917 battles at Arras, Messines, Passchendaele and Cambrai, and were weakened by the losses during the Third Battle of Ypres, and Lloyd George's reluctance to send reinforcements to France. There were also the problems caused by the division of command amongst the Allies. The Americans, under General Pershing, would not contemplate working with any of the other allied forces and, once the German attack had begun, the French refused to send any assistance.

It was not until 5 April that the German advance was halted by a combination of local leadership, stiffening resistance, and a breakdown in German logistics. By then the British had fallen back an astonishing 28 miles and the Germans were just 11 miles from Amiens. The Allies had been so shaken that they decided to pool their resources with the French general Ferdinand Foch in overall command.

But it was not over. On 9 April another huge attack was mounted in Belgian Flanders around the town of Ypres and the River Lys. This time the Germans were aiming to reach the Channel ports. On the 11th, with the British line forced ever westwards, General Haig issued a 'Special Order of the Day' in which he wrote:

> There is no other course open to us but to fight it out. Every position must be held to the last man: there must be no retirement. With our backs to the wall and believing in the justice of our cause each one of us must fight on to the end. The safety of our homes and the Freedom of mankind alike depend upon the conduct of each one of us at this critical moment.

Just four days earlier, Keyes had issued his own order, introducing the startlingly obvious code name for the operation:

> To all Ranks and Ratings concerned.
>
> Operation Z.O.
>
> The object of the Enterprise we are about to undertake is the blocking of the Entrances of Zeebrugge and Ostend. These ports are the bases of a number of Torpedo Craft and submarines, which are a constant and ever increasing menace to the communications of our Army and to the trade and food supply of our Country.
>
> The complete achievement of our aims would have the most favourable and far reaching effect on the Naval situation.
>
> I am very proud to command the Force which has the great privilege of carrying out this enterprise.
>
> Drawn as this Force is from the Grand Fleet, the Harwich Force, the Dover Patrol, the Three Depots, and the Royal Marine Artillery and Light Infantry, it is thoroughly representative of our Service.
>
> I am very confident that the great traditions of our forefathers will be worthily maintained, and that all ranks will strive to emulate the heroic deeds of our brothers of the Sister Service in France and Flanders.

It was, perhaps, a too matter-of-fact summation of the intended operation to merit a mention in any of the contemporary accounts of the events that were to follow. Its lack of Nelsonian or Churchillian rhetoric, or even of any 'with our backs to the wall' defiance, highlights Keyes' single-minded commitment to the task in hand. Now everyone knew the tactics, the strategy, the proposed outcome, the men doing it, and the example to follow. Any appeals to higher motives were simply unnecessary.

In preparation for the attack, and in order to allow the Germans to become used to such events, Keyes had ordered monitors to bombard the Belgian coast, the RAF dropped bombs on Zeebrugge and Ostend, and squadrons of CMBs roared up and down off the ports, the sound of their engines – hardly distinguishable from aircraft engines – being taken by the enemy as little more than a perpetual irritant. The CMBs also laid mines off the ports – a clear indicator to the Germans that there was no intention to send ships into the area. What the enemy did not realise, however, was that the mines were designed to sink after a specified time, presenting no risk to approaching vessels.

Another task that needed Keyes' close attention was ensuring that hospital facilities would be available to his wounded on their return. At Dover there was a forty-bed hospital ship, which had been built as a luxury steam yacht for the American newspaper publisher and eponymous prize giver, Joseph Pulitzer. The yacht had been purchased by Lord Tredegar and loaned to the Royal Navy with the peer himself in command as a Royal Naval Volunteer Reserve lieutenant. Clearly there was every possibility that Keyes' casualties would exceed the yacht's capacity and so he arranged for the Military Hospital at Dover, the Royal Marine Sick Quarters at Deal and the Naval Hospital at Chatham to be put on the alert for casualties 'from France', along with the supply of a hospital train to be ready at Dover.

During the forenoon of the 11th, Keyes sent a signal telling the ships to 'raise steam', followed shortly by the order to 'carry on'. Excess personal effects were

The monitor HMS *Erebus* with her two 15in guns. The shallow-draught monitors were designed to anchor close inshore to engage land installations. At Zeebrugge, however, they were kept well off shore to keep the risk from enemy coastal artillery to a minimum.

put into kit-bags and trunks and sent ashore as anchor-cables were first shortened then the anchors weighed. The sound of cheering rolled across a sea hardly troubled by the slight wind as the *Vindictive* led the blockships away from the Swin in line ahead. They had not travelled far when a fire was reported in *Vindictive's* gunner's store – the compartment containing hundreds of grenades and Stokes' mortar shells. The ship's gunner, Warrant Officer Gunner John Cobby, calmly organised teams of men to empty the store whilst the fire was being fought. With the alarm over and the danger dealt with there was a short pause as the *Vindictive* took the *Iris* and *Daffodil* in tow before the first of a series of marker light-buoys, laid down to provide a simple navigation path towards the targets, was met.

The marker buoys were laid down under the guidance of two Hydrographic Department officers, Captain Henry Douglas and Lieutenant Commander Francis Haselfoot. Now, with the operation under way, Douglas was given the job of guiding the Dunkirk-based monitors – *Terror* and *Erebus* – in company with their smoke-laying CMBs, to the position from which they would bombard Zeebrugge. Not only was accurate positioning vital for the ranging of their huge guns, but it was equally vital that they did not cross into Dutch waters, thereby causing an unnecessary international incident. Haselfoot was on his way to locate the positions for Aga flashing buoys. These had been obtained by Brock to be dropped closer to Zeebrugge as the fleet approached under the cover of darkness. The Aga buoys had been designed before the war by the Swede Gustaf Dalen, and every three seconds gave a three-tenths of a second flash. In years to come, Dalen would be better known for his invention of a cooker. Once the final buoy had been reached, the last 13 miles would be navigated by dead reckoning – a combination of speed and compass bearing, taking into account wind and local tide conditions. The responsibility for ensuring that the main force under Keyes arrived at each buoy at a predetermined time was given to Carpenter.

To the north, as the main force headed eastwards, the Harwich Force under Commodore Tyrwhitt took to sea to guard against any enemy interference from that direction. To the south, Keyes' chief of staff, Commodore Boyle, set off for 'position 'G' where a gap had been created in the net-mine barrage. It was at this point that the excess crews of the blockships would be taken off and the Ostend blockships would turn south. Boyle also had another, extremely important, role once he reached buoy 'G'.

Through wireless signals picked up by Naval Intelligence, Keyes could monitor the weather conditions at Zeebrugge. The Germans regularly informed their U-boats of the state of the weather and, once this information had been picked up by Room 40, they passed it on to Keyes by encrypted wireless message. Such information alone, however, could not be trusted as German Naval Intelligence was not averse to sending false information to cause confusion regarding shipping movements – something they could do just as easily with weather reports.

Consequently, Boyle was ordered to keep a close eye on the wind direction, reporting its current state at regular intervals by means of a screened signalling lamp. No wireless was to be used, and there would be no acknowledgement by a return flashing light.

At Dunkirk, under the cover of darkness, Commodore Lynes would lead his force out to meet the two Ostend blockships with Commander Hamilton Benn leading the CMBs. The Stroom Bank buoy was to be located and illuminated, light-buoys were to be laid at the entrance to the canal, and smokescreens laid down to prevent the blockships from coming under fire from the shore batteries.

When the *Vindictive* and the blockships reached 'A' buoy off the north Goodwin Sands after their voyage from the Swin, they found themselves surrounded by a scene of great activity. CMBs passed lines across to destroyers, which were to tow them across the North Sea to save fuel. Also taken under tow were the two submarines, *C1* and *C3* and Francis Sandford's picket boat, which he had commandeered in Vice Admiral Keyes' name (Keyes himself being unaware until the deed was done). Each submarine carried a dingy or 'skiff' secured to its after casing to assist in the escape of its crew. The fore-ends were stuffed with 5 tons of highly explosive amatol and each boat had been fitted with an auto-gyro steering system designed to steer the boats the final few yards towards their target viaduct. This, it was hoped, would enable the crews to get away before the explosion completed their work.

If there was to be one single cheering sight in the fleet, it was the arrival of the destroyer HMS *Warwick* – Keyes' flagship. The spirits of all were lifted by the sight of his flag flying from the foremast – not simply because it was the 'one ball' Saint George's flag of a vice admiral, but mainly because of its size. This was the silk flag that had been presented to Keyes by the ship's company of HMS *Centurion*. When they instructed him that the flag was to 'fly in battle', they had expected it to be flown from the mast of a 26,000-ton battleship. When flown from a destroyer the size of the *Warwick* (just over 1,000 tons), the flag appeared to be the same size as the whole of the ship's forward superstructure. The splash of pure white and bright red waving gallantly above the destroyer could leave no one could in any doubt where the admiral could be found. When presented to Keyes, the flag carried the 'two ball' design of a rear admiral. Lady Keyes had unpicked the ball in the lower hoist canton to transform it into a flag for a vice admiral.

The captain of the *Warwick* was Commander Victor Campbell. He had not only been the commanding officer of the Drake Battalion of the Royal Naval Division at Gallipoli (where he had earned the Distinguished Service Order) but, as a lieutenant, had been the 'Wicked Mate' on Captain Scott's 1910 *Terra Nova* expedition. Ordered to lead a northern party as Scott headed south, Campbell found himself having to spend the winter at a desperately remote spot with no hut and no supplies. The party dug a 12ft by 9ft cave into the snow as their shelter.

Campbell then drew a line down the centre of the cave declaring that one side was for the two officers and a civilian scientist, and the other side was for the three ratings. Anything said by the officers could not be heard on the rating's side, and anything said by the ratings could not be heard on the officer's side. After surviving the worst winter then on record (resulting in Scott's death), Campbell led his party on a 230-mile march back to the expedition base camp.

At 1930hrs that evening, Keyes gave the order to 'Carry on'. With Carpenter as the fleet navigator, and with the large ships of the main force in three line-ahead columns, the fleet of almost eighty vessels surged towards the Belgian coast. Around and inbetween the columns, the MLs growled, eager to be let free and reach the speeds of which they were capable. Above them, aircraft from Dover and Dunkirk flew to fend off any approaching enemy machines, and to watch out for German submarines and surface vessels. They would return to their airfields as soon as darkness had fallen over the scene.

Now determinedly under way, the diversion ships heading towards the Belgian ports prepared for the coming action. In the *Vindictive*, the landing brows were secured ready to be lowered on the top of the mole parapet, and the large flamethrowers checked and rechecked. Gun breeches were checked for operation, ammunition made ready, and small arms inspected. Fire hoses were run out and extinguishers positioned where needed. Demolition charges for use against the mole facilities were brought onto the upper deck and field dressings distributed. In case any of the navigating team were rendered *hors de combat* and the charts destroyed, instructions for the return course were painted on the inside of the conning tower.

'C' buoy was reached at 2300hrs with the wind still blowing gently from the north-west. Keyes ordered the first of a series of coded one-word signals to be sent. Operation Z.O. was on.

With darkness descended and 'D' buoy ahead, a flash of light off the starboard beam followed by the probing of searchlights, indicated that something was going on at Ostend – almost certainly Lynes and his vessels getting on station ready for the arrival of the *Brilliant* and the *Sirius*. Then, off the starboard bow, more lights, flashes, and searchlights showed that Zeebrugge was being attacked by the Handley-Page bombers of the RAF. Soon the rumble of distant gunfire could be heard as lines of glowing green 'flaming onions' arced upwards in search of the attackers. These anti-aircraft weapons were causing grave concern amongst the Allied pilots who believed that the shells were linked together by wire.

At 'D' buoy, the fleet slowed down to allow an ML to go alongside the blockships to take off the reluctant passage crews and transfer them to the *Lingfield*. As she did so, an air of increasing consternation grew on the bridge of the *Warwick*. Although no signal had been received from Boyle in the *Attentive*, it was clear to all that the wind had dropped. Even worse, the clouds, although made visible only by a weak light from a thin crescent moon, were slowly moving northwards. As the minutes passed, ensigns and pennants stirred limply in the same direction as the surface of the sea began to show the effects of a southerly wind. Then, out of the darkness ahead, a light flashed. It was Boyle. He had come to the inescapable conclusion that the wind was now holding firm from the south.

All eyes turned towards Keyes. The imperturbable Campbell, his old friend Tomkinson, his coxswain, Brady, who had been with him since his days in the *Fame*, all waited for his command. His men were eager to get to grips with the enemy, his ships were where he wanted them, but without the aid of a smokescreen both men and ships were at the mercy of well-sited heavy guns firing at practically point-blank range. Should he risk the Admiralty's refusal to remount the assault, or press on, trusting to 'the God of Battles and the good fortune of the British Navy'?

Keyes, despite being 'horribly tempted', gave the order to cancel the attack.

Suddenly, Carpenter was presented with a task, the like of which had never before been experienced at sea. He had to turn an entire fleet of seventy-seven vessels, many of them under tow, 16 points (180 degrees), in the dark, on the edge of a minefield with, apart from signal lamps, no lights. He had worked on a detailed scheme of retirement that had been approved by Keyes, and now it was about to be put to the test. The signal was sent by shaded flashing lantern or shouted across by megaphone and the enormous task set in motion.

For the most part, Carpenter's planning went well. One CMB was sliced in two by a larger ship but no lives were lost. Another had a hole rammed in her bows, her captain ordering one of his crew to sit over the hole until he could build up the speed. Once he had reached 27 knots the bows lifted clear of the water, relieving the human bung of his duties. Considerably worse happened when one of the CMBs, believing that he was about to be rammed, switched on his navigation lights. Other vessels, close by, under the impression that they had missed an order, switched their lights on in response. The scene suddenly looked like Brighton Esplanade before a sharp 'Out Lights' signal was flashed from the flagship. Keyes, ever positive in attitude, thought that the showing of lights at such a distance from the shore, 16 miles away, occasioned very little risk.

For whatever reason, the rushing train-like sound of heavy shells approached and four huge fountains of water surged up close to the *Warwick*. No further shells were fired, and Keyes was left wondering whether the firing had been in response to the lights, or if the already respected German wireless position fixing had been responsible. On the other hand, could it have been a new sound ranging system, such as had gained Brock's interest? Nevertheless, to the relief of everyone, the fleet's turn was successfully achieved and its component parts returned to their various starting points to await the decisions that were to follow.

The blockship *Thetis* only narrowly avoided problems of a different sort. When short-handed in the machinery compartments, it was usual for the engineers to call on the seamen to lend a hand with 'trimming' coal (balancing the coal bunkers). However, when Engineer Lieutenant Commander Boddie called for assistance, the seamen who turned up were clearly drunk. It turned out that the coxswain, a chief petty officer 'with an excellent war record' had broken into the spirit room, opened the rum cask, and poured out two days' supply of the powerful liquid for his seamen friends. The stokers were outraged – not necessarily because of the lack of assistance with the heavy work of trimming, but because they had not been invited to share in the rum. The coxswain was summarily dismissed on the ship's return.

There had been two other notable incidents during the night, both concerning CMBs, that showed both enterprise and initiative – and an appalling lapse of basic security.

One of the Dover CMBs had left with the others but had found herself with an engine defect and the captain was forced to persuade a trawler to tow him back into harbour. After five hours of frenetic work by the base engineers, the fault was rectified and the captain decided that he would take a direct path to Zeebrugge to rejoin the assault. At top speed in the darkness, skimming over shoals, nets, and minefields, the boat closed with the Belgian coast. In less than two hours after leaving Dover they saw searchlights sweeping the waters, bombs and shells exploding, and flaming onions reaching up into the black sky. They then saw something dead ahead that they had not expected – buildings. With the wheel wrenched over, the boat practically skimmed along the edge of Blankenberge beach, miraculously escaping grounding on the shallows, and very quickly found herself parallel with the Zeebrugge mole. At great risk of being picked up by the searchlights, the boat came under fire. By now, particularly as the bombing had quietened down, the captain began to realise that his boat was the sole representative of the Royal Navy immediately alongside the mole and, more to the point, he was not very welcome. As enemy ships emerged from the harbour, he opened his throttle, roared off into the darkness, and retraced his route back to Dover. The boat arrived at the harbour before Keyes and the main force had returned – the only vessel to complete the voyage to Zeebrugge and back that night.

On his return to Dover, Keyes telephoned Commodore Lynes to obtain an early report of the proceedings off Ostend. The Dunkirk force had arrived off the port at 2200hrs and the CMBs had closed with the canal entrance to lay down the flares needed to guide the blockships in. Behind them, the MLs laid down the smokescreen as Commander Hamilton Benn, in ML532, waited to pick up the escaping crew of the *Brilliant*. Lieutenant Commander Keith Hoare's ML283 would do the same for the *Sirius*, and Lieutenant Roland Bourke, the

Canadian farmer, stood by at the helm of ML276 in case he was needed to assist with the rescue.

The Stroom Bank Buoy had been located with little difficulty, as had a Bell buoy at the entrance to the canal. Inevitably, these activities came under fierce gunfire from the shore. Star shells, rocket flares and searchlights were followed by flaming onions and 2-pound tracer. Fortunately, however, the heavy guns sited along the shore and inland chose not to get involved – possibly preserving their ammunition in view of the shortages being experienced by Ludendorff's advancing army to their rear. Nevertheless, without any wireless communication, and with the destroyers hidden by smoke, Hamilton Benn's small craft had to endure the firing for two hours before a falling tide convinced him that the blockships were not coming and he ordered their withdrawal.

From Lynes, Keyes learned that one CMB had been sunk, and that another, *CMB33*, was missing. Two of the Handley-Page bombers used over Zeebrugge had not returned. In the normal course of events the loss of the aircraft and the CMBs would have been considered a sad, but nevertheless, inevitable cost of war. However, the disappearance of the *CMB33* turned out to be considerably more serious.

Lieutenant Robert Angus was not an officer on whom fortune smiled readily. In 1916, after mine-laying operations, two seaplanes were reported missing. Angus's *CMB8*, in company with *CMB13*, was sent to see if the aircraft could be found. Close to the Belgian coast *CMB8*'s steering-gear broke down and she was taken in tow by *CMB13*. Shortly afterwards the two vessels came under fire from the shore and an approaching German torpedo boat was seen on the horizon. At that moment, *CMB13*'s engines broke down. Angus restarted his engine and surged forward, only to have the tow-rope wrapped around his propeller. With the accuracy of the enemy gunfire rapidly improving, and the German ship closing at speed, it was decided to place charges in the bottom of *CMB8* and sink her. With this achieved, and everyone onboard *CMB13*, they raced away from the scene and arrived safely back at Dover.

By April 1918, Angus was back in command of a Dunkirk-based CMB – this time *CMB33*. What actually happened on the night of 11 April is not fully known but it appears that *CMB33* was separated from the other CMBs and ended up grounded on a sandbank close to the eastern pier at the entrance to the Ostend canal. Probably after being discovered by searchlights or flares, the boat came under fire with all six of the crew being killed (although some reports put three of the deaths down to 'exposure'). *CMB33* then either drifted in to the beach with the tide, or was towed there by the Germans. No doubt much to the enemy's surprise and delight, on searching the boat they came across a set of Z.O. operational orders. Keyes had been specific in his instructions regarding security. On no account were such orders to be carried by the small craft. Only signal books and orders relating to the individual vessels could be carried and they were to be destroyed 'on entering enemy waters'. Fortunately for his peace of mind, Keyes was, of course, completely unaware of this alarming development.

Matters were difficult enough for the admiral when he toured the ships at the Swin later that day. Not only was there an air of gloom throughout, he also felt strongly that the men were close to the opinion that he was not really up to the job. Keyes countered this by telling the ships' companies that he was interested only in a 'great success' not a 'heroic disaster'. He promised to 'take them alongside the enemy' but he had to have their trust in his choice of the right moment. He was rewarded with a 'shout of approval and ringing cheers'.

They did not have to wait long. On the following day, the 13th (and the last day of the dark period), the wind swung round to a northerly direction and Keyes gave the order to proceed. As *Vindictive* and the blockships left the Swin, a destroyer approached and passed across Brock – who only narrowly escaped missing the sailing – and a letter from Keyes. The message stressed 'We must push in tonight'. and was signalled down the line to the other ships. They had, however, reached no further than 20 miles from their anchorage when it became clear to everyone that the wind was far too strong to continue. The small boats, the MLs and the CMBs could not handle such a rising sea, and

CMB33 in the hands of the Germans, 12 April 1918.

getting the landing ships alongside the mole in such conditions would verge upon the impossible. Yet again, the lines turned north-westwards and returned to the Swin.

According to Carpenter, the men showed no discontent and 'endeavoured to appear unruffled'. Keyes, however, was not allowed a simple patient wait for another opportunity. The following day, the First Sea Lord arrived at Dover to tell him that the operation was cancelled.

Wemyss and the Admiralty Board had decided that the men were to be returned to the Grand Fleet, that the 4th Battalion was to be disbanded with the Royal Marines returned to their depots, and the ships would be paid off. The reasons for this decision were plain and straightforward. Several neutral ships had seen the fleet at sea, and word was bound to get back to the Germans. Furthermore, the next dark period was three weeks away and the men anchored in the Swin would not survive being cooped up onboard for that long. Keyes recorded the next part of their conversation:

> Keyes – 'Why wait three weeks, I want to try again in nine or ten days.'
> Wemyss – 'Why, it will be a full moon, as well as high tide about midnight.'
> Keyes – 'No, I always wanted a full moon, but I could not wait for it. Please go back and tell the Board that you approve of my carrying out the attack in the next period, when high tide occurs about midnight.'
> Wemyss (with a grin) – 'Roger, what a damned liar you are.'

The First Sea Lord promised his support but he still had to get the Admiralty Board around to his point of view. This was achieved by the unannounced visit of a destroyer from the Harwich Flotilla passing silently through the Swin anchorage. Onboard, without his flag flying, was Wemyss accompanied by the First Lord, Sir Eric Geddes. Moreover, devoid of any ceremony, calls were made upon the *Vindictive* and some of the blockships. Wemyss' stratagem worked. Within hours, Keyes' earlier request for an extra accommodation ship was granted with the dispatch of HMS *Dominion*, like the *Hindustan*, a pre-Dreadnaught, King Edward VII-class, battleship.

Whilst the waiting continued, the planners looked closely at the experience gained during the two failed attempts. The submarines' skiffs had both been washed overboard during the crossing and, although the crews were quite happy to go without their rudimentary primary escape equipment, Keyes insisted on a better arrangement. As a result, the submarines ended up looking like no other submarine in the history of underwater warfare. Each of them seemed to have acquired a pair of wings that jutted out from the top of their conning towers. From each 'wing' was suspended a skiff, powered by a petrol engine and supplied with a pump to help keep down the level of water in the fragile boat.

The gap in the minefield at 'G' buoy was to be widened and its edges marked by Aga buoys flashing red and white lights. Also, the time spent bombing the mole was to be reduced in order to lessen the risk to the airmen.

One clear weakness in the plan was the deployment of MLs and CMBs. When the sea surface was anything from calm to a modest chop, the small vessels performed superbly, but any conditions more severe brought a marked limitation to their deployment. Accordingly, Keyes had a number of P-boats and destroyers fitted with smoke-making apparatus to take over if the weather deteriorated. Under such circumstances, the only small boats to go with the fleet would be the MLs and CMBs, required to rescue the blockship crews.

Now all thoughts turned to the next period of high tide – the need for darkness having been removed by Keyes.

7

The Ostend Raid

With just a few days to go before 22 April – the start of the next period available to launch Operation Z.O. – Keyes received some disappointing news. Lieutenant Franks, the captain of the blockship *Iphigenia*, was taken to hospital with appendicitis. There was no possibility of his returning in time and no time to familiarise a replacement officer with the complexities of the assault on the Zeebrugge lockgates. A possible solution, however, came in the form of a hastily scrawled note written by Franks as he was on the way to the operating theatre. In it, he urgently requested that his command be given to his deputy, Lieutenant Edward Billyard-Leake. One of the first three cadets to be sent from his native Australia to England for entry into the Royal Navy, the violin-playing Billyard-Leake came from a wealthy family with vast acres of prime farmland

Lieutenant E.W. Billyard-Leake, captain of the *Iphigenia*, seated on the far left of the front row as a midshipman in 1914. While on board HMAS *Australia* he became firm friends with the Prince of Wales – seated in the second row on the far right. The civilian is Sir George Reid, the Australian High Commissioner, a former Prime Minister of Australia who later became a member of the British Parliament.

in New South Wales and Tasmania. Their English property included Harefield House, near Uxbridge. At the outbreak of war, the family turned the house over to the Australian military medical services as a hospital for their injured sailors and soldiers. The problem facing Keyes, however, was that Billyard-Leake was just 22 years old and with barely a year's seniority in his rank. He had, however, seen action during the Battle of Jutland. As he stood on the battleship HMS *Warspite*'s open bridge, a nearby ship (possibly HMS *Queen Mary*) blew apart and sank almost immediately. A senior officer, standing next to Billyard-Leake turned to him and said 'Are you ready, Leake? Our turn next.'

Iphigenia's navigating officer, Lieutenant Philip Vaux, was of a similar age to Billyard-Leake, but with even less seniority. Could Billyard-Leake lead men into such a hazardous situation as was inevitable at Zeebrugge? The answer came from a surprising source. A petition arrived on Keyes' desk signed by all the ship's company of the *Iphigenia* – they wanted 'Billy Leake' as their captain.

With Billyard-Leake appointed to the command of the *Iphigenia*, Keyes had a vacancy for a junior officer. He did not have to look very far. Sub Lieutenant Maurice Lloyd was kicking his heels on the accommodation ship *Dominion,* and he was desperately eager to get involved. As a 17-year-old midshipman he had been in the Gallipoli landing ship *River Clyde* and had earned a DSC by assisting in securing the lighters connecting the ship to the shore despite a storm of fire from many nearby machine guns. Now 20 years old, and having been turned down by Keyes when he first applied to take part in the attack, he found his chance had come.

Another officer upon whom fortune smiled was Sub Lieutenant Alfred ('Victor') Knight of the *Hindustan*. During the forenoon of the 22nd, the ship's captain, Davidson, called to see his old friend, Lieutenant Commander Hardy, the captain of the Ostend blockship *Sirius*. During the visit, Davidson learned that one of the ship's officers had been badly affected when a smoke-float misfired. On his return he sent for Knight and offered him the chance to go in the blockship. Knight needed no second asking and immediately crossed over to the *Sirius*. At the same time, Carpenter sent a signal by semaphore to the other vessels – 'Ships are warned that Chloro Sulphuric [*sic*] gas is dangerous.'

In all, the accommodation ships furnished twenty-two replacements for the assaulting vessel, plus an additional four cooks and officers' stewards who managed to persuade their superiors to let them go.

With his planned assault now back on track, Keyes continued to receive good news. At midnight on 19 April, patrolling drifters heard two large explosions and steamed immediately in the direction of the sound. There they found a great amount of oil and bubbles rising to the surface – another U-boat had fallen victim to the net-mines.

Two days later a newly designed 'indicator loop' was laid across the straits between the North Foreland and the Sandetti Bank. Designed by a Nobel Prize-winning physicist, Professor William Bragg, serving on the Admiralty Board of Invention and Research, the loop used pressurised quartz crystal to produce a sound. When the sound wave bounced off an object it was picked up by hydrophones and could be used to determine the distance and direction of the target. This design proved so effective that it became the basis for all subsequent Asdic and, eventually, Sonar equipment.

Then, in the early hours of 22 April, another U-boat was destroyed by the mine barrage. As this date was the start of the next tidal period, such an incident might have been regarded as an omen contributing to Keyes' 'feeling' that this was the day to mount his attack. Accordingly, at 1045hrs, he ordered Carpenter to be under weigh by 1300hrs, and the entire fleet to be ready to depart from 'A' buoy at 1700hrs. Within a minute, the vessels at the Swin received a signal sent by semaphore flags with the code-word 'Nascent'.

Tow-lines were sent from the *Vindictive* across to the two Liverpool ferries as the stokers and engineers in all the ships worked to build up the steam pressure. At the appointed time, under a pall of black smoke rising to a crystal-clear sky, the ships surged forward in a southwesterly direction, then towards the east, and finally southeasterly towards the assembly point.

In all, seventy-six vessels mustered at 'A' buoy. With the exception of the MLs, they were to arrange themselves into three line-ahead columns. The central

The *Vindictive* and other ships sailing toward Zeebrugge in a painting by Bernard Finegan Gribble. The *Vindictive* is on the right with the flagship HMS *Warwick* on the left flying the huge flag of Vice Admiral Keyes.

column consisted of the *Vindictive* towing the *Iris* which, in turn, was towing the *Daffodil*, herself towing the CMB responsible for dropping smoke-floats off Blankenberge. Then came the three Zeebrugge blockships, each towing a smokescreen CMB. Behind them came the Ostend blockships, both towing a single CMB armed with a Stokes' mortar for bombarding the mole gun positions. Bringing up the rear was the Royal Mail Ship *Lingfield* with the task of bringing home the passage crews.

With a single exception, the port column was made up of four destroyers and two P-boats, each towing a single CMB. The exception was a destroyer with the task of acting as close escort to the Ostend blockships. The starboard column was headed by two destroyers, each towing a CMB. They were followed by another two destroyers with a submarine at the end of their respective towing cables. Next came a destroyer towing the submarines' picket boat followed by two destroyers and two P-boats, each towing a single CMB. MLs were positioned between the columns, responsible for the rescue of the blockship's crews at the rear. Ahead of the starboard column, HMS *Warwick* with her giant vice admiral's flag flying, took up her position.

Steaming well ahead of the fleet, the 'Gap Patrol', made up of the scout cruiser, *Attentive,* and four destroyers from Harwich under the command of Commodore Boyle, were already on their way to open up the mine-net and to lay occulting Aga buoys at the gap's limits. To the north, the Harwich Force was setting off for its patrol work at the northern limit of the operation as three more Harwich destroyers escorted the two monitors, *Erebus* and *Terror*, to their bombarding positions off the mouth of the River Scheldt.

To the south-east, under the direction of Commodore Lynes, steam was being raised by the destroyers and monitors involved in the Ostend attack. The French were supplying five destroyers and four MLs. Inland from Dunkirk, the heavy naval guns of the Royal Marine Artillery siege trains prepared to open fire at the German coastal guns protecting Zeebrugge and Ostend. Final checks were being carried out on the RAF aircraft in preparation for the bombing raid.

As Keyes watched the ships take up their positions, a CMB came alongside bringing a gift from the admiral's wife. His coxswain, Chief Petty Officer Henry Brady, clambered onboard clutching two cork-packed 'life-saving waistcoats' manufactured by Gieves, the naval tailors. Sent by Keyes to collect them, Brady had returned to find that the admiral had left without him. Whether or not there was any underlying motive behind Keyes' action is not known, but it is likely that, with the coxswain having no particular role in the impending action, he had deliberately left him behind to keep him out of danger. When Eva Keyes discovered the distraught man still at the house, she put him in her car and drove him to the harbour where she found one of the last CMBs on the point of departure. Of course, the captain of the CMB was unlikely to refuse to run an errand for the admiral's wife, and so Brady and the life-jackets soon found their way on to the *Warwick*.

At 1700hrs, Keyes ordered the Yeoman of Signals to hoist the signal: 'Proceed'. The earlier clear skies had clouded over and the fleet sailed into a fine drizzle. It was not a good sign. The rain itself was of no consequence to the seamen and marines; after all, if it was raining at their destination, it was also raining on the Germans. But the band of rain stretched across the straits and put a halt to the RAF's preparations at Dunkirk. The Zeebrugge mole was not to be bombed that night.

As Carpenter concentrated on keeping as close to the buoy timings as he could, the ships made their final preparations. Fire hoses were run out, grenades and shells were fuzed, first-aid stations stocked, and emergency lighting and gas masks tested. Dead-lights were fastened into position behind scuttles to 'darken' ship. Clean underwear was put on to reduce the risk of wound contamination, and anti-searchlight and anti-gas goggles issued to those manning the guns and bridge.

After just 18 miles of surging through the waves, the tiny crew of Lieutenant Edward Hill's *CMB35* suffered a dreadful disappointment. An unsecured rope unwound itself and trailed behind them. Inevitably it wrapped itself around the propeller, the engine ground to a halt, and the motor boat's bows drooped to the sea. With all efforts to restart the engine failing, it was clear that they were to have no part in the approaching enterprise.

Below the decks of the *Vindictive*, the majority of men with little to do slept, played cards, sang, or listened to the gramophone. Wing Commander Brock, having checked the flamethrowers and smokescreen apparatus, wrote to his wife. If he was killed, he informed her, she should continue to press his claim that his anti-Zeppelin bullet had been responsible for many of the airships being brought down. The government had decided that each Zeppelin was worth £70,000 and that the pilot should be given a third with the rest awarded to the inventor of the bullet used. The pilots, however, had frequently used a mixture of Brock bullets and another type. Where that had happened, Brock had only received 31 per cent of the remaining money, whereas the other bullet manufacturer received 35 per cent. As both Brock and the pilots were convinced that it was entirely Brock's bullets that had defeated the airships, he felt sure that the claim should be pursued.

The Member of Parliament, Lieutenant Hilton Young, a poet of considerable talent, seemed to have thought there was a good chance he would not return alive. As the *Vindictive* advanced towards the twilight, he wrote:

I have no hope. No fear for my distress.
There is no man on earth so free.
Hope cannot vex one that is futureless;
Fear ends in certainty.

No hope, no fear, no triumph, no regret,
But darkness of the gathering shades.
What have I left to hold for comfort yet,
Now that the daylight fades?

I will think of all good things that I have known,
Of everything that I love best.
I will take all their beauty for my own
To be my strength and rest.

Vindictive steaming towards Zeebrugge, 22 April 1918.

Vindictive with major modifications identified.

Lancashire-born Private Harold Mercer, who was referred to by his local newspaper as 'an athletic young fellow standing 5ft, 11ins', had been turned down repeatedly in his attempts to join the Royal Marines. However, through sheer determination he had, eventually, been accepted by the Corps. Now the family's main provider, he wrote to his recently widowed mother telling her that 'we are going to make our name'. As the ships felt the gentle roll of a placid North Sea, the wooden arms of the signalling apparatus on the *Warwick's* bridge were seen to be moving. As Keyes had said farewell to his wife, she had reminded him that the next day would be 23 April – Saint George's Day. 'It is sure to be the best day for our enterprise. Saint George can be trusted to bring good fortune to England.' she told him. In consequence of these words, the heart-stirring signal that was semaphored from the flagship to the fleet read proudly, 'St George for England.' In reply, Carpenter, no doubt busy with his convoy navigational calculations, sent what he felt was an 'impertinent' reply. He told his Yeoman of Signals to send: 'May we give the Dragon's tail a damned good twist.' The signalman – probably having been brought up on strict Sunday School training, and as the King's Regulations and Admiralty Instructions demanded that all signals be recorded in the signal log – substituted the word 'darned' for 'damned'. When this was spotted, he was told to replace 'damned' – only to send the signal with a conscience-saving 'dammed' instead.

In fact, Carpenter's reply lacked the inspirational quality of the initial signal, which would have probably been best left unanswered (nobody had the temerity to answer Nelson's signal at Trafalgar). Keyes noted that it 'did not fit in with my mood'. (The admiral had not been the first with the signal. Three hundred years earlier, Captain John Smith – of Pocahontas fame – would celebrate victory by signalling 'Sound drums and trumpets: Saint George for England.')

With the twilight darkening, a full moon rose with a baleful glare that flooded the scene with alarming clarity but, by the time the ships had reached 'D' buoy, a comforting mist accompanying a slight drizzle reduced visibility to less than a mile. Captain Tomkinson, well aware of the extra risks of mounting an attack beneath a full moon, told Keyes that the Germans would never think that the Royal Navy contained such 'damned fools' who were prepared to launch an assault 'in bright moonlight'.

At the buoy, the ships slowed down to enable to passage crews of the blockships to be taken off. With the ML alongside the *Thetis*, the number of men ready to be disembarked seemed remarkably few. Many of the stokers could not be found, including all five of the Australians. A similar situation existed alongside the *Iphigenia,* and the ML had to pull clear leaving several men hiding about the ship desperately keen to get involved with the approaching action. Matters were even worse for the *Intrepid*. Her ML broke down and could not get alongside, leaving eighty-four men onboard instead of the fifty-four Carpenter had planned for, and which Lieutenant Bonham Carter expected.

The Ostend blockships *Sirius* and *Brilliant* experienced similar reluctance from their passage crews and by the time the ships had reached Commodore Boyle at 'G' buoy, the excess men left their hiding places and took their places by the guns and in the boiler and engine rooms. At that point, the two ships bid the Zeebrugge force 'Farewell and Good Luck' and turned their bows southwards towards Ostend, the 12-mile journey being paced to arrive at the canal entrance at midnight.

As the Ostend blockships and their escorting destroyers parted company with the Zeebrugge force, the Dunkirk force, under Commodore Lynes, had left harbour at 2100hrs and was on its way to take up station off Ostend. Flying his broad pennant in the destroyer HMS *Faulkner*, Lynes had under his command seven monitors, eight British and three French destroyers, twenty-four British and four French MLs, four French torpedo boats, and six CMBs. In addition, the Royal Marine Artillery batteries, based in the Dunkirk and Nieuport area, would engage the German coastal guns around the port. The RAF bombers based near Dunkirk, however, confirmed that they were prevented from taking part due to the weather.

On closing with the Belgian coast off Ostend, Lynes used his megaphone to hail Commander Hamilton Benn MP in *ML532* and tell him that he was to proceed with his orders. Hamilton Benn answered with a salute and the roar of his engines as he set off to lead his MLs in their vital role in the attack. On his way, he informed Lieutenant Francis Harrison, commanding the CMBs, of Lynes' order. The crew of *ML532* may be seen as typical of the small vessels that were employed in the raids. They were all from the Naval Reserves. The captain was a Member of Parliament and his deputy, Lieutenant Malcolm Kirkwood, came from New Zealand. The leading deckhand, William Wigg, was an experienced seaman who held a master's certificate. Deckhand (and ship's cook) Frank Bowles had been the cook on the Kaiser's schooner, *Meteor*, and had good reason to dislike the Germans. With the outbreak of the war, he had been allowed home – but without the £60 in wages owed to him.

The plan to block the Ostend canal was relatively straightforward. As the monitors opened fire on the coastal guns, Harrison, the captain of *CMB19* (who had already been awarded a DSO a year earlier), was to place a calcium light-buoy alongside the Stroom Bank buoy, another light by the Bell buoy near the mouth of the canal, and then mark the canal entrance with more light-buoys. As this was being done, the MLs, under Hamilton Benn's leadership, were to lay down a double-layered smokescreen parallel to the shore on either side of the canal entrance whilst ensuring that a gap remained open at the entrance itself. Other MLs, in company with CMBs, would lay down an avenue of smokescreens from the Stroom Bank buoy to the Bell buoy down which the blockships would pass. In accordance with Hamilton Benn's instructions, all the MLs carried a small red light at the top of their masts to help with identification in the darkness. On their arrival at the Stroom Bank buoy, the blockships would steam down towards the Bell buoy between banks of smokescreens, pick up the light-buoys at the canal entrance, penetrate the canal, and scuttle themselves, thus blocking the route to the sea. The obvious weakness in the plan was the smokescreen's dependence upon the wind direction but, in the final hour of 22 April, the modest breeze continued to blow from the north-north west, the ideal direction for the assault.

As the monitors reached their positions and began to lay down a barrage on the heavy coastal guns, Harrison in *CMB19* throttled up and shot off to locate the Stroom Bank buoy. To his bafflement, the buoy was not where he had expected it to be. To add to his confusion, he came under some very accurate fire from the shore. With the buoy nowhere to be seen, he dropped a calcium light-buoy and set off in search of the Bell buoy. Yet again, the buoy was missing. Convinced that he could not have made an enormous navigational error over such a short distance, Harrison decided that the Bell buoy must have drifted from its correct position, and dropped another light-buoy. As he did so, he came to the attention of several searchlights followed rapidly by pom-pom and machine-gun fire. Once again, it seemed as if the Germans were expecting enemy craft to be in particular positions and had zeroed-in their guns accordingly. Harrison still had to lay his light-buoys at the entrance to the canal and roared off whilst violently weaving about the surface of the water in an attempt to shake off the lights and guns. Suddenly, a scatter of machine-gun bullets sent his chief motor mechanic spinning to the deck. As the man fell, Harrison saw what he was looking for – the two curved piers jutting out from the canal entrance. Ignoring the heavy fire from the massed machine guns along the piers, he dropped one buoy off the eastern arm and two off the western pier. With that completed, Harrison raced off to find shelter in the towering smokescreen put up by the MLs and other CMBs.

Just before midnight, with precision navigation, the blockships arrived at the Stroom Bank buoy position – only, like others before them, to find that the buoy was nowhere to be seen. On the *Sirius'* port bow, Commander Godsal could see the yellow-orange flashes of numerous guns and hear the continuous thudding and rattling of their fire. Overhead, the sky was filled with bright white starshells, red tracers, rocket trails and the rising green strings of flaming onions. Convinced that the departure point at 'G' buoy had been in the wrong position (thus confusing his navigation), Godsal, followed closely by Lieutenant Commander Hardy in the *Sirius*, continued to steam on an easterly course. After no more than a minute, Godsal decided that he should turn to port and search out the Bell buoy but, just as he gave the order, his attention was brought to a light burning in the north-east. It was the Stroom Bank buoy. The ships swung around and headed towards the light. Once there, Godsal was joined by Hamilton Benn in *ML532* as the rescue craft, and *Sirius* was followed by Lieutenant Commander Keith Hoare in *ML283*. Hoare had recently had a busy time. Just over two weeks before the raid on Ostend, he learned he had been awarded the Distinguished Service Cross for his work with the Auxiliary Patrol during 1917. Less than a week later he was with another officer at Dunkirk when and explosion occurred on an ML in a busy waterway blowing several men overboard, the remainder escaping over the stern in a skiff. Then the cry went up that the petrol tanks were just about to explode along with a depth charge still in position. Officers ordered everyone to get clear, but it was obvious that many men on adjacent boats would not be able to escape. Hoare and his fellow officer jumped into a dinghy and pulled out to the burning boat. They clambered onboard and removed the depth charge, thereby possibly saving the lives of many men. For their action, both officers were awarded the Albert Medal.

As Hoare steered *ML283* in the wake of the *Sirius*, Lieutenant Roland Bourke volunteered to act as support in *ML276* and followed Hoare.

When the blockships had turned to make for the Stroom Bank buoy the wind appeared to have dropped, allowing the smokescreen to drift, although it was hoped that the increasing drizzle would help to hold it in place. The CMBs and MLs immediately set off to fill the gaps – but it was to no avail. Within minutes the wind had swung round to south-south-west. Now the blockships' approach to the canal entrance came under the full glare of searchlights and the full force

The aftermath of the first Ostend raid. *Brilliant* and *Sirius* are both aground, and fires have broken out in the *Sirius*.

of the enemy's massed firepower. Godsal, however, knew that all he had to do was to get on the correct bearing from the Stroom Bank buoy and, if he and Hardy could keep going, they would achieve their intention of sinking the ships in the canal. The task, nevertheless, was made considerably more difficult as the calcium light-buoys marking the piers of the canal had been shot out by the Germans.

The three supporting MLs were joined by Harrison in *CMB19*, taking station on the starboard side of the blockships. Hamilton Benn, stationed on the port side, could see that both blockships were taking a hammering from the enemy's guns – *Sirius* had been badly damaged, appeared to be on fire, and was taking in water. As a result, *ML532* surged forward to lay down a smokescreen across the bows of the *Brilliant*. Harrison also considered laying a smokescreen down. Being on the side from which most of the firing was coming, he not only recognised that the ships were being hit repeatedly, but that they were in the full glare of the enemy searchlights. Nevertheless, he hesitated on the grounds that, with the blockships on their way to the canal entrance, and with their gunners replying to the enemy gun flashes, any smokescreen would be a hindrance rather than a help. Accordingly, he stayed in his self-imposed position taking his share of the shelling and machine-gun fire directed at their location.

In the meantime, Hamilton Benn had pushed on ahead of the blockships, but had only gone a short distance when he saw something that made his blood run

The beached *Sirius* and *Brilliant* as seen from the shore.

cold. In the overspill of the searchlights he saw ahead of him, not the arms of the canal piers, nor even the Ostend esplanade, but a row of sand dunes. Such a sight could only mean that they were to the east of Ostend, and that the blockships were heading directly towards the beach.

In the tightest possible turning circle, Hamilton Benn spun the ML around and raced back towards the *Brilliant*, but he was too late. Just as he came up to her bows, the old cruiser ran aground and sheered round. At the same time a loud bang removed much of Hamilton Benn's bows along with *ML532*'s anchorwinch, anchor and chain. At first Hamilton Benn was convinced that he had rammed the *Brilliant* but it was later discovered that he had been hit by a shell.

Godsal, on the bridge of the first cruiser, heard the sound of breakers washing over the sandbank and gave the order 'Full astern!' just as the ship buried her bows into the obstacle. For a second it seemed as if she would break free, but a surge drove her deeper into the sand. Then, almost as if executing a *coup de grâce*, the *Sirius* rammed into *Brilliant*'s port quarter.

Hardy had seen the grounding and had also gone hard astern but the *Sirius*, sluggish with water below decks and with several compartments filled with concrete, could not respond quickly enough. Within moments, she had settled on the bottom and fires broke out in various parts of the ship. Even if her explosive charges were still capable of being fired, they would have been of no use. Hardy gave the order to get into the rescue boats.

With Hamilton Benn's *ML532* nowhere to be seen, Hoare in *ML283* went alongside the *Brilliant* as Harrison took his CMB and laid down a smokescreen between the crippled ships and the pom-poms firing from the eastern canal pier. From astern, Canadian Bourke raced in with *ML276* to collect the men from the *Sirius* as a heavy machine gun sprayed the scene from just 250 yards away and seven 8in guns fired from a range of 1,000 yards. Alongside them were two 11in guns, whilst 2 miles to the rear, a 15in gun battery joined in. Fortunately the Germans had released a counter-smokescreen which, thanks to the now offshore wind, helped to provide a dense shroud over the blockships and the rescue MLs reducing the accuracy of the enemy fire.

As would have been expected, Godsal, along with his first lieutenant Victor Crutchley, remained in the *Brilliant* until every man had left the ship. Most had boarded Hoare's ML, whilst others took to the ship's whaler, only to have it damaged by machine-gun fire. Hardy also checked his ship before boarding *ML276* but, as the launch left the scene, he counted the men clinging to her upperworks. There simply were not enough. A further check revealed that Engineer Lieutenant William MacLaren and several of the engine-room staff were missing. Hardy promptly flagged down *CMB10*, which had turned up to see if they could assist, and asked her captain, Sub Lieutenant Peter Clarke, if he would take him back to the *Sirius*. Clarke readily agreed and Hardy clambered onboard with his first lieutenant, Lieutenant Edward Berthon. Once they were disembarked, Hoare took *ML283*, with its seventy-five additional passengers crammed precariously on her upper deck, out to sea and back to Dunkirk.

Back alongside the cruiser, Hardy and Berthon scrambled onboard under heavy fire and, to the rattle and clanging of shells and bullets striking the sides and upperworks, searched the burning ship from end to end. No one could be found. Then it was noticed that the ship's whaler was missing. Despite this, and just to be certain, the two officers transferred to the *Brilliant* and diligently searched through her. Again, no one remained onboard. It later transpired that MacLaren and his stokers had taken to the whaler and rowed out to sea. After a few hours and 13 miles of hard pulling, they came across Commodore Boyle's ship, HMS *Attentive*, and were safely picked up.

Just before rejoining Clarke's ML, the smoke cleared enough for Hardy to get a clearer picture of the scene. Beneath the light of flares and starshells he could see the beach and, more importantly, the eastern pier of the canal entrance. It was about a mile and a half away. The blockships had been nowhere near the intended arrival point.

Meanwhile, Hamilton Benn and the crew of *ML532* were in desperate straits. Drifting in and out of clouds of smoke, and with only the thickness of an eighth-of-an-inch bulkhead stopping water from pouring in at the wrecked bows, the boat was in constant danger of capsizing. When the forepart of the launch had been blown off, the engines had shifted on their mountings and the exhaust pipes had broken. The exhaust gases had overwhelmed the two motor mechanics and, when signals to stop the engines failed to be answered, Lieutenant Kirkwood lifted the engine-room hatch and jumped down into the compartment. There he managed to stop the engines, but had to struggle out, reaching the deck before collapsing from the fumes. At this the deckhand/cook, Bowles, dropped into the engine room and single-handedly hauled out the two comatose men. Clearly the only options remaining to the men of *ML532* were death from the continuing fire of the Germans or capture. Hamilton Benn turned to his helmsman and said, 'It looks like breakfast on sauerkraut.' As he did so, and before the man could reply, Hamilton Benn spotted a tiny red light some way off in the darkness. It was one of the masthead lights he had ordered to be fixed on all the MLs. Risking the attention of the German gunners, Hamilton Benn switched on the boat's searchlight and flashed 'SOS, SOS, SOS'. Just seconds later, an acknowledging light flashed across in answer and, within minutes, the comforting growl of *ML276* could be heard and Bourke brought the boat alongside. He was already towing the bullet-riddled whaler from the *Brilliant*. A tow-rope was passed to the stricken vessel but it parted immediately. So did a second, and a third. Eventually, however, a rope held and, at much reduced speed, Bourke, *ML276*, and his charges, turned for Dunkirk. They had reached about half-way when, despite suffering from the effects of the exhaust fumes, the two motor mechanics managed to get one of *ML532*'s engines going with a bandaged exhaust pipe. As there were several wounded men onboard Bourke's boat and in the whaler, Hamilton Benn ordered him to cast off and proceed at his best speed. *ML532* limped into Dunkirk at midday on the 23rd, the last to arrive from the previous night's ordeal.

On his arrival, Hamilton Benn found a satisfying unity amongst the attack leaders. Godsal, Crutchley, and Hardy all agreed on one thing – the attempt to block the canal entrance must be renewed, and they were the men who should lead it. They had learned many valuable lessons during the failed attempt and, already new ideas based upon their experience began to form in their minds. Lynes, happy to concur with their eagerness to get back into the fray, had something else on his mind. He had to make a report of the night's events. How was he going to explain his force's failure to block the canal entrance? How had the blockships ended up a mile and a half to the east of their intended position?

The two most important apparent reasons were fully agreed upon by the senior officers present during the attack. It seemed to them all that the accurate German gunnery could only be accounted for by the enemy being warned of the attack. This had allowed them to zero their guns in on the original assembly points and areas of activity (Lynes and the other officers were not aware at this stage of the plans discovered in *CMB33*). Even more importantly, the Germans had moved the Stroom Bank buoy almost at the last minute. Inevitably, this action appeared to strengthen the argument in favour of previous knowledge of the attack. However, although a legitimate ruse of war, there were other sound reasons why the buoy could have been moved. It was known that the British had sown mines just off Zeebrugge – a clear indication that they had no intention of putting their own ships into that area (the Germans, of course, were not aware that the mines in question were designed to sink to the bottom shortly afterwards). If such mines had been laid across the Stroom Bank passage into Ostend, they represented a hazard to all shipping until they could be swept. Under such circumstances, and in the short term, it would be better to move the buoy to another passage. Furthermore, the sandbanks and the passages between them were not permanent features. A rough winter in the North Sea could easily change the routes through the shoals. This could be quickly discovered by a simple hydrographic survey, and a new passage located. Nevertheless, whatever the reason for the buoy's removal, a new means of approach to the canal entrance for any attempt by blockships had to be found.

But all attempts to seek such answers on the morning of Saint George's Day 1918 seemed almost academic without the answer to a much more important question – what had happened at Zeebrugge?

8

The Inferno

Even before the Zeebrugge and Ostend forces parted company at 'D' buoy, the submarine *C1* had suffered her share of misfortune. The sea conditions forced her towards her towing ship – the destroyer HMS *Mansfield* – and then dragged her back with equal force, causing the tow-line to repeatedly take the shock and strain. Inevitably, after this had happened several times, the cable parted. Rather than risk missing his appointment with the mole viaduct, her captain, Lieutenant Newbold, took the opportunity to get his craft's engines going with the intention of making his own way to the prearranged assembly point. He had not gone far, however, when it was realised that there was every chance that he was dragging his part of the separated cable beneath the submarine. The risk of continuing was obvious and the submarine came to a halt. Lieutenant Stephen Beyford, who had previously earned a Distinguished Service Cross by rescuing a picket boat whilst under fire, lowered himself from the conning tower onto the upper casing and made his way forward to the bows as the boat (not designed to operate comfortably on the surface of a choppy sea) rolled violently. Eventually, he cut the wire cable free – only to be swept overboard. A succeeding wave brought him close enough to grab a handrail and, moments later, he was back inside the conning tower with the submarine now safe to continue.

Lieutenant Commander Francis Sandford's picket boat had suffered a similar set of circumstances. Towed by the destroyer *Moorsom*, the stern sea caused her to pitch and roll so violently that Sandford later reported that 'it is by no means clear why she righted herself'. After 'D' buoy, the tow-rope became fouled and had to be cleared. Conscious that the picket boat's vital part in the rescue of the submarine crews depended upon accurate timing, once the cable was restored, the *Moorsom* increased her speed – only for the rope to part. At this, Sandford, with his younger brother well on his way towards the mole viaduct in *C3*, decided to make his own way to the supposed rescue rendezvous. It looked, however, as if he would be failed by the picket boat's maximum speed of 12 knots.

With all preparations made in the landing vessels, the storming and demolition parties slept, read, spun exaggerated 'ditties' or, with a fine disregard for the

King's Regulations and Admiralty Instructions, gambled their 4 shillings a week
on games of 'Crown and Anchor'. From 2000hrs the *Vindictive*'s 'Cooks of the
Messes' were informed that hot soup was available from the ship's galley. Even
better, at 2200hrs, as the ships passed through and over enemy minefields, bugle
calls and boatswain's pipes announced 'Splice the main brace' – it was time for an
extra rum ration. There had been the normal midday ration but an additional one
had been authorised. To the seamen involved, the arrival of rum was a normal,
though welcome, event. Generations of their forebears had evolved a system of
trading rum for favours or of illicitly storing it away to enjoy at a later time. The
Royal Marines, however, only enjoyed the rum ration when they were actually
serving onboard one of His Majesty's ships, and were much less used to the
subtleties of trading the 'tot' or of respecting its fiercely powerful strength. During
the failed attempt on the 11th it had been noted that several of the marines
were the worse for wear for having helped out their friends to drink their ration.
Now that there was an extra supply, and in an attempt to prevent such a thing
happening again, the Royal Marines' adjutant, Captain Chater, in company with
the sergeant major, toured the marines' messdecks (temporarily given the name
of 'barracks'). They were too late. As they passed through the accommodation a
voice shouted out with all the bravado of too much rum, 'We are just going over
the top. We are all equal now.' With the experience born of frequently being with
men just about to go 'over the top' Chater ignored the comment but noted the
name of the man.

'Action Stations' sounded at 2300hrs and the storming parties began to muster
on the main deck, by the ramps leading up to the false deck, and on the false
deck itself. Gun crews 'closed up' and Commander Osborne chose to head into
the foretop, where he was joined by Lieutenant Rigby of the Royal Marine
Artillery, eight marines and his gunnery petty officer. Osborne had given strict
instructions that no one was to open fire before the two pom-poms and six Lewis
guns stationed in the top.

With less than an hour to go before their intended arrival time at the mole,
the *Vindictive*'s cable used to tow the *Iris* and the *Daffodil*, parted. As the rain was
now heavier than it had been all day, and being surrounded by darkened ships, it
would have been an extremely hazardous enterprise to attempt to re-establish the
tow. Instead, the two Mersey ferries began to make their own way towards the
Zeebrugge mole.

At 2330hrs the blockships slowed down in order to adjust the timing of their
arrival whilst the CMBs and MLs bustled their way to the front of the larger ships.
Three of the CMBs surged forward until they reached a position where they
could switch on their smoke apparatus and lay down a bank of smoke to hide the
approaching fleet. A lone CMB readied itself to enter Zeebrugge harbour and put
down a screen to blind the torpedo boats alongside the inner mole. Another CMB

roared off towards Blankenberge where, having laid down her smokescreen, she would remain lurking outside to take on any of the enemy who emerged from that port. Two CMBs, led by Lieutenant Welman, left to take on the incredibly hazardous task of laying a smokescreen in front of the lighthouse extension guns. They were followed by two more CMBs with the job of lobbing Stokes' mortar bombs over the mole wall onto the guns of the fortified zone. Another pair of CMBs headed towards the harbour in the wake of the single CMB. They were to fire torpedoes at the German torpedo boats tied up at the inner mole.

Welman, in *CMB22B*, accompanied by Lieutenant John Annesley in *CMB22C*, streaked in front of the lighthouse extension guns, well within range of the machine guns and pom-poms. As they roared past they pumped smoke out of their exhausts and dropped smoke floats. They could clearly hear shouting in German – a sound quickly followed by the heavy, grinding, rattle of the guns as every barrel was aimed in their direction. Welman seemed to have a charmed life and, apart from some structural damage to his ship, he survived the passage in front of the guns. Annesley, on the other hand, came in for much more than his fair share. Soon every one of his upper deck crew was injured. The motor mechanics stopped nursing the engine and clambered on deck to take the place of the seamen. Very quickly they also fell to the hail of bullets. Then Annesley himself was hit. With every member of the crew injured one man lay on the deck beneath the ship's wheel, turning it with his undamaged arm; another jammed himself against a bulkhead in order to operate the throttle. Annesley, propped up against the shattered windscreen, calmly gave orders for a final run in front of the batteries.

Just a short way behind Welman and his boats came another CMB skimming over the surface and roaring defiance at fate. Astonishingly, this was *CMB35* captained by Lieutenant Hill. Dismissed as an unlucky accident by everyone else when his propeller was fouled, he had commandeered a drifter to tow him back to Dover. On his arrival, he had chased up anyone he could get his hands on to fix his boat. It had taken several hours to get the vessel back into a seaworthy condition but at 2140hrs, he left Dover and with due disregard for minefields, shallows and enemy ships, streaked across the North Sea determined to take his place in the fight.

Any response from the Germans seemed slow in coming, possibly as most of their officers were ashore attending a social event. A few searchlights flashed across the sky, doing little more than assisting the approaching ships in confirming their navigational fixes. Any lights searching towards the north of the mole lighthouse could see little more than a dense fog bank rolling in. The northerly wind, on which so much depended, had died down a little, but still held the smokescreen in position.

With a quarter of an hour remaining before the estimated time of arrival, flashes of light like distant sheet lightning could be seen to the north-east from the guns of the monitors *Erebus* and *Terror*. Their opening fire had been delayed through problems experienced with the tidal stream and the difficulty in locating the Oost Gat light, which indicated the limits of the Netherlands' territorial waters. These difficulties were compounded by the arrival of a torpedo boat bearing a Dutch admiral who insisted that the ships and their escorts were in Dutch territory. Commander Andrew Brown Cunningham (popularly known as 'ABC'), the captain of the destroyer, HMS *Termagant,* spent most of the night having a megaphone-assisted argument with the admiral to the accompaniment of the monitor's massive guns.

In the *Vindictive*, the flamethrower crews closed up in the large steel boxes fore and aft on the port side and checked their equipment. Wing Commander Brock took charge of the after flamethrower whilst the forward one came under the command of the raid's military representative, Lieutenant Eastlake of the Royal Engineers.

Lieutenant Hilton Young took up his position at the rear of the forward 6in gun. In the darkness, the gun crews felt their way around the breech-blocks to refamiliarise themselves with its interrupted-screw mechanism, locking levers and wheels. The 100-pound shells they were to fire had been designed for close-range work against torpedo boats but would serve perfectly well against the mole guns. As he carried out his own checks, Hilton Young caught sight of a number of cigarette ends glowing within the armoured gun shield. Although strictly prohibited he chose to ignore these breaches of the regulations as 'it seemed an occasion for a little relaxation in the rigour of the rules'. But there was another problem that was causing him concern. The upper deck had become crowded with seaman and marines and many were clustered around the rear of the gun. Several times he and the captain of the gun cleared the area but still they returned. Not only were they causing difficulty in loading the gun, but anyone in the path of the savage recoil would find themselves on the wrong end of several tons of armoured steel moving at considerable speed.

The Royal Marines' adjutant, Captain Chater, found himself with a quite different problem. Having made his way through the crowded upper deck towards the bridge to take up his position alongside the battalion commander, Colonel Elliot, he came across the second-in-command, Major Cordner, and asked him why he was on the bridge instead of taking up a position on the after end of the false deck. Cordner replied that he should be with Elliot until the ship was alongside, then he would go aft. Chater felt decidedly uncomfortable about the situation but felt he could not press the senior officer more forcibly to leave the bridge.

Beneath the quarterdeck, in the captain's cabin, the port scuttles were opened to allow the pyrotechnic party under the command of Lieutenant Graham Hewett to fire their flare rockets to light the way for the blockships. In the wardroom, Staff Surgeon McCutcheon prepared his operating instruments for their inevitable use as Surgeon Clegg mustered his team of stretcher bearers. Surgeon 'Jack' Payne, from Tasmania, set up a first-aid station just beneath the bridge. The Reverend Peshall said a prayer and prepared to do God's work wherever he could provide it.

With minutes to go before the estimated arrival time alongside the mole, Captain Carpenter crossed over from the conning tower to join Lieutenant Eastlake and his team in the forward flamethrower cabin. From his new position he could look along the whole of the port side, a situation that would greatly assist in bringing the cruiser alongside the mole wall. Above and ahead of him, all he could see was a thick wall made up of Brock's 'artificial fog'. Somewhere off his starboard bow he could hear large guns from a shore battery firing randomly into the smoke, the shells passing harmlessly overhead. Directly above them, starshells burst with a loud 'pock' sound. Astern, more starshells lit up a vast area, but it meant nothing as the smokescreen continued to hide the approaching ships. Once inside the smokescreen, the light from the shells merely lent a diffused glow to a scene limited by the dense smoke.

From his position in the flamethrower cabin, he was aware of the massed seamen and marines waiting in the darkness for the rapidly approaching moment when they would be let loose onto the mole. Orders had been given that the storming parties were to remain below decks until the landing brows had been secured, but no one could overcome the eagerness to get ashore. Captain Halahan, suffering from a swollen and cut left eye as the result of a stumble over a quarterdeck cable just minutes earlier, mingled with the seamen giving words of encouragement. By him stood the tall figure of Lieutenant Commander Harrison, eager to put his rugby-charge experience to good use should the Germans give him a chance. Then something happened that shocked all who saw it. The wind, which had been stilled for some time, revealed an unexpected malevolence. The smokescreen laid down by the CMBs to blind the Germans had now drifted to the south and the *Vindictive* emerged from the smoke directly in front of the German lighthouse extension guns.

It is difficult to know exactly how far away the mole was when the cruiser left the shelter of the smokescreen. Rosoman, the ship's first lieutenant thought it was 800 yards, Hilton Young decided it was 400 yards, but most witnesses put it at between 200 and 300 yards. For Carpenter it was 250 yards to the nearest enemy gun. The sudden exposure was a shock to both sides. The Germans, with no reason to expect a cruiser, had been anticipating more small craft.

Carpenter responded immediately, shouting towards the conning tower to port the helm and increase speed. This would bring the ship round to starboard and allow Hilton Young's 6in guns to bear on the lighthouse extension battery. Hilton Young himself was mentally shouting at the foretop marines to start firing but Osborne, up aloft with the marines, delayed giving the order to open fire. It was, he felt, more important to get as far across the front of the German guns before they spotted the ship. But the Germans did not oblige by delaying their response.

With an earth-shattering roar the three 4.1in and three 3.5in guns of the lighthouse extension opened fire. The shells crashed into the *Vindictive's* side and upper deck at point-blank range. The packed seamen and marines were felled like ripe corn before a passing scythe. Before anyone could recover, a second barrage fell among them – then a third. The massive onslaught by the heavy guns was augmented by numerous machine guns sweeping along the decks with streams of red tracer bullets. On the bridge, Chater picked himself up and saw that Elliot and Cordner both lay dead at his feet. He hurried off to inform Major Bernard Weller that he was now in command of the Royal Marines.

Among the many dead on the false deck was Captain Halahan. His deputy, Lieutenant Commander Harrison, had been struck on the head by shrapnel and lay concussed on the deck. Lieutenant Commander Harrington Edwards, who had been overjoyed at being selected to go, lay on the deck after being shot through both legs. Lieutenant Chamberlain, his upper body blown apart, staggered to the nearest first-aid post only to collapse and die as helpers ran towards him. At the forward 6in gun, Hilton Young, determined to make the Germans pay for the wind's mean-spirited reversal, urged his gunners on until a 'Titan blacksmith' struck his right arm with a sledgehammer. The blow sent him reeling to the deck where a nearby marine prodded him with his boot saying 'Why, whatever's the matter with you?'

Just before he was hit, Hilton Young saw a 'gallant act' that 'was glorious to see'. Lieutenant Hill steered *CMB35* straight for the gap between the extension and the ship and laid down a smokescreen before skimming off to disappear across the bows of the *Vindictive*. It truly was a brave act but, unsupported, the smoke thinned and drifted within seconds.

It took four minutes for the *Vindictive* to pass beneath the extension guns. Every second of those minutes saw the ship getting ever closer to the guns. The final gun was passed, according to Carpenter, at a range of 50 yards, although when later asked, a petty officer on the port after 6in gun, gave the range as about 'three feet' from the end of the muzzle.

Several things had saved the *Vindictive*. Carpenter's rapid action with course and speed played a major factor. So had the German response. The enemy gunners, overwhelmed by the sight of a cruiser bearing down upon them, simply fired directly at the ship. She was, after all, a target that could not be missed. Had they acted more rationally, however, they might have realised that what was needed was for their aim to be directed at the ship's vitals. It would not have taken many shells penetrating the boiler or engine room to have brought the ship to a halt. In fact, just a few shells anywhere below the waterline would have had the same effect. Yet for four minutes they blazed away at the upper works. The structural damage done was tremendous but none of it fatal. There was, nevertheless, an additional penalty to pay.

When Carpenter turned to starboard, and increased the speed, the *Vindictive* missed the position of the intended landing on the mole. This had been deliberately chosen to put the storming parties ashore on top of the fortified zone at the end of the mole proper. From there, the naval stormers would take on the lighthouse extension guns, whilst the Royal Marines would drop down directly onto the German defenders. Now safely beyond the firing arcs of the extension guns, Carpenter found himself almost 400 yards westward of the intended landing place. It was one-minute-past-midnight – Saint George's Day.

Once the ship had nudged the wall with its giant fenders, he ordered the engines to be put hard astern and the starboard anchor to be dropped, but the anchor reached only the level of the water and refused to go further, its cable jammed somewhere between the forecastle and the cable locker. At this, Carpenter sent Rosoman forward to the forecastle to let go the port anchor. With this successfully completed, the *Vindictive* went astern, veering out the anchor cable to its 100-yard limit. At this point the stern of the ship swung out from the wall. Putting the wheel to starboard brought the stern closer in, but held the bows so tightly to the wall that the landing brows could not reach the wall parapet. With the wheel amidships, a gap opened up between the ship's side and the mole, whilst putting the wheel to port merely brought the stern out again.

Whilst Carpenter desperately manoeuvred his ship beneath a hail of fire from every enemy gun that could be brought to bear, the *Iris* passed along her starboard side aiming to arrive at the wall 100 yards ahead. Just as she had cleared the *Vindictive*'s bows, salvation arrived in the shape of the *Daffodil*. Lieutenant Campbell, despite having been shot in the face and blinded in one eye, had steered his vessel so that it arrived bows-on against the cruiser's starboard side, just abaft of the conning tower. As he made contact, Warrant Gunner Cobby took a party of seamen and, with great difficulty, secured the ferry in position. He also delivered a request from Carpenter. It was necessary for the *Daffodil* to stay in position, probably for the entire operation, in order to keep the *Vindictive* firmly against the wall. This required that, in the ferry's boiler room, Artificer Engineer William Sutton maintained a boiler pressure of 160 pounds with equipment that was never intended to be at such a pressure. Undeterred, he and his team strove to keep the gauge needles well into the red, despite two shells punching holes in the boiler-room bulkheads. As he did so, members of the naval demolition party, followed by Royal Marines, scrambled over the ferry's bows and onto the *Vindictive*.

Even with the cruiser held against the wall there still remained other problems. The difficulty with which Cobby had to cope when securing the *Daffodil* came from a source unforeseen by the planners. When the *Vindictive* closed with the mole wall she created her own wash, trapping turbulent waters between her side and the wall. This caused the ship to roll violently at the same time as she rose and

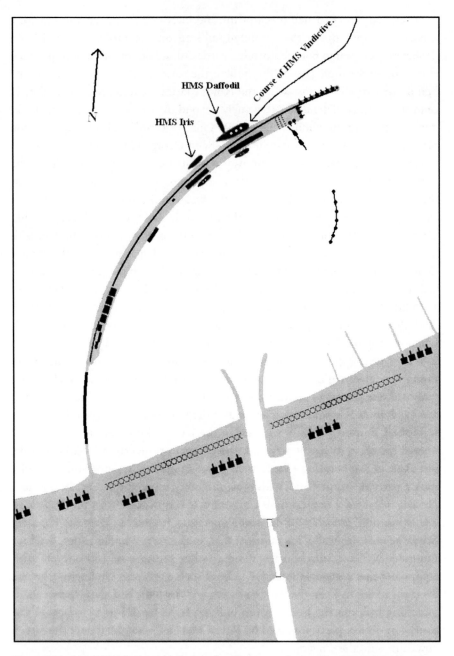

The arrival of HMS *Vindictive* and the two former Mersey ferries. The *Vindictive* should have gone alongside the mole level with the defended zone, but was forced by gunfire to go alongside further to the west. The *Daffodil* is holding the cruiser to the wall as the *Iris* takes up her position forward of the *Vindictive*.

fell. Beneath the waterline, the crunching collision of the port bilges against the stone foundation step at the foot of the wall could be heard and felt throughout the ship. The problem was exacerbated by the fact that, of the eighteen brows built to get the stormers ashore, only two had survived the shells from the extension guns (the ship's carpenter's, nevertheless, were already at work trying to increase that number). When the surviving brows were lowered onto the top of the parapet they sawed up and down or rose and fell with a jarring crash above the 30ft black chasm below.

Like the foretop gun position, the flamethrower cabins were high enough to gain no benefit from the protection of the wall beneath, which most of the ship sheltered. Sparks flew inside as machine-gun bullets and shrapnel travelled in all directions. Carpenter's cap was sent flying from his head as a bullet passed through, and his searchlight goggles and binoculars were both hit. It had been intended that, when the ship came alongside the fortified zone, the flamethrowers would be able to spray the trenches and machine-gun posts to drive the defenders out. With the ship far beyond the zone, it was decided to use the flamethrowers just in case there were any Germans sheltering out of sight behind the parapet or on the mole floor. Just as the order to 'fire-up' was given, a piece of shrapnel removed the nozzle from the forward flamethrower rendering it useless. Things were no better at the after flamethrower cabin. As the order to switch on was given by Commander Brock, the ignition system was destroyed leaving a pointless jet of oil shooting from the nozzle.

As the forward flamethrower was put out of action, another shell cut its oil supply pipes sending oil pouring into the first-aid post beneath the conning tower. Despite the high risk of the oil catching fire, Surgeon Payne simply added the 'dirty, stinking, black oil' to the 'cut water pipes' and other inconveniences from which he was suffering.

Undeterred by the lack of flamethrower support or the wildly bucking brows, Lieutenant Commander Adams, the senior uninjured naval officer of the storming parties, clambered over the dead men lying in heaps on the false deck and ran up the forward brow beneath a spray of cold water from a fractured fire main. At the top he stepped off the rearing gangway and onto the parapet, jumping down on to the walkway 4ft below. To his amazement he could not see a single German, despite the air above him crackling with machine-gun bullets. He also had difficulty in orienting himself regarding his position on the mole. All his training had been aimed at a landing on the lighthouse extension. Now, in the light of the starshells and flares, he found himself facing a large building occupying most of the far side of the mole (No. 3 Shed). To his right, about 300 yards away, stood a similar building (No. 2 Shed). Much more ominously, a number of torpedo boats could be seen tied up alongside the mole to the east of No. 3 Shed. Having taken all this in, Adams stood up to call for his men to join him but they were already following him onto the walkway. As they stepped off the false deck they had to climb over a number of dead at the foot of the brows. Carpenter, who had just left the flamethrower cabin, noticed that among the bodies was an officer who was still alive. It was Lieutenant Walker, the son of a general, whose left hand and lower arm had been smashed by gunfire. He was pulled clear only for him to drag himself up to a sitting position and wave his remaining arm shouting 'Good luck, good luck, boys.'

Adams and his men reached out over the parapet in an effort to grab hold of the forward parapet anchor dangling from its davits but it was a nightmare as the heavy twin-hooked anchor swung with the rise and fall of the ship. Several times it was grabbed only to be wrenched out of the seamen's hands. Other seamen climbed over the parapet to lend a hand and Rosoman tried to assist from onboard, but the combination of the davits crashing against the wall and the wildly swinging anchor defeated all attempts to secure the ship by that means. The *Daffodil,* with her boiler rivets straining under the pressure, would have to continue holding her to the wall.

The carnage on the upper deck continued despite the shelter from the mole wall. The forward 7.5in howitzer crew were all killed or badly wounded, and a replacement crew from Hilton Young's 6in gun suffered a similar fate. Stretcher parties under Surgeon Clegg dashed out into the open time and time again to bring in the wounded as the Reverend Peshall, acting as a one-man rescue team, hauled injured men to positions of safety. Surgeon Payne gave his impression of the scene:

> We surgeons could not do very much for the wounded, except to give them morphia, and to stop them bleeding. Between decks on the old *Vindictive* was too filthy for words, and was wet with oil and water from pipes being broken with shells, and there was very little space that was not covered with blood: and on deck above you would find bits of human beings plastered up against shells in racks, stanchions, deck houses, etc. One not having been through the whole night of it would probably turn tail and run from the sight of it all.

With the diversion ships coming under the fire of the shore guns, Lieutenant Gordon Maxwell, captain of *ML314,* decided to try a stunt that might relieve some of the pressure from the ships. Unable to find a light-buoy laid down by one of the CMBs, he had dropped off a smoke buoy after removing the light baffles as a substitute. His reward was a shower of shrapnel shells. Clearly the Germans were eager to fire at any illuminated target on the grounds that it might constitute an attack. Keen to test this idea, Maxwell roared off in the direction of Blankenberge. Just off the shore he dropped another smoke buoy after removing the baffles. Sure enough, searchlights swung around to the spot and the guns opened fire on glowing smoke. A second, and then a third, smoke buoy was dropped with the same result. Only a shortage of buoys prevented a continuation of the scheme. Nevertheless the guns on that part of the shore spent much of the remaining night watching out for a possible landing on the coast that was never to come.

High above the action in the *Vindictive*, Lieutenant Charles Rigby and his marines fired their pom-poms and Lewis guns from the foretop, greatly assisting the storming parties by keeping the mole defenders under constant fire. Behind them, mixing with the deafening sound of gunfire, was the clanging of the ship's funnels as the enemy's shells struck home with repeated violence. Inevitably, being in the only part of the ship that could take on the defenders directly, Rigby and his men were hit by two shells in succession. The foretop was reduced to a chaos of dead men and splintered wreckage. Incredibly, from the debris, Sergeant Norman Finch – badly wounded but still capable of mounting a Lewis gun – found one of the weapons amongst the ruins and quickly had it firing once again.

As the seamen struggled with the parapet anchors, Royal Marines under the command of Lieutenant Theodore Cooke charged past them. The marines had a particularly difficult choice to make regarding the action they should take. The original plan had been for them to land above the trenches and guns of the fortified zone at the end of the mole, but now they found themselves at least 100 yards closer to the shore with the possibility of the enemy advancing along the mole and setting up machine guns close by the *Vindictive*. If that happened, the chances of a successful withdrawal would be very slight at best. Major Weller decided to set up a defensive position to the west, i.e. to the right of the ship. With that flank secured an attack on the fortified zone could be carried out.

Cooke was accompanied by Chater who was concerned about the 15ft drop to the floor of the mole. When he saw that there was no permanent stairway available, he returned onboard and ordered Sergeant Major

Lieutenant C. Hawkings, second-in-command of the *Iris'* naval landing parties.

A painting by Charles de Lacy showing the *Vindictive* alongside the mole discharging the Royal Marines. The ship is being held alongside by the *Daffodil*.

John Thatcher to take some marines carrying hook ropes and follow Cooke's party. The ropes would enable the marines to get down to the lower level and, once they had been delivered, the sergeant major was to ensure that scaling ladders would be obtained to assist the withdrawal.

The fact that there were Germans forward of the *Vindictive* was in no doubt as the activities around the *Iris* had shown. Commander Gibbs had just as much difficulty in getting alongside as Carpenter had. Having arrived alongside the mole at about a quarter-past twelve, the ferry reacted wildly to the disturbed water trapped against the mole. Although the starboard anchor had been dropped successfully, the *Iris* pitched and rolled violently. Even worse, the seamen storming party responsible for securing the smaller, single-hook parapet anchors found that the scaling ladders, violently rising and falling, could not be held against the wall. Twenty-two-year-old Lieutenant Claude Hawkins, with the aid of some of his seamen, managed to get a ladder against the wall which, although rapidly rising and falling, stayed in place when held upright by the men. He climbed the ladder and, at the right moment, put his hands over the parapet, hauled himself up, and

Sergeant N. Finch of the
Royal Marine Artillery.

sat on the top. Turning towards the anchor davits he had reached out to grab the anchor cable and haul it towards himself when he turned back towards the mole, drew his revolver, and started firing at an unseen target. Within a second his body arched back and he fell lifeless onto the walkway.

Seeing his deputy killed did not deter Lieutenant Commander Bradford from making another attempt. Disregarding the ladders he climbed the anchor davits, found a foothold and, having hauled up the suspended anchor, steadied himself for a leap on to the parapet. The moment came and with superb timing Bradford landed on the top of the wall, hooking the anchor over the top. Just as he did so, a burst of machine-gun fire sent him tumbling into the clashing waters below. Immediately, and before anyone could stop him, Petty Officer Michael Hallihan jumped into the water in an attempt to save Bradford. But gallantry lies often in the act rather in the result, and the petty officer was swept away and drowned.

In the *Vindictive*'s wrecked foretop, Sergeant Finch was still firing his Lewis gun when another shell finally put paid to the work that could be done there. Badly wounded yet again, Finch fell back among the dead and dying, unable to take shelter from the continuing storm of shells and bullets.

9

The Mole

Just about a mile ahead of the action on the mole, a long black shape, powered by electric motors, surged quietly through the water. Submarine *C3*'s voyage since separating from her towing destroyer had not been without incident. At some stage she had lost her starboard skiff and would have to depend upon the one suspended from spars on her port side. As she had closed with the coast, a starshell had disclosed her presence to the enemy who promptly opened fire. Expecting the worst, Lieutenant Sandford pressed on as shells began to drop around him. Then, as the starshell faded, so did the shelling. The Germans may have decided that *C3* was, in fact, one of their own, or they may have believed that the submarine did not know that the way ahead was barred by a viaduct leading to a huge concrete mole. If that was the case, there was every chance of an easy capture.

As he approached his target, Sandford was assisted by the light of flares shining on the water through the iron piles of the viaduct. Final adjustments were made to the steering before the crew were ordered up into the conning tower. Sandford had decided not to use the gyro-assisted automatic steering system but to deliver the boat to its destination with its crew and himself still onboard. That way he knew the job would be done. To port, now hidden by the curve of the mole, an extraordinary, continuous barrage of sound and light told him that the diversionary force had fallen upon the enemy – and now it was his job to see that the Germans could expect no reinforcements from the shore. With just over 100 yards to go, two searchlights, and then a third, fell upon them. Still there was no firing despite the clear sound of German voices shouting, and even laughing. On they pressed at over 9 knots, until the viaduct reared blackly above them. Then the bows of the submarine rammed into the viaduct metal work, snapping the slender girders and forcing the piles apart. Having been warned of the impending collision, the crew hung on to any fixed support they could find, the only words spoken as the boat juddered to a halt was 'We're here all right.' As the bows of the submarine rose by 2ft and settled into its position the first lieutenant, John Howell-Price, led the way over the side and launched the skiff.

Sandford set the fuses for twelve minutes and followed. With all six men onboard the tiny craft, the engine was started – but the boat refused to move.

It did not take long for Sandford and the others to realise that either the propeller shaft, or the propeller itself, was damaged. There was nothing for it but to take up the two tiny oars and start paddling out in to the full glare of the searchlights as, less than 20ft away, machine guns and rifles were aimed at them. Seconds later, the Germans lining the viaduct opened fire. Bullet after bullet struck the craft and the surrounding water was churned into a foam. Stoker Henry Bindall was hit and fell forward. As he did so, Sandford reached out to support him, only to have a bullet pass clean through his hand. Engine Room Artificer Allan Roxburgh and Petty Officer Walter Harner paddled furiously against the tide in an attempt to distance themselves from C3 and the 5 tons of amatol packed into her bows. Still held by the searchlights, and with the air seemingly filled with bullets, Harner slumped forward. Leading Seaman William Cleaver snatched up the paddle and took the petty officer's place. At the same moment a bullet smashed through Sandford's thigh. Howell-Price pulled him clear from the skiff's stern and took his place at the tiller. With agonising slowness, the craft reached the curve of the mole, only to come under the additional fire of a pom-pom. Just as the heavier shells traced a line in the water towards them, an ear-shattering, bone-shaking explosion lit the night sky. A huge column of flame leapt upwards, taking with it men, guns, searchlights, and a substantial section of the viaduct. The waters around the skiff exploded in fountains and froth as metal and concrete fell from the skies, yet none hit the boat itself. Such was the shock that even those guns which had been able to continue firing at the skiff were silenced. Cleaver and Roxburgh continued paddling vigorously for the next few minutes without much further attention from the mole when out of the darkness surged a picket boat. It was the elder Sandford, come to pick up his brother.

Once onboard the picket boat, Richard Sandford insisted that the wounded Harner and Bindall were given first-aid before he was. As this was being done, Francis Sandford turned the vessel around and headed directly for Dover – their work had been done.

Out at sea, Lieutenant Newbold saw the bright flash of the explosion. Having earlier had the indignity of being fired on by the very destroyer that had towed him until they had separated, he now knew that any further progress towards Zeebrugge would be futile. Not only was he not prepared to put his crew's lives at risk in an operation that had already seen success, there was always the possibility that C1 could find similar employment in the future. Consequently, he had the helm put over and, with his disappointment tempered by pride in his fellow-submariner's achievement, also headed for Dover.

As C3 was just about to meet her appointment with the viaduct, events on and around the *Vindictive* continued to provide the distraction needed for the silently

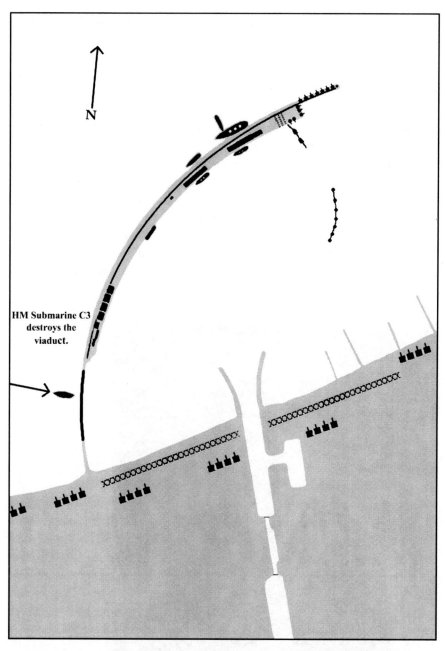

N

HM Submarine C3 destroys the viaduct.

As the storming parties land from the *Vindictive*, HM Submarine *C3* approaches the viaduct.

approaching blockships. Lieutenant Commander Harrington Edwards, lying on the false deck with bullet wounds in both legs, roared orders at anyone passing, demanding that he be taken over the brows and onto the mole. In the beginning his demands were ignored – it was far more important to get the even more seriously wounded to medical assistance than to pay attention to an outraged officer. Eventually, however, two seamen picked up the one-eyed, black-bearded Harrington Edwards and, ignoring his demands, took him below decks and put him into the hands of the sick berth staff.

Harrington Edwards had not been the only man desperate to get on to the mole. Seamen and Royal Marines almost competed with each other to get over the brows. By now the carpenter's crew had managed to repair an additional gangway, leaving three available for disembarkation.

The Royal Marines, having driven back a number of enemy snipers, were joined by reinforcements led by Captain Bamford and had established a strongpoint to the west to keep back any threat from that direction. Now they

Captain Edward Bamford of the Royal Marines.

were giving their attention to moving down the mole in the direction of the fortified zone at its end.

Mixed up with the seamen storming parties trying to get ashore was Lieutenant Dickinson and the remnants of his demolition party. Those in the *Vindictive* had suffered badly in the shelling during the approach and the remainder were still trapped in the *Iris* trying to get secured alongside. Their key initial task had been to destroy the lighthouse extension guns once they had been captured by the storming parties. With that part of their job clearly impossible, at least in the short term, Dickinson sought other opportunities to inflict damage on the enemy. Seeing that Sergeant Major Thatcher had already lowered scaling ladders down to the mole, he led his party on the mole floor and advanced on No. 3 Shed.

As Dickinson descended to the mole floor, Lieutenant Commander Adams took charge of the remaining seamen clustered on the walkway by the brows. The situation may have changed, but the target remained the same. The guns on the lighthouse extension had to be attacked and, if possible, put out of action. In his small group of seamen was Petty Officer George Antell who, despite having been wounded in the hand and arm during the approach, insisted on taking his place with the storming party. Leading Seaman William Childs, who had been put in command of the naval storming party's Lewis guns, was also wounded and had a narrow escape when he was 'knocked silly' by a bullet passing through his helmet. Many of the Lewis-gun crews had been killed or badly injured during the passage in front of the extension guns, leaving only himself and 19-year-old Able Seaman Albert McKenzie – the Grand Fleet lightweight boxing champion – on the parapet. McKenzie had also been wounded during the approach. Both were heavily weighed down with equipment, each having to carry two men's share of the Lewis gun's ammunition and spare parts.

Just as Adams and his party were about to advance towards the guns they were joined by the tall figure of Wing Commander Brock, armed with two revolvers and a cutlass. After a brief sprint of about 50 yards they came under fire from one or more machine guns, and Adams ordered Childs and McKenzie to set up their Lewis gun and engage the enemy. As they did so, the remainder, with the exception of Brock, continued their charge. The enemy machine guns turned their attention to Adams and his party as they raced along the walkway. Brock chose that moment to drop a hand grenade on the concrete bunkers beneath them. This resulted in a rush of Germans sprinting across the mole in an attempt to reach the destroyers tied up on the other side. Brock emptied his revolver into them as McKenzie let loose with his Lewis gun. Having shaken out the enemy, Brock set off to catch up with Adams. Moments later, McKenzie heard and felt the click that told him his magazine was empty. Raising the weapon, he began to remove the empty magazine when a bullet struck the gun sending it tumbling from his hands. On hitting the ground, the gun barrel separated from the pistol-grip and the stock. Seeing this, a German, looking 'too business like' for McKenzie, turned to raise his rifle. In response, the able seaman snatched up the gun stock and threw it down at the enemy. The German's attempt to avoid the missile gave McKenzie just enough time to draw his revolver, open fire, and bring the man down. Now without their Lewis gun, Childs and McKenzie threw the remaining ammunition over the parapet wall before descending an iron stairway onto the floor of the mole. There they fired their guns, bayoneted, punched or kicked the numerous Germans who were fleeing from the dark corners beneath the wall where they had hidden themselves away. Moving down the mole floor they were flushing out other Germans from their hiding places when, over their right shoulder, came the sound of a mighty explosion with towering flames, which Childs thought 'would never stop going upwards'. *C3* had blown up.

When Adams and his party charged down the mole with Brock in pursuit, they found themselves confronted by a barrier they had not expected. Built by the Germans across the walkway was the seaward side of the Friedrichsort battery's fire control position. The crews of the shore battery's 6.5in guns could not see how effective their gunfire was with the mole curving across 90 degrees of their firing arc. In consequence of this the concrete fire control position had been built so that observers could see and report the fall of shot. It was on the top of this building that the suspected sound-ranging system was believed to have been built. Openings on both sides of the building, combined with an inner passagway, allowed access along the parapet in either direction.

Adams arrived at the building after a run through a wall of sound provided by the *Vindictive*'s quarterdeck howitzer – its crews urged on by an indefatigable Captain Dallas Brooks – by the thump of the Stokes' mortars and by the illuminating rockets fired through the ship's stern scuttles. To his right-front, the mole-end guns were firing over his head at the *Vindictive*'s funnels and exposed superstructure. A grenade was thrown into the fire control station but a brief inspection showed that it was empty. Brock disappeared inside, ostensibly in search of equipment from the sound-ranging system believed to have been installed. As he did so, Adams led his men through the building's passageway to the far exit where he found he was about 50 yards from the end of the mole and about 75 yards from the nearest mole extension gun. Gathering a group of his seamen together, he led a charge out of the building, straight into the machine-gun and small-arms fire from the trenches of the fortified zone down on the mole to his right. By the time he had covered 40 yards several of his men had become casualties and it became clear that more men would be needed to carry the attack through to the guns. Ordering the survivors to lay down on the 80ft-wide walkway, thus gaining some shelter from the enemy fire below them, Adams ran back to the fire-control station. There he found more seamen had arrived, including a two-man Lewis gun team. These men were sent forward to join the party exposed on the parapet and to keep the Germans in the trenches of the fortified zone busy. Petty Officer Antell, who had done good work in encouraging the men remaining at the building, was doubled over with pain from his injuries. Adams ordered him to go back to the ship. Once again gathering his men around him for another charge against the guns, Adams' attention was drawn to an extraordinary, even improbable, sight. Just about to enter the building after a limping, weaving dash along the walkway, was Lieutenant Commander Harrison.

Despite the pain and the disorientation from his wounds, Harrison, after having been given first-aid, had hauled himself up, shaken off the immediate effects of concussion and clambered up the brows and over the mole parapet. From there he charged to the left – in the direction of the extension guns. With the guns in the foretop now silenced, the torpedo boats lined up along the inner mole opened fire with their machine guns but despite the streams of bullets fired at him, Harrison did not falter in his dash to join the naval storming party. He arrived at the fire-control building without further injury and joined Adams.

Once Harrison had heard his fellow officer's report, the first thing he did was send Adams back to the ship to summon more reinforcements. It had to be Adams as no one else had the authority to make such an urgent request directly to whoever could be found to provide extra men. As he left the fire-control station to make his dash back to the brows, Harrison emerged from the other exit of the building, leading his men in a charge along the walkway. His intention was probably to collect the men lying on the parapet and continue towards the guns. There were two reasons why Harrison led his charge immediately after Adams began his dash to reach the ship. In leading a group of men forward, they would distract the machine-gunners from the sprinting Adams. There was also the fact that, immediately in front of him, he could see that the blockships were entering the harbour. Whilst it appeared that the lighthouse extension guns had been abandoned, the guns at the end of the mole were perfectly sited to fire into the sides of the ships. If Harrison could distract the gunners and prevent the extension guns from being remanned, it would greatly improve the blockships' chances of success.

Onboard the *Vindictive*, Carpenter walked around his ship: shells from shore batteries were regularly striking her, the conning tower had been wrecked, as had the sick-bay. On the upper deck, in passageways and on messdecks, the dead and dying lay everywhere, but those who could, raised themselves up to ask 'Are we winning, Sir?' or cheered as he walked by. One officer had asked why a group of marines remained crouched at the bottom of one of the brows – only to be told that they were all dead. The funnels and many of the ventilator cowls were shredded by shells fired at short range, the impacts sending metal splinters to cause yet more casualties. Oddly enough, the funnel that had suffered least had Keyes' 'lucky' horseshoe bolted to it.

As Carpenter reached the port forward 6in gun, he came across Lieutenant Hilton Young, 'our Parliamentary representative'. Standing without jacket or cap, and with his right arm bandaged, Hilton Young blithely puffed away at an illicit cigar and continued with 'his self-appointed duty of cheering everybody up'. After being hit he had made his way down to the nearest first-aid station only to be knocked over once again by a shell exploding in the same compartment. Amidst a crowd of wounded men he had his arm dressed before making his way back to the upper deck. Finding he had emerged onto the false deck, he took the opportunity to climb one of the brows and stand looking at the scene around him. What surprised him the most was the lack of a vigorous German response to the attack. Everyone had expected the enemy to try to storm the ship but there was not a German to be seen.

Someone who Hilton Young may have seen was the Reverend Peshall. The chaplain, having helped Surgeon Clegg and his stretcher parties, decided there was good work to be done on the mole parapet. After climbing one of the brows he ran, first in one direction then in the other, picking up wounded men and carrying them back to the ship. Another officer who did not feel bound by his departmental responsibilities was Engineer Lieutenant Commander William Bury. With the boiler and engine rooms well led by their officers and artificers, Bury had seen that the numbers of injured were in danger of overwhelming the stretcher-bearers. Despite being injured himself (a bullet had buried itself in his thigh, taking a half-crown coin from his pocket with it), he seemed to be everywhere, lending a hand to get the wounded into the care of the medical teams.

During his rounds of the ship, Carpenter also visited the boiler and engine rooms to inform the engineers and stokers of the situation. Such visits were much appreciated and Stoker Alfred Dingle noted that his captain was 'full of enthusiasm' and he 'cheered us up wonderfully'.

Little could cheer up the seaman and marines onboard the *Iris*. The heavy rise and fall of the ferry had caused the parapet anchor placed by Bradford to be wrenched away, resulting in the vessel swinging away from the wall. Time and time again, Commander Gibbs tried to bring her back, but each time the ferry swung on the starboard anchor cable. In the end, Gibbs sent for Major Eagles, commanding the Royal Marines onboard, and told him that it would be a futile gesture to continue trying to keep the *Iris* where she was. Instead, he intended to bring the ferry around and put her alongside the *Vindictive*. Once this had been achieved, the storming parties could cross the cruiser and use her brows to get ashore. It was not, however, to be a straightforward task. It would mean that the *Iris* would have to enter the smokescreen still being laid down by the MLs to the west of the mole. Not only would Gibbs have to steer his ship through the pungent fog, he would have to bring her very carefully alongside a vessel that was being held against the mole by another ferry. There being no other option, he ordered the anchor cable to be slipped, put the helm to port, and ordered 'half ahead'.

As the *Iris* moved away from the wall there were about 300 Royal Marines already on the mole. Twenty of them were acting as back-up to the demolition party and Major Weller had sent Lieutenant Underhill and two platoons to follow Lieutenant Commander Adams, who was already returning to the fire-control building. They were to assist Lieutenant Commander Harrison and the seamen in attacking the extension guns. The remainder, led by Lieutenant Cooke with Captain Chater in support, headed in the direction of the shore. Some accurate rifle fire from the eastern end of No. 2 Shed required an assault on the position; several men were wounded, including Lieutenant Cooke.

With the arrival of reinforcements under the command of Captain Edward Bamford, Chater sent Cooke back to the ship to have his wound tended. As he left, Cooke picked up another wounded man and began to carry him towards the scaling ladders. He had not gone far, however, when he was struck in the head by

A photograph taken after the raid of the barbed-wire barricades at the defended portion of the mole, just before the start of the lighthouse extension. It was against these obstacles that Captain Bamford led his Royal Marines. It is almost certain that the bunkers beneath the mole wall are the ones that came under grenade attack by Wing Commander Brock, and the steps to the floor are the ones used by Childs and McKenzie as they attacked the enemy trying to escape to the destroyers tied up on the other side of the Mole.

another bullet and fell to the ground. Seeing this, his runner, Private John Press, dashed over, picked him up and carried him safely back to the ship.

Although Chater was the senior officer, his main role was to keep Major Weller informed of the progress of events, thus maintaining an overall picture of what was happening on the mole. Consequently it fell to Bamford to take charge of the next phase of the attack. The blockships were now well inside the harbour, but an assault still had to be made on the guns at the fortified zone, if only to distract them from the MLs attempting to rescue the blockship crews.

As Lieutenant Charles Lamplough established a strongpoint from which to keep the enemy at bay, and with the sky above him exploding with flares, starshells and strings of flaming onions, Bamford raised his lead-loaded ash plant and ordered, loudly but calmly, 'Fall in B Company'.

With his men, including Surgeon Colson, mustered behind him, Bamford stepped off as if about to embark upon a brisk after-lunch constitutional. His body erect, his stride unfaltering, and swinging his cane, Bamford provided a perfect example of courage under fire. The western end of No. 3 Shed was reached with just a few casualties but, once the shelter of the shed had been passed, they faced a 200-yard open area where they would be subjected to machine-gun and pom-pom fire from the torpedo boats to their right, and from the barbed-wire-protected fortified zone ahead. A group on the right broke away and attacked the torpedo boat with grenades, supported by the demolition party marines.

The marines' advance down the mole had caused problems for the demolition party. They had placed their charges but could not explode them with so many marines in the near vicinity. It was decided to abandon the idea, simply on the grounds that the German shore batteries were shelling the mole so heavily that they were managing to inflict as much damage on their own facilities as would have been done by Lieutenant Dickinson's team. The Demolition Party withdrew, Petty Officer Stoker Soan clutching an office sign marked with the word *Hafenkapitan* ('Port Captain') as his personal souvenir. Someone else returned onboard with a German alarm gong.

As expected, the advance of the Royal Marines towards the fortified zone was met by a furious fire from their flank and front, but still they continued, led by the seemingly imperturbable Bamford. Ignoring their casualties they pressed on, determined to get to grips with the guns that could do enormous damage to the rescue attempts. Then, an extraordinary sound, blending with the barrage of gunfire, fell upon their ears. It was a wheezing, gurgling, spluttering noise that did not belong in any battle. Chater, at the rear of the marines, turned and sprinted across the mole, clambered up a ladder and returned onboard. Finding Carpenter, he asked if the strange noise was the recall signal.

The original plan called for the seamen and marines to be recalled by waving the *Vindictive*'s two searchlight beams vertically whilst, at the same time, sounding the Morse letter 'K' (one long, one short, one long – 'K' for 'Keyes') on the siren. However, the searchlights had been destroyed by the ferocity of the German shelling and the steam to the wrecked sirens had been cut off. At ten-minutes-to-one, after forty-nine minutes alongside the mole, with no diminution in the gunfire that continued to shred the ship's upperworks – had the time come to clear the mole of the storming parties? The blockships had already entered the harbour and had either succeeded or failed. The plan of attack had originally stipulated that the mole should be cleared, at the latest, at 0120hrs, and that it would take twenty minutes to get the men back onboard. There were now thirty minutes remaining before the planned departure time, and the spare ten minutes could be used to let the demolition teams complete their work. The value of such work, however, had already been seen as minor and, when compared to the possible loss of the storming parties, seemed not worth the risk. As the clock ticked, Carpenter ordered Lieutenant Campbell in the *Daffodil* to use his battered, but just about working, siren to make the recall signal.

The signal had been sounding for just a short time, when the advancing marines saw in the glare of the starshells two of the seamen storming party coming towards them close under the shelter of the wall. It was the Lewis gunners, Leading Seaman Childs and Able Seaman McKenzie. The two men were waving and shouting that the strange sound they could hear was the recall signal. But the marines, still led by Bamford, ignored them and continued to move against the fortified zone.

It was at this moment that McKenzie was hit in the foot – a serious injury that shattered several bones. He continued, hopping and limping until the two of them reached the bottom of the iron stairway down which they had reached the mole floor. McKenzie tried to climb the steps but the pain in his foot was too much and he stopped, unable to move further. Childs, even though badly injured himself, half carried, half supported his shipmate up the steps. At the top, both men lay down exhausted before rolling over, rising to their knees, and crawling along the parapet until they reached the top of the brows. There they found willing help to get them onboard.

When Lieutenant Commander Adams returned to the fire-control station all that remained of that part of the seaman storming party were two wounded men. From them he learned that Lieutenant Commander Harrison had led a charge towards the extension guns. It was a charge neither of hope nor desperation, but with a clear principal aim – to distract the guns from the blockships. The chances of reaching the guns and putting them out of action were remote but Harrison and his men were undeterred by the odds. With the exception of the two survivors, no one else survived the machine guns. When they returned to the shelter of the fire-control station, they had turned to see Able Seaman Harold Eaves, despite his wounds, get up from the parapet floor and begin to drag Harrison's body. After just a few faltering paces, he fell as more machine-gun bullets smashed into him.

With the recall signal sounding, Adams ordered his few remaining men back to the ship as he descended to the mole floor to collect any straggling members of the seaman storming party. He eventually returned safely across the *Vindictive's* brows, the most senior of the naval officers to survive on the mole unscathed.

In the meantime, the Royal Marines, advancing like a black wave on to the fortified zone, were taking numerous casualties from the machine guns to their front and right flank, the only shelter coming from the occasional railway truck. Bamford still pressed on in the lead over the open ground until his attention was drawn to a figure running alongside them on the parapet waving his arms. It was Captain Chater, shouting that the retirement signal was sounding. Bamford halted in his tracks, turned, and waved his men back towards the modest shelter of No. 3 Shed. There, still well within the cone of fire from the machine guns in the trenches at the end of the mole, they were faced with a dash across an open space before they could arrive at the ladders placed against the parapet. The ladders themselves were easily covered by the machine guns, and would have to be climbed with the back towards the enemy. Even worse, Bamford was faced with a dilemma. All military experience had shown that the best way to get a large number of men across open ground was to charge in a single mass. To send men across in small groups would be like setting up a shooting gallery for the enemy who had simply to wait in expectation of the next rush with their guns lined-up and ready. If, however, they tried a single mass rush, there were too few ladders available, leaving a large group of men milling about in the open at the base of the parapet – an easy target for the machine guns.

Bamford asked Captain Charles Tuckey to lead the first rush. Tuckey gathered a small group around him, several of them carrying, or otherwise assisting, a wounded man. When they were ready, he led them across the mole and stood at the bottom of the nearest ladder, encouraging and helping the burdened men up. The hail of gun fire that greeted them brought several men down and a number of ladders were simply shot to pieces. Tuckey, disregarding the bullets flying past at close range, nevertheless, stayed where he was. In clear view of the machine guns, he used hand signals to bring the next few groups across whilst clearing bodies from the bottom of the ladders. Then, inevitably, a bullet found its mark and he fell down dead.

Captain John Palmer had the opportunity to cross the open ground to the ladders but chose not to do so. He had noticed that several of his men were missing, and he set off, determined to try and find them.

Aid eventually came to the marines from the parapet, where Chater had obtained some Lewis gunners and had them mount their weapons on the iron railing and open fire on the fortified zone. Gradually, the numbers remaining on the mole grew smaller until, taking up the rear of the final group dashing across the open ground, Bamford climbed up the ladder and crossed over the brows.

Chater found himself alone with the dead. Turning to go back onboard he became aware of a sharp pain in his right knee. Up until that time he had not realised that he had been wounded, probably when the first shells hit the ship, killing Colonel Elliot and Major Cordner. Once he was back on the ship he reported to Major Weller that, in his opinion, all those who were coming back were now onboard.

On the seaward side of the *Vindictive* Lieutenant Gordon Maxwell, the captain of *ML314*, had continued to lay down a close smokescreen. He had seen the activity up and down the parapet, and the withdrawal brought to his report of the event a concise description. 'It was' he wrote, 'bloody hell.'

Captain Carpenter and the remainder of the *Vindictive*'s company had found no relief from the fury directed at the ship. The guns at Blankenberge had soon found her range and large shells frequently struck home as the guns on the mole continued to shred her upperworks. Just as the recall was about to be sounded, a shell fell among boxes of fused Stokes' mortar bombs. The ship's coxswain, Petty Officer Edwin Youlton, who had steered the ship alongside the mole, bellowed to everyone within range to clear the area. In the absence of any surviving fire extinguishers, Youlton pulled burning boxes of ammunition clear and stamped on them in an effort to put out the fires. After a hectic few minutes it seemed as if he had succeeded but shortly afterwards they burst into flame once again. For a second time, Youlton, now assisted by Lieutenant Commander Rosoman, tackled the flames, this time successfully.

In the meantime, the *Iris* had completed her wide turn through the smokescreen and had come alongside the *Vindictive*. Unfortunately there was no one on the starboard side to see her arrive and it was several minutes before someone noticed her. Gunner Cobby took a party to assist her coming alongside. Again, the ferry bounced up and down with undiminished vigour and twice the hawser snapped as Cobby and his men tried to secure her. A few men jumped onto the *Vindictive* but just as a hawser was successfully passed across, the message came from the conning tower telling Commander Gibbs that the recall was sounding, and he should cast off and make his way home.

As the *Iris* left the side of the cruiser, Rosoman and Youlton met Carpenter outside the conning tower. They were discussing the plan for the departure when a large shell exploded nearby. Rosoman, whose right knee had been hit by a piece of shrapnel whilst he helped Youlton stamp out the mortar shells fire, collapsed as more shrapnel smashed into his left ankle. Youlton fell back as his arm was shattered and Carpenter reeled as shrapnel entered his left shoulder and, luckily, emerged without striking the bone.

Regardless of his wound, Carpenter climbed up one of the brows and stood looking out on to the mole. He was there to satisfy his own mind that no one was being left behind. He could see plenty of bodies but no one who moved. The time had come to go.

Gunner Cobby was sent for and told to slip *Daffodil*. Using his megaphone, Carpenter told Lieutenant Campbell to prepare a hawser to tow the *Vindictive*'s bows away from the mole. The forecastle party were ordered to slip the anchor cable. Returning to the conning tower, Carpenter encountered a limping Rosoman and suggested that he join Youlton in obtaining medical aid. Rosoman refused on the grounds that he had seen many men more badly injured than he was. It followed, he argued, that they needed the surgeon's attention more than he did. Once inside the armoured compartment, the first lieutenant even refused to sit down, remaining standing by an observation slit.

The conditions inside the conning tower were dreadful. Four wounded men lay among the remains of four dead men. Blood was splashed everywhere. The engine-room telegraph had been smashed and engine room orders had to be transmitted by the sole remaining working telephone. The ship's single surviving compass was wholly unreliable, a condition, as Rosoman pointed out, not helped by the number of steel helmets bending over it.

Some 200 yards off her starboard quarter, an Australian artificer engineer, William Edgar, urged on his boiler-room staff in his efforts to keep the *Iris'* steam pressure as high as possible. Commander Gibbs wanted to get his ship clear of the guns, both on the shore and on the lighthouse extension. He had, so far, only suffered three casualties, and he had no intention of adding to that total if he could avoid it. Grateful for any shelter he could find in the rolling banks of smokescreen against sporadic machine-gun fire, he ordered the navigator, Lieutenant George Spencer, to keep the bows pointing north-west, the best route to put distance between the ship and the guns. But it was too late. A large shell from the heavy shore guns hit the port control station – a weather-proof compartment on the same level as the bridge, used by the captain to view the ferry's port side when bringing her alongside. The blast destroyed Gibbs' legs and mortally wounded Major Eagles. Spencer lay badly wounded, although awake and trying to come to terms with what had happened. With a single exception, Signalman Thomas Bryant, the entire communications staff was killed. The coxswain, Petty Officer David Smith, was blown over by the blast but hauled himself to his feet and saw to his horror that the ferry was swinging to starboard – directly in line with the extension guns. Spencer raised himself to a sitting position and croaked out the bearing they needed. Smith responded immediately and the ferry turned away from the blazing guns.

The shell had started a fire beneath the port bridge wing, just where a large supply of Stokes' mortar shells and hand grenades were stored. On hearing shouts of 'Fire!' the first lieutenant, Lieutenant Oscar Henderson, raced up from below decks, grasped the situation and organised a party of firefighters. As he advanced against the flames, Henderson saw the wreckage on the bridge and went to investigate. There he found PO Smith steering with one hand, and with the other holding a torch to light the compass. Spencer was struggling to remain conscious but both Gibbs and Eagles were clearly dying. The surviving signalman, Bryant, had been taken below to receive medical help from Surgeon Pocock and his sick-berth team.

Checking that Smith could hold on a little longer, Henderson returned to the fire as more shells hit the ferry. Beneath the bridge he found that shrapnel had reduced the fire party to a single man, Able Seaman Ferdinand Lake who, with burnt and blistered hands was picking up mortar shells and grenades from the flames and throwing them overboard. Between them they managed to extinguish the fire by smothering it with sand before Henderson returned to the bridge taking Lake with him. There they found Spencer was just about to succumb to his wounds and Smith barely able to stand. Lake took over the wheel as another volley of shells fell on the ferry. The effect was devastating. One of the shells exploded in the passenger salon killing dozens of seamen and marines. The entire sick-berth staff were killed with the exception of Pocock. Such was the carnage that men had to attend to their own wounds or help each other if they could. Air Mechanic First Class George Warrington, who had been buried under wrecked corpses in the explosion, had been raised on a farm and understood basic animal husbandry – he did his best to help where he could.

Leaving his stokers to keep up the steam pressure, Artificer Engineer Edgar took Engine Room Artificer Stanley Odam with him onto the upper deck to see if there was anything they could do to help. There was. The *Iris'* smokescreen apparatus had been damaged, probably by earlier machine-gun fire. Ignoring the shards of shrapnel flying through the air, the two men set to work with their tools and in a remarkably quick time thick black 'artificial fog' was pouring from the equipment.

Help also came from another quarter. Lieutenant Commander Lionel Chappell, the captain of *ML558* (also carrying Keyes' flag-captain, Ralph Collins), had spotted the *Iris'* plight and roared directly into the path of the extension guns, laying down a smokescreen. As the smoke rose behind the ferry, *ML558* was hit several times and sustained considerable damage. Chappell, however, was not deterred and prepared to make another dash into the firing zone, only to hold back when the ferry's own smoke issued from her stern.

The *Iris* was, by now, almost a floating mortuary: 182 dead and wounded still lay mixed on the main and upper decks as Surgeon Pocock, with only the light of candles and a torch, struggled desperately to save lives. When word reached Signalman Bryant that the ship had been left without any means of

The return of the *Vindictive* from Zeebrugge, by Charles Dixon.

communication, he had himself carried along the deck and up ladders to the bridge, where he was propped up just a few feet from the bodies of Eagles and Spencer (Gibbs had been taken below decks). Almost fainting with pain he stood by to send any messages that Henderson required. He did not have long to wait. As soon as the first warship approached, Henderson ordered Bryant to send 'For God's sake send some doctors, I have a shipload of dead and dying.' Eventually word reached Keyes who ordered the surgeon from the monitor *Erebus* to assist.

Lieutenant Hilton Young, the pain from his wrecked arm dulled by morphine, walked around the *Vindictive*'s upper deck, making sure that only the gunners and the upper-deck seamen parties remained exposed to the continuing enemy fire. Everyone else was sent below. He had seen what had happened to the *Iris* and was determined to keep the number of casualties to a minimum. The cruiser was about to 'slip and proceed' and it would not be long before they came under the fire of the same guns that had caused devastation in the *Iris*. Hilton Young took his place at the port forward 6in gun, where he was joined by Gunner Cobby.

On the *Vindictive*'s forecastle, a party of seamen had sent a heaving line across to the *Daffodil* and were hauling a hawser across. Once the thick rope was in their hands, they dropped it over a bollard and signalled the conning tower that they were ready for the tow. Carpenter waved at Lieutenant Campbell on the bridge of the ferry, who responded by ordering 'Full astern'. The hawser tautened, the bows began to move – and the hawser parted. For just a second or two there was a flurry of action as efforts were made to send another hawser across. Carpenter had noticed, however, the bows were continuing to swing away from the wall. Without any hesitation he waved the *Daffodil* away and ordered 'Full speed ahead' over his telephone link to the engine room. Then, in the absence of the injured PO Youlton, Carpenter took the wheel himself, and turned it firmly hard to port. Almost immediately there was a great crashing and grinding sound as the brows slid off the wall, bringing lumps of concrete with them. At the same time the old mainmast, secured horizontally across the quarterdeck, proved its worth as it held the stern – and thus the propellers – clear of the projecting foundation step at the base of the wall. For one, almost heart-stopping moment, the ropes used to support the brows wrapped themselves around the port propeller but, after a juddering alarm, the great bronze screw resumed its steady rotation. The pressure, however, that came onto the horizontal mainmast as a result of the violent shaking caused the mast to be dislodged and the port propeller hit the foundation step. Great chunks were broken off the screw and its effectiveness was severely reduced.

At several points on the upper deck, smoke apparatus was switched on, a northerly breeze pushing the smoke along with the ship. Not that the cruiser's presence entirely vanished from the enemy's sight. Flames roaring up through the lacerated funnels, provided a flickering orange glow. Yet despite their best endeavours, the German gunners failed to hit the ship. Detonations and the sound of shells falling into the water nearby could be heard and felt throughout the *Vindictive*, but none were recorded striking their target.

After several tense minutes had passed, Hilton Young shouted up to Cobby, 'Where are we now?' The gunner replied, 'We are well away. Here come our destroyers.' The incredible had happened. Just when she was at her most vulnerable, when her sides were exposed to the enemy, when a single shell in the right place could have brought her to a halt, the *Vindictive* had escaped further damage. Not a single man was lost or injured in the withdrawal of a ship from an enemy waiting with loaded guns at point-blank range. And not just one ship – the *Daffodil* had also escaped without further harm.

The first destroyer to come alongside was the *Moorsom*. Carpenter, with all his signalling lamps destroyed, used a hand torch to flash a message across asking her to lead the way as his conning tower compass was proving totally unreliable. He then handed over the wheel to a quartermaster and went to do rounds of his ship.

Someone else doing his 'rounds' was Engineer Lieutenant Commander Bury. In one of the boiler rooms he found the stokers singing 'I want to go home' as they furiously shovelled coal into the boiler. He asked their leader, Warrant Engineer Dugald Campbell, 'What have you got to say about your men?' Campbell replied, 'I'm not going to say anything for them or against them, but if I was going to hell tomorrow night I would have the same men with me.'

Much the same could have been said of any of the men who had taken part in the attack on the mole, those who survived and those who died. Men like Harrison, Bradford, Hawkins, Tuckey, Hallihan, Elliot, Halahan, and Cordner. Men like the two unknowns whose bodies were photographed by the Germans lying on the mole at the spot where the *Vindictive*'s brows rested on the parapet wall. The closest to the camera was wearing a 'Class III' ('Men not dressed as seamen') uniform, the one furthest away is in a dark uniform but it is too indistinct to be recognisable. Neither man was intended for service on the mole or they would have been wearing khaki. The two men are, almost certainly, Shipwright Thomas Cochran and Stoker First Class, Jonathan Hughes. Both men were probably part of the *Vindictive*'s carpenter's crew, killed trying to repair the damaged brows.

Not all, however, were dead. Captain Palmer had found his missing men, but it was too late – the ship had sailed. A total of thirteen seamen and Royal Marines ended up as prisoners of the Germans. Another man who fell into German hands was Able Seaman Harold Eaves who had fallen to machine-gun fire whilst trying to bring back the body of Lieutenant Commander Harrison. Despite his injuries Eaves had hung on to life long enough to reach a German hospital where his numerous wounds could be treated. The day after the raid the Kaiser paid a visit to the mole and Captain Palmer was taken to meet him. When the Kaiser thrust out his hand to shake Palmer's, the Royal Marine stood rigidly to attention and refused the offer.

The chief mystery remained the question of what had happened to Wing Commander Brock. Last seen disappearing into the fire-control position, it was widely assumed that he had died whilst trying to obtain information about the supposed sound-ranging system installed in the building. Brock, however, was not a physicist or even a technician. His interest lay in chemistry – especially the kind of chemistry involved in pyrotechnics and munitions. At best, the fire-control position's role in sound-ranging would have been little more than an early warning listening post. The all-important microphones, stop watches and recorders were required to be sited hundreds of yards from each other, and would have been installed somewhere along the shore. On the other hand, probably less than a hundred yards from the building he had entered, Brock would have known that there was the answer to a mystery that had baffled experts amongst the Allies since the beginning of the war.

The much-feared German 'flaming onions' anti-aircraft fire had begun the war as a batch of five 37mm tracer shells fired from the five rotating barrels of a Hotchkiss revolving cannon. A later version was developed that used the 37mm single-barrelled Maxim gun, and it was well known that at least one of these guns was sited at the end of the mole. None of the guns nor any of the ammunition had ever been captured and it was widely believed that the glowing trail of light climbing into the sky was made up of shells linked together by chain or wire.

In February 1918 the Canadian air ace and Victoria Cross holder Major W. 'Billy' Bishop, described to an American audience the effect of being fired on by 'flaming onions':

> the first thing you see is a big cluster of six or eight whirling balls of fire coming at you from below ... They whirl rapidly about a common centre, with a lateral spinning motion, spreading out apparently by centrifugal force from some common hub or centre to which they are held in some way ... When you are well up and far within the Boche lines and you see one of these roaring aerial conflagrations mounting towards you, spurting fountains of fire in a big sort of spiral fifty or sixty feet across, it is somewhat disconcerting.

Even as late as 27 April 1918 *The Times*' description of flaming onions as 'a small incendiary shell fastened together in chains by wire which, on finding its target, winds round it and creates a fire' was fully believed.

There would have been few people on the side of the Allies who were better qualified, or with greater interest, in finding out what the flaming onions were or how they worked, than Brock. Being within close range of one of the weapons and with the opportunity to attempt to obtain a sample of the ammunition would have been an irresistible attraction to such a man. Nevertheless, had he lived, the question uppermost in his mind, and on the minds of all who took part in the diversion led by the *Vindictive*, would surely have been 'How are the blockships – did they get through?'

10

The Blockships

It was highly likely that any German on the Zeebrugge mole at 0015hrs on the morning of 23 April 1918 would have had his eyes firmly on the astonishing sight of the upper works of a cruiser towering over the mole wall. The hammering noise of the guns was appalling, searchlights probed drifting clouds of smoke and the skies were streaked and splashed with rockets, flares and starshells. It may have been some time before the German would have realised that, behind him, a flotilla of Royal Naval coastal motor boats had roared around the lighthouse and, although they were in the harbour with the intent of letting loose a smokescreen, were also eager to commit mayhem.

The word 'roared' is probably a little too strong for *CMB5*, under the command of Sub Lieutenant Cedric Outhwaite. He had not long left Dover when his engine began to smell of burning oil. An investigation revealed that one of the pistons was glowing red hot. Clearly the only answer was to return to port. Outhwaite, however, knew that common sense played little part in any battle and chose to continue, his engine racing violently with an ominous rattling noise.

CMB5 had barely entered the harbour when Outhwaite saw a German vessel, probably a torpedo boat but possibly a destroyer, underway to the north-east. He immediately set off in pursuit with the intention, no doubt encouraged by the poor condition of his engine, to 'cause a collision with the enemy destroyer'. Skimming across the surface of the harbour water, *CMB5* soon came under the attention of some of the mole guns. Then the target vessel joined in with a strange reversal of the usual defence against an approaching threat. First a searchlight found the motor boat, machine guns opened up, followed by the pom-poms, then the ship's main armament, her 3.5in guns. With the multitude of projectiles screaming around him and soaked from the splashes of near misses, Outhwaite reconsidered his options and came to the conclusion that if he continued on his present course he was unlikely to survive long enough to ram the enemy ship. Consequently he ordered a slight slowing down of *CMB5* and with the enemy 650 yards to his front, launched his torpedo from his stern. He then immediately increased his revolutions and put the helm hard over to port in order to get out of the way of the weapon. The torpedo hissed down his port side and vanished into clouds of drifting smoke. Outhwaite fancied that he heard an explosion above the din of battle going on to starboard and was pleased to see that the beam from the searchlight dimmed and died. With the whole craft shaking from the increasingly defective engine, Outhwaite emerged from the harbour and headed back to Dover. It was later confirmed that a German destroyer had been torpedoed and badly damaged at the spot reported by Outhwaite.

Entering the harbour in company with *CMB5*, Sub Lieutenant Leslie Blake, commanding *CMB7*, saw the net boom ahead of him and steered eastwards until he found a gap. With *CMB5* on her way to attack her destroyer target, Blake, aided by the light from German starshells, caught sight of a destroyer of his own secured alongside the mole. Putting his helm over, he closed to within 600 yards and released his torpedo. Then, despite the hail of fire falling about his ears, he stopped dead in the water to observe the results of his attack. A gratifying explosion abreast of the fore bridge rewarded his patience. Pleased with the outcome, Blake laid down a smokescreen before turning eastwards, skimming parallel with the shore at high speed until he ran head-on into a large buoy. At first it seemed to the crew of *CMB7* there was no option but to sink at the spot and hope to survive long enough to be captured. Blake, however, tried out the engine, found that it remained unaffected, and with enough speed could bring the cracked and crumpled bows clear of the water. This brought about a second option. The boat could head for Dutch waters. Such a decision would mean internment but with the possibility of escape back to England. Closing with the coast, Blake realised that he had a third option. With the engine running well and the bows remaining clear of the water he decided that he would make a dash for Dunkirk. Accordingly he increased speed to 32 knots and with the rolling thunder of gunfire and skies lit by flares and searchlights to port he roared off into the darkness. Within a very short time *CMB7* found herself with a similar activity continuing off her port bow. Blake had navigated himself into the raid on Ostend. Just as this became clear, an oil gland burst, the engine rumbled to a halt and the damaged bows returned to the water. Now there was just one option. Blake fired two red flares as his crew desperately bailed in a futile effort to keep back the water. No doubt to their intense delight the bows of a destroyer appeared out of the darkness and proved to be HMS *Faulkner*, carrying Commodore Lynes. Another ship, the destroyer HMS *Tetrarch*, was summoned and, with her bows hauled clear of the water, *CMB7* was towed safely into Dunkirk.

Following *CMB5* and *CMB7* into the harbour were *CMB32A* and *CMB27A*. Once they had found a gap in the boom, the captain of *CMB32A* decided that Captain Fryatt's former ship, the *Brussels* (now renamed the *Brugge* and used by the German Navy as a depot ship), would make an excellent target for his torpedo and roared off in her direction. *CMB27A*, under the command of Lieutenant Cuthbert Bowlby, a son of the clergyman headmaster of Lancing College and a distant relation of Eva Keyes, laid down a smokescreen until he arrived at a point some 70 yards off the mole seaplane base. Seeing activity around the hangar, Bowlby decided to exercise his Lewis guns and opened fire, causing consternation amongst the defenders preparing to meet an attack by the Royal Marines advancing down the mole in their direction. Bowlby was, almost certainly, unaware of the aid he was giving to the marine storming party and, no doubt, was happy to settle for the chance to have a go at the enemy. His unacknowledged work of distraction completed, Bowlby returned to his smokescreen duties.

Whilst the CMBs were carrying out their – mainly self-appointed – havoc inside the curve of the mole, three massive shapes were gliding though the dark waters towards the harbour entrance. In the first of the blockships, HMS *Thetis,* Engineer Lieutenant Commander Ronald Boddie had passed much of the voyage dining in the wooden shed that served as the ship's temporary wardroom. He feasted on grouse and other delicacies from a Fortnam & Mason picnic hamper supplied by the captain, Commander Sneyd. Now, having made himself a cup of soup, he dressed in his duffel coat and slung a knapsack over his back containing a first-aid kit, spare rations, a water bottle, a life jacket, a whistle, a pistol, and – being an Irishman – a shillelagh. Sneyd, in the meantime, was having great difficulty in locating the actual entrance. The lighthouse had of course long been extinguished and although the *Vindictive*'s pyrotechnic party continued to fire rocket flares from the ship's stern scuttles, the light provided was diffused by the drifting banks of smokescreen. Nevertheless, such a problem had been anticipated and *Motor Launch 110* raced towards the entrance to lay down calcium buoys as a guide for the blockships. When this was achieved, *ML110* was to enter the harbour and lay down more buoys at the canal entrance.

The captain of *ML110*, Lieutenant Commander Dawbarn Young, had volunteered for the duty of providing the light-buoys. He was a particularly popular officer, well-known for his eager enthusiasm and keen desire to get to grips with the enemy. A fellow officer considered Young to be 'a white man in the very best sense of the word [i.e. not upright and honest]'. He was a man for whom 'a mean or lying action was impossible to his nature' and no one had ever 'set or kept a straighter course than he'. But fate shows no respect for human superlatives and 400 yards from the entrance three heavy shells hit the bridge of the motor launch. Young's left arm and right leg were smashed and a shell splinter ripped through his left lung. The coxswain was killed outright and Lieutenant Leonard Lee – who had volunteered for service in *ML110* when his own ML was found to be defective – suffered a badly injured arm. Astonishingly, although standing next to Young, the first lieutenant, Lieutenant George Bowen, remained unscathed and, with the boat taking on water, managed to get the ML's tin dinghy over the side. Then, with the help of other unwounded men, he got all eight survivors into the tiny craft. Returning onboard, Bowen wrenched off the ship's compass and passed it down into the dinghy. He then loaded two magazines into a Lewis gun and fired the bullets through the bottom of the boat, completing the job with an axe. When he returned to the dinghy, he found that only he and the chief motor mechanic were capable of rowing. They began pulling away from the entrance with Lee gripping the compass between his knees, lighting the needle with a torch held in his undamaged hand. Three CMBs passed at high speed without catching sight of them or hearing their cries for help. Eventually they were spotted by another ML. The transfer to the rescue vessel was too much for Young. He died as he was being passed across.

The situation in which Commander Sneyd found himself was getting increasingly complex. Peering through his binoculars from the bridge of the *Thetis*, he knew that he was close to the harbour entrance but despite the continuing flashes from gunfire, flares and starshells, the drifting clouds of 'artificial fog' persisted in obscuring his vision. To his surprise and concern, the flares of the calcium buoys were nowhere to be seen. Any unease he felt would not have been helped by the fact that his responsibilities included the *Intrepid* and the *Iphigenia* following closely in his wake. Like the *Thetis*, both ships were weighed down with cement and concrete and answered their helms with sluggish reluctance. The chances of instant 'Grand Fleet' manoeuvring, should they find the mole itself rearing up just beyond their bows, were remote. Suddenly the answer appeared in the shape of *ML558*, fresh from helping the *Vindictive* with her smokescreens. She was carrying Captain Ralph Collins, Keyes' flag-captain, who was in overall command of the motor launches. Word had reached him that the calcium buoys had not been laid close by the lighthouse entrance to the harbour. Accordingly he asked Lieutenant Commander Chappell to take him to the spot from where he calculated the course and distance the blockships would have to travel to enter the harbour. Arriving alongside the *Thetis*, Collins shouted the directions through a megaphone, waving the cruiser good luck as he returned to his duties monitoring the activities of the MLs.

On approaching the lighthouse the *Thetis* came under fire from heavy shells and flaming onions but neither did enough damage to deter Sneyd's intention of heading straight into the harbour. Just minutes later, at twenty-five minutes past midnight, the bows of the cruiser appeared round the end of the lighthouse extension, her once elegant lines marred by two steel girders bolted to her forecastle and projecting over her bows. After a life of modest activity she was within a nautical mile of sacrificing herself by charging the outer gates of the canal lock, her battering-ram-like girders assisting in the destruction of the Bruges canal system and the end of submarine and destroyer access to the North Sea. Following in her wake, the *Intrepid* and the *Iphigenia* were to slew themselves across the canal as a means of adding to the enemy's misery. All they needed was for the fortunes of war to be scattered in their favour.

The entire length of the *Thetis* had hardly penetrated the harbour when she came under a savage onslaught of gunfire. Most of the firing came from the extension guns, which found themselves with a target hardly more than 100 yards away. The guns at the end of the mole were, for the most part, silent, their crews more concerned with the seamen on the parapet above them and the Royal Marines advancing along the mole. *Thetis's* 6in guns barked back in reply and a gun sited on the end barge of a barge-boom extending from the shore was silenced when the cruiser ran the barge down, sinking it. Suddenly, as if reeling from the hammering by the enemy's heavy guns (but more likely affected by a damaged steering system), the *Thetis* lurched rapidly to port. Sneyd struggled to control the ship but the massed weight of concrete made her responses slow. With the helm hard over, the ship eventually began to answer – but it was too late.

With its northern end less than 200 yards from the southern end of the barge boom, a buoyed net-boom ran north–south for about 400 yards. As the ram-shaped bows of the *Thetis* finally swung slowly to starboard they hit the net between the two most northerly buoys, the nets hooking onto the bulging ram at the base of the bows. Despite this extra burden, the cruiser continued her turn to starboard. Sneyd brought her back on course, the ship surging forward towards the canal entrance, but if control of the *Thetis* was difficult before it was now almost impossible. The close-range firing from the extension guns had breached her sides at several points, water was flooding in and she had an already pronounced list to starboard. Nevertheless the cruiser pushed on, dragging the net-boom with her. But success in bringing the ship round to starboard (and thus back into the dredged channel) brought its own penalties. The manoeuvre caused the starboard propeller to come into contact with the writhing wires of the net-boom. Inevitably the wires wrapped themselves around the propeller and with a grinding sound that shuddered throughout the vessel, the starboard engine crashed to a halt, followed moments later by the port engine. Once again, the ship reeled to port. With just 300 yards to go to the canal entrance, the *Thetis* ran aground on a sandbank.

In such a situation, Sneyd – by now wounded in both legs – knew that he had to do one thing above all others. The *Thetis* and the area around her was blanketed in smoke, both from battle damage and from smokescreens. Many of the ship's pipes had been cut and steam shrieked out of the holes, adding to the already poor visibility. In addition, searchlights to the east and west of the canal were sending their baleful beams directly at his ship. It would be near impossible for the following blockships to locate the canal entrance. Sneyd ordered the lighting of the starboard navigation lantern. The green light glowing through the smoke and steam did its job perfectly, and the *Intrepid*, followed by the *Iphigenia*, swept past to cheers from all the ships.

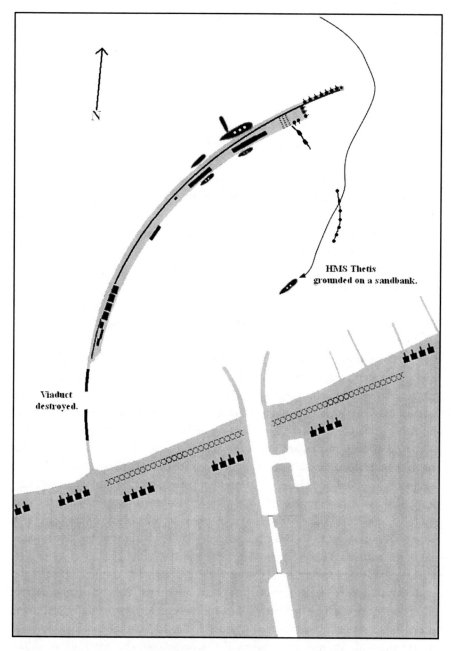

N

HMS Thetis
grounded on a sandbank.

Viaduct
destroyed.

As the landing parties try to distract the Germans, HMS *Thetis* rounds the lighthouse and enters the harbour. She nevertheless comes under heavy fire and her steering gear is damaged, causing her to hit the net boom and ground to a halt on a sandbank.

Unable to make contact with the *Thetis'* bridge, Boddie sent a stoker to find the captain to ask for instructions. When, after ten minutes, the man failed to return, he sent another. With the failure of the second stoker to return he was forced to assume that the captain and other officers were either dead, or incapable of giving instructions. Consequently he decided to open the seacocks and blow the explosive charges. Once water was pouring into the engine spaces, Boddie made his way to the quarterdeck where he found a number of stokers and seamen waiting to be given their orders. Making his way forward, he came across the 20-year-old, newly promoted Lieutenant George Belben, who told him that the captain was wounded but still in command. Lieutenant Francis Lambert, who had volunteered at the last moment from the monitor *Sir John Moore*, had his lungs filled with fumes from an exploding shell and was incapable of speech. One of the only two boats available had been destroyed and one of the funnels had been brought down by shellfire. As he heard this news, Boddie was approached by a seaman with a message from the captain saying that he 'would like the engines to go ahead if possible'.

Firmly believing that he was wasting his time, Boddie collected as many of his engine-room artificers as he could and returned to the engine room to turn off the seacocks. With Chief ERA Gale he 'wrestled' with both engines and, to his 'great astonishment' managed to get them slowly turning over. What he was unaware of, however, was that Sneyd had sent the request down with the seaman messenger at least fifteen minutes earlier and, on receiving no acknowledgement, had assumed that either Boddie was unable to comply or that the engines were incapable of being restarted. Consequently he had made his way painfully down to the main deck in preparation for abandoning the ship. There, much to his surprise, he realised the ship was moving forward – with no one on the bridge. Again he hobbled and dragged himself up the ladder he had very recently descended but it was too late. After surging forward for about 500 yards the ship ran into the western side of the cleared channel, partially blocking the canal exit. Now all that was left to be done was to explode the charges to blow the bottom out of the battered *Thetis*.

Sneyd ordered everyone up from below decks and gave the order for the explosive charges to be detonated. It was then discovered that the petty officer in charge of the firing keys had been killed and no one knew where the keys were. Sneyd reacted quickly and had the charges exploded from an auxiliary position. As the satisfying thumps from below decks confirmed that the bottom of the ship had been blown out, Sneyd ordered the surviving ship's boats to be lowered and the remaining smoke canisters discharged. Unfortunately, both Sneyd and Lambert were badly affected by the dense smoke and collapsed gasping for air. As a result, command during the attempted escape fell upon Lieutenant Belben. His chief concern was that the only surviving boat turned out to be the ship's cutter. Already holed in several places, and intended for no more than twenty-two passengers and crew, Belben had to get forty men – including five wounded – into the vessel at the same time as the ship was under fire from vessels alongside the mole, from shore batteries, and from machine guns less than 100 yards away. Having succeeded in getting everyone onboard, Belben found that the boat was in imminent danger of sinking beneath him and ordered everyone who could to bail the vessel out with anything they could find, including their cupped hands.

In true naval tradition, despite his injuries and his breathing difficulties, the last to leave the ship was Commander Sneyd. Leaning away from the ship's side, he took hold of one of the boat's falls and attempted to climb down the rope, but the effort was too much for him and he fell into the water. He was swiftly hauled out and Belben gave the order to pull clear of the ship. Surrounded by smoke they pulled in what they hoped to be the direction of the harbour entrance.

This was just the moment for which Lieutenant Hugh Littleton, the captain of *ML526* had been waiting. His vessel had been one of four that had been intended to follow the blockships in, but Young's *ML110* had been sunk, and another ML had engine failure. Only *ML282* was able to accompany *ML526* into the harbour. In following the *Thetis* into the harbour, Littleton had experienced all the alarms occasioned by accurate gunfire, the net-boom and the groundings. Now he was peering into the smoke-engendered gloom with his first lieutenant, Lieutenant Lefroy Geddes, an Ottawa-born lawyer. Their efforts were rewarded by the sight of an overloaded cutter emerging from a bank of smoke. Within minutes the wounded were passed over, followed by the remainder of *Thetis*' survivors. They sat, stood or laid down where they could as Littleton turned *ML526* about, preparing to leave the harbour, when someone spotted another cutter appearing out of the smoke. Littleton closed with the boat and found she had come from the *Intrepid*. Taking the men onboard, *M526* found herself with over sixty passengers in addition to her crew of nine. It was clearly time to leave the bullet-splattered waters of the harbour, but not before stopping to pick up another man who had fallen over the side of the *Intrepid*'s cutter and who was thought to have been killed. Having some experience of first-aid, Littleton set about helping the wounded as Geddes took over the bridge and powered the boat out of the harbour beneath scores of guns attempting to bring her exit to a halt. The boat only slowed down after covering well over 100 miles, having reached the pier at Dover, bearing the marks of just one machine-gun bullet through the after hatch, and a shrapnel tear in the roof of the bridge.

When Lieutenant Bonham Carter took the *Intrepid* down the starboard side of the *Thetis*, he had found himself with an interesting conundrum. With the Germans on all quarters concentrating their fire on the lead ship, the *Intrepid* had escaped any serious harm. The way to the canal was clear ahead and, once inside, there was nothing to stop the *Intrepid* from charging down the canal and ramming the lockgates. Less than half a mile on a straight course would bring the ship bows-on to the gates. The structural damage combined with the bottom of the ship being blown out would present the enemy with a complex and difficult task, and probably render the canal totally useless for several months. On the other hand, if he was brought to a halt by the weight of enemy gunfire as he charged towards the lockgates, the *Intrepid* would almost certainly find herself lying along the axis of the dredged channel, and offering little difficulty for enemy vessels wishing to pass her on either side. Furthermore, Bonham Carter's orders – given verbally by Keyes himself – were to sink his ship across the canal, just inside the entrance. With this achieved, the inevitably rapid build-up of silt at the point of blockage would (according to Belgian sources) add significantly to the enemy's difficulties. Furthermore, as a junior officer, Bonham Carter would have been aware that he might not be in possession of all the details of the entire raid. Was there anything else being carried out of which he was not aware, and which depended for its success upon his carrying out his orders to the letter? He decided to follow his orders.

With the curved entrance piers on each beam, Bonham Carter ordered the engines 'Full speed astern', leaving him just enough headway on the ship to reach the position where the canal breached the harbour wall. He then ordered 'Full speed ahead starboard, full speed astern port, helm hard-a-starboard.' Slowly the *Intrepid* began to swing to port when, to the surprise of all, the ship grounded fore and aft with no more than 10 degrees of turn having been achieved. It became immediately clear that the Germans' lack of attention to harbour maintenance had allowed a build-up of silt that far exceeded anyone's expectations. Consequently the navigable channel at the entrance to the canal was much more narrow than had been believed. Bonham Carter tried to nudge the ship ahead and astern to see if a greater angle could be achieved but when it became obvious that little more could be done, he ordered the upper-deck parties to get into the ship's boats along with as many of the engine- and boiler-room staff as possible. He knew that evacuating the ship would not be as straightforward as it should have been due to the fact that – thanks to the 'disinclination' of the spare watch of stokers to leave the ship earlier – he now had eighty-seven officers and men to disembark instead of the expected fifty-four.

To add to Bonham Carter's problems, the enemy had suddenly realised that their chief target within the harbour was not the battered *Thetis* but the two ships that had appeared at the entrance to the canal. The *Intrepid* had been hit a number of times by heavy shells that had penetrated her starboard side, and machine guns sent streams of bullets rattling about her upper works. Bonham Carter ordered the smoke canisters to be turned on and within seconds the *Intrepid* was enveloped in a cloud of thick grey-black smoke. At this he slotted in the explosive charge firing keys and set off the alarm gongs to tell the engine-room staff to clear the compartment. Whilst mentally calculating the time it would take for the men to get clear before he fired the charges, Bonham Carter was stunned by a very loud 'clang' from forward followed by the ship lurching, Even worse, he then realised that the *Intrepid* was now beginning to swing to starboard – putting her back in line with the dredged channel. With no other option open to him, Bonham Carter turned the firing keys and blew the bottom out of the ship, to the considerable discomfort of the engine-room staff. The *Intrepid's* dislodgement from the silt had announced the arrival of her fellow blockship, HMS *Iphigenia*.

Like the *Intrepid*, the *Iphigenia* had attracted little attention compared to the pounding received by the *Thetis*, but that changed immediately as she passed Sneyd's battered ship. Three large shells – probably intended for the *Thetis* – hit her starboard side. Shrapnel from one of the shells severed a steampipe, and a huge cloud of blanketing steam covered the bridge and conning position, obliterating the view forward. Her captain, Lieutenant Billyard-Leake, his navigating officer, Lieutenant Philip Vaux, and Leading Seaman William Potter at the wheel, looked out urgently for any sign that would give them a clue as to their position. They did not have to wait for too long. The steam cleared, revealing that the *Iphigenia's* bows were just about to collide with the western entrance pier. Billyard-Leake shouted, 'Helm hard a starboard! Full astern both!' There was just enough time to bring the bows around to port and enough way on the ship to see her scraping her starboard side down the pier structure. Ordering a return to full speed ahead, Billyard-Leake then found himself faced with a dredger tied up to a barge dead ahead. The *Iphigenia* collided with the dredger (which subsequently sank) and found herself encumbered by the barge snarled up with her bows. A burst of forward speed with the starboard engine eventually shook the barge off, leaving Billyard-Leake just able to make out the shape of the *Intrepid* through the cloud of smoke ahead of him. As he approached, a slight thinning of the cloud revealed that the first blockship into the canal had grounded, apparently leaving a gap on the eastern side. Unaware that this 'gap' was, in fact, blocked by silt, Billyard-Leake decided to try and fill the opening with the forepart of the *Iphigenia*. However, having reacted quickly enough to avert the threat of collision with the western pier, the cruiser now reverted to her sluggish response. The result was a heavy glancing blow to the *Intrepid's* port bow. In addition to nudging the other cruiser off the silt, the *Iphigenia* had also lost headway. When he realised this, although the alarm gongs were sounding, indicating that the explosive charges were about to be fired, Billyard-Leake sent Vaux to the engine room with the order that Engineering Mate Sydney West and his team of stokers, were to remain at their stations. He then ordered 'Astern both, port your helm.' The cruiser shuddered backwards until, within the narrow limits open to him, he considered he had enough space to build up speed. Ordering 'Full speed ahead both, helm amidships' he took the ship forward. There was never going to be enough time or space to

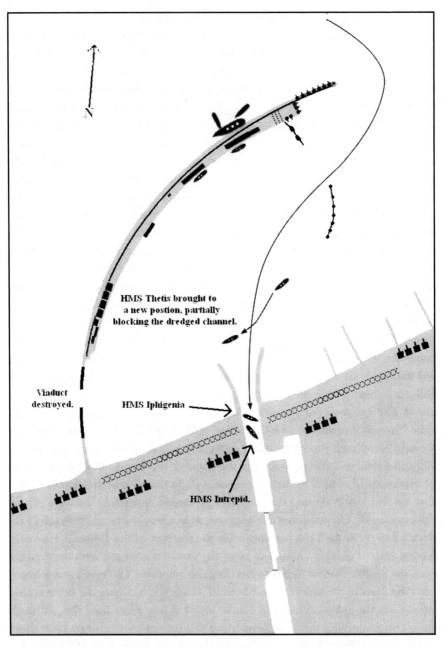

N

HMS Thetis brought to
a new postion, partially
blocking the dredged channel.

Viaduct
destroyed.

HMS Iphigenia

HMS Intrepid.

The *Iris* leaves her position forward of the *Invincible* and arrives off the cruiser's starboard quarter as the blockships *Intrepid* and *Iphigenia* enter the harbour. The two cruisers, guided by a starboard light on the *Thetis*, enter the canal and are sunk in the dredged channel. As their bottoms are blown out, the *Thetis* frees herself from the sandbank and is scuttled in the harbour channel.

build up the sort of speed that he would have wanted, but once he had thousands of tons of steel and concrete going forward at the best speed he could expect, Billyard-Leake ordered 'Full astern port, helm hard a starboard!' With just yards to go, the bow of the cruiser swung to port and buried itself in the silt. *Iphigenia* was firmly across the canal. With a twist of the firing keys, Billyard-Leake blew out her bottom and she settled on the canal floor, her upper works almost level with the surface of the waterway. Satisfied with his work, he then ordered everybody to be crammed into the surviving ship's cutter.

As they pulled clear of the ship's starboard side they were surprised to hear, coming through the clamour of gunfire, an alarmed shout followed by a splash. Leading Seaman Albert Davis had been told to remain by his gun until ordered to leave it. In the noise and confusion, however, the order to abandon ship had not reached Davis and he had stood at his station until, by the light of a starshell, he saw the cutter being rowed from the ship's side. Despite the close-range fire of enemy small arms, the cutter waited patiently until the leading seaman swam to the boat's side and was hauled inboard.

Once again the cutter was pulled clear of the ship but after just a few strokes, someone spotted the forepart of *ML282* appearing round the bows of the *Iphigenia*. The boat was immediately rowed in the ML's direction only to find it stopped in the water. A large number of men scrambled across to the ML until

Lieutenant P. Dean, captain of the rescue vessel, *ML282*.

The northern canal lock gate looking to the north. In the background can be seen the sloping eastern bank and the large posts at the position where the *Intrepid* and the *Iphigenia* were sunk. At the time of the raid there would have been the western bank of the canal where, today, large ships are tied up alongside modern facilities. To the left of the lock gate is the bombproof shelter into which the gates could be withdrawn when under attack.

an order was shouted for them to stop. The captain of the ML, Lieutenant Percy Dean was concerned that, thanks to the build-up of silt, the depth of water was too shallow to take yet more men onboard without the risk of grounding. Those left in the cutter were told to take the boat around the stern of the cruiser. When this was done, *ML282* was found waiting and the transfer of men continued – until a skiff containing sixteen men from the *Intrepid* arrived and began to board on the other side. With increasing attention from close-range machine guns, Dean decided to modify the arrangements and ordered the few remaining men in the cutter to pull around to the ML's bows and tie the boat's bows to the ML's stem. With this done, Dean went astern, towing the cutter. They had just about reached the end of the curving piers that guarded the entrance to the canal when an unwelcome flare suddenly bathed the entire area in a hard bright light.

When Bonham Carter ordered his men into the boats, the *Intrepid* had two cutters and a skiff remaining seaworthy. One cutter was filled with the

The site of the entrance to the canal where the blockships were sunk. The eastern bank remains the same, and the vessel leaving the canal is at approximately the same position as the western bank in 1918.

engine- and boiler-room staff under the command of Engineer Sub Lieutenant Edgar Meikle. After pulling clear of the canal entrance, Meikle's cutter was spotted by Littleton's *ML526*. The *Intrepid*'s men were taken onboard and all the way back to Dover. The other cutter likewise pulled clear of the canal, crossed the entire harbour without injury and, once beyond the lighthouse extension, had the luck to be seen by the destroyer HMS *Whirlwind*. All were taken onboard.

With the departure of the two cutters, Bonham Carter was left with two officers and twenty ratings. Sixteen of the men were crammed into the skiff and paddled off around the stern of the *Iphigenia* where they were confronted by the sight of Dean's *ML282* being boarded by men from the *Iphigenia*'s cutter. Before long they were all sitting on the deck of the ML as the boat slowly backed out of the canal towing the cutter and bearing an astonishing load of ninety-four men.

Having sent the skiff away, Bonham Carter was left with his first lieutenant, Lieutenant Alan Cory-Wright, his navigator, Sub Lieutenant Dudley Babb, and four petty officers. All that was available to them as a means of escape was a small Carly raft – a wide metal tube bent into an oval shape and covered with packing and canvas, the decking was simply a wooden lattice. The seven men jumped into the raft and paddled around the bows of the *Iphigenia* unaware, thanks to the great clouds of smoke, that *ML282* was just about to leave the canal entrance ahead of them.

It was possibly the wash created by *ML282* as she backed out of the canal that caused what happened next. The Carly raft had a Holmes light onboard, a calcium carbide-based flare that operated when brought into contact with water. By one means or another, water sprayed onto the light's calcium phosphide, causing it to ignite. This, in turn, lit the acetylene gas being given off by the calcium carbide. From being hidden in the drifting smoke, the Carly raft and its occupants were instantly given away by the unquenchable, dazzling light in their midst. The response of the machine guns lining the canal banks was immediate and Bonham Carter and his companions had no other choice than to jump overboard to try and avoid the hail of machine-gun bullets that fell around them.

The Germans, however, were not the only ones to have spotted the light. Lieutenant Dean had just set the cutter adrift from his bows and was about to make a high-speed dash out of the harbour. When the flare burst into light, the occupants of the raft could be seen taking to the water. Dean promptly headed back into the canal and, within a very few moments, had plucked a further six men out of the water. Believing this to be the total number needing rescue, he began, once again, to back out of the canal. As he did so, one of the ML's deckhands spotted someone hanging on to a rope that had been left trailing over the bows. Having been assured that there were a lot of Germans in the area – and not all of them friendly – the deckhand picked up a boathook and was about to fend off the intruder when a bellow from the water introduced him to Bonham Carter – most definitely a cricket-playing Englishman. The deckhand clambered over the many men hanging onto the upper-deck fittings and told Dean that there was another man in the water. The ML was immediately slowed down and Dean looked over the side – there was no one there. Then someone spotted Bonham Carter swimming towards the shore. Yet again, Dean took *ML282* back into the canal, hauled the *Intrepid's* captain out of the water and, once again, reversed out of the canal.

This time, convinced that there was no one left to rescue, Dean spun the craft around so that her bows were heading directly towards the harbour entrance. At that moment, just as he was about to ask for maximum revolutions, his quartermaster informed him that the steering gear had jammed. Dean was faced with a crucial decision. He could manoeuvre the boat by alternately using the port and starboard engines, but this could not be done at high speed and a slow passage across the harbour would make him an easy target for the heavier guns on the mole and the extension. Instead, he decided to use the engines to steer the boat on a course close to, and parallel with, the mole itself. Although he would come within easy range of every machine gun and pom-pom on the mole and on the destroyers alongside, he would be so close that the heavier guns could not be depressed far enough to be used against him.

ML282 had not gone far on her precarious route towards the harbour exit when she came under fire from the mole. An early casualty was the quartermaster, relaying Dean's orders to the engine room via the telegraph. He was killed outright, his place being taken by the *Iphigenia's* quartermaster, Leading Seaman Potter. Dean's first lieutenant, Lieutenant James Keith Wright was badly wounded, as was Sub Lieutenant Maurice Lloyd. Keith Wright had begun the war as an experienced Chief Petty Officer with the Royal Naval Volunteer Reserve. At that time he was well-known for training teams for the annual Field Gun competition. Under his direction, one team had even reached the final against the favourites, HMS *Excellent*. He was standing at the bows of the ML, helping to guide Dean with his steering when he was hit. Lloyd had volunteered when the original captain of the *Iphigenia* was struck down by influenza and replaced by Billyard-Leake. As the *Iphigenia* was abandoned Lloyd, who had been awarded a Distinguished Service Cross as a midshipman at the Gallipoli landings, grabbed the ship's white ensign and wrapped it around his waist. Now, as the ML zigzagged off the mole, the ensign was soaking up 20-year-old Lloyd's blood. The situation was not improved when a bullet hit a smoke canister. The smoke poured out across the boat, gassing everyone who breathed it in.

Eventually, despite the best efforts of the Germans to stop his ML, Dean brought the boat around the lighthouse and out into the North Sea. He had not gone far when, to a loud cheer from both vessels, a destroyer bore down on the heavily overloaded motor launch. It was not just any destroyer, but the *Warwick*, flying the flag of Vice Admiral Keyes. After all that had happened, Dean and his many passengers very nearly met an abrupt end as the destroyer approached. The Torpedo Control Officer, Sub Lieutenant John Cowie, seeing a strange shape loom out of the darkness assumed the newcomer to be a German destroyer. With the torpedo tubes already loaded, he had the tubes swung out and was about to give the order to fire when, just in time, he heard the sound of cheering.

As *ML282* came alongside, Keyes used a megaphone to ask Dean how many people he had onboard. Dean replied, 'About seventy, Sir.' In fact, 101 men were taken off the boat. Both the blockship captains made their way to the destroyer's bridge to report to Keyes. He, in turn, noted the difference in appearance between the two officers. Billyard-Leake 'might have stepped straight out of a military tailor's shop, equipped for the trenches, leather coat, shrapnel helmet all complete, very erect and absolutely unperturbed'. Bonham Carter, on the other hand, was bareheaded, wet through, soaked in oil, and wearing 'a dirty wet vest and trousers'. But it was not appearances that counted. Both officers could report that their ships were across the canal's dredged channel with their bottoms blown out. They then retired to the wardroom where, over several stiff drinks, Bonham Carter got into a ferocious debate with an engineering officer over whether or not he should have fired the *Intrepid*'s explosive charges with the engineers still in the engine and boiler rooms.

Keyes went below to meet the wounded. The surgeon informed him that Wright and Lloyd were both severely injured and unlikely to survive. When he spoke to Keith Wright, the lieutenant told him that despite his wounds, he 'would not have missed it for anything'. Lloyd, on the other hand, appeared to be reconciled to his impending death but was, nevertheless, 'perfectly happy'. He was also 'fearfully proud' of bringing away the *Iphigenia*'s ensign. Keyes acknowledged Lloyd's gallantry by telling him that he could keep the blood-soaked emblem of his courage.

For Dean, once rid of his charges, there was nothing more to do but fix his steering gear and head off for Dover, happy in the knowledge that he had played a vital part in the saving of so many men's lives.

It was not, however, the end of the action.

Two destroyers, the *North Star* and the *Phoebe* (designated 'Unit L' by the planners) were ordered to patrol an area close to the lighthouse. Their role was to tackle any enemy destroyers leaving the harbour to attack the diversion ships, to lay down smokescreens where required, and to keep the heads of the German gunners down. They would probably be joined for part of the action by Keyes' flagship, HMS *Warwick*, as the area by the lighthouse was the best position from which the admiral could control events. As the *Vindictive* and the two Mersey ferries headed for the outer mole, the three destroyers were swallowed up by the massive smokescreens laid down by the small craft buzzing around the lighthouse extension.

Lieutenant Commander Kenneth Helyar, captain of the *North Star*, soon lost sight of his accompanying destroyers, but kept on steadily with the course he believed to be the right one. Sure enough, a gap in the screen revealed two destroyers ahead, and a relieved Helyar tucked himself in behind them. Surprisingly, however, the two other ships seemed to be continuing much farther to the east than he expected. The surprise was considerably increased when the sternmost of the two ships flashed a discreet signal at him saying 'Who are you?' He then very quickly discovered he was following two destroyers of 'Unit R' – HMS *Melpomene* and HMS *Morris* – whose job was to patrol the eastern approaches to the harbour. Having apparently abandoned his 'chummy' destroyer right under the eye of the flagship, Helyar was extremely keen to set matters right: he swung the ship around and set a course that would take him back to the lighthouse area. Unfortunately, not only was he much further east than he believed but his turning circle brought him close to the coast. Unaware of his precarious position, Helyar cautiously headed towards the bright lights and diffused glow immediately beyond his bows. Suddenly a searchlight was switched on and caught the *North Star* in its beam. Then, in the light reflected on the water, the track of a torpedo could be seen heading towards the ship. It missed and Helyar fired one back in the general direction it had come from before turning out to sea.

Once clear of the searchlight, Helyar turned back, still trying to find a recognisable landmark from which he could navigate back to his proper station. To his surprise, the sight that greeted him consisted of houses lining the beach. Hauling off, Helyar decided to run alongside the coast as a means of getting back to the lighthouse area. He also gave his gunners orders to open fire with machine guns and pom-poms at any tempting target. The destroyer had not gone far when the funnels of a cruiser were silhouetted ahead – it was the stranded *Thetis*. By now it was obvious to all that the *North Star* was well inside the curve of the mole and heading in the general direction of the viaduct. Helyar had the wheel put hard to port. As the ship swung to starboard, she came, once again, under the glare of a searchlight, and every enemy gun that could be brought to bear, opened fire. The *North Star* dashed for the lighthouse with all guns firing and with torpedoes launched one after the other in the general direction of the mole. All the weapons were under the direction of Gunner (Torpedo) Thomas Galletly, who set a remarkable example to his men by passing constantly and calmly between his gun and the torpedo tubes to check that all was well.

The punishment the *North Star* was taking as she raced towards the lighthouse was astonishing. Before she had reached the end of the mole her after funnel had been sent crashing down, a heavy shell crashed into her bows, the wireless room was destroyed and much of the port side riddled with bullet and shell holes. And then she came within 200 yards of the mole and extension guns.

Helyar had more to consider than just the enemy's guns. The barge-boom, although shortened by the collision with the *Thetis*, was still a dangerous barrier that could bring a destroyer to a fatal halt. Peering ahead through air filled with smoke and flying splinters, Helyar guided the ship to starboard with such success that the northern end of the boom bobbed down his port side. From there it was just a short distance to the lighthouse. With the towering structure almost on her port beam and her battered bows pointing to the north, the *North Star* suffered a hammer blow amidships. High explosive shells had smashed into the engine and boiler rooms. The boilers exploded in an eruption of steam, boiling water, and hot coals. The engines noisily reduced themselves to a pile of scrap metal. The headway on the ship continued until she wallowed to a halt about 400 yards north of the lighthouse – now little more than a helpless target for the German gunners.

As more shells hit the ship in a relentless barrage, the wounded were brought up from the wrecked machinery compartments. The chief mechanician, the chief stoker and two stokers were dead, but Artificer Engineer Percy Brooker and Chief Engine Room Artificer George Carter refused to leave the engine room as they scrabbled around by the light of torches trying to get one of the auxiliary engines to work.

The crippled destroyer's exit from the harbour had not gone unnoticed. Her 'Unit L' partner, HMS *Phoebe*, had continued to patrol the lighthouse area in accordance with her instructions and, by the light of a searchlight and numerous starshells and flares, saw the battered *North Star* emerge round the lighthouse extension. Dashing to her aid, the *Phoebe's* captain, Lieutenant Commander Hubert Gore-Langton, put his ship between the *North Star* and the extension gunners before encircling her with a smokescreen. He then came alongside and edged forward until a towing wire could be passed across. As this was being done, Gore-Langton climbed down from the compass platform and ran to the quarterdeck from where he was able to have a shouted conversation with the first lieutenant of the stricken ship, 22-year-old Lieutenant Charles Paynter. From Paynter, Gore-Langton learned the dire condition that the *North Star* was in.

With the towing wire secured, the *Phoebe* began to pull ahead but a gust of wind not only blew away the smokescreen but also pushed against the *North Star's* battered bows. The wire snapped. Yet again, Gore-Langton brought his ship around to lay a smokescreen before returning to the *North Star's* bows, but even the wind's efforts to break it up were rendered pointless when an exploding shell sent splinters singing through the night air. One splinter cut the lanyard holding the *Phoebe's* steam siren valve down. A continuous high-pitched shriek immediately informed the enemy exactly where the ships were. Once again, a towing wire was passed but it parted immediately on coming under load.

Gore-Langton then decided to try something different. He came alongside the *North Star* and passed wires across with the intention of taking the other ship side-by-side out of the danger zone before attempting another stern tow. A new development, however, put paid to the idea. The German shore batteries had begun to join in the attack on the two ships and a heavy shell from one of these guns tore between the ships, sheering the side rails and severing the wires. It then exploded against the *North Star's* capstan, killing Lieutenant Paynter.

Although the situation was deteriorating fast, Gore-Langton persevered and came alongside once more. Again wires were passed over and secured but just as the *Phoebe* was ready to steam slowly ahead, another barrage of shells hit the *North Star*. This time the damage seemed fatal as the ship rapidly took on a pronounced list to starboard. Gore-Langton had no choice but to release the wires holding the ships together. He then shouted across to Helyar with the suggestion – put as gently as the circumstances permitted – that he should consider abandoning ship. The *North Star's* captain reluctantly agreed, his decision supported, in part, by the fact that the *Phoebe* was continuing to put herself in danger and, whilst it was difficult to lose his own ship, to contribute to the loss of another was unthinkable. He ordered the surviving ship's boats to be lowered as Gore-Langton ordered his ship's whaler away to assist. Five men from the *North Star* took to the ship's dinghy only to have it capsize when a shell fell close by. They survived to spend the rest of the war as guests of the Germans.

Gore-Langton closed with the *North Star* one more time, encouraging the men from the ailing ship to jump across. The last to leave was Helyar himself, although, just as he crossed, a figure appeared on the upper deck. The men on the *Phoebe* shouted and waved at him to jump. He began his run towards the ship's side when a shell landed beside him. He was never seen again.

The *Phoebe* hauled clear of the *North Star* until she was broadside on and within striking range of her torpedoes. Gore-Langton, with the support of Helyar, decided to sink the ship rather than risk her falling into the hands of the Germans. Just as he was about to give the order a large number of heavy shells fell around both ships. The *Phoebe* emerged unscathed from the huge fountains of water thrown up by the shells, but of the *North Star*, there was no sign – the Germans had done Gore-Langton's work for him. The *North Star* had been sunk at 0200hrs, less than two hours after the *Vindictive* had arrived alongside the mole. With nothing more left to be done, the *Phoebe* turned her bows towards Dover, and headed for home.

11

Preparations for the Second Ostend Raid

Once clear of the mole and the surrounding enemy minefields, every vessel returning from the raid piled on maximum revolutions in an effort to reach Dover as early as possible. For some, such as the motor launches and coastal motor boats, there was little difficulty as they skimmed across the grey waters. For others, especially the *Iris*, it was not so straightforward. The *Daffodil* had been taken in tow by the destroyer *Trident* but although several attempts were made to secure a tow to the *Iris*, her flooded compartments rendered her so sluggish that the tow-lines continually parted and she was forced to make her way back entirely under her own steam.

The original plan of withdrawal called for a muster of all the vessels at a rendezvous point known as the Thornton Ridge, some 19 miles north of Ostend. This had been a defensive plan based on mutual protection should a pursuit by German warships take place. Not a single enemy ship, however, came after them. Keyes, with the *Vindictive* already on her way, and bearing in mind the number of wounded that were onboard some of the remaining ships, ordered a dash for Dover. As a rearguard he left Captain Boyle in HMS *Attentive* along with the monitors, just in case the Germans decided to show up.

Just before arrival at Dover, Keyes, still flying his huge flag in the *Warwick*, passed the *Vindictive* and signalled 'Operation successful. Well done, *Vindictive*.' The destroyer's company manned the upper deck and cheered wildly, the cheering being echoed by the men in the battered cruiser. Above them the early morning light held a strange glow from the flames and sparks still pouring from the *Vindictive*'s funnels.

On arrival at the port, the *Warwick* went alongside the hospital yacht *Liberty* to pass over the wounded as Keyes sent a signal to the Admiralty:

Some of the *Vindictive*'s officers after the Zeebrugge raid. From the left: Surgeon Payne, Surgeon W. Clegg, Commander E.S. Osborne, Captain A.F. Carpenter, Staff Surgeon G. McCutcheon, Assistant Paymaster E.G. Young, Gunner J.H. Colby.

A group of seamen and stokers stand amidst the wreckage of the *Vindictive*'s upper deck. The seaman on the right is holding a cutlass.

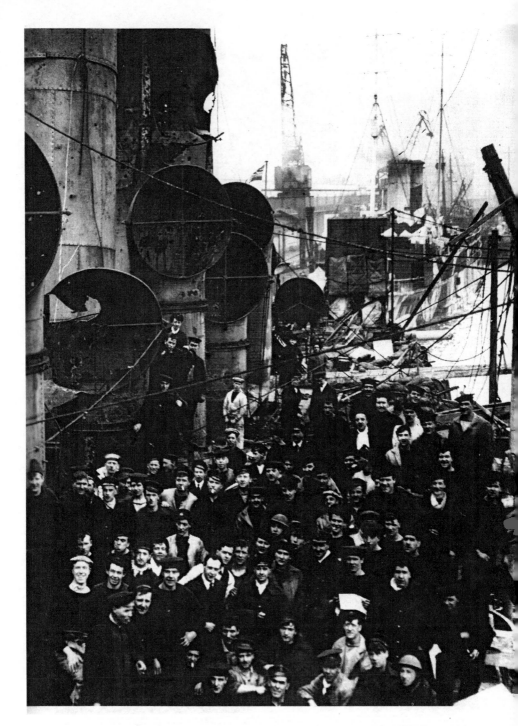

A large group of seamen and stokers stand on the wrecked false deck on the port side of the *Vindictive*. The square structure to the rear is the stern-most flame-thrower cabin.

A group of seamen pose light heartedly around an Mk I 7.5in howitzer on the forecastle of the *Vindictive*. To the left, two bowler-hatted press photographers can be seen hurrying to take their photographs. The howitzer was eventually presented to the Imperial War Museum along with Stoke's mortars, portable flame-throwers, a rum measure, an alarm gong and a chunk of the mole masonry.

Operation carried out at Zeebrugge in accordance with plan, except that aerial attack was not possible owing to mist and rain. The *Vindictive, Iris* and *Daffodil* remained alongside Mole about an hour. Casualties believed to be about 400. The three ships were successfully withdrawn and are returning. *Thetis* grounded to the eastward of the canal entrance. Captains of *Iphigenia* and *Intrepid* consider that their vessels were sunk in correct positions. Seven officers and 87 men (of whom one officer and 17 men are wounded) of these two ships were brought away by a motor launch. One officer and 60 men not accounted for. No news of *Thetis* crew yet. All destroyers and most of the small craft are believed to be returning. *C1* did not reach destination and is returning. *C3* was blown up apparently in the correct position. Visibility very low. Search is being made for stragglers. Further report follows.

A small group of seamen stand between the bullet-riddled funnels of the *Vindictive*.

The port side of the *Vindictive* on her return. The damaged brows can be seen hanging from the false deck. One of the failed parapet anchors can be seen suspended near to the bows of the cruiser, whilst large fenders used to protect the ship from a collision with the mole are still in position.

The starboard side of the *Vindictive* after the raid. The foretop where Sergeant Finch continued to fire his Lewis gun can be seen rising from behind the conning tower; both are still draped in their splinter mats.

A graphic view of the damage done to the *Vindictive*'s superstructure. The central funnel was the least damaged – seemingly protected by a 'lucky' horseshoe presented by Keyes and secured to it before the raid.

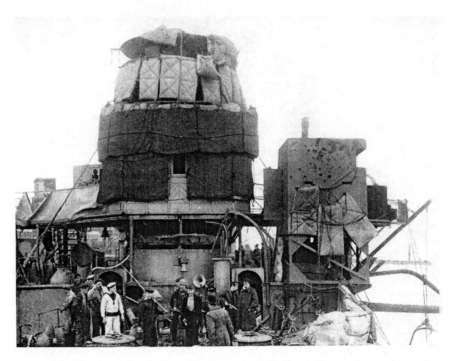

The conning tower with the foretop to its rear seen from the *Vindictive*'s forecastle. To the right can be seen the forward flame-thrower cabin used by Captain Carpenter to bring the cruiser alongside the mole. To the bottom right a parapet anchor can be seen hanging.

With the signal dispatched, Keyes watched as, at 0800hrs, the *Vindictive* came alongside the Admiralty pier. As he did so, Commander de Berry, one of the Dover Patrol's transport officers, approached him and asked what had been going on? When told, de Berry went pale with the shock. His son, Lieutenant Hubert de Berry, was in command of No. 7 Platoon of the 4th Battalion. His responsibility had been to put in place the scaling ladders needed by the Royal Marines to get from the parapet to the floor of the mole. His father had every reason to be concerned. A long hospital train was waiting for the cruiser to be berthed and ambulances queued up along the jetty. Royal Army Medical Corps teams were everywhere, overseeing the discharge of the wounded. A line of lorries waited quietly to take the dead to the mortuary. The ship itself was an absolute shambles with the upperworks riddled with shell and bullet holes and wrecked brows crumpled and drooping along the port side. Engineer Lieutenant Commander Bury recorded a brief glimpse of conditions onboard:

We had no room to separate out the dead from amongst the living, so thickly were they packed. At daybreak the upper deck was a dreadful sight, truncated remains, sandbags, blackened corpses, represented the howitzer and Stokes' gun crews. All but one were blown to bits in the fore top, where they did good work with their pom-poms.

Although Commander de Berry's immediate shock and concern was an obvious reaction, he need not have worried – his son survived intact. Keyes, on the other

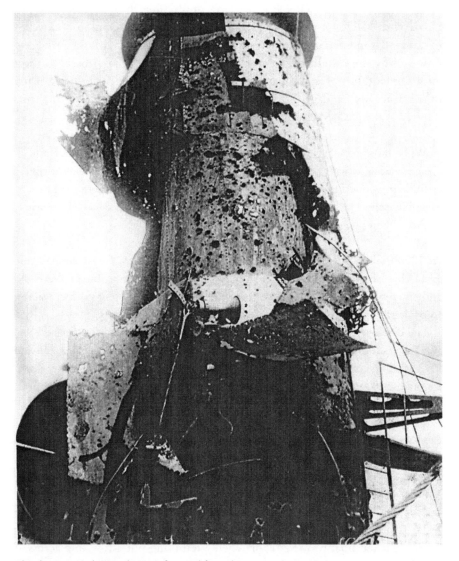

The damage to the *Vindictive's* forward funnel.

hand, was delighted by this evident proof that the security so vital to the success of the operation had held, even between a serving father and son.

Another example of the tight security was revealed when Captain Carpenter's wife was sent a telegram by a fellow officer on the grounds that she would be relieved of her natural concern on hearing of his survival. However, the telegram read – 'Operation successful. Husband quite all right' and Carpenter's wife – who know nothing of the raid – assumed that he had suffered from appendicitis.

The sombre business of removing the dead was distracted by the sudden noise of a number of MLs appearing out of the sea mist and passing round the end of the breakwater. Like schoolboys let loose at playtime, they had raced towards Dover with *ML314* – under the command of Lieutenant Gordon Maxwell – in the lead. On entering the harbour Maxwell steered towards the *Vindictive* followed by the others, their intention being to cheer the cruiser. To their astonishment, however, the large numbers of men on her upper deck, many of them heavily bandaged or with their arms in slings, broke out into cheers directed at the MLs. Maxwell noted:

> We could scarcely believe our ears, that these men, whom we felt we ought to be cheering, actually got in first with a cheer for the MLs who had helped them in their wonderful achievement. That cheer went straight home to the heart, and its echoes will sound there to my dying day … I am not ashamed to own that a lump came into my throat.

At 1225hrs Lieutenant Newbold brought the submarine *C1* into the harbour. Elated by the success of *C3*, yet disappointed not to have contributed, Newbold and his crew were ready and eager in case there remained another viaduct waiting to be destroyed.

The destroyer *Trident* returned to the port at 1300hrs towing the *Daffodil*. She was followed ninety minutes later by the last of the small craft, the *MLs 252* and *420*. *ML252*, commanded by Lieutenant Trevor Hedberg, had been laying down a smokescreen to protect the *Daffodil* when he picked up a distress signal from *ML420*, at that time close inshore off Blankenberge.

As soon as it was safe to do so, Hedberg set off to try to find his fellow ML. He came upon her close inshore just as the rising sun was casting its unwanted light across the water and burning away the protective fog. He found that Lieutenant Herbert Tracey's *ML420* had collided with something (probably a buoy) in the darkness, leaving the bows completely smashed in. Fortunately the forward bulkhead had survived and the engines remained in good working order. Consequently, rather than risk being spotted as they transferred the crew of the stricken boat to *ML252*, or when attempting put a tow-line across, it was decided to take *ML420* as quickly and carefully as possible away from the

A cartoon from the magazine *Punch* a week after the Zeebrugge raid.

coast and its menacing guns. The bulkhead continued to hold for the next hour and a half as the mist lingered long enough for them to get beyond the range of most of the enemy's guns. Having got that far, Tracey was reluctant to sink his vessel and transfer into *ML252*, and Hedberg was willing to keep his ML standing by. Then someone came up with an idea. The canvas recognition signal bearing a red, white and blue roundel secured across the top of the bridge house was removed and draped around the bows, its corners secured to the foredeck. This helped to reduce the water pressure against the bulkhead but the maximum speed permitted still remained at 'Dead slow'. They gurgled gently into Dover harbour at 1430hrs with *ML420*'s brightly coloured canvas-wrapped bows being considered as 'certainly something new in camouflage'.

Shortly after his return Carpenter, his arm in a sling as a result of his shoulder injury, took a boat across to the *Warwick* and made his report to Keyes. The captain of the *Vindictive* expressed mild irritation that having put the cruiser alongside the mole in the face of appalling close-range gunfire, the Dover Port authorities had insisted that he hand over control of the ship to a civilian pilot to bring her alongside the harbour's railway jetty. Nevertheless, in the absence of any additional confirmation, he was able to tell Keyes that the reports from the blockship captains indicated that the operation had been a success.

Keyes then went ashore to his office and telephoned the First Sea Lord. He told Admiral Wemyss as much about the action as he was able before making a most unusual request. With the sole exception of the Victoria Cross, no decoration for gallantry could be awarded posthumously. Now, however, with two of his officers on the verge of death, he was desperate to have each of them immediately awarded a Distinguished Service Cross. Wemyss agreed to make a direct approach to the king.

After breakfast with his wife, who had gone to bed in the early hours of the morning 'with a strong feeling that all was well', Keyes received a telephone call from Wemyss. The king had instantly approved the award of the DSCs to the two officers and could 'only hope that they would live to wear them'.

Eva Keyes joined her husband as he returned to the *Liberty*, clutching armfuls of red roses obtained during a purchasing raid on the Dover florists. They first called upon Sub Lieutenant Maurice Lloyd who, after rescuing the *Iphigenia*'s white ensign, was hit by machine-gun fire whilst escaping on *ML282*. Keyes told him that he now had a second DSC to go with the one he had earned on the beach at Gallipoli.

The next visit was to Lieutenant James Keith Wright, who had also been hit by machine-gun bullets as he helped Lieutenant Dean steer *ML282* along the inner curve of the mole. Both he and Lloyd were 'fearfully pleased' to hear of their award. However, Lloyd died before the day was out. Keith Wright's health, on

The two Mersey ferries after their return from the raid. To the left, the *Daffodil* seems to have sustained damage to her bows after holding the *Vindictive* alongside the Zeebrugge mole.

the other hand, 'improved from that moment' and he survived despite his terrible injuries.

Having distributed red roses to the other wounded on the hospital yacht, Keyes and his wife visited the hospital train. There they found Lieutenant Commander Harrington Edwards still depressed at failing to get into the action on the mole due to his injuries. He cheered up, however, when he heard that the blockships had done their job and that two of them were actually sitting on the bottom inside the canal.

The roses that remained were handed out on the train. As they were distributed, Keyes noted that several of the men were clutching pieces of concrete taken as souvenirs from the mole. A particularly large piece had been knocked onto the *Vindictive* by a shell fired from one of the shore batteries. Carpenter was particularly pleased with this as it would be used to counter any German suggestion that the ship had not been alongside the mole. It eventually ended up in the collection of the Imperial War Museum.

Shortly afterwards, Keyes received a telegram giving him a souvenir of his own. The king, in addition to granting the award of a DSC each for Lloyd and Keith Wright, had authorised the expedition leader to be appointed a Knight Commander of the Order of the Bath. A visit to Buckingham Palace was all it would take for him to become Vice Admiral Sir Roger John Brownlow Keyes KCB CMG DSO. In addition, Keyes obtained a confirmation in the rank of

The upper deck of the *Iris*. The damage to the port side of the bridge and below can clearly be seen.

captain for Carpenter and a promise that Commander Sneyd (who had been senior to Carpenter as a commander) would be promoted to captain when the honours list was published – and have his promotion back-dated to 23 April.

At 1455hrs that afternoon the battered *Iris* limped into Dover, escorted by a host of smaller vessels clustered protectively around her. In the main saloon Surgeon Lieutenant Pocock still struggled to save lives as the dead lay in rows on the after deck. A burnt and blood-stained Lieutenant Oscar Henderson brought the ferry into the harbour and once again the medical teams found themselves separating the dead from the wounded.

Many of the officers were given beds in Keyes' home. Lieutenant Billyard-Leake was due to go on leave the following day and refused to have his leg injury attended to. He told Keyes' wife that the house at which he was spending his leave had been taken over as a hospital and he would be looked after there. In fact, a piece of his trousers had been forced into his leg by the shrapnel and the wound was much more serious than he, or anyone else, suspected. He ended up spending a considerable time in a hospital bed. Lieutenant Harold Campbell, the captain of the *Daffodil*, chose to ignore his eye wound but told his hostess that he would visit an eye specialist the following day. When he did so, he was placed in a darkened room for three weeks to save the sight in the eye.

At dinner that night, Keyes read out a telegram he had received from the king. It read:

> Most heartily congratulate you and the forces under your command who carried out last night's operation with such success. The splendid gallantry displayed by all under exceptionally hazardous circumstances fills me with pride and admiration.

The return of the *Iris* was just one of the many things that required Keyes' attention but there was one above all others. After personally thanking the Royal Marines as they boarded the train to Deal, he tried to concentrate his mind on the problem of Ostend. He had spoken to Commodore Lynes, who had told him of the failure caused by the German removal of the vital Stroom Bank buoy. Unwilling to draw a line under the event whilst a canal passage remained available to the North Sea, Keyes was keen to have another go. In this he was overwhelmed with support from those who had taken part in the Ostend raid. Commodore Lynes supported the idea and both the blockship captains, Commander Alfred Godsal and Lieutenant Commander Henry Hardy, were eager to mount another attack. Godsal's first lieutenant, the bulky, bearded Lieutenant Victor Crutchley, was also desperate to be involved. Already there were suggestions that the *Vindictive* should be used as a blockship for another attempt at Ostend.

The following morning, after an inspection had shown that the *Vindictive* could be prepared for a Channel crossing in a very short time, Keyes telephoned the First Sea Lord and told him that, subject to Wemyss' approval, he intended to use the cruiser as a blockship in another attack against Ostend. Wemyss gave his immediate support and Godsal was appointed captain with Hardy as his first lieutenant. Crutchley was also selected but the final seaman officer who had taken part in the Ostend raid under Godsal, a very young Sub Lieutenant Angus MacLachlan, was ordered to be replaced by another officer due to his age. The maximum number of ratings that would be allowed was thirty-nine, the foremost of whom was Petty Officer Joseph Reed, who had greatly impressed Godsal on the first attempt. It had been expected that the *Brilliant's* engine- and boiler-room staff would take over the same spaces in the *Vindictive*, but Engineering Lieutenant Commander William Bury badgered Keyes with demands that he be allowed to remain in the cruiser, if only on the grounds that the engines in the ship were very difficult to control (which Keyes believed to be 'sheer nonsense'). Bury was given permission to take part, along with four of his engine-room artificers.

To operate at the damaged bridge compass and other navigation instruments in the *Vindictive*, Keyes needed a navigation specialist. He chose Lieutenant Sir John Alleyne, the 4th Baronet of Four Hills in the Island of Barbados, DSC, the son of the designer of the roof of Paddington Station and manufacturer of the curving steel beams used in its construction. Although short in stature, Alleyne had more than his share of courage, and had been awarded his DSC for his services in the monitor HMS *Lord Clive* off the Flanders coast. When he learned that the *Vindictive* was to be used for another raid on Ostend, he pleaded to be allowed to take part, putting forward his special knowledge of the shoals and sandbanks off Dunkirk and Ostend as a reason he should be chosen. Keyes, easily persuaded by buoyant enthusiasm, granted him permission and appointed him in place of the disappointed Sub Lieutenant MacLachlan.

Major General Sir Bernard Hickie had just taken over as the garrison commander at Dover and introduced himself to Keyes, mainly for the chance to offer his congratulations. Keyes took the opportunity to explain that there was to be a second attack using the *Vindictive* but that he was hampered by the shortage of manpower to prepare the cruiser as a blockship. The general immediately (as Keyes had hoped) offered to lend the men under his command in any way that they could help. Soon hundreds of soldiers were toiling on the wharfside filling the ship with sand, cement and rubble as explosive charges were fitted to blow out the bottom when she arrived at her destination. Finally the ship was stripped of everything that might be of use to the enemy, the fittings and furniture being given away to the dockyard stores and offices ashore with a view to accumulating a large number of favours that could come in useful in the future. As this was being done, Godsal and Bury were visiting the destroyers and monitors in the harbour, selecting stokers and seamen from the large number of volunteers who had come forward.

In the meantime, the messages continued to pour in to Keyes. Admiral Beatty sent congratulations from the Grand Fleet – 'Well done, Roger. We anxiously await news, and were with you in spirit.' His old submarine command told him that, 'We are proud that our Commodore should have delivered the goods,' and his time at Gallipoli was recalled when his then commander-in-chief, Admiral de Robeck, signalled congratulations 'from your old comrades on the Staff and myself'. Even the army joined in with messages from all along the Western Front, including one from Field Marshal Sir Douglas Haig:

> On behalf of the Army in France, please accept for yourself and all ranks engaged, our most hearty congratulations on the success of your operation against Zeebrugge and Ostend. St George's Day was indeed a fitting date for such a daring feat of arms.

The most welcome messages, however, were from his friends throughout the Royal Navy. Their view of the events may be summed up in a letter from Rear Admiral Walter Cowan, who was serving with the Grand Fleet:

A funeral procession for the raid's dead passing through Dover.

The graves of the dead from the Zeebrugge and Ostend raids in St James' cemetery, Dover.

Dear Roger,

You've written a very glorious page for us, and straight back to the old splendid Nelson sort of days. I'd gladly have finished my life to have spent that day with you, and shall ever be the bit sadder that I'd no part in it. It's done more for the honour and reputation of the Navy than anything else in this war, and seldom has a Knighthood been so well won. God bless you.

Yours ever,

Walter C.

Also, by now, aerial reconnaissance photographs were beginning to arrive, clearly showing the blockships in the canal and the destruction of the viaduct. Most important of all, however, were the images of destroyers, torpedo boats and submarines trapped at Bruges looking 'like salmon in a pool'. This information caused Keyes to urge Brigadier General Lambe of the Royal Air Force (who had previously been under his command as Commodore Lamb of the Royal Naval Air Service) to unleash his bombers in constant raids on the Bruges basin. The new RAF, however, had different ideas, and had deprived Lambe of many of the bombers that could have been used. Consequently a few raids were made but only succeeded in driving the trapped vessels to take refuge in canals surrounding Bruges. For Keyes, the major irritant caused by the recent creation of the RAF developed rapidly into a tactical disaster.

A further annoyance arrived with the large numbers of journalists and photographers who descended upon Dover. Keyes and his chief of staff, Commodore Boyle, refused to be interviewed, as did the blockship captains. Other officers were ambushed before breakfast. They told the journalists to wait until later that morning – and promptly caught the first train out of town. Permission was given, however, for the press to go onboard the *Vindictive* where Carpenter told them – in great detail – the part the ship had played in the raid. When the story appeared in print it seemed to be entirely concentrated around the cruiser at the expense of the achievements of the blockships and the submarine *C3*. This, Keyes felt, was 'boastful' and when combined with several clearly exaggerated claims, caused him considerable embarrassment.

Keyes still had, nevertheless, much to do that would take his mind off such distractions. It had been hoped that the *Vindictive* would be prepared in time for the last few days when the weather, wind and tide conditions would be right. Such hopes, however, were dashed when the weather deteriorated. This meant there would be no raid on Ostend until the next suitable period, beginning on 8 May. It also meant that the number of blockships involved could be increased.

Launched in 1891, HMS *Sappho* was a 300ft long, second-class cruiser. She had seen service in the Second Boer War and, after the outbreak of war in 1914, had been converted to a minelayer. By 1918, however, she had been reduced to a depot ship in Southampton Waters. Authorised by the Admiralty, Keyes had her brought round to Chatham to be fitted out for her new task, and gave her command to Lieutenant Commander Hardy, who summoned all his officers who had served with him in the ill-fated *Sirius*. The rest of his crew were made up of volunteers from the Dover Patrol.

Three days after his return from Zeebrugge, Keyes crossed over to France, where he met Field Marshal Haig. There, a sombre possibility that had previously been discussed at the Admiralty was underlined as a probability. German pressure, which had already caused massive retreats along the Allied front, was continuing to build up and there was every likelihood that the French would be pushed even further back. Haig was convinced that he had no choice if such a retreat took place – he would have to maintain contact with the French Army and retreat with them. This meant that Dunkirk would have to be abandoned and, with Dunkirk in enemy hands, the loss of Calais would be sure to follow. Keyes replied with a copy of a memorandum he had written to the First Sea Lord when the magnitude of the German advance became apparent. In it he had penned:

> The loss of Calais and consequent loss of the control of the Straits would be, in my opinion, nothing short of disaster … it would be as well to make absolutely certain that we would be able to maintain the British Army in France, without the control of the Straits, under the conditions which would then exist in the Channel.

A pre-war photograph showing the width of the Ostend canal entrance between the piers.

The implied threat suggesting that the British Army would be stranded in France if Dunkirk and the other ports fell may have had an impact upon Haig. In his later report on the German Spring offensive, Haig revealed that he had placed half his strength south of Arras to repel any attempt to separate the French and British armies but maintained the numbers of troops needed, along with adequate reserves, to protect the Channel ports as 'Little or no ground could be given up on this front …'

On the afternoon of Saturday 27 April the dead from the raid, whose bodies had not been claimed by their families, were laid to rest in a single long grave on a green, wooded, hillside at Dover cemetery. In all, two officers and sixty-four ratings and other ranks were interred that day as huge crowds bowed their heads in heartfelt and grateful tribute to the fallen. Flowers and wreaths arrived from many parts of England. Keyes' wife, Eva, placed a large arrangement of red and white roses in the shape of a St George's cross on the grave. Others planted the gentle blue of flowers of 'Forget-me-not'.

The following day saw a service of remembrance held at Dover parish church. The chaplain, the Reverend Francis Jackson, had served under the unfortunate Captain Halahan with the naval siege guns. He chose as the theme of his sermon a passage about Henry V from Edward Hall's *English Chronicles* of 1542, which ended with:

> King Henry caused the Te Deum with certain anthems to be sung, giving lauds and praisings to God, and not boasting nor bragging of himself, nor his human power.

Keyes approved and noted that he hoped that the sermon 'would be taken to heart by some people, who had been talking too much'.

Keyes was back in France on 9 May, the first day of the next period when, it was hoped, the tide and wind conditions would allow the second Ostend raid to take place. His reason for being in France, however, was not directly related to the intended raid. He, along with Lynes, had been invited across the Belgian border to lunch with the king and queen of that country. The royal family maintained a home at La Panne, a coastal village about 8 miles east of Dunkirk, and a mile-and-a-half inside Belgium. The king wanted to consult Keyes on some matter and Lynes was invited along as a matter of courtesy.

Over lunch the conversation was dominated by Lynes' love of birds and, with the meal over, it was decided that the party would go for a walk along the sand dunes. As they did so, the king gently pulled Keyes to one side and handed him the star of a Grand Officer of the Order of Leopold along with the thanks of his people. Keyes was honoured by the award and was expressing his gratitude when he noticed something of considerably greater importance – the breeze was blowing in from the sea.

After a dash back to Dunkirk, Keyes left Lynes to set his forces into action as he returned to Dover in the *Warwick*. He arrived at the port just as the *Vindictive* and the *Sappho* – alerted by wireless and telephone from Dunkirk – were leaving the harbour. The *Warwick* was steered alongside the *Sappho* and Keyes shouted his best wishes through a megaphone to Hardy. He then closed with the *Vindictive* and climbed onboard to talk to Godsal, Crutchley, and Alleyne. As he was doing so, he noticed the tall figure of Sub Lieutenant MacLachlan trying to hide himself away in the background. Having expressly ordered that the young officer should hand his place on the ship to Alleyne, he asked him what he was doing onboard. MacLachlan replied, 'Sir, I found my gear had been put onboard, so I thought I ought to go with it.' Once again, having accepted 'sheer nonsense' from Bury and his artificers, along with Alleyne's bursting enthusiasm, Keyes gave way and allowed MacLachlan to remain onboard.

Wishing them all good luck, Keyes landed and dined with his wife as the destroyers *Trident, Velox* and *Whirlwind* were prepared to join the *Warwick* in forming a defensive line between Zeebrugge and Ostend. Recent evidence of German destroyer and submarine activities in the area (six British ships had been sunk and two U-boats destroyed) highlighted the risk of enemy vessels falling upon the ships attacking Ostend. Keyes was determined not to get caught out.

His wife told him that she had been visited by Godsal and Crutchley, bringing with them the *Vindictive*'s bell, which they did not want to fall into German hands. She also mentioned something that had crossed Keyes' mind when he had shook hands on parting from Godsal in the cruiser. Eva Keyes had noticed in Godsal a calm acceptance of an unknown but imminent, fate; her husband had also felt that he and the commander would 'not meet again in this world'. Crutchley, on the other hand, revealed no such expectant fatalism and remained imperturbable and rock solid.

Keyes and his wife walked down to the jetty where she waved him goodbye as his giant silk flag was broken out at the masthead. With him was his staff: his old friend Captain Tomkinson (in command of the destroyers); Commander Osborne, the former gunnery officer in the *Vindictive* who had now rejoined the staff; and the Reverend Jackson, who – no doubt stirred by the words of Henry V at the memorial service – had pleaded to be taken along.

12

The Reckoning

At Dunkirk, Commodore Lynes' staff had been augmented by the addition of Lieutenant Commander Francis Sandford, who's planning and deeds had enabled his brother to destroy the Zeebrugge mole viaduct. In the second raid against Ostend he had been given responsibility for the smokescreens intended to hide the approach movements of the blockships. Along with the other members of the staff, he joined Lynes onboard the *Faulknor* just before 2200hrs on the night of 9 May. The two blockships were expected within the hour and Lynes wanted to be sure that, once the steaming crews had disembarked, the operation could get under way. He had issued a memorandum with orders that it was to be read by all who were taking part. It read:

> The luck of the wind and the shifting of the buoy – whether by chance or enemy design – foiled our last Ostend blocking enterprise. To have thus failed was the fortune of war, and need dishearten no one. None could have carried out their duties more admirably than did the Ostend forces on that occasion.

> Our new endeavour to block Ostend with *Vindictive* and *Sappho* gives us another chance to equal the splendid success of the Zeebrugge Forces, and I am confident that the spirit and the work of the Forces it is now my privilege to command, will achieve its objective this time, if it is to be done.

> I wish all hands to realize that the success of our enterprise will have a wide and important influence on the conduct of the whole war.

The blockships arrived at 2245hrs and discharged their steaming crews. In the *Vindictive*, word reached Lieutenant Alleyne that Keyes' chief of staff, Commodore Algernon Boyle, on hearing that the navigator had embarked in the *Vindictive* and, wanting him back in the *Lord Clive*, had demanded his removal at Dunkirk. On receiving the information, Alleyne ensured that no one could find him to hand over any official message.

As the cruisers rode at anchor they were passed by seven destroyers, three to guard the northern approaches to Ostend (with Keyes and the Dover destroyers close at hand), the other four to carry out the same duty to the south. They were accompanied by the motor launches, again under the command of Commander Hamilton Benn MP. He was to control his boats from *ML105*, commanded by Commander William Watson. Shortly afterwards the monitors *Prince Eugene*, *Sir John Moore*, and *M27* left Dunkirk under the command of Captain Ernest Wigram in the *Prince Eugene*. His orders were to get his ships into position but not to open fire until ordered to do so by Lynes or when the Germans opened fire on the attacking vessels. They were escorted by the coastal motor boats, commanded by Lieutenant Arthur Welman, eager to build on his experiences at Zeebrugge. In the meantime the naval siege guns, just inland from Dunkirk, began to aim their barrels at Ostend's heavy gun batteries as 214 Squadron's Handley-Page bombers were armed in readiness to attack the same area.

The blockships sailed at 2330hrs followed by the *Faulknor* flying the commodore's pennant. The sea was calm and the wind blew gently from the right quarter. It looked as if all the conditions were just right for the attack. Then a serious blow fell. Less than half an hour after departure, a boiler manhole joint in the *Sappho* blew out. The cruiser's speed was immediately and dramatically reduced. Quite clearly she could now no longer reach Ostend in time to take part in the blocking operation – timed for 0200hrs. Lynes reacted directly by ordering *Sappho* to return to Dunkirk and by informing Keyes that he intended to continue with the attack. The original plan had allowed for one blockship – and they still had one blockship.

Lynes took the *Faulknor* ahead of the *Vindictive* and laid a flashing Aga buoy 4½ miles to the north-west of the canal entrance. It had been decided that, after the problems experienced in the first Ostend raid when the Stroom Bank buoy was removed by the Germans and relaid in a different position, all other buoys would be ignored. In fact, almost as if to help, the Germans had removed all the buoys in the approaches to the port. Many, in particular Alleyne in the *Vindictive*, were expecting the buoys' removal. What neither he nor the others expected was that when light-buoys were placed in the position of the removed buoys, their glare would indicate to the Germans that the enemy was approaching. Once the brilliance of the lights penetrated the smoke they opened fire with their previously laid and ranged heavy guns. Unaware of this, and to help with the final navigation to the canal entrance, *ML105* dropped a Holmes light where the Stroom Bank buoy would have been, and a CMB marked the position of the Bell buoy with two more Holmes lights. As they did so, the *Faulknor* steamed off to join the northern destroyer screen.

The *Vindictive* reached the Aga buoy at 0137hrs and Godsal turned the ship to starboard, heading towards the Stroom Bank Holmes light down an avenue of smoke laid down by MLs and CMBs. As she approached, Lynes ordered the monitors to open fire. The German batteries replied with a heavy fall of shells on and around the light-buoys leading to the canal entrance. Star shells soared upwards accompanied by strings of flaming onions as random machine-gun and pom-pom tracers spat through the smoke.

In the middle of this barrage, Lieutenant William Bremner in *CMB22* bore down on his target. With Lieutenant Welman onboard, he had been given the job of reaching the site of previous blockships, the now grounded and abandoned *Brilliant* and *Sirius*. Once he had located them he was to fire a succession of red flares as an aid to the *Vindictive's* navigation. Such an action might also serve as a distraction to the enemy. Edging forward cautiously through heavy smoke and the suggestion of fog, Bremner heard waves breaking on his starboard side and turned away to port. As he did so he was suddenly confronted by the outline of a ship. But it was not one of the grounded blockships – it was a German torpedo boat. A searchlight beam flashed out and lit up the CMB, followed by the barking sound of a pom-pom. Bremner responded by ordering 'Full speed ahead' and the boat surged forward with all of its four Lewis guns firing – one of them manned by Welman. Almost immediately the searchlight was extinguished and the torpedo boat retreated into the smoke and left the scene in a hurry. By his action, Bremner had almost certainly deflected an attack on the *Vindictive* as she approached the coast.

Lieutenant Archibald Dayrell-Reed, who was serving in Submarine *D3* when Keyes was commodore of submarines and already held a DSO and a *Croix de Guerre*, now commanded *CMB24A*. Emerging from the smoke at high speed he found his target – the eastern pier at the canal entrance – on his starboard side. He also found himself under heavy fire from a machine gun and immediately put the helm hard over. Taking his boat to port in a tight circle, he re-emerged from the smoke and headed directly at the pier end and its machine gun, which was instantly joined by another machine gun and a pom-pom. Staying on a straight line despite the air being filled with flying bullets, he got to within 200 yards before releasing his torpedo. Wrenching his boat to starboard he saw the torpedo pass down his port side and, within a very few seconds, was relieved to see an explosion that destroyed the two machine guns. Dayrell-Reed then tore off to lay smoke floats in front of the batteries to the east of the canal.

He was followed into the canal entrance by Lieutenant Albert Poland, who had orders to attack the western pier. Poland found himself directly facing his target and raced forward undeterred by the amount of machine-gun and pom-pom fire being aimed exclusively in his direction. He got to within 700 yards before releasing his torpedo. Once again, a loud bang and a tall column of water announced the success of his attack.

The *Vindictive* in the meantime was advancing steadily toward the hoped-for mouth of the canal. The two Holmes lights dropped to mark the Bell buoy position were clearly visible but at the same time attracting a large amount of enemy gunfire. Any gaps in the smokescreen would have put the cruiser at great risk. To counter this, *ML556*, commanded by Lieutenant Rawsthorne Proctor, broke away from laying smokescreens to protect the monitors and raced across to the lights. Reaching the position before *Vindictive's* arrival, Proctor set about laying smoke floats to keep the east and west screen intact whilst, at the same time, trying to ensure that the smoke ahead of the cruiser did not build up into an impenetrable barrier. Not only was this an extremely difficult task, it was also highly dangerous, with the Germans continually laying down a pre-prepared barrage of heavy shells exactly on the position of the missing Bell buoy.

On the open bridge of the *Vindictive* the navigator, Alleyne, unable to see the canal entrance, was using dead reckoning to reach his target. This combination of speed, time, tide and compass bearing was made even more difficult by the fact that, instead of the precision instrument he normally employed, he had to rely upon his pocket watch. Nevertheless, there was no reason to expect that he would be too far from his intended destination.

At this stage the cruiser was under close escort by three CMBs, with two MLs well astern, ready to act as rescue craft. Forward of her was *CMB26B*, racing ahead to take on anyone who might be a threat to the blockship. Her captain was Lieutenant Cuthbert Bowlby, who had last been in action against the seaplane hangars on the Zeebrugge mole. As he shot out of the smoke he saw the eastern pier ahead and came under machine-gun and pom-pom fire – he had found his target. Charging directly at the guns he closed the range as much as he could before releasing his torpedo. The boat swerved violently to starboard to get out of the path of the weapon but had hardly gone a few yards when there was a huge bang on the port quarter. The CMB was lifted off the surface of the water and Bowlby and his crew were thrown into the air and badly shaken. When they had regained their feet they found that the engines had stopped and water was pouring into the boat. The torpedo had exploded by hitting an underwater obstacle or the canal bottom; or it might even have been defective. Bowlby, on the other hand, was in no position to carry out an enquiry as the pier guns returned to pour fire down upon him. His Lewis guns replied as others grabbed buckets to bail out the sinking boat. Chief Motor Mechanic Eric McCracken, despite being badly shaken by the explosion, set to work and managed to get six of the port engine cylinders to fire. That was just enough to take them back into the smoke and out of sight of the pier guns. They managed to cover about 3 miles before the engine seized up. Again a hand-held torch blinked out in the darkness. Minutes later, the destroyer HMS *Melpomene* came alongside, took them off and towed the crippled CMB back to Dunkirk.

CMB25BD, off the starboard bow of the *Vindictive,* chose a more cautious approach towards the canal entrance – with good reason. The smokescreen, which had worked so well for the approaching blockship, was now joined by a dense wall of fog against which all starshells and flares failed. Her captain, Lieutenant Russell McBean, switched on his stern lights to help guide the cruiser in. Just as he did so, a storm of heavy shells from the shore batteries fell about the area. Even a near miss from one of the guns would have swamped McBean's boat and he had no option but to weave his way out of the danger. When he looked back, to his surprise he saw the *Vindictive* steaming to the west – away from the canal and parallel to the coast. Another turn brought McBean out of the fog bank, revealing the entrance to the canal. He immediately set off in pursuit of the cruiser, firing green flares to try to attract her attention.

It was not the fall of shot that had caused Godsal to change course but Alleyne's firm conviction that, with the conditions turning out as they had, it would be better to approach the mouth of the canal by means of a wide zig-zag. This manoeuvre would increase the chance of making a coastal sighting on which they could fix their position. Godsal also had his own experience when he last tried to take a blockship into Ostend. Rather than risk another grounding as had happened with the *Brilliant,* it would be far better to confirm his approach. He would miss his planned time of arrival but the loss of a few minutes was nothing compared to the ignominy of yet another blockship stranded near the beach. He had only gone a short distance when a break in the smoke gave him a glimpse of the shoreline. It was enough to confirm that he was to the west of the canal entrance. Godsal turned the ship through 16 points (180 degrees) and headed eastwards.

When McBean saw the *Vindictive* turn and begin her return journey, he assumed that it had been as a result of his green flares and decided he could press on with his own instructions. Carrying two torpedoes, *CMB25BD* shot out of the fog and smoke and fired the port torpedo at the eastern pier. Ignoring the steams of tracer bullets fired in his direction from fore and aft, he turned the boat and raced off towards the western pier, his Lewis guns firing both ahead and astern. At about 250 yards from the pier he let loose his starboard torpedo. As he did so, a storm of machine-gun bullets fell onto the boat. The Chief Motor Mechanic was killed outright and McBean, fighting to stay conscious after being hit, slumped into a corner of the deck-house. Sub Lieutenant George Shaw abandoned his Lewis gun on the forecastle and took over from McBean, aware that he had to stay on station until the blockship entered the canal. Suddenly an almost blinding bright light flared up and with its aid Shaw saw the bows of the *Vindictive* emerge from the smoke and enter the waterway. With both his torpedoes launched, with injured men onboard, and with the blockship in view of her destination, Shaw took the bullet-riddled boat into the safety of the smoke.

In fact Godsal had missed the canal entrance for the second time. Once again he had turned through 16 points and headed towards the west. With Bowlby and his battered *CMB26B* already out of the area, and McBean busy torpedoing the canal piers, Godsal's final option was to rely on Lieutenant the Honourable Cecil Spencer in *CMB23*. He gave the 'Last Resort' signal, which sent Spencer dashing off to find the entrance.

With as much speed as he could safely muster, Spencer weaved about in the fog and smoke until, at last, he found himself at the entrance. Finding the best position he could in the short time available to him, he lowered one of Brock's fearsome million-candle-power flares over the side. With just thirty seconds to get clear before it ignited, Spencer shot off into the smoke. Suddenly, at 0220hrs, at the mouth of the canal, a brilliant bright light lit up the entire area, its core easily seen through the thick smoke and drifting fog.

With the appearance of the dazzling light to his left, Godsal ordered the ship to port in as tight a turn as could be managed. He only just made it. Barely escaping a collision with the western pier as the ship continued to turn to port, Godsal was now faced with a problem. He had to bury the bows of the ship in the silt that had accumulated alongside the western pier. With that achieved, the strong eastwards-flowing tide would swing the ship's stern round to block the channel and the explosive charges could be fired to blow the cruiser's bottom out.

As he approached the start of the narrow part of the canal, Godsal could see that the only way he could get the ship to ram the silt at the base of the western pier was to take the ship towards the eastern pier and, at a finely chosen moment, bring her sharply to starboard. This would bring her bows round to face the western pier. The Germans, however, were in no mood to make this an easy matter. Exposed on the upper bridge, Godsal, Crutchley, Alleyne and others were coming under fire from close-range machine guns firing from the piers. The captain ordered everyone into the conning tower. As he dropped down the ladder to the bridge wing, Alleyne collapsed. Trying to regain his feet he found that one of his legs refused to work. Nevertheless, aware of the air being full of machine-gun bullets, he dragged himself into the conning tower where he hauled himself into a sitting position. There, to his 'slight relief', he discovered that a bullet, after having passed through one of his uniform jacket buttons, had entered his stomach.

Godsal, in the meantime, knew that the *Vindictive* was rapidly closing with the eastern pier and the time to turn the ship was just about upon him. He stepped out of the conning tower to get a better view of the situation and had only been outside for little more than a second when he realised that the moment was already upon him. Remaining outside, he shouted the order 'Hard-a-starboard!' Just as he completed the order there was a shattering bang as a shell hit the conning tower. Godsal vanished in the explosion and everyone inside the compartment staggered and reeled from the blast. Lieutenant Crutchley gathered himself together and looking out of the observation slit shouted, 'Full astern port!' It was the right order. By the time he had shaken off the effects of the blast, the cruiser was almost on the eastern pier. It was far too late to turn her bows to starboard as she was about to bury them deep into the silt at the base of the pier. However, on grounding, with the helm to starboard and with the starboard engine going ahead, and the port engine going astern, the ship should swing slowly to starboard. With luck, she could still end up blocking the channel. In the event, it added little, if anything. The port propeller, damaged when she left the mole at Zeebrugge, had remained in its broken condition. During the preparations for her new role as a blockship there had been no time to put the *Vindictive* into a dry dock to repair it.

With the ship grounded at an angle of about 25 degrees to the eastern pier (Crutchley's own estimate of 'about three points' – almost 34 degrees – was optimistic) there was only one order left to be given – 'Abandon ship'. Because of the new circumstances this was to be more difficult and dangerous than anticipated. Under the original plan the cruiser's starboard side would have been facing out to sea and all the escape cutters were suspended from davits on that side. Now they were facing the western pier and its machine guns.

An artist's impression of the second Ostend raid with the *Vindictive* under heavy fire and with *ML254* (Lieutenant Drummond) and *ML276* (Lieutenant Bourke) in attendance to rescue the cruiser's crew.

Lieutenant Sir John Alleyne's pocket watch, which stopped at exactly the time he entered the waters between the Ostend piers. It was the only instrument available to him to help navigate the *Vindictive* to the entrance to the Ostend canal. Also shown is a jacket button that Alleyne was wearing when he was shot and wounded. The bullet hole is clearly visible. (Courtesy of Rev. Sir John Alleyne)

Acting in response to the order to abandon ship, Sub Lieutenant MacLachlan, manning the after control position with his men, informed the conning tower 'All out here'. He took his men forward and reached the engine-room casing when they were struck by a large shell. None survived.

Lieutenant Commander Bury, on receiving the abandon ship order, ordered the machinery spaces to be cleared, leaving the starboard engine running half ahead and the port engine full astern. Once his petty officers had reported that all the engine- and boiler-room staff had left, Bury climbed out of the engine room. On reaching the upper deck he was met by a terrifying sight. The ship was being repeatedly hit by shrapnel shells and pom-pom and machine-gun bullets that made 'a noise just like pneumatic caulkers'. The air was full of red and green tracer bullets with showers of sparks flying off the metal superstructure where they struck. By the light of searchlights, starshells and flares, he could see seamen and stokers lying on the deck, hiding behind the flimsy protection of steel wire torpedo netting. He also noticed something else – the ship was not slewing to starboard as he had expected. Knowing that whoever was in the conning tower would not blow the forward explosive charges until the after and main charges were detonated (thus indicating that all the engineering staff were out of the engine spaces), and fearful that any delay might lead to the severing of the electrical connections between the triggers and the explosives themselves, Bury raced aft along the upper deck. Reaching the compartment containing the 'dynamo-exploders' he cranked the handles and was rewarded by a loud bang that sent parts of the port engine spinning into the night sky, followed by a jarring crash as the ship's stern settled on the bottom. Seconds later there was another explosion and crash as the forward charges were detonated. Returning to the upper deck, Bury saw that the men were abandoning their sheltered positions and scrambling over the ship's side.

Lieutenant
Rowland Bourke.

A later photograph
of Lieutenant
Geoffrey
Drummond.

On hearing the charges explode, Petty Officer Reed abandoned his position at the ship's wheel and, ignoring the machine-gun fire, half-carried and half-dragged the semi-conscious Alleyne out of the conning tower. Rather than risk Alleyne being further wounded as he tried to descend the ship's ladder into the water, Reed laid him down and rolled him over the side. Then, returning to the conning tower, he led two wounded seamen to the boat deck with the instructions that they were to join the navigator in the water and to do what they could to get the officer and themselves to one of the expected rescue launches. They both jumped in and, as they surfaced alongside Alleyne, one of them cried out as if in surprise,

'We meet again, Sir.' Reed returned to the conning tower to help Crutchley in getting the remainder of the crew away.

The *Vindictive* had been followed into the canal entrance by two MLs. In the lead was *ML254*, commanded by Lieutenant Geoffrey Drummond, who had so badly damaged his neck in a fall when he was aged 9 that it took the manipulations of a Swedish doctor before he could get past the naval medical examination. His first lieutenant was 'one of the most glad-hearted men', Lieutenant Gordon Ross, a Canadian from Toronto who had been the first from that country to join the Royal Naval Volunteer Reserve. He had taken part in the Zeebrugge raid and had volunteered for the second attempt against Ostend. On receiving no confirmation of his request he personally cornered Commander Hamilton Benn and pressed his case to the point where Hamilton Benn simply could not refuse. Just before departure he had written a letter to his parents, signing off with, 'Well I have to get under-weigh early, so will just say "Chin Chin."'

The second motor launch was *ML276*, still under the command of Lieutenant Roland Bourke, who had distinguished himself in bringing off many of the *Brilliant*'s crew in the first attempt against Ostend. His first lieutenant was Sub Lieutenant James Petrie, who had volunteered when he heard that the boat was to be used for rescue work.

Drummond took *ML254* inbetween the piers and made for the *Vindictive*. He immediately came under heavy fire. Ross manned one of the Lewis guns and began to fire back. Suddenly a shower of bullets struck the boat and Ross shouted 'For God's sake, coxswain, keep your head.' They were to be his last words. Both he and Deckhand John Thomas were killed immediately. Drummond was hit in the thigh, the bullet breaking the bone. The coxswain, Leading Deckhand David Rees, lost part of his hand. As Drummond held on to the telegraph he was hit twice again but remained standing on his uninjured leg. Then, to add to their difficulties, a 6in shell struck the forepart of the boat and they began to take on water.

Under Drummond's direction, Rees steered the battered boat alongside the cruiser until it was bows-on to one of the ship's cutters. Instantly men began to drop from the ship's side and crossed the cutter to climb over the ML's bows. Many were hit as they clambered onboard but all were dragged onto the forecastle and then aft. The last two to board were Bury and Crutchley, the latter not before he had searched the ship for survivors and set off the remaining smoke canisters. Altogether, the ML had taken off two officers and thirty-eight ratings. Assured that no one was left onboard, Drummond went astern and began to back out of the canal. He had not gone far when, at last, he collapsed and Crutchley – by now wounded himself – took over as another of the *Vindictive*'s survivors relieved the coxswain. Bury was unable to help, a machine-gun bullet had sent him tumbling to the deck.

ML254 had almost reached the safety of the smoke when it was rocked by the wake of *ML276* racing past. Bourke had decided that he could give covering fire to the crippled boat as she limped backwards out of the harbour. He also wanted to pay a final visit to the blockship just in case anyone had been missed The Germans switched their fire to the newcomer and before she could come up alongside the cruiser the coxswain, Leading Deckhand Joseph Hamshaw, and Deckhand William Hutchinson both lay dead.

Bourke and his surviving crew shouted above the clamour but there was no reply. As he did so, two more motor launches, *ML283* commanded by Lieutenant Commander Hoare, who had seen close action during the first Ostend raid, and *ML105* under the command of Commander William Watson, and carrying the flotilla commander, Commander Hamilton Benn MP, roared into the canal and opened fire on the piers.

With no response to his shouts Bourke powered *ML276* away from the grounded cruiser and turned his bows towards the canal entrance. He had not gone far when he fancied, amidst the noise all around, that he heard cries coming from the general direction of the *Vindictive*. Once again he returned to her side and cruised up and down for the best part of ten minutes whilst the enemy machine-gunners sprayed the air and sea around him with constant streams of red and green tracer bullets. Eventually it was clear that there was no one left and he ordered his replacement coxswain to turn for the entrance. As his order was being carried out he heard yet again a cry for help. Once more he turned and this time decided to risk the firing from the western pier and take a look at the cruiser's starboard side. Under the direct glare of searchlights *ML276* passed around the stern of the blockship. There, about half-way along the ship's side, a figure could be seen hanging on to a rope, supported by two more figures. Bourke manoeuvred the launch towards them as Sub Lieutenant Petrie stepped onto the bullet-swept forecastle. At great risk to himself Petrie reached down and hauled them one after the other onto the forecastle. They turned out to be Alleyne and the two wounded ratings Petty Officer Reed had put over the side. Once they were onboard, Bourke went hard astern until he had passed the cruiser's bows, then spinning the launch to port, went full ahead and shot towards the smoke as every gun on the piers fired in their direction. A 6in shell went through the dinghy, fortunately without exploding, and the coxswain's wheel splintered into fragments in his hands as it was hit by machine-gun bullets. Seconds later none of it mattered as they disappeared into the fog and smoke. Even then, fate was unkind and kept them circling around in the fog and darkness for almost an hour and a half until they chanced upon the monitor *Prince Eugene*, which took the ML in tow and brought her back to Dunkirk despite having fifty-five bullet holes in her hull.

HMS *Warwick* in a floating dock after the second Ostend raid. The mine explosion almost removed her entire stern.

For a man like Keyes, being away from the action was 'hateful'. He was convinced that the Germans would come out with their destroyers and make a fight of it. But just as had happened at Zeebrugge, not one of the enemy had shown up. He had ordered the firing of large red recall rockets at 0230hrs in accordance with the plan, but their glow was lost in the fog. Consequently the action was still continuing and in any case no one would have broken away whilst there were still men to be rescued. Keyes ordered Commander Campbell to take the *Warwick* closer to the shore in case there were stragglers who needed help.

At 0310hrs look-outs on the bridge of the flagship reported the flickering of a feeble light. Through binoculars the light could be seen to be repeatedly sending the signal 'SOS'. The destroyer closed with the light and discovered *ML254* wallowing hull down. Some of her unwounded were using buckets and other containers in an unavailing attempt to bail her out, whilst others were tackling a fire that had broken out. Waist-deep in water and bellowing encouragement whilst taking charge of everything at the same time, was Lieutenant Crutchley.

First the wounded were put onboard the *Warwick* and were soon in the hands of the ship's surgeon and the chaplain – the same Reverend Francis Jackson who had officiated at the Remembrance Service and who had volunteered to come along. Once the launch was empty Keyes ordered his staff torpedo officer to use explosives to destroy it. He did not want it to drift into the hands of the Germans, who would undoubtedly announce that they had captured it after a great battle in which they emerged victorious.

As Keyes and Captain Tompkinson watched the torpedo party begin to fend the motor launch off, they were joined by the *Warwick*'s first lieutenant, 24-year-old Lieutenant Frederick Trumble, a cricket-playing only son of a widowed mother. Looking over the side he suddenly said, 'We had better save this' and reached down to lift a Lewis gun off the boat. As he grabbed the gun by the barrel and pulled, the gun fired and Trumble fell to the deck, shot through the forehead.

Shortly after the loss of Lieutenant Trumble at about 0400hrs, Keyes was in the charthouse talking to Crutchley. The lieutenant had just removed his blood-soaked life jacket when a very loud, bone-crunching crash shook the ship violently. As the vessel heeled over to port, Keyes remarked calmly, 'Victor, you had better put it on again.' Crutchley, despite his wound, quickly made his way to the forecastle where, in the absence of the recently departed first lieutenant, he organised the forecastle party in preparing the ship to be towed. The destroyer, according to Bury, had 'walked on a mine'.

Below decks, Keyes' gunnery officer, Commander Osborne, was in the wardroom talking to the injured Drummond, captain of the scuttled *ML254*, when the explosion happened. Water immediately flooded in, blocking off the access to the companion hatch. Osborne managed to open a manhole used for the transfer of ammunition and pulled Drummond through to safety. He left in the wake of the wardroom dog – a terrier – which found itself taking an unexpected, and protracted, swim before anyone could come to its aid.

As Keyes made his way to the upper deck he passed through a large compartment below the forecastle where most of the wounded were lying. As he passed through he heard one of the injured say, 'O my God, in the ditch after all!' This, in turn, earned the reply, 'That's what comes of shipping a parson, the Admiral ought to have known better.'

Once on the bridge, Keyes learned that the mine had struck the ship close to the stern. The engine-room bulkhead had held and had been shored up by a damage control party. The *Warwick* had come very close to sinking by the stern, and had been saved mainly by Engineer Lieutenant Commander Robin Rampling, who had promptly transferred the fuel oil from the port to the starboard side, thus trimming the vessel. Keyes ordered the destroyer *Velox* to be secured alongside. She would serve to keep the *Warwick* afloat, whilst the *Whirlwind* took the two

The *Vindictive* remaining in the entrance of the Ostend canal as 'an insult' to the enemy. The Germans rigged an anchor and cable at her stern to prevent her drifting with the tide across the channel. They also removed her funnels and the foretop to prevent their use by enemy warships as an aiming point.

ships in tow. The destroyer *Trident* was ordered to keep station to the east in case the Germans decided to put in an appearance. If that did happen, the *Velox* and the *Whirlwind* were to cast off the crippled *Warwick* and engage the enemy.

All the wounded, with the exception of Crutchley, were transferred into the *Velox*. Crutchley had volunteered to remain as the temporary first lieutenant of the *Warwick*. Keyes, although unlikely to have paid much attention to the wounded man's comment regarding 'shipping a parson', also sent the Reverend Jackson into the *Velox*. When Jackson stepped across to the supporting destroyer he turned to Keyes and with a grin said, 'Is this what you call a "quiet night"? You told me we should probably only be spectators in the offing.'

As it was, the night was not yet over. The ships had first to get clear of the coast and the enemy guns capable of firing 40,000 yards. Even with this achieved there was every expectation that German destroyers could show up. At least nine were known to have been driven into Zeebrugge after falling in with destroyers from the Dover Patrol. At 0700hrs Keyes decided to send a signal asking for help from anyone in the area. With all the signal books destroyed at the outset of the raid, the signal had to be sent in plain language. Instead of using the ship's names, Keyes used the names of their captains in the hope that, by the time the Germans found a copy of the Navy List, it would be too late. Clearly, not everyone agreed with him, for it seemed as if every ship in the Dover Patrol had raced to the rendezvous position eager to get involved if the Germans decided to come out. Keyes found himself surrounded by a 'formidable array of monitors and destroyers'. As they circled protectively around, he had the *Velox* replaced by another destroyer, sending her off to take the wounded to the hospital yacht *Liberty* where, according to Lieutenant Commander Bury, 'the doctors had a field-day cutting up uniforms, doping with chloroform, etc.'

Keyes wished he could have transferred his flag into the departing *Velox* but felt he could not leave 'my wounded *Warwick*'. Eventually the admiral and the broken ship arrived alongside the Admiralty Pier at 1630hrs to be greeted by an anxious wife and a youngest daughter who was clearly displeased that, despite a promise to attend, her father had managed to miss her birthday teaparty. He also had to deal with about forty news reporters to whom he gave the basic outline of the operation, only on the condition that they did not mention that the *Warwick* had been mined or that he had given them an interview.

Across the Channel, Lynes sent out his own version of events to his command:

The *Vindictive* has been definitely located by air reconnaissance well inside the harbour, and although her angle is not enough to entirely block the harbour, she will hamper the enemy movements. Moreover she provides a constant insult to him.

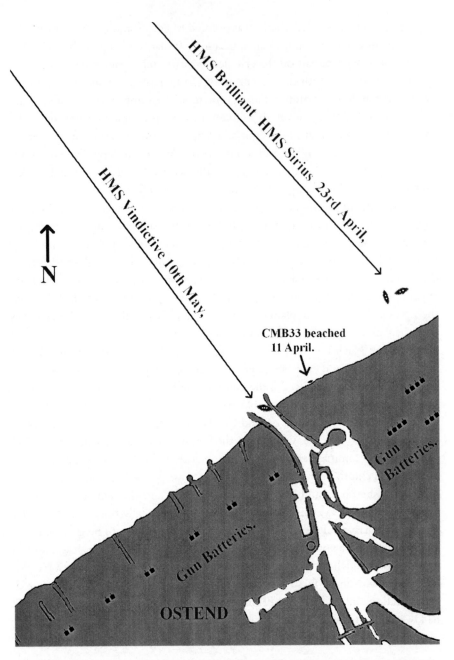

The Ostend outcomes. In early April *CMB33*, containing the plans for the raid on the 23rd, was hit by gunfire and her wreck fell into German hands. On 23 April, the two blockships, *Sirius* and *Brilliant*, misled by the altered position of a navigational buoy, ran aground and were scuttled. The following month, the *Vindictive* was sunk between the canal piers.

Just as followed the Zeebrugge raid, so the second raid on Ostend brought its own rush of congratulations. Sir Douglas Haig wrote, 'The whole Army has heard with enthusiasm the good news of your action at Ostend.' The Lord Mayor of London joined in to tell Keyes that all his citizens 'have been filled with enthusiastic admiration of the brilliant exploits of the officers and men of the Royal Navy under your command'. The War Cabinet sent, 'The country owes you, and the officers and men under your orders, its warmest thanks for the successful efforts you have made to deal with the submarine menace at its source.'

If the 'successful efforts' praised by the War Cabinet caused Keyes some embarrassment, the Admiralty released an account that caused him to be outraged.

When the *Velox* had been sent off to land the wounded, Keyes used her replacement to send a signal to Commodore Lynes – already back at Dunkirk with his force – giving him the details of Crutchley's report. Lynes replied to Keyes' Dover office where the flag-captain, Commodore Boyle, read that the *Vindictive* had entered the canal at Ostend and 'slewed about 40 degrees athwart and sunk herself'. Delighted at the news, Boyle sent the report on to the Admiralty who, in turn, issued a press release with a first paragraph that read:

> The operation designed to close the ports of Ostend and Zeebrugge was successfully completed last night, when the obsolete cruiser HMS *Vindictive* was sunk between the piers and across the entrance of Ostend Harbour.

Keyes was furious. He knew that the operation had not been a success. Ostend had not been closed. Equally as damning, the report sent by Boyle had not given the Admiralty justification for the release of such a communique.

When he heard that the Admiralty's claim had been repeated in parliament, Keyes sent a telegram to their lordships explaining that he had never claimed that the raid was a success. Not only was his telegram unacknowledged, it was also ignored. Keyes' riposte was typical. If the Admiralty was claiming that he had successfully blocked Ostend, then he ought to set about making it so.

After discussing his idea with the First Sea Lord, Keyes submitted his plan. Two vessels were to be used as blockships, the *Sappho*, which was already prepared, and the *Swiftsure*, a battleship launched in 1903 and sold to the Chilean Navy as the *Constitucion*. Her 11,800-ton displacement and heavy armour made her a good choice against the 6in guns mounted by the Germans at the harbour entrance. To lead the blockships and command the *Swiftsure*, Keyes selected Commander Andrew Browne Cunningham ('ABC') who had been the captain of HMS *Termagant* as she guarded the northern monitors during the Zeebrugge raid. The command of the *Sappho* went to Lieutenant Aubrey Newbold, the unfortunate commander of the submarine *C1*, also at Zeebrugge.

Rear Admiral V.
Crutchley VC.

The volunteer crews came from Chatham Barracks ('a wild lot' according to
Cunningham) and included many who had taken part in the earlier raids. Among
them was Petty Officer Reed who had steered the *Vindictive* into both Zeebrugge
and Ostend. The doctors, however, refused their permission for Reed to take part
on the grounds that he should not suffer a third raid despite his desperate efforts
to be involved.

The plan of attack had evolved from the experiences gained in the first two
raids. A half-mile chain of coastal motor boats would direct the blockships to
the canal entrance. The *Swiftsure* would be the first in, followed by the *Sappho*.
Cunningham would take the battleship to the western pier and bury her bows in
the silt. The cruiser would then follow and ram the battleship's starboard quarter,
driving her across the channel. Both ships would then explode their amatol
charges, blowing the bottoms out. The dredged channel would then be securely
and unquestionably blocked.

The Director of Naval Intelligence, Rear Admiral Hall, took a different view.
Six weeks after the Zeebrugge raid, the Germans were claiming that they had
managed to clear a channel past the *Intrepid* and the *Iphigenia*. If true, it could

only be used at high tides, and then only by the smallest submarines and torpedo boats. As these were the only vessels that could have gained access to the English Channel and the North Sea via the Ostend canal, there was no point in risking men and ships for no obvious purpose. Furthermore, there was no evidence that the Germans were, in fact, using the Ostend canal, but there was evidence that they had heavily mined the approaches to the port. When Hall reported his findings to the First Sea Lord, Wemyss had no option but to telephone Keyes with the news that the proposed raid was to be cancelled.

Keyes 'hated' having to abandon the raid, especially as the assembled crews 'were all terribly disappointed'. He, nevertheless, admitted being relieved of the prospect of risking 'any more of my gallant people, in an unnecessary and exceedingly dangerous undertaking'.

Again, if the German reports were true, the flow of submarines, destroyers, and torpedo boats from their base at Bruges had been reduced to an insignificant trickle. When combined with the newly completed deep minefield barrage and the endurance shown by the trawlers and drifters of the Auxiliary Patrol, the passage through the Channel was effectively blocked. Looking at all sides of the raids, the satirical magazine *Punch* noted – with its tongue firmly in its cheek – that 'Sir Eric Geddes has given unexpected support to the allegations that the German pill-boxes were made of British cement. At least he admitted that the port of Zeebrugge was positively congested with shiploads of the stuff.' The magazine then – having removed its tongue from its cheek – went on to comment about the

… incredible valour of the men who volunteered for and carried through what is perhaps the most astonishing and audacious enterprise in the annals of the Navy.

The pageantry of war has gone, but here at least is a magnificence of achievement and self-sacrifice on the epic scale which beggars description and transcends praise. The hornets' nest that has pestered us so long, if not rooted out, has been badly damaged; our sailors, dead and living, have once more proved themselves masters of the impossible.

13

The Defence Against Disenchantment

Shortly after his return from the raid on Zeebrugge, Keyes had set in motion his application to the Admiralty for the award of decorations in appreciation of the gallantry displayed during the night's events. His time as chief of staff during the Gallipoli campaign had served as a warning that the question of awards was not simply one of great courage but was subjected to the dead hand of administrative proportion and scale. Keyes had seen an example of difficulties put in the way of the army's efforts to get the great gallantry demonstrated at one of its engagements during the landings on the peninsula in April 1915 recognised by the award of six Victoria Crosses. After the landing on 'W' Beach (afterwards known as 'Lancashire Landings'), six names were put forward for the award. All were rejected by the War Office. The senior military officers then reapplied on the grounds that Rule 13 of the Victoria Cross regulations had been used to select the men. This allowed the use of a ballot in circumstances where, as the very highest level of courage had been shown by all who took part in the action, it was impossible for the senior officers to select individuals. Even then, the War Office only granted the decoration to three of the names submitted and it took another two years of pressure before the final three Victoria Crosses were awarded – the whole thus becoming the famous 'Six VCs before breakfast'.

Keyes knew he had to work fast as the 4th Battalion of the Royal Marines Light Infantry was ordered to be broken up within days of its return from Zeebrugge. He sent for Major Weller and told him that he should organise a ballot of all the Royal Marines who took part in the raid. They would then chose one officer and one man from the other ranks. Unfortunately, by the time the message reached the battalion, a mistake in transmission had reduced the number of awards to one. The ballot was held with Captain Bamford given the task of making the count. When it was completed, Bamford informed Weller that the chosen Royal Marine was Sergeant Finch, the Royal Marine Artillery gunner who had continued to fire his foretop gun until overwhelmed by his injuries. On Keyes' arrival to address the men, thanking them for the great courage they had shown, and to announce the name of the officer and man who had been chosen by the ballot, he found that only one name had been selected. After a hurried recount it was clear that the next highest number of votes had gone to a somewhat embarrassed Captain Bamford.

Keyes then telephoned the First Sea Lord to tell him what he had done. He also asked Wemyss to get the king's opinion and to allow him to do the same for the naval people involved. The king approved of the method and the same balloted choice of one officer and one rating was given to those naval officers and ratings who had taken part in the raid. Their choice descended upon Captain Carpenter (with Lieutenant Harold Campbell of the *Daffodil* second, and Lieutenant Commander Bryan Adams third), and Able Seaman Albert McKenzie – the Grand Fleet boxing champion who, despite his wounds, attacked any and every enemy with whom he could get to grips.

Keyes then resorted to Rule 7 of the Victoria Cross regulations. Under this rule, as the act of extreme valour was done 'under the eye and command of an admiral … commanding the forces' he could instigate the award 'subject to the confirmation by us' (the sovereign). His task was extremely difficult for the number of acts of sheer heroism were many. Eventually he selected Lieutenant Richard Sandford, the captain of the submarine *C3*; and Lieutenant Percy Dean, captain of *ML282* who had been foremost in the rescue of the blockships' crews. He also proposed two posthumous Victoria Crosses, one for Lieutenant Commander George Bradford, for his inspiring attempt to fix the *Iris'* grappling anchor on the top of the mole wall; and the other for Lieutenant Commander Arthur Harrison who, whilst seriously injured, led a stirring charge at the enemy guns on the lighthouse extension.

After the 10 May raid on Ostend, Keyes added three more names – Lieutenant Geoffrey Drummond, who although seriously injured had put his motor launch *ML254* alongside the *Vindictive*, rescuing her crew; and the mild-mannered, bespectacled Lieutenant Roland Bourke who, not content with playing a leading part in the rescue of the *Brilliant*'s crew on the first Ostend raid, had gone under intense fire with *ML276* to rescue Lieutenant Alleyne and two seamen from almost certain death. The final recommendation for the Victoria Cross bore the name of Lieutenant Victor Crutchley, whose leadership and example had kept the crippled *ML254* afloat after Drummond had collapsed from his injuries.

The eleven Victoria Cross recommendations were accompanied by no less than five recommendations for Companions of the Order of the Bath, three Companions of the Order of St Michael and St George, thirty-one Companions of the Distinguished Service Order, forty Distinguished Service Crosses, eighteen Conspicuous Gallantry Medals, 206 Distinguished Service Medals, and 340 Mentions in Dispatches. Furthermore, Keyes recommended instant promotions for fifty-five officers. He did not inform the Admiralty that the King of the Belgians had given him a *Croix de Guerre* with an unspecified number of others to be awarded as he thought fit. Nor did he mention that the French Chief of the Naval Staff had presented him with the insignia of a Grand Officer of the *Legion D'Honneur* and a French *Croix de Guerre* – along with another fourteen to be awarded at his discretion. To have told the Admiralty before they had agreed to the British decorations would, he felt, have seen them reducing the number and substituting the French and Belgian decorations.

Just as he had anticipated, the Admiralty was appalled. How could Keyes possibly request more decorations for three actions whose combined duration was less than four hours, than some army divisions had earned in almost four years? How could Bamford and Finch, neither of whom was even mentioned in Keyes' dispatches, be recommended for a Victoria Cross? Why should all the ratings in the submarine *C3* be awarded the Conspicuous Gallantry Medal? If a blockship captain was to be given a DSO, why should the other officers have a DSC, and why should the blockship ratings have so many DSMs? There was even a complaint that the recommendations were not written in the heroic language that had become the practice with the military. Keyes thought that the Admiralty were 'so infernally rude' that he determined to take on those responsible personally.

To draw attention to his displeasure, Keyes, a keen naval historian, resorted to a method used over a century earlier. Having fought with great distinction at the Battle of the Glorious First of June in 1794, Captain Cuthbert Collingwood was appalled when his name was not on the list of captains to receive a gold medal. It was not a question of merely adding a glittering trinket to his uniform, but the fact that the award of the medal reflected the courage of his ship's company during the fight. Almost three years later, Collingwood again distinguished himself at the Battle of Cape Saint Vincent. This time, however, his name was on the list for the award of the gold medal. When told this by Admiral Jervis, Collingwood refused to accept the medal on the grounds that he had been refused the earlier distinction. Jervis immediately contacted Lord Spencer, the First Lord of the Admiralty and, somehow, word also reached the king. Within a very short time, Collingwood received a package containing two medals along with a grovelling apology from Spencer. Keyes merely adapted Collingwood's method to his own circumstances. Whenever he received an invitation to Buckingham Palace to receive his knighthood, he was always to be found involved in something that required his personal attention.

It was not long before the king wanted to be taken over to France, and Keyes was invited to accompany him. As they talked, the king mentioned that he had heard that Keyes had 'been having trouble' over his recommendations. Keyes agreed that he had, and explained his problem which, by now, had boiled down to the removal of three names and the award of a promotion at the same time as a decoration. In his reply, the king stressed his eagerness to have Keyes finally knighted.

A few days later, on the evening before the *London Gazette* was due to be published with the list of the approved awards, Keyes received a proof copy of the publication. To his fury, he saw that another six names had been omitted. He promptly telephoned Rear Admiral 'Blinker' Hall to tell him that he was going to the Admiralty the following day, and that Hall should warn the first lord, Sir Eric Geddes, that he was going to receive a visit from a very angry Vice Admiral Dover.

The next morning, after a few opening civilities, Geddes, dressed in the uniform of an honorary vice admiral, found himself on the receiving end of a sharp reminder of what had been achieved during the raids – achievements that had come at a significant cost in lives and injuries, and only existed through the display of extraordinary courage. When Keyes had finished, Geddes sent for the officer responsible (who happened to be a friend of Keyes) and told him that the names were to be replaced. The officer replied that, regrettably, it was too late as the *Gazette* had already been published. Geddes, however, by now fired up by Keyes' enthusiasm, ordered the publication to be halted. As they waited for confirmation, the first lord suggested that Keyes give the list of omitted names to the other officer. He did so, and then, with a grin, added the three that had been earlier removed. Keyes had got his list.

Medals and decorations, however, record courage and initiative. They do not confirm the reason for the action or its outcome. The benefits of the use of blockships instead of continuing to pour shells and bombs down on the lockgates at Zeebrugge – as stoutly maintained by Vice Admiral Bacon and his supporters – was confirmed by an attack on the gates by the RAF early in June. The lockgates had been damaged by aerial bombing as far back as September 1917 but were soon back in service. The gates were designed to be withdrawn into concrete channels when open for the passage of vessels or when under attack. During the June bombing raid the southern gate was hit. Within hours the Germans had a crane alongside, lifting out the damaged gate ready to have a replacement installed. Even so, by then there was no certainty that anything but the smallest vessels were able to use the canal to enter, or withdraw from, the North Sea. Whereas Bacon had deluged the area with shells for years with just the occasional missile getting close to the target, Keyes had taken less than four months to block the canal. If Lieutenant Bonham Carter had not stuck to his instructions and taken the *Intrepid* just an extra 500 yards, he would have rammed the lockgates and the question of access to the North Sea would have been settled once and for all. Keyes was later to say 'Bonham Carter ought to have used his common sense; he is as brave as a lion but has no brain. I ought to have had Billyard-Leake in the *Intrepid*.'

If ever there had to be a great vexation in Keyes' role as vice admiral of the Dover Patrol, it had to be the creation of the RAF just a little over three weeks before the first raids. Even before the birth of the RAF on 1 April, Keyes had been ordered to hand over several of his Handley Page bomber squadrons to the army. On that date he was left with a single reconnaissance squadron, one anti-submarine squadron and three fighter squadrons. Furthermore, the Dunkirk RAF bomber squadrons, now under the command of the sympathetic Brigadier General (formerly Commodore) Lambe, had been drastically reduced by the Army's demands for bombing operations against the still advancing Germans, and by the equally strong demands of the RAF's 8th Brigade – about to be reborn as the Independent Air Force (created for strategic bombing) under the command of Major General Hugh Trenchard.

On 16 May a reconnaissance flight confirmed that twelve destroyers, eleven torpedo boats and at least seven U-boats were 'bottled up' at Bruges. It was also probable that more U-boats were tucked away inside the harbour's submarine pens (at least twelve could be sheltered under their protection). At Dunkirk, Lambe was doing his best to try and attack these targets, but the army's demands greatly weakened his efforts. It was clear that 'golden opportunities were missed of inflicting heavy losses on the enemy'. A furious Keyes sent telegrams in all directions and, when they did not work, wrote to the Admiralty on 28 May. He told their lordships that his previously excellent organisation at Dunkirk had 'been entirely disintegrated'. He wanted his bombers back:

> … without interference from the General Officer Commanding the RAF who does not seem to understand the elements of the Naval requirements on the Belgian Coast, or the great importance of its bearing on the general conduct of the War.

There were a few slight improvements but Keyes felt that the RAF's supporters 'had sections of the Press behind them, and carried more guns than the Admiralty'. Another reconnaissance flight on 15 June revealed that exactly the same number of enemy vessels were in the Bruges area, but spread out along the canals in an attempt to escape the bombing of the harbour. Just as interesting, however, was a report from an RAF flight that took place on 31 July – more than three months after the Zeebrugge raid. The airmen noted that the canal was 'still completely shut off by our sunken ships' and that the lockgates had been damaged by recent bombing. This was supported by Press reports from Amsterdam, which talked of 'German efforts to restore the passage, which remains closed'.

The first enemy wireless message intercepted by naval intelligence after the raid had warned:

Until further notice, the canal-entrance at Zeebrugge is blocked at low water and obstructed at high water. U-boats will use alternative ports.

This was confirmed less than two weeks later when two German airmen were captured after their seaplane came down in the North Sea. When mixed with other German prisoners, their conversation was covertly documented and forwarded to Keyes by Naval Intelligence. The airmen had told their countrymen that:

The blockships at Zeebrugge were sunk in the canal entrance, effectively blocking ingress and egress of even small craft. The sand is silting up, despite dredging, and the general opinion is that dredging is hopeless. It is intended to blow up the blockships.

Furthermore:

The Germans admit that the raid on Zeebrugge was completely successful, and they regarded the effective blocking of the canal as a serious mishap. There were a considerable number of submarines at Bruges at the time of the raid.

As it was, such information had already been confirmed by aerial reconnaissance photographs. These showed quite clearly that the bows and sterns of the *Iphigenia* and the *Intrepid* were in direct contact with the banks of silt that had been allowed to build up on both sides of the canal. In addition, the ships' bows were close to the eastern bank – a concrete-covered, man-made construction that sloped down towards the bows putting any dredging operation on that side out of the question. The approach towards the western bank from the direction of the lock was partially blocked by two small jetties that had been built to allow the loading of vessels with draughts too deep to go alongside the sloping bank on that side. Even if the jetties were removed (which photographs show never to have happened) to allow a channel to be dredged which would enable shallow-draught vessels to pass the stern of the blockships, the dredging itself would be no easy matter. The very fine silt that had built up alongside the banks was notoriously difficult to dredge. If a 'scoop' dredger was used, the silt simply flowed out of the scoop with the water. A chain-bucket dredger also lost most of the silt it picked up, and the hole it made immediately filled with more silt.

It was not just the *Intrepid* and the *Iphigenia* that were causing problems. Commander Sneyd had rammed the *Thetis* into a sandbank that had bordered the dredged passage at the exit to the canal. Almost immediately silt began to build up around the cruiser and when the Germans tried to sluice the silt away by opening the lockgates it merely caused more silt to pile up against the *Thetis*, significantly reducing the channel. (The lessons may have been learned by the Germans when faced by the formidable problems caused by the rapid build-up of the silt. When Zeebrugge was eventually evacuated, they towed the *Brussels* to a position near to the lighthouse and sank her in the dredged channel – knowing that the silt would soon prevent any passage.) Clearly, it would take a considerable time before a dredged channel past the blockships could be put into operation – and yet the Germans claimed that they had sent destroyers out at high tide the following day ('high tide' was frequently claimed by the Germans as a means of getting vessels out). Just two days after the raid it was claimed that a U-boat had left the canal.

Although considered a small submarine, *UB16* was 105ft long. She had been converted to a minelayer, which involved the replacement of her bow section. The modification had increased her length from her original 91ft, 6in. She had a beam of 10ft 6in and a draught of 9ft 10in (although this may have increased slightly on her conversion). For the Germans to claim to have been able to send their longest Bruges-based submarine (the length of three London buses) out of the canal, yet kept seven others – some even shorter than *UB16* – unprotected in Bruges, verges on the absurd.

If *UB16* had left via the Bruges Canal it would have been a propaganda triumph with at least one photograph being taken to record the event. There was no shortage of photographers, the Kaiser and Hindenburg had visited Zeebrugge only the previous day. There remains, however, not just a shortage of photographs – but a total absence. There were, in addition, a number of other ways that *UB16* could find her way into the North Sea.

She could have been disassembled and 'portaged' around the blockship to be reassembled on the other side. That, however, would probably have taken longer than two days. She could also have been taken along a canal to Ghent and then to the Dutch port of Terneuzen. From there it was a mere 12 miles of the River Scheldt to the North Sea. As for the problem of Dutch neutrality, it was in both Germany and the Netherlands' interest to keep the latter neutral, and neither was keen to antagonise the other. Germany was being supplied with food and raw materials by neutral ships using both the Rhine Delta and Antwerp. They knew that an assault on the Netherlands would result in the Scheldt being mined by the British. The Dutch had little time for the Belgians with rivalry between Rotterdam and Antwerp constantly on the boil, and the Belgians' refusal to turn stretches of the Meuse into canals, thus improving the transport of coal, was a major irritant for the Dutch. Both the Germans and the Dutch had tested each other's resolve. In January 1917 the Dutch arrested the German ship *Ursular Fischer* as she tried to reach Antwerp via the Scheldt, and followed this by interning two U-boats. The Germans responded by taking the Dutch mail steamer *Prinz Hendrie* into Zeebrugge. Later the same month, despite having rattled their sabres at each other, the Dutch allowed the German destroyer *V-69*, damaged by a

British cruiser, to undergo repairs at the port of Ijmuiden. It would have been a small thing to have put *UB16* onto a barge, covered her with tarpaulins, and towed her to the North Sea whilst persuading the Dutch to look the other way. It is interesting to note that on 24 April – the day after the raid – the *New York Times* headline read – 'Berlin Demands War Help From Holland'. Two days later, on the 26th, the following press report appeared in London:

> The Dutch Foreign Minister has announced that the issues with Germany in regard to the sand and gravel questions are very serious. He added that he could not make a fuller statement.

> The Washington correspondent of the United Press Association says that Washington officials believe Holland will not accept German demands for the supply of sand and gravel to Germany if the British have succeeded in bottling up Ostend and Zeebrugge. It is believed the Germans will feel forced to take drastic action against Holland to save the submarine campaign.

Sand and gravel had been allowed to pass in great quantities through Holland from Germany to Belgium, with some of the gravel being provided directly by the Dutch. The Germans claimed that the supplies were for the repair of harbours and roads, but they could equally have been used to build machine-gun bunkers, strongpoints, trench dug-outs, runways, and even submarine shelters. It was, however, clearly important enough to threaten a rupture between the two countries, both of whom had an obvious interest in keeping trade communications open. The only answer was for the Germans repeatedly to deny that Zeebrugge had been blocked. Whatever the outcome, the Dutch, with the Germans in full retreat, eventually refused to oblige and, in October and November, several destroyers were scuttled at Ghent and in the Ghent-Terneuzen Canal. At the same time the Germans were claiming that such ships had been regularly clearing the canal at Zeebrugge.

If such a route had been used to get the U-boat into the North Sea, it may have been the opening round of negotiations between the Germans and the Dutch. Neutral diplomats, including the Dutch, were told by the Germans in Brussels on 9 June:

> We must admit that Zeebrugge and Ostend will temporarily be of little use to the submarine war. Zeebrugge, in fact, is of no use at all and Ostend is very little. But there must be no mistake about this. The day that Ostend and Zeebrugge are completely blocked we shall, cost what it may, make use of the Scheldt as a submarine base. We know that the Scheldt question involves Dutch neutrality, but this would not make us shrink from our decision.

The report appeared in the *Daily Express* and the *New York Times* the following day.

Nevertheless, the best answer to the question of *UB16* appearing in the North Sea on 25 April was that she was probably never at Bruges during the time of the raid. It is known that she sank a fishing smack, *Ruth*, on 13 April. If she returned to Zeebrugge on the 23rd or 24th, it would have been a simple matter to have hidden her beneath the submarine shelter (which had survived the raid unscathed), provided her with fuel and supplies and sent her back out to sea once again trumpeting triumphantly that she had managed to squeeze past the blockships. There was, however, no trumpeting when *UB16* was sunk by the British submarine *E34* on 10 May.

Curiously, the flawed reasoning that had claimed *UB16* had escaped from Bruges only two days after the raid appeared to have been noticed by Captain Karl Schultz who, using the official German archives to write an account of the raid, amended the submarine's pennant number to *UB15* – a shorter vessel. The only problem with this change was that *UB15* had been sent to the Austro-Hungarian Navy in 1915 and served in the Adriatic during the war.

Schultz, however, did reveal one interesting fact. He confirmed that *CMB33*, which was missing after the aborted raid at Ostend on 11–12 April, had provided the Germans with a plan of the raid. Consequently, he claimed, the Germans had worked out when the attack would take place. This, however, made matters even more confusing. At Ostend, action seems to have taken place to thwart the impending raid, with the most important and effective being the removal of the Stroom Bank buoy. At Zeebrugge, on the other hand, it appeared that most of the officers were ashore enjoying a party in the early hours of the morning of the 23rd. This may have accounted for the strange lack of German aggression during the raid. No direct attack was made on the landing parties, no assaults were led against the diversionary ships, and there was no angry pursuit afterwards. Those defenders caught sheltering on the mole fled immediately the Royal Marines began to drop to the mole floor. The remainder stayed in their trenches and machine-gun positions and used their weapons to defend themselves rather than taking the fight to the enemy. This tactic failed them as a defence against the blockships but served them well in terms of casualties. The most reasonably calculated numbers of casualties sustained by the British during the combined raids is in the region of 204 killed, 412 wounded, and 13 taken prisoner. The Germans reported a combined loss of 11 killed and 24 wounded.

It is worth considering whether or not any of the German reports can be relied upon. Admiral Alfred von Tirpitz's official report on the Zeebrugge and Ostend raids, 24 April 1918, reads as follows:

During the night of April 22–23 an enterprise of the British naval forces against our Flanders bases, conceived on a large scale and planned regardless of sacrifice, was frustrated.

After a violent bombardment from the sea, small cruisers, escorted by numerous destroyers and motorboats, under cover of a thick veil of artificial fog, pushed forward near Ostend and Zeebrugge to quite near the coast, with the intention of destroying the locks and harbour works there.

According to the statements of prisoners, a detachment of four Companies of the Royal Marines was to occupy the Mole of Zeebrugge by a coup de main, in order to destroy all the structures, guns, and war material on it and the vessels lying in the harbour. Only about forty of them got on the Mole. These fell into our hands, some alive, some dead. On the narrow high wall of the Mole both parties fought with the utmost fierceness.

Of the English naval forces which participated in the attack the small cruisers *Virginia* [sic], *Intrepid*, *Sirius* and two others of similar construction, whose names are unknown, were sunk close off the coast. Moreover, three torpedo-boat destroyers and a considerable number of torpedo motor-boats were sunk by our artillery fire. Only a few men of the crews could be saved by us.

Beyond damage caused to the Mole by a torpedo hit, our harbour-works and coast batteries are quite undamaged. Of our naval forces only one torpedo-boat suffered damage of the lightest character. Our casualties are small.

So it appeared that the admiral, even if he knew the point of the distraction forces and the blocking ship, did not want to draw attention to them. The blockships are claimed as being sunk by the Germans. Only forty of the enemy got onto the mole, and they were all killed or captured (a complete fiction). Three torpedo-boat destroyers were sunk (in fact only one – the *North Star*), and a 'considerable number of motor-boats were sunk by our artillery fire' (just two MLs were lost – both were damaged by the guns on the lighthouse extension but scuttled by their own crews). According to the admiral, the viaduct was destroyed by a 'torpedo hit' rather than explosive packed into the fore-ends of the submarine *C3*.

Another report, this time by the commander of the mole guns, spoke in vivid detail of how his guns destroyed a coastal motor boat. The vessel was so completely destroyed that no fragment remained, either in German or in British records. All the CMBs in action at Zeebrugge returned to Dover.

To be fair, overstatements were not confined to the Germans. Keyes had been annoyed by the official communique issued after the second Ostend raid ('successfully completed'). Also, there were plenty of British exaggerations and fictions published, particularly in the popular press. In one version, an entire battalion of German cyclist troops pedalled to the aid of their comrades under attack on the mole, only to plunge into the gap created by the exploded *C3*. In another, two British sailors ran the whole length of the lighthouse extension and raised a Union Flag on the lighthouse. Not to be outdone, a further Union Flag was claimed to have been raised and left on the mole by the Royal Marines. Whilst these flags were being raised, according to a newspaper report, the seamen 'captured the German guns on the breakwater and turned them around, firing them on the German fortified positions'. There was even one such story that might be true. The officers of the *Vindictive* were known to have attached their visiting cards to a board with the letters 'R.P.C.' ('Request the Pleasure of your Company') painted on it. After the raid the board was never seen again and may well have been taken ashore but no one could be certain. Clearly, the difference between these stories and the German version of events is that the latter were

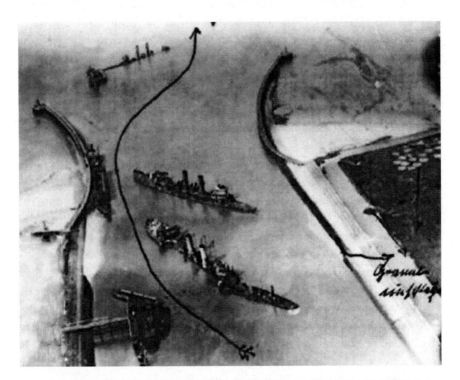

A German postcard produced shortly after the raid. The amateurish drawing of a line claims to indicate the route taken by U-boats proceeding to sea. To make this more plausible, a continuation of the sandbank alongside the western (left-hand) pier appears to have been photographically edited out. The loading jetty at the bottom left-hand corner of the photograph still remains in position. Part of it was later removed in an attempt to allow passage. The handwritten words to the right are '*Granat einschläge*' ('grenade/shell impacts'). The propaganda value of such an image would have been considerably enhanced by a photograph of a U-boat actually passing under the stern of the blockships.

official reports. At no subsequent stage was any retraction or correction ever issued by the Germans regarding any of the wholesale inaccuracies in their reports and accounts. And yet, incredibly, despite the evidence of the aerial photographs and the accounts of reliable eye-witnesses, it was the German version of events that gradually gained dominance.

At the time (with few exceptions) no one on the Allies' side doubted the success of the raids. Winston Churchill wrote – 'The raid on Zeebrugge may well rank as the finest feat of arms in the Great War, and certainly as an episode unsurpassed in the history of the Royal Navy.' The *New York Times* bore the headline – 'British Naval Raid Bottles Up U-boat Base'. The French newspaper *Le Matin* claimed that 'These attacks of the Flanders coast are the finest feat in the naval history of all times and of all countries.' The Australian press noted that 'gallant and daring in extreme as were many of our naval exploits, there is hardly one in the long record that rivals in audacity and brilliance Admiral Keyes' sensational dash on Zeebrugge and Ostend.' The Australian poet Annie R. Rentoul composed verses such as:

> Old worn-out ships,
> That venture forth for England's sake to die,
> Immortal shall ye live on England's lips,
> Named by immortal names of long gone by;
> Young hero-hearts, O young and eager feet,
> To swift to cross the hushed and misty wave,
> Your cradle and your home, old England's fleet,
> Old England's sea your grave!

In a similar vein, the anonymous 'A.L.B.' wrote:

> Hats off, gentlemen, to the *Vindictive*,
> And ladies, shout 'Hip! Hip!'
> She's gone below, but as long as we live
> We'll bless the grand old ship.
> We thought that our fleet had no peers,
> Now we know it's true. 'Three cheers!'

> Hats off, gentlemen, to the noble dead,
> And, ladies, do not cry,
> When their souls went out, straight aloft they sped,
> Oh, heroes never die.
> Honour their name, their victory,
> Thank God that such men can be.

Although not yet low tide (the *Thetis'* quarterdeck is still below water), the real extent of the sandbanks on both sides of the canal can be seen. Twice each day the tide would deposit more silt around the blockships. The barge-boom can be seen at the point where the mole ends and the lighthouse extension begins.

With the *Intrepid*'s stern to the right, the full length of the *Iphigenia* can be seen. With a low tide revealing the true situation, such a photograph could have been taken to impress upon superiors the great difficulty in obtaining a passage past the blockships.

Here footprints show along the edge of the sandbank and the *Iphigenia* is embedded in the canal bottom, exhibiting the shallow waters between the ship and the western bank. Taken at low water, the tidal rise never put the starboard upper deck of the *Iphigenia* under water. The Germans claimed to have sailed a U-boat with a length of over 100ft and a draught of over 10ft through the gap.

Judging by the condition of the *Iphigenia*, this photograph was taken some considerable time after the raid. The silting up of the entrance has either remained the same or has been increased. There is no evidence of any attempt to clear a channel. A mast for night warning signals has been raised on the quarterdeck of the *Iphigenia*.

Even a breezy song was composed by Reginald A.A. Stoneham with the refrain:

> We're steady, lads, and ready,
> From Tops to down below,
> The guns are bright, the night is right,
> We're off to find the foe.
> Our job, to block the channel,
> And keep them where they lie.
> We're off to greet, the German fleet,
> And bottle them up, or Die.

Such was the acclaim surrounding the raids that on 8 May the *New York Sun* was telling its readers that the Americans had taken part at Zeebrugge. They would, no doubt, have been welcomed by Keyes – but were, in fact, not made available.

The operations against the Flanders ports were successful on several levels. They achieved the immediate aim – blocking the passage of enemy shipping out of Zeebrugge. How long it remained blocked, or even if it was ever truly opened, remains as difficult to say today as it was in 1918. The only claims of breaching the blockage come from the Germans, but they are hollow claims without evidence from lock usage records, from photographs or from the many hundreds of Belgians drafted in as forced labour to help clear a passage. The only way that the U-boats, torpedo boats and destroyers trapped at Bruges could reach the North Sea was by the Ghent–Terneuzen Canal (needing Dutch agreement or German pressure), by the shallow and much longer Bruges–Ostend Canal (almost impracticable and certainly inconvenient) or for the smaller craft, breaking down and reassembling in Zeebrugge harbour (equally inconvenient and liable to exposure by air reconnaissance). As for Ostend, even if the *Vindictive* had left a gap that would admit vessels into the port, the existence of a Royal Navy ship permanently inside the canal entrance would, as Commodore Lynes noted, 'hamper the enemy movements' and provide 'a constant insult to him'.

The raid had shown the British and Empire soldiers that they were not alone in their fighting in Flanders and Northern France. Driven back by the spring onslaught and facing battle-hardened troops newly arrived from the Russian Front, to learn that the Royal Navy had delivered a stunning blow far behind the enemy lines gave great encouragement.

But it was on the home front, throughout the empire, and even in the United States of America, that the news received its greatest welcome. For years the much-vaunted reputation of the Royal Navy had lost its shine through its

There is clearly no passage down the eastern side of the canal exit. Although not yet low water, the vessel to the right has already grounded. The sloping wall of the canal side continues beneath the water until it meets a sandbank which is exposed at low water. When attempting to dismantle the *Iphigenia*, German workers could walk across to the blockship's bows and use a ladder to board.

apparent inactivity. The crushing defeat of the German High Seas Fleet had not happened, eastern coastal towns had been bombarded and the U-boat blockade was clearly having an effect upon food supplies. Suddenly the events at Zeebrugge and Ostend burst like a brilliant flare in the all-pervading gloom. The Royal Navy had shown that it could still take the fight to the enemy and deliver a blow that echoed round the world. The prime minister spoke for the entire nation when he described the raids as 'one of the most gallant and spectacular achievements of the War'.

Then there was the other side of the coin. When morale soars on one side, it is very likely to plummet on the other. On the very day that Keyes sailed with his ships towards Zeebrugge, the Berlin police president, Heinrich Von Oppen, noted that, thanks to the German Army advances:

The mood is one of jubilation. People are following the victorious advance on France [*sic*] and Belgian territory with the greatest and most confident expectations. The final bloody reckoning with the English is seen here as the order of the day.

The *Iphigenia* from the eastern bank with the stern of the *Intrepid* just in view on the left. This picture was taken when the tide was within inches of being at its highest (the upper deck of the *Iphigenia* – where the cut-down funnels are lying – was usually awash at high tide). The sandbanks on the western side can be clearly seen in close proximity to the sterns of the blockships. On the far right, just off the starboard stern of the *Iphigenia*, a post can be seen possibly acting as a tidal gauge to assist small craft in passing the sterns of the blockships. Visible in the distance is the gap in the mole viaduct caused by the detonation of the explosives on board submarine *C3*.

However, it was already well-known in Germany – suffering severely from food shortages – that the advancing German Army had discovered, to its consternation, that the British and Empire troops were well provisioned in both food and weapons. Supplies were getting through despite the U-boats' attempts to stem the flow. Now Zeebrugge was closed off and, when combined with the effectiveness of the mine-barrage across the straits, the numbers of U-boats attempting to pass through the English Channel had dropped almost to vanishing point – a fact reflected in German morale. The Germans had tried to counter the British achievements by producing photographs of the blockships at high tide, which hid the sandbanks and appeared to show a passage around the ships' sterns. Keyes answered this by having leaflets dropped over German areas showing the same sight at low tide.

It is possible that the Germans tried to manufacture further photographic evidence that could have been used for propaganda purposes. A photograph exists that claims to show a U-boat returning from patrol shortly after the raid. The vessel, with the blockships to its rear, appears to be just about to enter the northern lockgate during slack water around the time of high tide. The most obvious question is, why was no picture taken of the U-boat passing the blockships? Cameras were not a rare commodity; another photographer can be seen behind his tripod on the eastern bank. Clearly the 'return' is a very subdued affair. There are no officers manning the upper conning tower and no flags or ensigns are being flown. A desultory group of seamen are lined up on the eastern bank, again without any evidence of flags or handkerchiefs to greet the arriving vessel. Or are they merely waiting for the swing bridge to close in order to cross over to the western bank? Most peculiar of all, however, are the three fenders hanging from the eastern lock wall. Was this where the U-boat was tied up before being moved beyond the lockgate to be photographed? If so, the vessel would have prevented the lockgate from being closed with the result that the lock would have been put out of action – a decision that could have only come from a senior authority for a particular, defined, purpose. It would not be at all outlandish to suggest that the U-boat had been towed down the canal from Bruges, secured alongside the eastern wall of the lock whilst extra men were put onboard and final preparations made, before being moved (either by tow or under its own power) to a position just beyond the northern lockgate. The photograph was then taken before the vessel returned to the lock wall, discharged its temporary crew, and was towed back to Bruges.

Despite such widespread recognition of the results of the raids, it is astonishing to learn that, just over twenty years later, in October 1940, Viscount Maugham, a former Lord Chancellor, with no experience whatsoever of naval or military matters, could stand up in the House of Lords and, in the convoluted manner of a lawyer, address Their Lordships with the words:

A German propaganda photo purporting to show a U-boat returning from patrol after the sinking of the blockships (seen in the background). The vessel was probably towed down the canal from Bruges by the vessel from which the photograph was taken, before being returned by the same route.

The operation against Zeebrugge, as we now know, was very greatly unsuccessful; but it was not one which ought not to have been undertaken. We did not close Zeebrugge, and we completely failed to close Antwerp; at the same time, it was an operation which did the country good in all sorts of indirect ways.

The words 'very greatly unsuccessful' almost suggest a failure on an epic level. How could such a phrase be used about an event that had earned the praise of so many political, military and naval leaders? Even excusing Maugham for his error in confusing Antwerp with Ostend, it seems astonishing that such a comment should be made publicly.

The answer to such a reversal of perception lies in the usual human frailties of envy and resentment, along with an extra ingredient – Keyes himself.

Inevitably the softest target for the critics was the numbers of casualties, and much was made of the 204 British deaths compared to the Germans' 11. This, of course, overlooked the fact that, during the same period, the British Army was suffering an average daily loss of 334 soldiers killed – or 10,000 men a month. Even more pertinently, perhaps, were the losses that could be expected at sea. When the armoured cruisers *Aboukir, Hogue* and *Cressy* were sunk by the submarine *U9* in September 1914 the number of British sailors killed totalled 1,459. The German losses were nil.

Vice Admiral Bacon, still seething at being replaced by Keyes, was unstinting, but partial, in his praise. In his book, *The Dover Patrol*, he wrote:

> The operation was carried out with the greatest pluck and heroism. The handling of the *Vindictive* was beyond all praise, the plucky example of persistence and cool-headedness on the part of her captain will never die, and the successful handling of the blocking ships is a glory to the Navy ... The use of a submarine loaded with explosives to blow up the jetty connecting the mole with the shore was an admirable conception heroically carried out.

However, carefully avoiding any mention of Keyes by name, Bacon tells his readers, with an almost disdainful comment:

> At Zeebrugge, when blocked in 1918, the stern of the important blocking ship was close to a pile jetty, the removal of which and the opening up of the Channel to destroyer traffic was a most simple engineering operation.

Whatever Bacon meant by the 'important' blocking ship, he at least admits that the canal exit was blocked. He then goes on to give the German version of events leading to the creation of a passage within a day or so of the raid. Just to compound matters, Bacon then produced a diagrammatic drawing showing the *bows* of an unidentified blockship with a submarine passing ahead through a dredged channel. Even the Germans never claimed such a feat. To have done so would have required the removal of silt that came so close to the bows of the *Iphigenia* that, at low tide, the Germans could use a ladder from the surface of the silt to reach the forecastle of the ship. Even more, the bank at that point consisted of a concreted slope on top of a base of rubble, the removal of which would have been anything but a 'simple engineering operation'.

Bacon continued to condemn the landing of seamen and Royal Marine parties on the mole as a failure despite their intention to distract the enemy whilst the blockships entered the harbour having proved to be a complete success. He then goes on to denounce the blockships as 'useless', notwithstanding having earlier agreed that the canal was 'blocked'. Bearing in mind that the main objective of the operation was to block the canal, it is strange to deny the fact that the blockships not only blocked the canal but remained in situ until after the armistice.

From Bacon, the trail leads easily to admiral of the fleet, Lord Fisher, who had been bruised in a personal conflict with Keyes over the production of submarines. Fisher also resented the way matters were handled when he tried to get rid of Keyes as commodore (submarines). The first lord – Winston Churchill – simply sent Keyes out as chief of staff at the Dardanelles, a theatre of war bitterly opposed by Fisher, and one that led to his resignation as First Sea Lord. Furthermore, Fisher was notorious for his feuds with fellow officers and would not hesitate to destroy the career of anyone who disagreed with him. Keyes, however, had managed to avoid giving Fisher the satisfaction of finishing him off. When he came to write about Zeebrugge in his *Memories*, Fisher raged almost to the point of apoplexy:

> Brock was lost to us at the massacre of Zeebrugge – lost uselessly; for no such folly was ever devised by fools as such an operation as that of Zeebrugge divorced from military cooperation on land. What were the bravest of the brave massacred for? Was it glory? Is the British Navy a young Navy requiring glory? … for sailors to go on shore and attack forts, which Nelson said that no sailor but a lunatic would do, without those on shore of the military persuasion to keep what you had stormed, is not only silly, but it's murder and it's criminal.

Fisher was, of course, being disingenuous. Nelson went ashore to attack forts on more than one occasion, and Keyes had no intention of keeping hold of the mole. Oddly enough, later in the same book, Fisher describes anyone 'who never will runs risks' as an 'effete poltroon'. He, nevertheless, also revealingly complains that,

'I have not had even one single "thank you" for anything that I have done since King Edward died.'

In the end Fisher had one final shot in his locker – he was great friends with Sir Julian Corbett, who was to become the official naval historian of the war. Corbett's ideas on naval strategy had little to do with fleet engagements or tackling the enemy head-on, but concentrated on keeping sea communications open whilst blockading the enemy. He certainly would have had little time for a short, sharp action that involved blockships and men landing on a harbour wall. Despite being on friendly terms with Keyes, and possibly because of Keyes' own changing views of the raids, Corbett considered the Zeebrugge and Ostend raids as little more than a minor indicator ('prevision') of inevitable victory.

Keyes had begun to reassess the overall outcome of the raids as a result of two of his fellow officers. Bacon's surly mutterings were disregarded as blatant self-advertising. When his book *The Dover Patrol, 1915-1917*, appeared, it was soon lampooned by anonymous officers as *Admiral Sir Reginald Shakespeare's epoch-making revelations entitled 'How I won the War'*.

Admiral Jellicoe, on the other hand, was a different matter. In his book, *The Grand Fleet,* Jellicoe had written of the blocking of Zeebrugge, saying – 'The scheme was eventually approved by me in November 1917 and the training of the storming party and selection of the block ships taken in hand.' This clearly took away Admiral Wemyss' share of the event. In a letter of icy politeness, Keyes suggested that Jellicoe might like to amend the 'error' as 'I feel sure you are anxious to avoid all risk of giving rise to controversy.' Keyes then pointed out that, in his opinion, Jellicoe was taking 'the chief credit and responsibility for an operation, for which the preparation of material, and organisation and training of personnel, were taken in hand after you left the Admiralty, and the execution of which took place nearly four months after your responsibility ceased.' Jellicoe replied that he was 'not quite clear what you wish me to do' and offered a minor amendment in a footnote. Keyes, who felt that Jellicoe was being 'outrageously unfair', was forced to turn his firepower in another direction.

From the very day that Captain Carpenter returned from Zeebrugge, he had annoyed Keyes with his tendency towards self-publicity. The Admiralty, on the other hand, felt that such an attribute could be employed in explaining to the people of North America the purpose and outcome of the raids. Before leaving, Carpenter had approached Captain Cyril Fuller, the Director of the Plans Division, for his advice on what to do and say whilst in America and Canada. Fuller told Keyes that he had 'impressed on him the necessity of being careful how he worded his lectures & to make it quite clear as to what his position had been, & that the expedition had not been "his show"'. Unfortunately, judging from reports of the lectures given by Carpenter, the captain of the *Vindictive* was becoming almost the prime mover and central figure in the operation. In

Fuller's opinion, the appreciative audiences listening to Carpenter had 'turned his head a bit'.

Even worse, the British ambassador, and the commander-in-chief, North Atlantic, had taken exception to one of Carpenter's activities during his tour and demanded his return. What had caused such outrage was Carpenter's auctioning of Zeebrugge souvenirs to raise funds for a specific naval charity – the Dover Patrol Fund. The charity had been created by the mayor of Dover to provide instant funds for the dependents of naval personnel who had been killed, or to allow families to visit the injured. With the end of the war the charity was closed and the surplus funds sent to help with the education of orphaned children. Not only was Carpenter asking foreigners for money on behalf of a defunct Royal Navy charity, he was also using Keyes' name to support his plea. Agreeing with the ambassador and the commander-in-chief, Keyes told the British provost marshal in New York, Colonel Norman Thwaites – 'We in the Navy think that Captain Carpenter's proceedings in a foreign country brought contempt and discredit on our Service.'

The demand for Carpenter's return was opposed by the governor-general of Canada, the Duke of Devonshire; and the colonial secretary, Lord Milner. They argued that to cancel Carpenter's tour would result in an economic loss and, on those grounds, they won the argument. Keyes then rounded on Carpenter, telling Thwaites of

> … the fact, patent to all who took part, that owing to the *Vindictive* overshooting her assigned position by 400 yards, the assault of the Mole was an heroic failure. Fortunately, however, this did not affect the achievement of our objective, which was to sink Blockships in the Bruges Canal. I feel very strongly that a great deal too much has been made of what is known as the Zeebrugge Raid. After all, it was only akin to scores of similar unadvertised enterprises which have been carried out by the Army throughout the war, and all the advertisement, at home and abroad, undertaken no doubt for propaganda purposes, is very distasteful to me, and, I think, I can say without exaggeration – to every other officer who took part. That a Naval Officer should behave as Carpenter is doing has disgusted our Service …

To Carpenter himself, an 'incensed' Keyes wrote that the captain clearly had a 'weakness for modest self-advertisement' and that:

> the raising of money in a foreign country for a British Naval Charity by means of lectures delivered and relics auctioned by a Captain in the Royal Navy in uniform was derogatory and entirely foreign to the high traditions of the Service.

Far worse, however, Keyes used the phrase 'the failure of the assault' three times in his letter.

Keyes, of course, was referring to the attempt to distract the enemy from the blockships moving into the harbour behind them. The chief aim of this distraction had been to capture and destroy the guns on the lighthouse extension. Despite the sheer gallantry shown by Harrison, Adams, McKenzie and others, this had failed, but enough of a distraction had been created to enable the blockships to be sunk in the canal entrance – the raid's overall aim. It follows, therefore, that Keyes' definition of 'failure' was, in this instance, provoked by Carpenter's apparent desire to place himself at the centre of events.

Inevitably, once word leaked out that Keyes himself had admitted that the assault had been a failure, and when combined with the numbers of casualties involved and the various degrees of attack by Bacon, Fisher, Jellicoe and others, the sum total was a gift to the burgeoning 'Disenchantment School'. This loose grouping of academics, war poets, socialists and middle-class writers poured out an unremitting stream of literature about the war. Despite having gained the victory, all generals and staff officers were cowardly incompetents, and all the working-class soldiers were lumpen lambs plodding their way to slaughter through knee-deep mud. The glint of courage was ignored, the gleam of sacrifice ridiculed and the ideal of duty denigrated. All battles were nothing more than the death and mutilation of thousands of men in exchange for a few feet of sodden earth. Thus, in time, emerged the standard image of the First World War.

The raid on Zeebrugge was an early victim. The sneers and contempt shown by distinguished senior officers, the wholesale acceptance of the German version of events, and the wide disparity of the casualties, made the event an easy target for the disenchantment lobby. Even Keyes' comments about the failure of the mole attack were soon stretched to include the whole battle. Instead of a singularly courageous and successful assault high up on the enemy's flank, which stunned the Germans and cheered the British people, it became, in many people's minds, little more than a costly failure. In almost every account the British effort is belittled whilst the German response is treated as gospel truth. Even in the first few years of the twenty-first century, a book was published that treated the Royal Navy's effort with sarcasm and disdain, and distorted the German response beyond recognition.

With such reactions in mind it is worth revisiting the views of people who were there at the time and felt the wider effects of the raids. Firstly, a Belgian military point of view from Colonel G.M. Stinglhamber DSO, who later became a student of the Zeebrugge Raid. He wrote:

Zeebrugge was not only a brilliant feat of arms, it also had a very important bearing on the fortunes of the whole war. Zeebrugge was the only outlet to the great system of canals which connected Belgium with Germany. Bruges had been turned into a formidable dockyard and refitting base for the lighter craft of the German Navy. In blocking this outlet not only were the ships actually in the canal system at the moment put out of action, but the whole system of inland waterways was permanently closed to all future traffic. Germany could no longer count on sending her ships into the Channel in safety, she would have to run the gauntlet of a long passage on the open sea.

It takes just two comments sent to Keyes to show the wide range of British society's response. The first is from the Secretary to the Dover & District Trades and Labour Council. He wrote:

At the last meeting of the above Council I was directed to write you a letter of thanks and congratulations for the gallant exploit of Zeebrugge, carried out by the men of the Dover Patrol under your command. As representatives of the working men of the town our praise may not amount to much amongst the congratulations received by you from all quarters. But that you may know that the general opinion is unanimous, I may say, Sir, we are proud of you and the Dover Patrol.

The second came from the Archbishop of Canterbury, who spoke of the news of the raid being

... the sort which makes a man 'hold his breath' in admiration of the magnificent courage and skill involved in such an enterprise.

I should like, on St George's Day, to say to you and to your brave men how intensely we appreciate the heroism of such deeds, and how proud we are of those who are thus adding lustre to the long and varied records of English seamanship and naval prowess ...

In those comments lay the true voice of the British people. The last word, perhaps, should belong to one who gave his life onboard HMS *Vindictive*, and is buried in the communal grave at Dover. On the tombstone of Able Seaman Yeardon are the words:

He sleeps with British heroes in the watchful care of God.

On learning of their actions against a formidable, entrenched, and heavily armed enemy, there can be no doubt that all who took part in the raids were heroes. They were heroes who faced fearful odds, determined in the demands of duty, and resolute in the face of death. The corrosive mutterings of those who were neither there at the time, nor understand what they went through, should be condemned to wither away beneath the flame of freedom set blazing by the courage of such men. As observed in an editorial by the Australian press on the anniversary of the raids:

> The record of such a deed can never die. And when the nation itself is ashamed of it, then the nation is doomed.

Taken from the lighthouse extension looking towards the Friedrichsort battery fire control building. It was from the exit adjoining the parapet wall that Lieutenant Commander Harrison led the charge against the extension guns.

The graves of British dead in Zeebrugge churchyard. They lie close to the graves of their enemies.

A memorial plaque in Zeebrugge churchyard in memory of three missing officers – Brock, Harrison and Hawkings – and one rating, Mechanic Second Class J. Rouse.

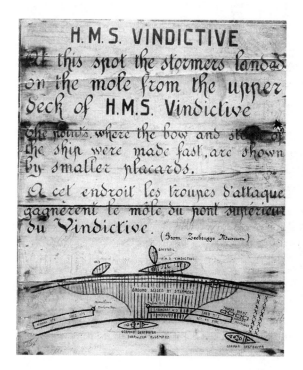

The first memorial. A wooden painted board was placed at the point the *Vindictive* lay alongside the mole. Co-incidentally, the board shows the approximate location where the fire-control position was placed across the mole, impeding the route of Lieutenant Commander Adams' first advance against the lighthouse extension guns, and from where Lieutenant Commander Harrison led his charge against the guns.

TO COMMEMORATE   THE BLOCKING OF

ZEEBRUGGE

BY A BRITISH NAVAL FORCE UNDER
THE COMMAND OF VICE-ADMIRAL ROGER KEYES
ON ST GEORGE'S DAY, APRIL 23 RD 1918.
HERE
H.M.S. "VINDICTIVE", CAPT. A.F.B. CARPENTER "IRIS", COMDR
V.F. GIBBS AND "DAFFODIL", LT. H.G. CAMPBELL
LAY ALONGSIDE FOR SEVENTY MINUTES WHILST STORMING THE MOLE IN THE FACE
OF CONCENTRATED FIRE FROM THE GERMAN GUNS

A bronze plaque unveiled by Prince Charles Theodore of Belgium in June 1926. It replaced the original wooden board marking the position of the *Vindictive* during the raid.

German naval officers on board the *Vindictive*. The bullet-riddled forward flame-thrower cabin is still in position.

The *Vindictive* being raised from the canal floor in 1920.

The bows of the *Vindictive* when first preserved as a memorial in Ostend.

The bows of HMS *Vindictive* at the new site in Ostend after renovation in 2013. The bows are now much closer to the scene of her attempt to block the canal.

The original, 70ft-high memorial at Zeebrugge. It bore a bronze statue of St George killing the dragon and the words, 'In memory of St. George's Day, 1918, when every moment had its deed and every deed its hero'. The memorial was unveiled by King Albert of the Belgians on 23 April 1925. It, like other Zeebrugge memorials to the raid, was destroyed by the Germans during the Second World War.

The Zeebrugge memorial to the attack against the mole viaduct by Lieutenant Sandford in *C3*. Rising from the smoke of the explosion, a female figure points towards England with her right arm while, in her left hand, she holds a Victoria Cross.

Medal replicas of the *C3* memorial were made and presented to the surviving crew members.

Epilogue

Part 1

By the end of the first decade of the twenty-first century, Zeebrugge had developed almost beyond recognition by anyone who knew the port only from 1918. Where there was once nothing but sand dunes, trenches, machine guns and heavy artillery, there now exists a smart, bustling, town with wide roads, shops, cafes and bars.

The port area has grown to a degree almost unimaginable a century earlier. Where the *Vindictive* was held against the mole wall by the *Daffodil*, a modern road now leads to huge dock installations to the west of the wall. The viaduct, once blown apart by the submarine *C3*, has entirely vanished. The mole floor itself remains and the site of the seaplane base is used by ferries plying between Hull and Zeebrugge, but there is no evidence of the activities carried out on the mole in 1918.

The great mole wall with its parapet, shelters and observation station has almost completely disappeared. There remains, however, one singularly important section – the lighthouse extension. Anyone arriving at the port onboard one of the ferries will sail past the lighthouse, exactly following the route where the blockships entered the harbour. Although there has had to be much restoration after the Germans caused extensive damage at the end of both world wars, the proportions and design of the extension remain exactly as they were on St George's Day 1918. The tower of the lighthouse is modern but the base still has the same doors and inner rooms that were in use on the day of the raid. The passageway leading through the extension still exists and can be entered by the same doorway close by the stone stairway that was in use in 1918.

The curving piers extending into the harbour from the mouth of the canal have gone, and the western bank of the canal at its entrance has been entirely removed to allow for a massive expansion of wharfs capable of being used by large vessels. The eastern bank, on the other hand, remains almost identical to that which existed in 1918. The underwater limit of the sloping bank is indicated by a number of upright timber baulks projecting above the surface. They also show the approximate position of *Iphigenia*'s bows when she was finally scuttled.

A little over 500 yards from the blockship's final position, the northern lockgates still operate by sliding in and out of a concrete channel designed to protect it from shelling or bombs, just as it did in 1918. Standing by the lockgate and looking towards the canal entrance it is quickly realised that it would have taken Lieutenant Bonham Carter a few short minutes to have reached and destroyed it. Disobeying orders in such a manner would have counted highly in Keyes' opinion of such an act.

Alongside the red-brick church at Zeebrugge, some of the British casualties of the raid are buried side-by-side with their German opponents. A large plaque remembers the sacrifice of Wing Commander Brock, Lieutenant Commander Harrison and others whose bodies were never recovered.

Ostend, even in the early part of the twentieth century, was a popular seaside resort with strong royal connections. There had been considerable damage from bombing and shelling during the war but not to the extent of causing population flight. Today it remains a beautiful town with its mixture of ancient and modern architecture. After the war, the Belgians were given the raised blockships to dispose of as they wished. Two masts were removed from the Zeebrugge blockships and the entire bow section of the *Vindictive* was cut away and preserved. All were then brought together at a site by the canal at Ostend and mounted in a beautiful garden area that was kept in pristine condition by a grateful Belgian nation for many years. In 2012 the bows were removed for restoration before being moved to a new site at the city's modern development at Oosteroever. A re-dedication ceremony on 26 May 2013 was attended by King Albert II and Queen Paola and descendants of several of those who took part in the second raid.

A towering memorial, topped by a bronze statue of St George defeating the dragon, was erected at the landward end of the mole and dedicated by King Albert I on 23 April 1925. In August 1927 the Belgian people erected a memorial on the mole to Lieutenant Richard Sandford and the crew of the submarine *C3*. A bronze panel, 8ft high, depicted a female figure rising from the smoke of the explosion. With her right hand she pointed towards England, whilst in her left hand, she carried a representation of the Victoria Cross awarded to Sandford. Small plaques of the same design were presented to the survivors. Another bronze memorial panel – replacing an earlier wooden version – was placed on the parapet wall where the *Vindictive* had come alongside. The tower and all other memorials to the action erected near to the Zeebrugge mole were destroyed by the Germans in the Second World War.

Many memorials to the raids were erected throughout Great Britain. One poignant instance may serve as an example for all. Lieutenant Charles Paynter

One of the *Vindictive*'s parapet anchors, now in the grounds of the Royal Marines Museum at Southsea, Portsmouth.

A parapet anchor from one of the Mersey ferries mounted as a memorial at Dover. Its bullet-scarred condition suggests that it could be the anchor that Lieutenant Hawkings and Lieutenant Commander Bradford lost their lives in trying to secure the *Isis* to the mole parapet. The inscription is incorrect in suggesting that it was used by the *Vindictive*.

died when a shell exploded on the forecastle of HMS *North Star*. His father, the rector of All Saints church at Chelmsford, erected a green-and-white marble tablet, which recorded that his son 'Gave his life his life for England on St George's day, April 23rd, 1918, in the glorious naval attack on Zeebrugge, aged 22. "Faithful Unto Death".'

A possibly unique memorial exists in St Ann's Church in the Royal Naval Dockyard, Portsmouth (now known as HM Naval Base, Portsmouth). The dead from the second Ostend raid had been interred with full honours by the Germans in an Ostend cemetery. During a visit to the graves by Major General Sir Fabien Ware, the vice chairman of the Imperial War Graves commission, he noticed that, when the wooden crosses erected over the graves by the Germans had been replaced by 'Commission pattern' gravestones, with the exception of a single example, the wooden crosses had been removed and discarded. The sole exception was in a very poor condition, but the words 'Unknown Stoker' had survived. The general had the Commission's workshop make a reproduction of the cross and presented it to the commander-in-chief Portsmouth – Admiral Sir Roger Keyes. With the costs approved by the Admiralty, Keyes had the cross embedded into the floor of the dockyard church just in front of the lectern, where it became known as 'The Memorial to the Unknown Stoker'.

The two Mersey ferries that had played such a significant part at Zeebrugge were destined to take up once again the task for which they were originally designed. After repairs at Chatham, the ferries returned to Liverpool, where Lieutenant Oscar Henderson presented the Mayor and Mayoress of Wallasey with a bouquet made up of daffodils and irises. In return, both he and Lieutenant Harold Campbell were presented with inscribed gold cigarette cases. Keyes wrote to the ferry owners saying:

> I am sure that it will interest you to know that your two stout vessels carried Bluejackets and Marines to Zeebrugge, and remained alongside the Mole for an hour, greatly contributing to the success of the operation ... The damaged [sic] caused by enemy gunfire has been repaired.

There was another, even more pleasing recognition of the work done by the two ferries. The King authorised the vessels' names to be changed to *Royal Iris* and *Royal Daffodil*.

After sixteen years further work on the Mersey, the *Royal Daffodil* was sold and worked on the Thames between Rochester and Southend. She was sold to the Belgians in 1938 and scrapped. The *Royal Iris* was sold to an Irish ferry company in 1932 and was renamed the *Blarney* in 1946. She was broken up in 1961.

After being succeeded by Keyes, it was not long before Vice Admiral Sir Reginald Bacon decided the time had come to seek solace in retirement. He was promoted to admiral on the Retired List in September 1918 and turned to writing books on naval history and technical matters (such as *The Motor-Car and How it Works*, and *A Simple Guide to Wireless, For All Whose Knowledge of Electricity is Childlike*). A long-serving and steadfast acquaintance of Admiral Jellicoe, Bacon decided that his friend was receiving too much of the blame for the failure to annihilate the German Fleet at Jutland, and reasoned that Beatty should shoulder more of the responsibility. To that end, in 1925 he wrote *The Jutland Scandal* to redress the balance. The result was a great deal of apoplexy throughout much of the fleet. In an appraisal of the book in *The Naval Review*, the reviewer thundered that Bacon's 'mentality is that of a fanatic ... with the conviction that no submarines are passing Dover Straits'. Bacon had turned on Beatty and made him 'a target of vulgar and vicious attack'. The entire book was one of 'unscrupulous inaccuracy'. A correspondent in the same edition fumed that Bacon had sunk to 'the level of blind abuse' and 'violent personal attack'. The writer went on to say that, thanks to the book's 'flavour of sensation and its offensive title' it had 'received more prominence than it deserved'.

Bacon continued to write on other subjects, including biographies of Jellicoe and Fisher, and an account of his own naval career. A reviewer of the latter chose a rather toe-curlingly egotistical example of Bacon's prose to highlight his style. Fisher, as commander-in-chief, Mediterranean, had let it be known that any ideas on the deployment of the ships of the fleet would be welcome from junior officers. Bacon noted:

> I sat down and sketched out a programme suitable for the rather antiquated craft we had at Malta and sent this to him. Next morning I was considerably astonished to receive a long signal eulogising me and my screed and ordering me to call at Admiralty House at noon ... Every officer with ideas was consulted and their views assimilated, till Sir John became the embodiment of the advanced ideas of all classes of officers of the fleet ... I cannot translate accurately into words the buoyant joy and relief I felt when I found that at last I was serving under a master mind ... It seemed as if the Navy at last was to be roused from its lethargic condition, that shortly it would arise and stretch itself, and throw off the old tradition and become a real live fighting service.

Admiral Sir Reginald Bacon died in 1947.

Captain Arthur Carpenter returned from his speaking tour of North America and, despite his bruising encounter with Keyes over the matter of auctioning Zeebrugge mementos for a naval charity, was appointed to command the cruiser HMS *Carysfort*. The following year, 1922, saw the publication of his book, *The Blocking of Zeebrugge* – dedicated 'To the Man-in-the-street as a representative of the British Public'. In the book, Carpenter makes no mention of any conflict with Keyes and, with its light tone, avoids any self-aggrandisement. After a period in charge of the Portsmouth Senior Officer's Technical Course, he was reassigned and felt the effects of the 'Geddes Axe' – a money-saving weapon wielded by the former first lord of the Admiralty, Sir Eric Geddes. Carpenter found himself appointed to Chatham as captain of the dockyard, deputy superintendent and king's harbourmaster – once three separate jobs now rolled into one as an economy measure. In 1927 he was given the command of the battleship *Benbow* before transferring to her sister-ship *Marlborough*. Carpenter was placed on the Retired List as a rear admiral in 1929 and, five years later, promoted to vice admiral on the same list. During the Second World War he served in the Home Guard, commanding the 17th Gloucestershire (Wye Valley) Battalion. He died in 1955.

Lieutenant Commander Bryan Adams, the senior surviving officer from those who volunteered from the Grand Fleet, the first officer to land on the mole from the *Vindictive*, and the officer who, 'with great coolness and bravery', led the first charge towards and beyond the look-out station, was awarded membership of the Distinguished Service Order and given special promotion to commander, to date from the day of the raid. Though born in Australia he remained with the Royal Navy when the Royal Australian Navy was set up. He married, first Audrey Marshall who died in 1929 – their daughter was a Leading Wren in WW2 – and secondly, Pamela Drury-Lowe, a senior WAAF Officer, and daughter of Admiral Sydney Drury-Lowe. Adams was transferred to the Retired List with the rank of captain in 1933 and worked on the Disarmament Section of the League of Nations Permanent Advisory Committee. With the outbreak of war in 1939 he returned to the Royal Navy as commandant of the Cabinet War Room No. 1. In 1942 he was appointed to HMS *Canopus*, the Alexandria naval base, as chief staff officer and flag-captain to the flag-officer Mediterranean Training Establishments. The following year he was reappointed to a similar position in HMS *Assegai*, the South Africa training base. His experience with the League of Nations was called into use when, later in 1943, he was appointed to create and run the Naval Section of the Control Commission intended to run Germany after the war. His chief responsibility prior to the end of the war was to consider the effects of any German armistice proposals and the immediate takeover and control of the German Navy. So well did he organise the section that it was eventually considered to be too important to remain under the command of a captain and the whole section was taken over by his boss from his League of Nations days, Rear Admiral Roger Bellairs. In 1945 he was offered the job of commanding officer of Danube Shipping but he preferred to retire. He died in 1971.

Lieutenant Edward Hilton Young MP, the *Vindictive*'s 'parliamentary representative' who, despite his severe injuries, had taken on the 'self-appointed duty of cheering everybody up', had his arm amputated immediately after the raid. In recognition of his 'indifference to suffering and danger' he was promoted to lieutenant commander and awarded a bar to the Distinguished Service Cross he had earned in Serbia. He went on to be made a member of the Distinguished Service Order after showing 'great initiative, gallantry and dash' whilst commanding an armoured train during fighting against the Bolsheviks near Archangel. Remaining in politics after the war, Hilton Young was made financial secretary to the Treasury before marrying Kathleen Scott, the sculptor and widow of Captain Scott, the Antarctic explorer. Later the same year he was appointed as a privy counsellor. Between 1926 and 1928 he served as the British delegate at the League of Nations and was knighted in 1927. In 1931 he was appointed as the minister of health, serving in that capacity until 1935 when he retired from politics and was created the 1st Baron Kennet, taking his seat in the House of Lords and returning to his League of Nations role. During his parliamentary career he found time to establish Iraq's Currency Board, institute the Iraqi monetary system, and even design the banknotes used in that country. He also did a similar service to Poland, helping to establish the *Złoty*, and chaired the Royal Commission on Indian Finance. In 1937 he was appointed to chair the Capital Issues Committee which advised the Chancellor of the Exchequer on significant movements of capital being invested abroad. With the outbreak of war two years later, the committee's work was expanded to include advising the Treasury on 'applications to raise capital for any purpose anywhere'. Lord Kennet remained as chairman of the committee until 1959. He died the following year. His step-son, Sir Peter Scott, the artist, ornithologist and founder of the World Wildlife Fund, was also a decorated naval officer.

An extraordinarily symmetry of fate affected both Adams and Hilton Young. The latter's son married one of the former's daughters. The only son, among five daughters, of this union, went on to marry a granddaughter of Admiral Keyes. The children of this marriage are probably unique in having three great-grandfathers who took part in the Zeebrugge raid.

Captain Reginald Dallas Brooks, commander of the Royal Marine Artillery howitzers in the *Vindictive*, was awarded a Distinguished Service Order and promoted to major for having 'imbued his men with the highest degree of devotion to duty'. Despite the injuries he had suffered in Gallipoli, he returned to the sports field, playing cricket for Hampshire, the Royal Navy and the Combined Services. He also played golf and hockey for the Royal Navy. His service career prospered likewise and, during the Second World War, he was appointed as deputy director general (military) at the Foreign Office's Political Warfare Executive. Ending the war as a major general, he was appointed the following year as the commandant general Royal Marines, with the rank of lieutenant general. Dallas Brooks was appointed governor of the Australian state of Victoria in 1949. He retired to that country and died in 1966. The Dallas Brooks Centre in Melbourne is named after him, as are one of the city's suburbs and several public highways.

Lieutenant Commander Robert Rosoman, the *Vindictive*'s first lieutenant, was specially promoted to commander. The ship's gunnery officer, Commander Edward ('Seymour') Osborne was awarded the Distinguished Service Order and went on to be promoted to vice admiral before dying in 1956. Engineer Lieutenant Commander William Bury was promoted and mentioned in dispatches for his 'great bravery' in helping to bring in the wounded whilst the *Vindictive* was alongside the mole. He was made a Companion of the Distinguished Service Order for his 'gallant' work on the second Ostend Raid.

Lieutenant Sir John Alleyne, badly injured in the *Vindictive* at Ostend and already the holder of a Distinguished Service Cross, was awarded the Distinguished Service Order for his 'great coolness under a very heavy fire' and for his vital navigational skills. Alleyne's perils had not ended with his being dragged out of the water onto Bourke's *ML276*. Once safely onboard it was seen that his wounds were very severe and he was carried to the after battery compartment of the launch. There he was laid down and covered with a blanket. Shortly afterwards a shell hit the launch allowing seawater to flood into the compartment. This produced a toxic gas, which Alleyne was aware of but to which he was unable to respond. Suddenly the compartment hatch was opened followed by the sound of someone shouting 'Anyone there?' Again, Alleyne was unable to reply and the hatch slammed shut. Luckily someone else decided to investigate, entered the compartment, and the navigator was 'fished out' just in time. On his return to Dunkirk he was put into hospital only to have the ward visited by naval and civic dignitaries eager to heap praise upon the gallant wounded from the attack. Unfortunately, Alleyne had to lie on his bed hearing everyone else being lauded for their efforts whilst he was ignored. This, of course, was because he should not have been in the *Vindictive* and he was not listed as having taken part in the action.

Despite his injuries, Alleyne was eager to get back in the war and, having been promoted to lieutenant commander, he was appointed as navigator in the light cruiser HMS *Carlisle* four days before the Armistice was signed. Two years after being promoted to commander in 1924, he was sent on a staff course at the Royal Naval College at Greenwich before being appointed to command the sloop HMS *Lupin*, on the Far East Station. Alleyne returned to England in 1930 to take up the appointments as staff officer (operations and intelligence) on the staff of the commander-in-chief, Portsmouth. Unfortunately, although recommended for promotion to captain, the recommendation was lost in the administrative system and not forwarded to the Admiralty. As a result all he received was a personal apology from the c-in-c. Once again in the Far East, Alleyne took on the appointment of king's harbour master and commander of the dockyard in Singapore in 1933. Three years later, at his own request, he was placed on the Retired List with the rank of captain.

Shortly after the outbreak of war, on 1 March 1940, the now 51-year-old Captain Sir John Alleyne was recalled to service and appointed to the command of the armed merchant cruiser HMS *Salopian* (originally the passenger ship *Shropshire*). Thirteen months later, with a cargo of empty beer barrels, and escorting a convoy some 400 miles off the coast of Greenland's Cape Farewell, the *Salopian* was zigzagging through the cold, foggy North Atlantic waters when two torpedoes from *U98* just missed the ship. Shortly afterwards another two torpedoes also shot past without making contact. The captain of the U-boat decided to make yet another effort and reloaded his forward tubes before running on the surface to catch up with the *Salopian*. This time, firing on the surface, he was successful and one torpedo struck amidships, the other forward. Forced to dive by the ship's guns opening fire, the U-boat sent another two torpedoes in, both exploding in the engine room. Now Alleyne ordered the ship's company into the ship's boats but still tried to fend off the submarine by ordering his launch to lay down a smokescreen around the ship. But it was to no avail as yet another torpedo struck, breaking the ship in half and sending her to the bottom within two minutes. The action cost the lives of one officer and two ratings, with 277 men being saved and taken to the combined US and British naval base at Hvalfjord on the west coast of Iceland. Alleyne served in command of two more armed merchant cruisers before being appointed in September 1943 as flag-captain to the flag-officer commanding West Africa based at the naval base at Freetown, Sierra Leone. On his return to England in May 1945 he was sent to Versailles to join the staff of the Allied Naval Commander Expeditionary Force (ANCXF). From there he was sent on to Flensburg, where he was put in command of the *Oberkommando der Marine* (the German Admiralty). After just over a week, the German commander-in-chief, *Generaladmiral* Hans-Georg von Friedeburg, an ardent Nazi, committed suicide. Within a few hectic days Alleyne oversaw the takeover of *Generaladmiral* Otto Backenkohler as von Friedeburg's replacement before Backenkohler was himself replaced by *Generaladmiral* Walter Warzecha. At the same time, the rapid dissolution of the German Navy had begun. Alleyne returned to the Retired List in April 1946 and took up, once again, his pre-war interest in horse-riding. He also became involved in charity work, chairing a county organisation dedicated to the resettlement and accommodation of former prisoners. Captain Sir John Alleyne OBE, DSO, DSC died in December 1983, aged 94.

After being saved from being trampled by Royal Marine boots on one of the *Vindictive's* landing brows, Lieutenant Harold Walker had no intention of letting the loss of his left hand interrupt his career. 'Hooky' Walker (a traditional Royal Naval name for anyone named 'Walker') went on to command the battlecruiser HMS *Hood* and the battleship HMS *Barham*. He transferred to the Retired List as Admiral Sir Harold Walker, Knight Commander of the Order of the Bath, and died in 1975.

Keyes' 'one-eyed, bearded warrior', Lieutenant Commander Patrick Harrington Edwards, recovered from the leg wounds that had prevented his landing on the mole and collected a second mention in dispatches oak leaf for his work on the preparations for the raid. By the time of his presentation he had been promoted to commander and appointed as commanding officer of the Allied Naval Brigade in Northern Russia (August 1918). In May 1919 he was awarded the Distinguished Service Order 'As recognition of his valuable services as Commanding Officer of the Allied Naval Brigade in North Russia between August 1918 and February 1919' and for 'very good work under difficult circumstances'. So well did he perform in what was, essentially, a military rather than a naval operation, that he was seconded to the army with the rank of lieutenant colonel (his service documents were promptly annotated 'Officer to be paid from Army funds with effect from 20 February 1919'). Nine months later, in February 1920, Harrington Edwards was awarded a bar to his DSO, this time for 'distinguished service in connection with military operations in Archangel, North Russia'. He was demobilised in June 1920, having lost the sight of an eye and with the scars of fifty-two other wounds obtained at Gallipoli, on the Western Front, alongside the mole at Zeebrugge and in Northern Russia. He had been injured so badly during the final phase of the Battle of the Somme that, as he lay in the Duchess of Westminster Hospital at Le Touquet, the order had been given that he 'May be visited' – a dreaded permit granted only to those considered unlikely to survive. In addition to his DSO and Bar, his two mentions in dispatches and his war service medals, Harrington Edwards also wore a French *Croix de Guerre* with bronze star; the Russian Order of St Vladimir (4th Class) with swords; and the Russian Order of St Anne (2nd Class) with swords.

Chaplain The Reverend Charles Peshall earned a Distinguished Service Order for his 'cheerful encouragement', 'calm demeanour', 'strength of character', and 'splendid comradeship' for his 'superhuman work in carrying the wounded from the mole over the brows into *Vindictive*'. In 1933 he was appointed venerable archdeacon and chaplain to the fleet. The same year he was appointed as an honorary chaplain to the king. He was made a Commander of the Most Excellent Order of the British Empire in 1935. The Venerable Charles Peshall died in 1957.

Commodore Hubert Lynes, already a Companion of the Order of St Michael and St George, was appointed a Companion of the Order of the Bath for his work at Ostend. He was appointed to the Retired List of the Royal Navy in 1919 with the rank of rear admiral and, being already a well-known expert in the field of ornithology, spent much of the next twenty years researching the birds of Africa. At the outbreak of the Second World War Lynes was appointed as senior naval officer in North Wales, but a debilitating disease he had picked up in Africa overwhelmed him and he died in 1942. His obituary described him as an 'outstanding character who had ideas of his own and carried them through, devoted to duty, a man of great generosity and the best of companions'.

Another leading figure in the Ostend part of the story was Captain Ion Hamilton Benn MP. For his command and leadership of the motor launches and coastal motor boats he was appointed a companion of the Distinguished Service Order. At the end of the war, he returned to politics, was knighted in the 1920 Birthday Honours list and retired from parliament at the 1922 General Election. Hamilton Benn entered the business world with great success and became involved with naval charity work at the Greenwich Dreadnaught Hospital. He lost his first wife in 1948 and demonstrated his indefatigable spirit by marrying a Canadian lady two years later when he was 87. He remained a director of the Port of London Authority until 1960 when he was aged 97. He died the following year.

Having brought the *Iris* back to Dover, Lieutenant Oscar Henderson was awarded a Distinguished Service Order for quenching a fire that had broken out amongst the ammunition and for taking command on the death of the captain. Promoted to lieutenant commander in due course, he was placed on the Retired List in 1922 in order to take up an appointment as comptroller and private secretary to the 3rd Duke of Abercorn on the duke's appointment as the first governor of Northern Ireland. During his service in that office Henderson was appointed a Commander of the Royal Victorian Order and a Commander of the Order of the British Empire. On retiring from the governor's service, Henderson took on a senior managerial role in journalism, helping to found Northern Ireland's first Sunday newspaper. He also became one of the founders of Ulster Television, which was launched in 1958. Oscar Henderson died in 1969.

Captain (later Vice Admiral) Ralph S. Sneyd DSO ADC. (Courtesy of Commander R. Wykes-Sneyd AFC)

Surgeon Frank Pocock, who alone faced piles of dead and injured in the *Iris* with only torches and candles with which to try and save as many of the casualties as he could, had already earned a Military Cross on the Western Front, saving lives in the trenches. He was awarded the Distinguished Service Order for his work in the ferry and returned to the Drake Battalion of the Royal Naval Division, fighting their way through Flanders. Pocock was killed in September 1918. He was 27 years old.

After taking part in both the Zeebrugge raid and the second Ostend raid in CMBs, Lieutenant Cuthbert Bowlby was awarded the Distinguished Service Cross. With the end of the war he remained in the Royal Navy and just before the outbreak of the Second World War was a commander in Naval Intelligence, where his striking good looks and wavy hair earned him the nickname 'Curly'. During the war he was promoted to captain and put in control of the Middle East section of the Secret Intelligence Service (SIS – later MI6). Bowlby and his team soon gained a reputation for being splendidly dismissive of political intrigue. One of his agents in Greece complained that, at the Cairo Headquarters, the leadership consisted of people whose 'whole professional upbringing had schooled them to treat politics as an arcane art, best left to others'. Nevertheless, during his time with SIS, Bowlby was made a Companion of the Order of St Michael and St George, and appointed Commander of the Order of the British Empire. With the peace in 1945 Bowlby became the director of personnel at the SIS. During his time with Naval Intelligence he served with Commander Ian Fleming. It may be fanciful to note that Bowlby's second middle name was – Bond.

For his work in 'greatly contributing to the success of the operations', Captain Arthur Chater of the Royal Marine Light Infantry was appointed a Companion of the Distinguished Service Order. He went on to have a distinguished career with the Royal Marines, serving with the Egyptian Army and the Sudanese Army – at one time commanding the Sudanese Camel Corps. During the Second World War he was the military governor and commander of British Somalia. After a short period as commander of the Portsmouth Division of the Royal Marines, he returned to the Middle East as director of combined operations for India and South East Asia. With the war's end he was appointed as commander of the Chatham Group Royal Marines before retiring as a major general to take up an appointment as one of the Honourable Corps of Gentlemen at Arms. As one of the sovereign's bodyguards he was promoted to the office of 'Harbinger' – an ancient post originally intended to act as a vanguard and to ensure accommodation was provided for the Corps.

For behaving with the 'greatest courage and dash despite being wounded', another Royal Marine officer, Lieutenant Theodore Cooke, became one of only three Royal Marine lieutenants to be awarded a Distinguished Service Order during the whole of the First World War (the other two were pilots with the

Royal Naval Air Service). His injuries, however, were so severe that he never fully recovered and, although he survived until 1958, he lived much of the rest of his life as an invalid.

The leader of the Zeebrugge blockships and captain of the *Thetis*, Commander Ralph Sneyd, already the holder of the Distinguished Service Order, was promoted to captain with the seniority date of 23 April 1918, awarded the French *Croix de Guerre*, and appointed an Officer of the Belgian Order of Leopold. In 1922, whilst commanding the light cruiser HMS *Comus*, as part of the escort to the Prince of Wales on his world tour in HMS *Renown*, a cousin named Wykes-Finch died and left a Devon manor house named North Wyke to the family. To continue the tradition of keeping the name in existence, Sneyd changed his name to Wykes-Sneyd. After commanding the new cruiser HMS *Berwick* in the Far East, he moved to the Retired List as a rear admiral in 1929 and was promoted to vice admiral in 1934. He died in 1951. Vice Admiral Wykes-Sneyd's son became a captain in the Royal Navy and his grandson was decorated for gallantry as a lieutenant commander leading 820 helicopter squadron in HMS *Invincible* during the Falklands War.

When the captain of the *Intrepid*, Lieutenant Stuart Bonham Carter, returned to his home at Buriton, near Petersfield in Hampshire, he was greeted by schoolchildren waving flags and singing 'Heart of Oak'. He would have probably felt more comfortable with the ripple of applause during a cricket match. After the war he played cricket for the Royal Navy and became an accomplished golfer. In 1925 he invited the Cambridge University cricket team down to Portsmouth to play against the Royal Navy, using as bait the promise of being 'well entertained'. It was later recorded that the promise was 'the greatest understatement since Nelson's time'. Bonham Carter was awarded the Distinguished Service Order for his 'great skill and coolness' at Zeebrugge, the Italian Silver Medal for Military Valour, and noted for early promotion. That promotion came through just a year after the raid, along with an appointment to command HMS *Petersfield* on the South America and South Atlantic Station. His first lieutenant was Lieutenant Victor Crutchley and he may have been somewhat annoyed by the fact that, when visitors met the solidly built, towering and bearded Crutchley with his Victoria Cross ribbon, they tended to assume that he was the captain. Nevertheless, Bonham Carter began a steady rise through the ranks that saw him made a Commander of the Victorian Order, and promoted to rear admiral just before the outbreak of the Second World War. After a year in command of the 3rd Battle Squadron (during which time he was made a Commander of the Order of the Bath) he was appointed to the command of the 18th Cruiser Squadron, eventually flying his flag in HMS *Edinburgh*. In April 1942 the *Edinburgh* was ordered to escort Convoy 11 out of Murmansk whilst carrying 4½ tons of gold ingots. Two days later she was torpedoed by a U-boat. Although the ship stayed afloat her engines and steering gear were so badly damaged that Bonham Carter had no option but have her finally sent to the bottom by a torpedo from one of his own destroyers. The gold went down with her. Promoted to vice admiral a month later, Bonham Carter was reappointed as flag-officer, Malta. He was made a Knight Commander of the Bath in the 1943 New Year's Honours List but succumbed to an illness that forced his return home and transfer to the Retired List. At the first opportunity he returned as a captain and later as a commodore in charge of convoys. He died in 1972.

After the Zeebrugge raid, Lieutenant Edward Billyard-Leake was 'noted for early promotion', awarded the Distinguished Service Order, made a *Chevalier* of the Legion of honour and awarded the French *Croix de Guerre*. Two years later he was presented with the Belgian *Croix de Guerre*. In 1920 he was appointed as aide de camp to Edward, Prince of Wales – probably as a result of the friendship he had made with the prince during the royal visit to HMAS *Australia* in 1913. He accompanied the prince on his 1920 tour to Australia and New Zealand in

Captain Edward Billyard-Leake RN DSO. (Courtesy of Charles Britten-Long Laird)

HMS *Renown*, refereeing the ship's boxing tournaments and taking the job of general manager of the ship's concert party. For such sporting and other activities Billyard-Leake was made a member of the 'Order of the Crusted Barnacle' at the Crossing the Line ceremony. On arrival in Australia he gave 'lantern lectures' at several of the east coast cities and towns on the subject of the Zeebrugge raid. These talks probably made a welcome break from the hectic social life required of an officer, particularly those on the Prince of Wales' staff. A press report noted that, after a dance onboard the *Renown*:

> Those who were there at the end will never forget the ham and eggs party in the ward-room afterwards. Those who were left just filled the two big tables, and as the eggs were a little slow in appearing, someone started a poi dance (twirling weighted cords from the hands) on one table, and a first-class 'rag' was soon in progress. Bread and nuts were hurled through the air, and everyone was nearly sick with laughing. Then someone started a poi dance on one table, and the girls promptly started an opposition one on another table. The captain and Lieutenant Billyard-Leake gave us a Maori 'Haka' with great success, and the evening reluctantly ended somewhere about 3.30 a.m., while one of the girls was still struggling with a fork which had been put down the back of her dress, and which she was eventually obliged to 'souvenir'.

During the visit to New Zealand, the *New Zealand Observer* described Billyard-Leake as 'sharp-featured, brisk and manly', a suitable description for the role of Lieutenant Snooker Pool RN he played in the ship's musical 'The Voyage of the Ditty Box, or, Nothing Serious' as they steamed through the Pacific.

On his return to England Billyard-Leake entered the Submarine Service and was promoted to lieutenant commander in March 1925. Appointed as flag-lieutenant to the commander-in-chief, Portsmouth, he married Edith Winifred ('Winney') Laird, the granddaughter of Sir William Laird, a former chairman of the North British Railway, in September the following year. The newlyweds settled into Holybush House, a substantial property in Ayrshire. In December 1928 he asked to be placed on the Retired List and entered fully into the world of sporting activities, ending up as chairman of the National Sporting Club (his green 8-litre, six-cylinder, Bentley was a constant fixture at the nation's major sporting events).

In an effort to be seen as more than merely a wealthy playboy, Billyard-Leake sought a business opportunity and was appointed as a director and chairman of the board of Anglo-Eastern Tin in May 1931. Within eighteen months the company's capital had increased by a third.

In 1932 Billyard-Leake was approached by Maundy Gregory, an unsavoury character who made a fortune selling peerages and other titles to raise funds for the Liberal politician and former prime minister, David Lloyd George. Gregory offered Billyard-Leake a knighthood in return for a 'donation' of £12,000. Billyard Leake expressed an interest and asked for a letter of confirmation. When the letter arrived he promptly handed it over to the Treasury Solicitor and the matter was placed in the hands of Scotland Yard, thus putting an end to Gregory's career.

In October 1934 he and his brother, Charles, sold 'Kenyu', the 11,212-acre family estate in New South Wales. Shortly afterwards his marriage was dissolved by the Scottish courts and, two years later, he provided the financial backing for Percival Aircraft Ltd – a company founded by the Australian aircraft designer, Edgar Percival. So successful was the design of the first aircraft – the Percival Gull – that it evolved into the Percival Proctor, an aircraft used world-wide for training pilots and with examples still flying well into the twenty-first century.

During a trip to Kenya to visit his brother, Charles, in January 1935, Billyard Leake ('the millionaire sportsman' according to the press) married Betty Chester, a beautiful light comedy actress with both film and stage experience. His Best Man was Josslyn Hay, the 22nd Earl of Erroll, a leading member of the 'Happy Valley set' who was later murdered, probably as a result of a dissolute lifestyle.

With the outbreak of war in 1939 Billyard-Leak re-entered the Royal Navy with the rank of commander and was appointed as assistant naval attaché at Lisbon. His time there was marred by his wife's prolonged illness followed by her death in January 1943. Shortly afterwards he was promoted to captain and appointed as naval attaché to Chungking, in China. In this new position he was able to immerse himself in his work to the degree that he was awarded the Special Rosette of the Order of the Cloud and Banner by a grateful Chinese government.

At the end of the war, Billyard-Leake returned to the Retired List and purchased the leasehold of a property in London's Belgravia. Two years later he married Muriel Brown before moving to Kenya. There he drove around in a Rolls Royce Silver Dawn, an elegant vehicle based on the design of the Bentley Mark VI that proved (according to a later owner of the same car) to be perfect for Kenya's 'rough dirt roads'.

Captain Edward ('Teddy') Whaley Billyard-Leake RN DSO died in May 1956 after a life full of activity, interest and glamour. Shining out above all, however, as with all the blockship captains, was his courage. He would have found especially pleasing the eventual use found for Holybush House, his Ayrshire property. His father had offered the substantial Harefield House for use as a hospital for Australian and New Zealand wounded during the First World War (it later became a famous tuberculosis sanatorium and, eventually, a National Health Service hospital specialising in heart and lung transplants). By the turn of the twenty-first century, Holybush House had developed into a care home for ex-servicemen suffering from combat stress. As someone who had witnessed the cold detachment of a long-range sea battle at Jutland and the red-heat of close combat at Zeebrugge, Billyard-Leake would certainly have approved.

Although not a blockship captain, Lieutenant Victor Crutchley had taken command of HMS *Vindictive* during the last moments before she had her bottom blown out in the entrance to the Ostend canal. He had then suffered under very trying circumstances during which time his actions and leadership had seen the award of the Victoria Cross. After serving under Bonham Carter in the *Petersfield* he served in a variety of vessels including two royal yachts. Promoted to lieutenant commander in 1923 he was sent to the Mediterranean the following year where the commander-in-chief was Vice Admiral Sir Roger Keyes. Being a polo player, Crutchley soon found himself playing alongside the c-in-c and, on one occasion in 1927, played in a team containing Keyes, the Duke of York, and Lieutenant Lord Louis Mountbatten. He was promoted to commander the following year for his skills in leadership and the handling of men.

After service in the New Zealand, Crutchley was promoted to captain in 1932 and appointed to the command of the 1st Minesweeper Flotilla followed by a short period as Captain Fishery Protection and Minesweeping. In 1937 he was appointed to command the battleship HMS *Warspite* and was sent to the Mediterranean as the station's flagship. With the outbreak of the Second World War, the *Warspite* was sent to Scapa Flow and attached to the Home Fleet, taking part in the Second Battle of Narvik.

Appointed to the temporary rank of commodore (2nd class) in May 1940, Crutchley was sent to the Devonport Naval Barracks where he spent much of the time agitating for a return to sea. His efforts were rewarded within two years when he was promoted to rear admiral and given an appointment with the Royal Australian Navy. In August 1942, whilst attached to the American force covering the landings on Guadalcanal, the Americans decided to remove their aircraft carriers. This led the American admiral in charge of the landings to decide that he should pull back now that he was without air cover. Accordingly he ordered Crutchley to join him with his flagship, HMAS *Australia,* to discuss the matter. Crutchley did so, only to find that, in his absence, a Japanese cruiser force attacked his ships, sinking the cruiser HMAS *Canberra* and three US cruisers. There was an attempt in some quarters to blame Crutchley for the incident, but this was brushed aside by the Americans to the extent that, on his return to England in 1944, he was presented with the US Legion of Merit with the grade of Chief Commander – an honour only normally bestowed on heads of state. Not to be outdone in his own country, Crutchley was appointed as a Companion of the Order of the Bath in the 1945 New Year's Honours List, promoted to vice admiral eight months later and, in the Birthday Honours List the following year, was advanced to Knight Grand Cross of the Order of the Bath.

After the end of the war, Crutchley served as flag-officer, Gibraltar, before retiring from the service. He settled in Dorset where he served as high sheriff and deputy lord lieutenant, being promoted to admiral on the Retired List in 1949. After a long and active retirement, Admiral Sir Victor Crutchley VC CB KCB DSO died in January 1986, aged 92.

Whereas Crutchley bristled with leadership and command, Lieutenant Roland Bourke was almost exactly the opposite. A naturally gentle and unassuming spirit, when his Victoria Cross was presented by the king in September 1918 he asked his family to keep the news out of the newspapers. With the end of the war he married an Australian woman and returned to his fruit farm in Canada. Although successful in his farming, he also took on the responsibility for the navigation buoys and lights on his area of Kootenay Lake. He reluctantly agreed to go on a lecture tour of New Zealand in 1920 – where he may have encountered Lieutenant Billyard-Leake. The experience, however, seems not to have improved his enjoyment of public adulation and nine years later he found a succession of suspect excuses keeping him from attending a very grand event put on by the Prince of Wales in London for all living holders of the Victoria Cross. Even pleas by local civic leaders and the offer of free travel by the Canadian Pacific Railway failed to persuade him.

In 1931 his already weak eyesight began to deteriorate and, concerned that he was about to go blind, he gave up farming and moved to Victoria on Vancouver Island, where he found employment in the Royal Canadian Navy's Esquimalt dockyard. On the outbreak of war in 1939 he volunteered his services and, promoted to acting commander, created the 'gum-boot navy' – a patrol service made up of fishermen that was employed in guarding the coast of British Columbia. At the end of the war Bourke had the rare distinction of having a British Columbian mountain named Mount Bourke in his honour. Roland Bourke died in 1958 and was buried with full naval honours in Victoria. He had once told an enquirer that he had only won the Victoria Cross because his eyesight was so bad that he 'couldn't see well enough to get out of the way'.

After some months in hospital recovering from the serious injuries he had received during the rescue of many of the *Vindictive*'s men during the second Ostend raid, the newly promoted Lieutenant Commander Geoffrey Drummond VC married the daughter of the owner of Claysmore House, near Enfield, where he had spent part of his boyhood. He was then sent on mine-clearance duties to Queenstown in Ireland. With the ending of the war he left the Royal Navy and eventually obtained work with the newly formed Imperial Chemical Industries. In 1939 he tried to re-enter the Royal Naval Volunteer Reserve but was rejected on account of his age and the infirmity as a result of his injuries. Undeterred he joined the Thames River Emergency Service as a 'second hand' where, amongst his other duties, he recorded the position of parachute mines as they fell into the river.

Still determined to return to the RNVR, he sought the help of Admiral Sir Roger Keyes and Captain Hamilton Benn only to have his efforts overtaken by tragedy. In April 1941, whilst carrying a sack of coal onto his vessel, his left leg – severely injured off Ostend – gave way and he fell striking his head. He never regained consciousness and died shortly afterwards. His son noted that:

> He was a man [with] a great charm and humour and he had a great many friends. He had a strong religious belief and a strict sense of honour and duty to his country and his family. He never hesitated to do what he felt was right.

Able Seaman Albert McKenzie receiving his Victoria Cross from King George V.

Wearing his Victoria Cross, Able Seaman Albert McKenzie is feted by the people of Southwark.

Drummond's tombstone at the church in Chalfont St Peter's in Buckinghamshire records that he died as a 'Second Hand ... (Late Lieutenant Commander RNVR)' – an order of events that this officer of 'indomitable courage' would almost certainly have approved.

When the war ended, Lieutenant Commander Percy Dean VC stood for parliament as a Coalition Conservative in his home town of Blackburn. He defeated the sitting member – the pacifist Phillip Snowdon – and was selected as one of two members of the House to make the Loyal Address. However, it seems that he became quickly disillusioned with being a Member of Parliament. He spoke only a few times in the House during his first year – and then said nothing for the next two years. When an election was called in 1922, he stood down and returned to his pre-war occupation as a slate merchant, becoming the managing director of three slate firms and the chairman of the board running a slate quarry. He died in March 1939 and his ashes were buried in Golders Green crematorium, London.

Sadly, not all those awarded the Victoria Cross as a result of their actions during the raids lived long enough to enjoy life after the war. Able Seaman Albert MacKenzie, still undergoing recovery from his wounds, was presented with his VC by the king at Buckingham Palace. Accompanied by his mother and sister to the ceremony, MacKenzie climbed the steps of the dais using crutches but managed to stand tall and proud as he received the decoration. Returning to the Royal Naval Hospital at Chatham he contracted septicaemia, which dramatically weakened his immune system. At the same time he fell victim to the flu pandemic that was sweeping the world in 1918. Ironically, although many – possibly most – of the flu victims were young adults, they died as a result of their immune systems violently overreacting to the contagion. MacKenzie, on the other hand, with his immune system already laid low and incapable of such a reaction, probably died from the septicaemia. He was buried near his home in Camberwell. The funeral was attended by Captain Carpenter VC who told MacKenzie's mother, 'The splendid example which your boy set at Zeebrugge will be accorded a high place of honour in the naval records of the British Empire.' A message from Buckingham Palace expressed 'the sympathy of their Majesties with the widowed mother and family. Their Majesties were grieved to hear of his untimely death and to think that he had been spared so short a time to wear the proud decoration which he had so nobly won.'

By 1 November 1918 Lieutenant Richard Sandford had recovered from the wounds he had received whilst paddling away from the mole viaduct and his highly explosive submarine C3. On that date he received a temporary appointment as the captain of submarine G11 based at Blyth, Northumberland – G11's captain had fallen victim to the flu. Sandford repaired onboard as quickly as he could, knowing that he was expected to sail on 19 November and he knew little about the boat or its crew. He had not been onboard long when he was struck down by a severe illness and taken to the depot ship sickbay. There it was discovered that he had contracted typhoid fever. He was rushed to the fever ward in a hospital at nearby Grangetown but nothing could be done for him. Sandford died on the 23 November, just twelve days after the Armistice, and the day after G11 was wrecked on the rocks off the Northumberland coast. His brother Francis, who had come to his rescue in the picket boat, served in HMS *Repulse* before being promoted to captain in 1926. Shortly afterwards, whilst appointed to the Admiralty, he visited Switzerland where he died of septicaemia. Both bothers are remembered on a memorial plaque in Exeter Cathedral.

On returning to the Corps after recovering from his severe injuries, Sergeant Norman Finch VC was promoted to colour sergeant in 1920, and to quartermaster sergeant five years later. On 9 November 1920 he was a member of the guard of honour mustered at Westminster Abbey during the internment of the Unknown Warrior. Other members of the guard included Captain Carpenter

VC, Lieutenant Dean VC MP, and Able Seaman Ferdinand Lake, who had been awarded the Conspicuous Gallantry Medal after taking over the wheel of the ferry *Iris* despite his hands being burned and blistered from throwing burning ammunition overboard.

Finch retired from the Royal Marines in 1929 and worked, firstly, as a postman, and then as a bank messenger. In 1933 he was granted a special distinction by being appointed as a member of The King's Bodyguard of the Yeomen of the Guard. This entailed wearing a distinctive Tudor-style uniform as escort to the sovereign on several occasions throughout the year. With the outbreak of war in 1939 Finch returned to the Royal Marines as a quartermaster sergeant and was promoted to temporary lieutenant in 1943 in charge of stores. After the war he returned to The King's (later Queen's) Bodyguard and in 1961 was promoted to divisional sergeant major. He died in 1966.

Whereas Sergeant Finch had been selected for the award of the Victoria Cross by his fellow Royal Marines on account of his indomitable spirit despite being badly wounded, Captain Edward Bamford DSO VC was chosen for his award of the decoration on the grounds of his 'magnificent example' of leadership under fire. At the end of the war, among his other decorations were the French *Legion d'Honneur* (Officer); the Russian Order of St Anne (3rd Class) with Swords, and the Japanese Order of the Rising Sun (4th Class). He remained in service with the Royal Marines and was promoted to brevet major shortly after his return from Zeebrugge with the rank being confirmed in due course. In early September 1928, he was serving in the cruiser HMS *Cumberland* when she visited the Chinese port of Weihaiwei. There he became sick with an unspecified illness. It was decided that the ship should head for Hong Kong, where he could be placed in the care of the British Military Hospital. As the ship called in to fuel at Shanghai on 29 September, the 41-year-old Bamford died. He was buried in the port's English Cemetery. Sadly the cemetery was destroyed during the Cultural Revolution and the site was afterwards covered by a shopping centre.

Part 2

By the end of September 1918 Vice Admiral Sir Roger Keyes was eagerly cooperating with the British and French armies as they launched an attack along the Belgian coast. Although there was to be no military landing on the coast, naval activity could convince the Germans that such a landing was possible – even probable. In addition, the monitors could bring their heavy guns to bear on the retreating enemy. Keyes, unable to bring himself to be absent whilst the chance of action existed, was always close at hand with his flag flying in the destroyer HMS *Termagant*, captained by Commander A.B. Cunningham.

Early on the morning of 17 October Keyes was asked by the French to close with Ostend to assess the situation in the port. As he approached the entrance to the canal, Keyes could see the thrilling site of Belgian flags flying everywhere and crowds of people lining the canal piers. Keyes decided that he and Captain Wilfred Tomkinson would go ashore in the ship's whaler (to avoid putting *Termagant* at risk from mines). Before leaving, however, he sent a message to the Belgian king and queen suggesting that if they cared to join him later that day, they could land in the newly liberated Ostend. As a destroyer left with the message, the whaler's crew pulled Keyes and Tomkinson into the canal and past the battered *Vindictive* with her decks covered with Belgian boy scouts and other children waving flags. Eventually, a vertical iron ladder was found and Keyes climbed up to be greeted with wild cheering and a huge crowd trying to shake his hand. The excitement had not lasted for long when a shell from a German field battery fell nearby, followed in quick succession by more shells. Keyes shouted to the civilians to take cover and that he would be back later in the day.

On his return to the flagship, Keyes headed for Dunkirk to make sure that the Belgian king and queen did not take up his offer. He found, instead, that their majesties were equally determined that they would make the landing at Ostend – shelling or no shelling. Failing to persuade them of the risks, Keyes returned to the port after dark, where he heard the news that, this time, the Germans had definitely abandoned the town. Locating the same iron ladder that had been used earlier in the day, Keyes and his royal charges climbed safely up to the quay, but the king's equerry fell into the canal.

It was not long before the royal couple were recognised and a cheering crowd accompanied them to the *hotel de ville*, where they found the city council celebrating the German withdrawal with champagne. The celebrations grew even more enthusiastic with the presence of the king and queen, but Keyes, continually concerned over their safety, finally managed to coax them back to the quay and onboard the *Termagant*. Returning to Dunkirk, Keyes decided that the two motor launches that were acting as escorts should be used to get the king and queen to the port more quickly. As the transfer was being made, the equerry, by now dried off and in dry clothing, once again managed to fall into the water. Far worse, however, was to follow. Travelling at 40 knots in the dark, the two MLs lost sight of each other. Shortly after the separation, the ML carrying the king, the queen and Keyes, surged to a halt, its engine broken down. For Keyes, the possibilities were of the worst nightmare proportions. The risk of collision on a blackened sea, or the chance encounter with an enemy warship would be disastrous. He decided to risk using the ML's signal flares but the boat's entire supply was exhausted without summoning any sign of assistance. The ML drifted at the mercy of the wind and tide for well over an hour before the sound of an engine was heard. It proved to be a Royal Naval vessel, one of many sent out by Tompkinson (who had been travelling in the other ML). He had been greatly alarmed on reaching Dunkirk to find that Keyes and the royal couple had not arrived before him. The king and queen, however, were entirely unperturbed by their experience and invited Keyes to join them on horseback in the procession as they led the Belgian Army into a liberated Brussels.

In early 1919, Keyes escorted the king, the Prince of Wales, and Prince Albert (later King George VI) across the Channel and, at the king's request, and in company with the King of the Belgians, he took them on a visit to the mole at Zeebrugge. On the way back to Dover, the king awarded him the distinction of a Knight Commander of the Royal Victorian Order (KCVO).

Two important events then followed in quick succession. Firstly, Lady Keyes gave birth to a son named Roger, as a brother to Geoffrey, who was still under two years old and, secondly, Keyes was appointed to command the Battle-Cruiser Squadron, flying his flag in HMS *Lion* with his old friend Tomkinson as his flag-captain. Seven months after his arrival, Keyes was further honoured by being created Sir Roger Keyes of Zeebrugge and Dover, Baronet – a hereditary honour that made him senior to all knights of the realm with the exception of Knights of the Garter and of the Thistle.

After two years with the Battle-Cruiser Squadron, Keyes learned that he was to be put on half-pay for a year. Rather than be dismayed, he looked upon the opportunity to be able to relax with his family for twelve months with a great deal of pleasure. There was, however, to be a possibly even greater reason to enjoy the long break. He was told that, once the year was over, he would be appointed as deputy chief of the Naval Staff and a lord commissioner of the Admiralty. This, in effect, meant that he would stand in as required for the First Sea Lord, the position currently held by his long standing friend Admiral of the Fleet the Earl Beatty. Matters, however, were to move more quickly than anyone anticipated. The current holder of the post of DCNS, Vice Admiral Sir Osmond Brock, fell ill six months before he was due to leave, Keyes was summoned to London and informed that his time on half-pay was to be ended immediately and he was to take over the appointment.

It was an interesting time to take the DCNS's chair. The Washington Treaty placed restrictions on the building of aircraft carriers, battleships and battle-cruisers, and limited the displacement of cruisers and smaller vessels. Keyes sat on the Committee of Imperial Defence with the role of explaining the new restrictions to the politicians. He was also directly involved in negotiations with the Turks over the question of the passage of foreign warships through the Dardanelles. When faced with implacable Turkish intransigence and lukewarm support from the British government, Keyes solved the problem by booking a seat on the next train home. When the Turks refused to believe that he would actually leave, Keyes boarded the train and left. Greatly perturbed by this demonstration of determination, the following morning the Turks agreed to everything he had demanded.

Almost certainly, however, the greatest concern to Keyes was the threat to naval aviation posed by the complete control of everything to do with the air being in the hands of the Royal Air Force. In late 1922, spurred on by a comment made by his wife's brother-in-law, Air Chief Marshal Sir Hugh Trenchard, threatening him that, if the Royal Navy caused any difficulties, the Air Ministry would start building its own aircraft carriers, Keyes had accompanied Beatty to a cabinet meeting. The First Sea Lord reminded Lloyd George, the prime minister, that the creation of a separate air service was nothing more than a temporary arrangement meant to deal with the problems exposed during the war. After three years, the new organisation, if not failing utterly, was certainly operating to the detriment of the Royal Navy. Lloyd George agreed and an inquiry was held which, instead of arriving at a conclusion which restored the future of naval air-warfare, proved to be a botched compromise offering dual control. Beatty threatened to resign unless the arrangement was considered to be 'experimental'. Eventually Keyes was made a member of a three-man committee under the chairmanship of Lord Haldane with the aim of reaching a workable compromise. The other member was Trenchard. An agreement was made that Keyes felt was 'fairly workable'. In reality the agreement was a tangle of compromises that satisfied neither side and, Keyes believed, was 'full of anomalies and certainly does not make for efficiencies'. He fully agreed with the view that the resulting system only worked because of the 'good fellowship of the officers and men of the two Services'. In all events, naval aviation continued to suffer for the succeeding decade and beyond.

In May 1925 Keyes left England to take up the appointment of commander-in-chief, Mediterranean, the prime operational appointment open to the Royal Navy's flag-officers and the one considered to be the final step before reaching the pinnacle of First Sea Lord. The appointment had come at a difficult time on the diplomatic front with Turkey, shaking off its defeat during the war, now threatening to invade Iraq, a British protectorate – and grab the oil-rich region of Mosel. In typical Keyes manner, the new c-in-c decided that the Mediterranean Fleet should carry out exercises close to the Turkish shore. This led to a flurry of diplomatic activity resulting in a telegram from the Admiralty to Keyes demanding that the 'utmost care' should be taken not to give the Turks cause for complaint. Keyes replied that it was all the fault of the Turks for not allowing his ships to visit Gallipoli and the British war graves.

Notwithstanding his activities afloat with the fleet, Keyes was also able to follow two of his favourite interests. His love of polo was expanded to become almost an instrument of naval training for up-and-coming young officers. Keyes encouraged such potential leaders to take up the sport on the grounds that it encouraged dash and instant decisions. Not everyone, however, agreed and there were dark mutterings in some quarters about favouritism and, even more absurdly, the unfounded and malicious rumour that one of the rating's football pitches on Malta had been commandeered as a polo ground.

His other main interest was naval aviation. Keyes kept a very close eye on the 'dual control' with the RAF that governed all air operations. In late October 1925 he decided to pay a visit to the aircraft carrier HMS *Eagle*, from which he watched his 'splendid young Naval Officer pilots proving themselves Second to NONE'. On completion of his visit he took off in an aircraft piloted by a young RAF officer with the intention of arriving back at Malta in time for lunch. With the wind from astern, the aircraft was still within range of the carrier when the engine failed. The pilot turned the aircraft to take advantage of a head wind but the aircraft stalled and plummeted perpendicularly 100 feet into the sea. Keyes was badly injured and knocked unconscious, his life being saved by the pilot who unstrapped him and dragged him out of the cockpit and into the sea. Amazingly, despite his pains, Keyes felt for those on the ship he had so recently left, 'It was awful for the poor *Eagle* to watch.' Equally amazingly, the 'vets' who tended to his injuries found no permanent injuries and, in less than three weeks, he was writing to the Admiralty Secretary listing the many reasons why complete control of naval aviation should be removed from the RAF and handed over to the Admiralty.

As his time in the Mediterranean drew to a close during the early part of 1928, Keyes found himself implicated in a series of incidents over which he had responsibility as C-in-C, but with no personal involvement. The second-in-command of the fleet's 1st Battle Squadron, Rear Admiral Bernard St George Collard, an officer with a history of causing discontent amongst those beneath him, had a complaint lodged against him by his flag-captain, the captain of HMS *Royal Oak*. Two months earlier, Collard had publicly abused the ship's bandmaster, the splendidly named Percy Barnacle. The matter was allowed quietly to submerge for a time but returned with a vengeance when Collard turned viciously on the ship's commander (executive officer) over the matter of a ship's ladder not being lowered ready for the admiral to descend. The commander complained to the captain, who forwarded the complaint on to the squadron's senior flag-officer. This in turn was sent to Keyes. After a Court of Inquiry looked into the matter, all three officers were found to be guilty of poor behaviour. Keyes ordered Collard to haul down his flag and return to England, the other two officers were dismissed from their ship and sent home. Unfortunately the press had got hold of the story and questions were asked in the House of Commons. The Admiralty delayed releasing the facts of the matter, and unfounded rumours began to implicate Keyes. Eventually, even the king told Keyes that he thought the Admiral had made 'a balls' of the affair. Collard was put on the Retired List and the captain and the commander were court-martialled and sentenced to be severely reprimanded. The former accepted an eventual appointment at sea whilst the latter left the service for a job in journalism.

It seemed, nevertheless, that Keyes' career was still on track. Having been promoted to Admiral in 1926, he could have been reasonably secure in the belief, supported by Beatty, that he would take over the role of First Sea Lord. There had been an opportunity whilst Keyes was c-in-c Mediterranean when Beatty decided to resign but Keyes was not keen to leave the appointment early and suggested the role should go to Admiral Sir Charles Madden – a flag-officer considerably older than him and unlikely to remain too long in the position.

At the end of his time in the Mediterranean, Keyes returned home and was appointed commander-in-chief, Portsmouth. He took over in April 1929, safe in the knowledge that Beatty, Madden and the First Lord of the Admiralty, had all indicated their support for his eventual appointment as First Sea Lord. It was, in consequence, all the more disappointing when Madden's surprise suggestion that his former chief of staff, Admiral Sir Frederick Field (who had taken over as C-in-C Mediterranean from Keyes), should be his replacement, was accepted. Keyes' hope, aspiration and ambition were all crushed.

The reasons given for the rejection of Keyes usually congregate around a build-up of envy over his polo playing, the *Royal Oak* affair, and the entirely probable likelihood that, as First Sea Lord, he would have proved a very difficult obstacle in the way of the newly elected Labour government's plans for naval disarmament. Of at least equal importance – and possibly looming above all the other reasons – was Keyes' position in the Jellicoe-Beatty conflict. He had always strongly supported Beatty and had brushed aside and humiliated one of Jellicoe's firmest allies, the former commander of the Dover Patrol, Admiral Sir Reginald Bacon. Now Beatty had gone and Keyes' future had landed in the grip of Madden – who was married to Jellicoe's daughter.

In true Keyes style, and echoing his actions on being dismissed from command of his ship, *Fame,* thirty years earlier, he responded by going straight to the prime minister, Ramsey MacDonald. They met at Chequers on the afternoon of 2 March 1930 and Keyes persuaded MacDonald to see if the new first lord, Albert ('A.V.') Alexander, would delay any announcement – but it was to no avail. The following day Alexander wrote to Keyes with the numbing words – 'You must please regard the matter as now closed.' The announcement of Field's appointment had been rushed through with unseemly haste.

Although the appointment of First Sea Lord had been snatched from him, there was to be a consolation prize. Less than two months later, at the age of 57, Keyes was promoted to admiral of the fleet, the highest rank possible in the service. He also received the signal honour of being appointed as the honorary colonel commandant of the Royal Marines Portsmouth Division, an appointment he held until he was required to resign having reached the age of 70. Keyes remained at Portsmouth before hauling down his flag on 9 June 1931, retiring to write his memoirs at his home in Tingewick, Buckinghamshire.

Ordained fate and inevitability saw to it that Keyes would not quietly fade away. In January 1934 the Member of Parliament for Portsmouth North was elevated to the House of Lords and suggested to Keyes that he might like to take his place in parliament. Not seeing himself as a natural politician Keyes at first hesitated but then realised that, if elected, he could continue to represent the Royal Navy in a new, if somewhat different, way. After a sweeping victory at the polls, Keyes entered the House on 19 February, supported by Winston Churchill.

Within three weeks of his arrival, Keyes was to be found roundly informing ministers during the debate on the Naval Estimates that, thanks to the reductions to the fleet accepted by the government as a result of the defence-shrinking Treaty of London, the nation's naval requirements were no longer decided by the nation's need – but by the terms of a treaty. Thus, even at an early stage in his parliamentary career, Keyes was firmly charting the course he intended to steer.

That course was to have a great effect upon naval efficiency and effectiveness over the next few years, and to bring a hammer blow that made its mark upon world history. Regarding the former, Keyes never rejected an opportunity to stand up in the House and demand that the Fleet Air Arm should be removed from RAF control and handed back to the Admiralty. In late 1935 a naval lieutenant wrote to him from HMS *Courageous*, a former cruiser converted to an aircraft carrier. According to the officer, the idea of taking over the Royal Navy's own aircraft was extremely popular – 'In this ship everyone is screaming for it.' Presenting Keyes with 'rather a sad shock' he continued to explain that, at Alexandria, he had seen a merchant ship employed by the RAF as a flying boat depot ship – 'at her stern she flies the RAF ensign'. It looked as if Trenchard's threat to give the RAF its own aircraft carriers was on its way to becoming reality.

Every aspect of the current state of naval aviation, from the strategic use of maritime aircraft, to the RAF's refusal to train 'our splendid petty officers' as pilots whilst sending non-commissioned RAF pilots to serve at sea were brought to the floor of the House. In November 1936 Keyes told the House in no uncertain terms that 'the unfortunate experiment should now be terminated'. Five months later, the Minister of Defence Co-ordination, Sir Thomas Inskip, when asked by another former naval officer what he intended to do about the Fleet Air Arm, replied:

As a result of my consideration of this question, I have decided with the aid of the Chiefs of Staff Sub-committee and the other responsible authorities concerned, to conduct a systematic investigation of the important factors involved in this matter …

The result was the 'Inskip Award', which handed the ailing Fleet Air Arm over to the Admiralty. It was not a complete success, as Coastal Command aircraft and crews, including flying boats, remained in the hands of the RAF, but it gave Royal Naval aviation a chance to survive. Despite having to start with poor-quality aircraft, chaotic training facilities and a chronic lack of funding, the Fleet Air Arm emerged by the end of the Second World War as a leader in its field having replaced the battleship with the aircraft carrier as the prime surface capital ship. Keyes' persistence, in company with the efforts of other enlightened naval officers, had paid off.

Admiral of the Fleet Sir Roger Keyes MP wearing the admiral's 'undress' uniform, which he wore to address the House of Commons in May 1940.

Naval activities on the outbreak of war in September 1939 convinced Keyes that he had to get involved as quickly as possible. The German invasion of Poland was expected in all quarters but, to Keyes' fury, no ships had been dispatched to the Baltic to make an instant response. If just a few destroyers had been off the German Baltic coast, they could have done enormous damage but, by the time that such ships had been made available, their way was barred by newly sown minefields.

With Churchill returned to the Admiralty as first lord, Keyes held on to the hope that he would be given a 'mission'. When, however, his help was requested, it came, not from the Admiralty, but from King Leopold of the Belgians. Regardless of any views the king might take of his situation he had to support his ministers. They were holding out for a policy of strict neutrality and the king, much to French annoyance, made no public announcement that contradicted the Belgian government's position. He did, however, ask Keyes if he would visit him privately to act as a liaison between Brussels and London. With permission from the Admiralty and the Foreign Office, Keyes arrived in Belgium in mid-October.

He was informed by Leopold that, in the king's opinion, if the Germans invaded the Belgian Army would be able to hold the line long enough for the French and British to be rushed to the front in support. Keyes then asked for the disposition of the Belgian Army and the plans made for a defence against invasion. This placed the king in a difficult situation. He had assumed that the British already knew of the Belgian dispositions and their plans – after all, the French had been informed. For him to reveal them now, and if news of that handing over of information reached the Germans, it would be seen as a dangerous breach of neutrality. In an attempt to ease the problem, Keyes arranged for lines of communication to be opened between the British military attaché and the king's military staff. He also arranged for British staff officers to visit the country in civilian clothing. News of his activities, however, reached the French, and they demanded similar facilities. The Belgian government refused and Keyes was ordered home.

Without the job he so desperately sought with the navy, despite being restored to the Active List as an admiral of the fleet, parliament was the right place at the right time for Keyes in May 1940. On 9 April the Germans had invaded Denmark and Norway and were occupying the strategic ports on Norway's western coast. After the Royal Navy had sunk several enemy ships during the First and Second Battles of Narvik, some 400 miles to the north, the most important harbour as far as the British were concerned was Trondheim, and a plan was hastily put together to land troops 80 miles to the north and 150 miles south of the port. They were intended to close in on the city's flanks as naval vessels charged into Trondheim Fjord, sank the German destroyers and destroyed the enemy garrison. Troops would then be landed to capture the local airfield. Unfortunately, the commander-in-chief of the Home Fleet decided on the 14th that German air superiority put his ships at too great a risk and the naval attack was abandoned. Instead, the troops to the north and south would have to capture the port in a pincer movement.

On the 16th, Keyes managed to get an interview with Churchill and begged to be allowed to lead an attack on Trondheim with old ships. He not only guaranteed success but, in a later note, said to the first lord 'Pity we can't be ready on St George's Day. Why not?' (It was 22 years since his attack on Zeebrugge). Three days later, on the 19th, the original naval attack was cancelled. After a brave attempt to complete their task without artillery or vehicles, and always under the threat of air attack, those troops that could be, were evacuated.

Just a week later, on 7 May, a packed House of Commons was surprised to see Keyes arrive and take his seat wearing the 'undress' uniform of an admiral of the fleet. The flash of gold lace on the cuffs, the sparkle from the aiguillettes of an aide de camp to the sovereign, and the blaze from a chestful of medal ribbons put out the perfect signals for a member who wished to catch the Speaker's eye. But Keyes had not worn the uniform just to stand out in a crowd of dark suits – he had worn it 'because I wish to speak for some officers and men of the fighting, seagoing Navy who are very unhappy.' Nor was the speech he intended to make concerned purely with the Royal Navy or the events in Norway. A group of parliamentarians from both Houses, known as the Watching Committee and under the leadership of the Marquess of Salisbury and other members of the highly influential Cecil family, had decided that the prime minister, Neville Chamberlain, had to be replaced by either the foreign secretary, Lord Halifax, or the first lord of the Admiralty, Winston Churchill. Keyes was not a member of the committee (probably because Trenchard had been co-opted), but was a keen ally and supporter of its central policy of removing Chamberlain. If selected by the Speaker, his speech would prove to be more than just a grumble about the inadequacies of the Norwegian campaign.

Chamberlain opened the debate with an almost lacklustre speech that followed the expected pattern. First the gushing praise for the services involved, in case there may be any reflected glory – the 'remarkable skill of our naval and military Forces', the 'magnificent gallantry' and 'great traditions of the Service', the men of which, despite being unquestionably outnumbered and outgunned, 'performed great achievements'. Next came the reasons why it was almost a success – 'There were no large forces involved. The fact was, it was not much more than a single division, and our losses, therefore, were not really great in number, nor was there any considerable or valuable amount of stores left behind.' True, the country had 'suffered a certain loss of prestige' but that was only because the enemy 'prepared for war whilst we were thinking only of peace'. All in all, Chamberlain thought that 'the implications of the Norwegian campaign have been seriously exaggerated'.

After two attempts to end with a rallying call, he finally ended with the leaden plea – 'Let us then, before these trials come upon us, put all our strength into the work of preparing for them, and we shall thus steadily increase our strength until we ourselves are able to deliver our blows where and when we will.'

The House was not impressed.

A succession of speakers followed Chamberlain. Many on the opposition benches such as Lloyd George, Herbert Morrison and Clement Atlee, resorted to political point-scoring dressed up as concern for the troops involved. They were followed by Colonel Josiah Wedgewood, a former Liberal who had transferred his loyalties to the Labour Party. Wedgewood had served both as an army and as a naval officer, earning a Distinguished Service Order when in command of machine guns on the forecastle of the landing ship *River Clyde* during the Gallipoli landings. Wedgewood's speech raged at 'facile optimism' and underlined the dangers faced by the country. His references to the Norwegian campaign were few, and he mainly talked about his ideas such as arming civilians. Part of his ire, however, was aimed at the Royal Navy, claiming that 'at present the Fleet can save us from starvation, but it cannot save us from invasion'.

Vice Admiral Ernest Taylor, the Member for Paddington, rose to remind Wedgewood that Britain still had a Navy 'to prevent the invasion of this country'.

The Member for Newcastle under Lyme retorted with a sneering, 'The British Navy could perfectly well defend this country if it had not gone to the other end of the Mediterranean to keep itself safe from bombing' before returning to his notes. A gasp of 'No!' shot around the Chamber and several members rose to their feet, among them Keyes. Wedgewood, however, ignored them all and continued to speak. Eventually he gave way to the Secretary of State for War and to two other members, none of whom referred to his comments about the navy. Keyes continued to rise to his feet until, after a considerable time, Wedgewood gave way. Clearly annoyed, Keyes told the house that they had just heard his 'Right Honourable and Gallant Friend' tell the House that 'the British Navy ran to the Eastern Mediterranean and had gone to Alexandria because they were frightened of bombs.' Pausing for effect, he then added in un-parliamentary language that was ignored by the Speaker, 'That is a damned insult.'

Wedgewood, trying to take the edge off the situation, replied as if he had been challenged to a duel – 'I am quite prepared to meet the Gallant Admiral with anything.'

Keyes remained on his feet and brushed Wedgewood aside with 'I have much more respect for my Right Honourable and Gallant Friend as a machine-gunner in the *River Clyde* than as a strategist and a speaker in the House of Commons.' Having held the floor, Keyes then turned to the speech he had prepared. Being unsure of himself on such occasions, he had taken the advice of the experienced back-bencher, Harold Macmillan, that a speech previously prepared and read out, was better than attempting a meandering discourse that could be easily interrupted by members out of mischief. Now, at last, having almost had his planned speech entirely derailed by Wedgewood, he could press on with the vital matter that had brought him to the House that day. Speaking for officers and men of the Royal Navy who had been disappointed with their leadership during the Norway campaign, he began:

> I want to make it perfectly clear that it is not their fault that the German warships and transports which forced their way into Norwegian ports by treachery, were not followed in and destroyed as they were at Narvik. It is not the fault of those for whom I speak, that the enemy have been left in undisputable possession of vulnerable ports and aerodromes for nearly a month, have been given time to pour in reinforcements by sea and air, to land tanks, heavy artillery and mechanised transport, and have been given time to develop the air offensive which has had such a devastating effect on the morale of Whitehall. If they had been more courageously and offensively employed, they might have done much to prevent these unhappy happenings, and much to influence unfriendly neutrals.

To a silent House, Keyes stressed that 'the capture of Trondheim' was imperative, and that it was 'surely worth almost any risk to win so great a prize'. Such views did not come from abstract opinion but were based upon the fact that 'the naval hazards would have been trifling compared to those overcome in other operations I have organised and led'. Despite being 'a shocking story of ineptitude' the Trondheim situation 'could have been retrieved by immediate action'. The faint-hearted approach shown both by politicians and naval leaders had been the cause of the present situation, not by the men prepared to do the fighting. A couple of days earlier, the prime minister had 'told us that the evacuation of southern Norway was made imperative by the air menace' yet subsequent evidence 'showed the amazingly low percentage of hits achieved by the German aircraft in the face of opposition'. He had interviewed one officer from an anti-aircraft cruiser who had been involved in the fighting and was told that 'they had had about 120 heavy bombs dropped around the two convoys which she escorted into Namsos; no damage was done, and the only diving attack which was made was beaten off, and five German aircraft were destroyed.' 'The war,' Keyes stressed, 'cannot be won by committees, and those responsible for its prosecution, must have full power to act, without the delays of conferences'. He then referred to his old friend, the first lord of the Admiralty, Winston Churchill, and the problems he had encountered during the Gallipoli campaign:

Now, however, he has the confidence of the War Cabinet, as was made abundantly clear to me when I tried to interest them in my project; he has the confidence of the Navy, and indeed of the whole country, which is looking to him to help to win the war ... I beg him to steel his heart and take the steps that are necessary to ensure that more vigorous Naval action in Norway is no longer delayed. If he does, he will have the Navy wholeheartedly behind him.

Finally, and almost inevitably, Keyes looked back to the hero shared by both Churchill and himself – 'One hundred and forty years ago, Nelson said, "I am of the opinion that the boldest measures are the safest," and that still holds good today.'

As he sat down, the House erupted in loud cheers accompanied by the waving of order papers. The right words had been said at the right time and the speech had struck home just as he had intended. Another MP, General Sir Edward Spears (a member of the Watching Committee) wrote that Keyes 'was cheered and cheered again'. Harold Nicholson, a former diplomat and now the Member for Leicester West noted in his diary that it 'is by far the most dramatic speech I have ever heard, and when Keyes sits down there is thunderous applause'. Keyes received over 400 letters as a direct result of the speech – all of them applauding his words, and many thanking him for bringing Churchill's name to the forefront of potential leaders. But it was to be some time before Keyes could find an opportunity to read the letters. On 9 May, two days after Keyes' speech, Salisbury called upon Halifax and, after declaring the inevitability of Chamberlain's removal from office, offered him the position of prime minister. Halifax, despite Salisbury's attempt to persuade him to the contrary, demurred on the grounds that, whilst it was possible for a member of the House of Lords to be Prime Minister, it would be very difficult under the current situation. The following day, Churchill replaced Chamberlain just as the Germans invaded the Low Countries. Keyes found himself, once again, heading for Brussels, this time as Churchill's Special Liaison Officer to the King of the Belgians.

After paying a visit to General Lord Gort VC – the Commander of the British Expeditionary Force – and a brush with suspicious Belgian officials, he reached the British Embassy. The following day he joined the king and heard the appalling news of the German advance. Key Belgian fortifications had been captured, bridges across the defence line of the Albert Canal had fallen to the enemy and the German Air Force dominated the skies. The British and French armies were advancing into Belgium across the Franco-Belgian border as the Belgian Army took the brunt of the fighting. But neither the French nor the British were aware that the Germans were poised to race westwards across their rear, thus trapping them.

By the 13th, with much of the French Army heading north with the intention of holding a line in central Belgium or Holland, other French forces, remaining in the south to defend the French fortress at Sedan on the River Meuse, found themselves under an attack, the like of which had never been experienced before. Having crashed through Luxembourg and the Ardennes forest, German armour attacked the town, the way cleared by 540 bombers and 370 fighters. As elsewhere in Belgium, the Germans had turned air superiority into air supremacy. Sedan fell and the Meuse was crossed as French communications broke down. An artillery section, mistaking French tanks for the enemy, reported that they were about to be encircled by German tanks. They were ordered to withdraw, the action contributing to a rising panic and causing the suicide of the artillery colonel. Soon the roads heading south, already full of civilians fleeing the area, become so clogged that French reinforcements could not get through. Chaos reigned as the Germans, ignoring the risk of extended and exposed flanks, dashed for the Channel coast, intending to trap the British and French armies.

Two days earlier it had been obvious to King Leopold and to Keyes that it was the lack of air opposition that was allowing the Germans to move with such rapidity. Keyes had contacted the chief of the air staff – Marshal of the Royal Air Force Sir Cyril Newall – and pleaded with him to send aircraft. Newall tried to assure him that, as they spoke, RAF aircraft were operating over Belgium, but refused to give any details. Unconvinced, Keyes left a message for Churchill explaining that, without air defence, the situation was dire. The following morning, RAF planes were seen overhead, accounting for several aircraft before returning to their bases in eastern England.

The following day, whilst Sedan was under pressure in the south, the northern French Army had been roughly handled by the Germans and was falling back in disorder. The Belgians, however, were holding their ground and, when the king learned that the Belgian Cabinet intended to leave Brussels, and that they had suggested that the British and French ambassadors should also leave, he demanded that at least four of his ministers should remain. He also asked Keyes to try and persuade the ambassadors to stay at their posts. Keyes convinced the British ambassador who, in turn, persuaded the French ambassador and the Belgian foreign minister to remain in Brussels. The arrangement, however, was short-lived. Two days later all were gone. The French prime minister had already told Churchill that, for France, the war was over and, on the 16th, the Germans entered Brussels.

By the 18th, with half of Belgium overrun by the enemy, the Belgian and British armies had withdrawn to a new defensive line, where they were constantly bombed and strafed by German aircraft. Keyes went with the king to the new headquarters established in the castle at Loppem, just to the south of Bruges. After visiting Ostend and Zeebrugge, Keyes was asked by the king to visit Lord Gort to find out what his plans were for the British Expeditionary Force.

Arriving at Gort's headquarters, Keyes found the general in a realistic mood. The French high command had just paid a visit and were full of gloom over both immediate and long-term prospects. All the French soldiers were desperately tired, short of ammunition, and dispirited by the air attacks. They had been ordered to launch an attack to the south. Gort had offered British help and, if the attack succeeded, there was just the possibility that the Germans could be trapped when the north and south allies linked up. Nevertheless, as he thought that such a success was unlikely, Gort otherwise intended to fight his way south until he could form a defensive line on the River Somme. If that could not be done, the only remaining option was to fall back to the coast and hope that the Royal Navy could lift the army off the beaches. To help with his decision, General Ironside, the chief of the imperial general staff, was coming from England the following day with instructions from the War Cabinet. Keyes was invited to stay overnight to attend the meeting.

The following morning, 20 May, Ironside told Gort and Keyes that the British Army was to make its way to the south of the River Somme. If the Belgians wished to join them they could, otherwise they would have to make their own arrangements. Gort's latest information, however, revealed that the British were in contact with the Germans all along their line and any withdrawal ran the risk of turning into a rout – especially without air cover. Furthermore, later that day, it was learned that the Germans had reached the outskirts of Boulogne – the way south was completely sealed off.

After discussions with the French, who promised to provide two divisions of troops and air cover, it was decided that an attempt would be made to punch a hole through the southern German lines. The attack took place on the afternoon of the 21st: 400 Germans were captured but because the French failed to arrive in any shape or form, the British were forced to withdraw. All that remained was a retreat towards Dunkirk.

Keyes had spent the day with King Leopold in Ypres at a meeting with French Army commanders. Nothing was achieved as the French were so disorganised that they had nothing to offer other than a vague idea that an attack should be made on both flanks of the German thrust to the coast. The Belgian monarch left the talks disappointed at having found his allies, at best, 'confused'. Lord Gort's ADC was more blunt. In company with Keyes, he told Anthony Eden, the secretary of state for war, that the French, 'were not prepared to fight, nor did they show any signs of doing so'. The king's disappointment continued at his meeting with the British. The best Gort could offer was a withdrawal to a new line of defence, taking the Belgian Army with him to cover his left flank. Leopold reluctantly agreed. There was also little comfort to be had from his ministers – they were preparing to leave the country in order to set up a government-in-exile in England, and they wanted the king to leave with them. He, however, was determined to stay with his people.

Keyes remained in contact with Churchill by using the only line available – from the queen mother's quarters at La Panne. This entailed dangerous journeys from Bruges to the palace along roads packed with refugees. The French supreme commander – General Billotte – had been already been killed when his car collided with a French lorry. Keyes' transport and communication problems were exacerbated on the 23rd when he ran into thousands of French soldiers who were both advancing on – and retreating from – the front. The cause of the chaos turned out to be rumours that the Germans had already arrived in Dunkirk.

Churchill persisted in demanding that an attack be mounted against the German flank to the south, a wholly impractical proposition when the British Army was running out of ammunition, the Belgians were coming under huge pressure from the Germans, and advances claimed by the French had no reality outside the mind of the French military leadership. Keyes, in the meantime, was constantly on the telephone to the air minister – Sir Archibald Sinclair (who had been in office for less than two weeks) – demanding and pleading for air support, especially for the Belgians. What little support did come had to come from airfields in England and was mostly ineffectual whilst the RAF concentrated on equally ineffectual bombing raids on the Ruhr. Lieutenant Colonel George Davy, the senior British Army liaison officer at the Belgian headquarters noted 'the disappointed and frustrated expressions of the officers of GHQ as the BBC announced that the RAF had bombed the marshalling yards at Hamm and other remote places deep inside Germany'.

The rumours that had caused the French disarray on the road travelled by Keyes were suddenly found to be closer to the truth than many had realised. On the 23rd, German tanks were closer to Dunkirk than the majority of the British troops (in fact some tanks had entered the Dunkirk suburbs before being ordered to retire) but, that day, the German commander-in-chief had ordered a halt – a remarkable order that was confirmed by Hitler on the 24th.

Keyes spoke to Churchill that afternoon, emphasising King Leopold's probable decision to remain in Belgium with his troops. The following day, the War Cabinet met and decided that the king should follow his cabinet and cross to England. To this end they promised a naval vessel would be sent to pick up the royal family. In addition, Churchill had arranged to talk to Keyes that evening. He would stress the importance of the king going to England. On no account should Leopold arrange a separate peace agreement with the Germans, which would be 'a disaster for the Allied cause'.

It was all too late. The previous evening, Keyes had sat down and helped the king to write a letter to his cousin, King George. In it, Leopold wrote – 'In spite of all the advice I have received to the contrary, I feel that my duty impels me to share the fate of my army and to remain with my people.' The king, the queen mother (Leopold's queen had died in a car accident in 1935), and Keyes then sat down to dinner before listening to a speech by King George to the British people.

On the 25th Keyes visited Zeebrugge to see if two blockships he had ordered had arrived. He was keen that the port, along with Ostend, should not be left in working condition for the enemy's use. To his annoyance he found that the French naval officers at the port had not informed the French Army of the approach of the blockships. Consequently, the army had opened fire on the ships which, with the reasonable assumption that the Germans had taken over the port, returned to England. Keyes then arranged for the outer lockgate to be blown up. Luckily he turned up at the canal mouth to check the damage only to find the French just about to blow up the inner lockgate as well, despite vigorous Belgian complaints that such an action would flood the area to the east – which was full of French and Belgian troops. Instead, whilst under heavy air attack, Keyes arranged for a large floating crane to be sunk in the canal entrance. Afterwards he noted that 'it was easier to block these two ports against the opposition of the Germans, than to do it with the cooperation of the French!'

From first light on the 26th, the Belgian Army again came under a continuous and heavy aerial bombardment. They were still holding the line but German pressure was mounting. That afternoon Keyes telephoned Churchill, who was presiding over a meeting of the War Cabinet. The minutes of the meeting recorded that:

> During the latter part of this discussion the Prime Minister was called out of the room to speak to Sir Roger Keyes, who had a message from the King of the Belgians. The King was determined to stay with his Army. There was, perhaps, a chance that he might be persuaded to leave at the last minute. The Belgians were determined to act as the left flank to assist our re-embarkation. Sir Roger Keyes said there was nothing in Ostend to prevent it being taken. The Menin Gate was being shelled that afternoon. He had been at Lord Gort's headquarters when orders had come to march to the coast. It was clear that these orders had been received with acclamation at G.H.Q., where it was held that the march to the South held out no prospect of success.

The previous evening Gort had decided to ignore any demands for a defence line to be established along the Somme. The French were already casting about trying to find reasons to blame the British for an impending defeat and, with the chaotic French Army being more likely to impede any attack to the south than assist, he chose to try to save the British Army by falling back on Dunkirk.

When Churchill had finished speaking to Keyes – having been told that the Belgian Army 'had been subjected all day to the most frightful aerial bombardment from low-flying German bombers, unmolested by the Royal Air Force' – he handed the telephone over to the secretary of state for air. Keyes took the opportunity sharply to inform Sinclair that 'unless the RAF could do something to counter the German low bombing attacks, and lighten the Belgian Army's burden, it was bound to crack, and was unlikely to stand another day, having endured three without respite'. In fact there had been RAF air activity over the battlefront but it had been in such small numbers that, despite considerable gallantry by the airmen, it had been wholly ineffective.

Keyes then telephoned Vice Admiral Tom Phillips, the vice chief of the Naval Staff, to request 'two or three Motor Torpedo Boats' (MTBs) to be sent to Nieuport to collect himself and any others he could bring with him – as the War Cabinet minutes had suggested, there was always the chance that King Leopold might change his mind.

Early the next day, Keyes received a telegram from King George that was to be passed on to King Leopold. The British King laid out for Leopold all the arguments that had earlier been put forward by Churchill and the British government, but nothing was going to change the Belgian king's mind. Keyes telephoned Churchill with the king's response and emphasised that he did not think the Belgian Army would last out the day. On his return to Bruges, the king handed Keyes a message for Lord Gort. It told the British commander-in-chief that, after four days of continuous fighting, with no reserves or air cover, and with ammunition almost depleted, the Belgian Army could no longer defend themselves or the British. Civilians fleeing the advance of the enemy were being bombed and strafed, and lives were being lost to no good purpose. In his position as commander-in-chief of the Belgian armed forces, the king would issue an order to his army to lay down their arms.

Keyes dashed back to La Panne with Lieutenant Colonel Davy to inform Churchill and the War Office of the situation. The prime minister replied with an off-the-cuff note for Keyes to deliver to the king. It was yet another plea to Leopold not to allow himself to fall into the hands of the Germans. Churchill then told Keyes that he was also to endeavour to get the king to leave the country.

On their way back to Bruges, Keyes and Davy saw German paratroops dropping just to the south of Nieuport – clearly with the intention of gaining the bridges giving access to the port. They immediately stopped the car and opened fire with rifles until Belgian troops, charged with guarding the bridges, ran forward and joined them. Continuing on to the provincial governor's palace at Bruges, they found that the king's whereabouts were unknown, but the queen mother told them that she would not be leaving the country, nor did she expect the king to change his mind. Shortly afterwards, the king's location was discovered and Keyes prepared to set off to find him and hand over Churchill's note. Before he did so, he told Davy to make his way to Middlekirk to ensure that the staff of the British Military Mission were taken onboard the merchant steamer *Aboukir*, which had arrived with supplies for the British Army and would be sailing at midnight.

Keyes met the king shortly before 10 p.m. As the queen mother had suggested, Leopold was adamant that he would not desert his people. That being the case, there was little more Keyes could do but offer the king his best wishes along with the sure and certain knowledge of the ultimate victory over the Germans. Just as he was about to leave, the king asked him if he would write down Rudyard Kipling's poem 'If'. It was the final service Keyes was able to do for the Belgian sovereign.

In company with a member of the *Sûreté de l'Etat* – the Belgian State Security Service – provided by the king, Keyes arrived at Nieuport harbour at about 1 a.m. and found Davy there along with a major from the Military Mission. Both officers had remained behind to see if they could help Keyes escape, an act that may have saved their lives – the *Aboukir* was sunk with a large loss of life.

With no sign of the requested MTBs, the group searched among the vessels tied up in the harbour. Most had been disabled to prevent their use by the enemy but one fishing boat was found with two of its crew sleeping onboard. When asked to take the officers to England, the fishermen refused. Keyes promptly changed the request to a peremptory demand strengthened by the promise of a considerable cash reward. Such a persuasive manner changed the fishermen's attitude and they were just about to set sail when a deep rumbling sound announced the arrival of thee MTBs. Shortly afterwards, with dawn just breaking over the horizon, Keyes and his party set off for Harwich.

Behind them, all along the Belgian Army's line, the only sound that could be heard was from German aircraft circling overhead. No guns were fired, no bombs were dropped. A wireless message had been sent to the Germans that said – 'Laying down arms. Cease fire at 4am (Belgian time) 28th May. Envoy will cross German lines at 5am.' As expected, an unconditional surrender was demanded and accepted. After the war, criticism of King Leopold's decision to prevent the needless loss of life (including criticism from Churchill in an attempt to boost French morale) led to his abdication in favour of his son, Prince Baudouin, in 1951. Keyes, however, never lost an opportunity to defend the king, telling anyone who would listen that 'King Leopold will be proved a worthy son of his father. He sacrificed his army to try to save the BEF before *it deserted* him.'

Once back in England and approaching his sixty-eighth birthday, Keyes found himself with nothing more to do than attend the House of Commons where Chamberlain – unforgiving of Keyes' role in his overthrow – 'cuts me dead'. With the war's prospects seeming to be more and more perilous, he fretted at his inactivity and wrote to Churchill saying 'is the country so flush of people with the experience I possess … that you can afford to ignore me in this critical hour?' An answer came almost immediately.

In June, the chiefs of staff had appointed the adjutant-general of the Royal Marines to be Commander of Raiding Operations. Initially intended to mount raids against German-occupied Norway, Churchill decided that the role should be widened to attack all of occupied Europe. Accordingly, a small raid was mounted against the French coast that resulted in the deaths of two German soldiers (the results of which were greatly inflated by the national press). A second raid against Guernsey went disastrously wrong. Churchill, gravely disappointed by these 'pin-prick raids', offered the job to Keyes.

Needing no second asking, Keyes leapt at the opportunity. Armed with the title of Director of Combined Operations (DCO), he set to work with a will and energy that soon transformed attitudes and behaviour. Within a month he had established a training centre for his 'Commandos' and moved his office away from the Admiralty to escape the risk of interference from unwelcome influences. In the meantime he set about devising plans to take the war to the enemy.

Unfortunately, nothing was to be quite as straightforward as Keyes would have wished. The Chiefs of Staff eyed his position with deep suspicion and rapidly began to erect barriers against his designs on their men and equipment. The First Sea Lord, and former member of his staff, Admiral of the Fleet Sir Dudley Pound, had a particular antipathy towards the new DCO. Still smarting from the attack by Keyes on the Royal Navy's performance during the Norway Campaign, he farmed out all suggestions by Keyes to committees of relatively junior naval officers who could be guaranteed not to risk their careers by taking sides against the First Sea Lord. Keyes was particularly angered by not being consulted about the seaborne attack on the Vichy French forces at Dakar in Senegal. The failed assault had led to a humiliating withdrawal and the French bombing of Gibraltar.

Other difficulties continued to pile up. In September all Combined Operation forces were taken away and given to the commander-in-chief, Home Forces, in case of invasion. Much time and energy was spent on preparing plans to capture the Spanish Atlantic islands of Cape Verde, the Canaries, and the Azores, in case Spain entered the war on the side of the Germans and attacked Gibraltar. Spain, however, stayed clear of direct involvement.

With the threat of invasion averted, Keyes' forces were returned to him towards the end of 1940. Accordingly, with Churchill's encouragement, he turned his attention to a new scheme that had been occupying his mind. The Mediterranean island of Pantellaria, situated between Tunisia and Sicily was occupied by the Italians. Its capture (with him directly in command) would extend the range of aircraft from Malta and Allied convoys could be protected whilst enemy shipping plying between Italy and Libya could be attacked from its airfields.

Although the Chiefs of Staff had been persuaded by Churchill to support the scheme, their enthusiasm was, at best, shallow, and Keyes was appalled when he found, yet again, that hastily thrown-together sub-committees were coming out against the idea. Catalogues of objections were raised. Landing parties would be wiped out before they could get ashore. Even if they did land and actually took the island, it would then have to be defended. Where were the extra aircraft coming from? How would we feed the islanders? Not only were the chiefs of staff starting to come out against the idea, Admiral Cunningham, the commander-in-chief in the Mediterranean (who had done well during the attack on Zeebrugge), wrote to Churchill saying 'The hard fact is that my resources are strained beyond their limits already and the extra burden means that something else will have to suffer in consequence.' Nor was he very keen on the idea of Keyes going out to take charge – 'The organisation for command appears likely to lead to awkward and unsatisfactory situations.' Under the weight of these objections, along with military successes in North Africa, the proposal was postponed until January 1941 then, shortly afterwards, cancelled altogether.

Keyes promptly proposed a landing on Sardinia but it never got beyond the speculative phase. Matters improved greatly, however, in February, when he was allowed to mount (but not accompany) an attack on the Norwegian Lofoten Islands, north of the Arctic Circle. The islands were home to several fish oil plants, a valuable commodity from which the Germans extracted glycerine – an important component of explosives and propellants such as gelignite and cordite. Rapidly planned and organised, the raid was intended to land commandos and Norwegian troops at four fishing ports on the islands to destroy the fish-boiling plants and any shipping that happened to be in the ports. The outcome was a welcome success with eleven factories destroyed, 800,000 gallons of fish oil ruined and almost 20,000 tons of shipping sunk or wrecked. Some 225 enemy prisoners and 12 collaborators were captured, whilst several Norwegians (including women) volunteered to board the assault ships and join the fight against the Germans. The spirit of the commandos was demonstrated by one group taking a bus to attack a nearby German seaplane base, whilst a signaller sent a message to Adolf Hitler using enemy communications to ask where the German troops were? The only British casualty was an officer who accidentally shot himself in the leg. One unexpected bonus was a set of spare rotors for a German Enigma coding machine, which was immediately sent to the decoders at Bletchley Park.

German successes in North Africa brought back the possibility of Spain joining the Axis powers and the likelihood of an attack on her Atlantic islands. Keyes took the view that, particularly concerning Gran Canaria, the islands should be taken regardless of Spain's current neutrality. In his view, the possession of the islands was 'infinitely more important' to the Battle of the Atlantic than any risk of upsetting the Spanish. No one else, however, could be persuaded towards this view and the emphasis returned to cross-Channel raiding or an assault on Sardinia. To this end, an exercise was mounted at Scapa Flow to test the Commandos. The result, according to the military and naval leaders, was 'confusion and chaos'. All blamed the 'divided control' for the problems and urged a return to dealing

Admiral of the Fleet Sir Roger Keyes with his eldest son, Geoffrey. Newly commissioned into the Royal Scots Greys, Geoffrey Keyes became the youngest lieutenant colonel in the British Army and was awarded a posthumous Victoria Cross after leading an attack on Rommel's North African headquarters. (Courtesy of Josephine Keyes)

solely with 'Service Ministries' rather than an 'outside Directorate'. The vice chief of the Imperial General Staff wrote that 'Roger Keyes is a great nuisance' who 'continually interferes' and 'continually criticizes' matters that were 'no business of his whatsoever'. Emboldened by this change in fortunes, the Chiefs of Staff persuaded Churchill that Keyes' role should be changed from 'Director of Combined Operations' to 'Advisor on Combined Operations'. Not unnaturally, this prompted a swift letter to Churchill from Keyes telling the prime minister that he could not 'accept such a sweeping reduction of status and an absurd title which means nothing ...' Churchill's reply was blunt and uncompromising – 'In all the circumstances I have no choice but to arrange for your relief.' Keyes was relieved by Captain Lord Louis Mountbatten on 19 October 1941.

The following month, Keyes addressed the House of Commons, telling the members that he had been 'frustrated in every worth-while offensive action I have tried to undertake'. Not only was he to remain frustrated for the immediate future, he also suffered a grievous tragedy in his personal life. His two sons were both serving their country. Roger, the youngest, was an officer in the Royal Navy, whilst his eldest son, Geoffrey, at 24 years old the youngest lieutenant colonel in the British Army, was attached to the Commandos. Already having been awarded a Military Cross for his actions against the Vichy French in Lebanon, Geoffrey Keyes volunteered to lead a detachment of commandos in an attack on General Rommel's headquarters. With just one other officer and a single NCO, Keyes launched the attack with the intention of killing or capturing the general. The raid failed and Keyes was killed. Nevertheless, such was his example of courage, initiative and leadership that he was awarded a posthumous Victoria Cross.

Whatever despair may have been felt by his father, he did not allow it to overwhelm him, but continued with his parliamentary role. During most of 1942 he also toured the country urging people to invest in National Savings and adding his status to 'War Weapons Weeks' and 'Navy Weeks'.

In the 1943 New Year's Honours List Keyes' name appeared amongst the newly elevated peers. Taking the title 'Baron Keyes of Zeebrugge and Dover in the County of Kent', he was introduced to the House of Lords by Admiral of the Fleet the Earl of Cork and Orrery and Lieutenant Colonel Lord Lovat (one of the commandos who had taken part in the Lofoten raid). Also sitting in the House that day was Keyes' brother-in-law, Lord Trenchard. He was not there to greet and congratulate the newly elevated Lord Keyes, but to speak in the debate which, that day, concerned the Fleet Air Arm. Trenchard lost no time in blaming the Royal Navy for its poorly performing aircraft and continued, 'the best way of making certain that the Fleet Air Arm is properly equipped is for it to be taken over by the Royal Air Force, who have the knowledge to re-establish this branch on a sound footing.'

This was too much for Keyes who, ignoring the tradition that new peers do not speak in the House on the day of their introduction, replied to his 'Noble Friend' by saying, 'if the Navy had been allowed to develop its aviation and had not been deprived of it in 1918, we should have been in a very different position today'. His reply to Trenchard brought Lord Cherwell, the paymaster-general, who had spent the First World War at the Royal Aircraft Factory, to his feet with the comment about Keyes, 'We are pleased to see that he is faithful to his habit. He starts by closing with the enemy and lets off his broadside as soon as he has an opportunity.'

In July 1944, after a visit to the D-Day landings, Keyes took up an invitation by Churchill to visit the USA, Canada, Australia and New Zealand, having agreed on the condition he could take Lady Keyes as his 'secretary'. At Washington he met President Roosevelt along with senior naval and military officers. During the course of these meetings, Lady Keyes was made an honorary member of the US Naval Reserve (Women's Reserve) – or 'Waves' – in order that she could fly in military or naval aircraft. Keyes also used the contacts he had made gently to push forward the suggestion that he be allowed to see the carrier-borne aircraft of the USN in operation.

During his tour of Canada, Keyes met several survivors from the Zeebrugge and Ostend raids in-between, amongst other engagements, giving lectures, making broadcasts and inspecting the Naval College. After a flight to Hawaii, Keyes met Admiral Nimitz, the commander-in-chief of the US Pacific Fleet, and spent a day at sea with one of the US Navy's large aircraft carriers, followed by an inspection of a smaller escort-carrier. An even greater excitement was promised when Nimitz asked General MacArthur and Vice Admiral Thomas Kinkaid – the commander-in-chief of the US 7th Fleet – to allow Keyes to witness any operations that were being carried out whilst he was in their area.

To his immense delight, after two weeks of making speeches in Australia – and on his seventy-second birthday – Keyes left his wife behind as he flew to Hollandia (Jayapura, Indonesia) accompanied by 29-year-old Lieutenant William Tapp of the Royal Australian Navy, who was to act as his flag-lieutenant. On arrival they were met by Admiral Kinkaid who, in turn, introduced them to Rear Admiral Richard Conolly (known as 'Close-in Conolly' from his belief that shore defensive positions could only be destroyed by ships firing at the shortest possible range).

Just ten days later, Keyes found himself in Leyte Gulf, a wide stretch of water penetrating the Philippines some 400 miles south-east of Manila. It is difficult to imagine him wanting to be anywhere else in the world on that day and at that time. On the bridge of Conolly's flagship, the USS *Appalachian*, he was surrounded by over 700 ships carrying and guarding 100,000 soldiers about to land. To the north, the US Third Fleet with its numerous aircraft carriers sat waiting to pounce on any enemy ships that attempted to impede the landings. Altogether there were 2,800 naval aircraft available to the commanders and there was promise of even more for the British visitor. Once the troops were ashore on Leyte Island, Keyes was to transfer to the USS *Tennessee* – a battleship ready to take on any Japanese battleships and cruisers that decided to get involved. However, a cruel twist of fate intervened.

Following a four-hour bombardment, the US and Filipino troops landed with such success that, by early afternoon, General MacArthur could wade ashore declaring 'I have returned!' Shortly afterwards, the fleet off shore was attacked by Japanese torpedo planes and dive bombers. The attack was pressed home with determination and a cruiser, close by the *Appalachian*, was hit by a torpedo. With troops still embarking into landing craft, Conolly decided to order the laying of smoke floats in an attempt to hide the ships from the enemy aircraft. Tactically, such a decision was a sound reaction. Unfortunately, however, the floats were using a new, untested type of chemical smoke that proved to be poisonous when breathed in. Several senior officers on the bridge of the flagship, including Keyes, had their lungs filled.

Keyes was taken below and given oxygen. He recovered from the immediate effects of the smoke but remained very ill for several days, much to his chagrin missing the subsequent action of the Battle of Leyte Gulf in which the *Tennessee* played a significant part.

Forced by his medical condition – particularly the damage to his heart – Keyes returned to Australia to continue a lecture tour before moving on to New Zealand. Before he left, he found time and energy to challenge the Australian trades union leadership who, he felt, were betraying their country's servicemen and women by not encouraging their members to commit to 'one hundred per cent activity on the home front'. When an outraged, and vigorous, response threatened to overwhelm him, he simply replied, 'If this seems too direct, I would point out that my own war experiences, my own personal losses, and my own desires that others should suffer as little as possible, must be my excuse.'

Following a busy time in New Zealand, Lord and Lady Keyes flew back to Sydney with the intention of continuing his lecture tour but his condition declined to the point where medical advice insisted that he should spend a month in bed. Before going to Adelaide, where the governor general had invited him to convalesce at Government House, Keyes was visited by the deputy prime minister who admitted 'admiration' for the way he 'had taken on the Trades Union leaders'.

The long rest proved entirely beneficial and in mid-March 1945 Keyes and his wife flew to Ceylon, where they met Mountbatten, now commander-in-chief, South East Asia Command. Before returning to England they diverted to Benghazi to visit the grave of their eldest son, Geoffrey.

On his return, Keyes became embroiled in the controversy over the return of King Leopold to Belgium, which was most vigorously opposed by Paul Henri Spaak, the socialist Belgian foreign minister. Spaak had tried to persuade Leopold to flee at the approach of the Germans but having failed, fled himself, first to France and then to England. Whilst in France he had tried to negotiate with the Germans to allow his return to Belgium to take a place in the Belgian government during the German occupation but his attempt was rejected. During a speech that was reported in *The Times*, Spaak referred to Keyes as 'a fine soldier' who gave 'horrible political advice'. Keyes responded immediately with a letter reminding everyone that 'the fate of the small British Army, during their retreat, depended on the steadfastness of the Belgian Army on their flank.' For that 'resolute steadfastness … we have to thank King Leopold'. If the king had fled with Spaak and his cabinet colleagues, 'many thousands of British soldiers, who escaped to Dunkirk, would surely have perished or been captured'.

Having seen the enormous improvement in the Royal Navy's Fleet Air Arm during the war, and the impressive capabilities of the United States Navy's air operations, Keyes never failed to take up the torch on behalf of naval aviation. When news arrived that the dropping of two atomic bombs on Japanese cities had brought the war to an end, Keyes wrote to a friend and fellow Admiral of the Fleet telling him that the war would still be continuing if Admiral Nimitz had not led his vast fleet of aircraft carriers and battleships

> … across the Pacific by a series of daring amphibious operations – capturing islands and potential airbases with troops and marines, landed under cover of his gigantic sea-borne air force, and supported by the gunfire of ships, thousands of miles out of reach of the US Army Air Force.

In the same letter, Keyes even managed to have a parting shot at the RAF: 'I see that Bomber Harris (the head of the RAF's Bomber Command) announced that battleships are the dodos of the war!'

By now utterly exhausted and broken in health, Keyes was once again ordered to rest. After a quiet Christmas with his family, Admiral of the Fleet the Lord Keyes closed his eyes for the last time and died in the early hours of Boxing Day 1945.

With the news of Keyes' death, tributes came from all points of the compass. Churchill wrote, 'We have lost one of the great sailors of the Royal Navy, who embodied its traditions and renewed its glories. It was by men like him, in whom the fire and force of valiance burned, that our Island was guarded during perilous centuries.' One old friend regarded Keyes as 'the voice of England', whilst another spoke of his 'Nelson spirit'. Yet another told Lady Keyes that 'He never, in any stroke of war he planned or took part in, even thought of the possibility of

Admiral of the Fleet Sir Roger Keyes Bt MP, 1st Baron Keyes of Zeebrugge and Dover, GCB, KCVO, CMG, DSO, D.Cl, LL.D, GC of Leopold, GO Legion of Honour, Croix De Guerre, DSM, 4 October, 1872–26 December 1945. (Courtesy of Josephine Keyes)

The memorial stone over Lord Keyes' grave at Dover. He is buried alongside the men he led.

defeat.' Admiral Nimitz wrote of 'his outstanding qualities of leadership, brilliant handling of naval problems, and his fearless, driving personality'.

There was talk of burying Keyes in St Paul's Cathedral, where he would join Nelson, Collingwood, Jellicoe and Beatty. The Admiralty, however, objected on the grounds that Keyes had never commanded a great fleet in action.

Keyes' body, the coffin draped in the Union Flag and guarded by servicemen, rested in Tingewick church, close to his home. On a nearby wall was displayed a wooden cross originally placed by General Rommel on the grave of Keyes' eldest son, Geoffrey. A memorial service was held at Westminster Abbey after a procession from Horse Guards Parade, his coffin mounted on a gun carriage drawn by seamen from the Royal Navy marching to the beat of muffled drums. The coffin was escorted by six admirals of the fleet (Cork and Orrery, Cunningham, Somerville, Chatfield, Forbes, and Tyrwhitt). They were joined by Field Marshal Alexander, and Major General Robert Laycock, who had been appointed to Combined Operations by Keyes, and who was now their chief. During the service in the Abbey, Robert Louis Stevenson's poem *Requiem* was sung:

> Under the wide and starry sky
> Dig the grave and let me die.
> Glad did I live and gladly die,
> And I laid me down with a will.
>
> This be the verse you grave for me;
> 'Here he lies where he longed to be,
> Home is the sailor, home from sea,
> And the hunter home from the hill.'

And it was to be 'Under the wide and starry sky' that Keyes' body was taken to Dover and laid to rest alongside his men, who had given their lives in the Zeebrugge and Ostend raids. The grave site was marked by a large memorial stone bearing a carving of Saint George defeating the dragon.

Roger John Brownlow Keyes defeated numerous dragons of his own during his lifetime. The petty-minded were easily dealt with; those who depended upon their rank and status were shocked into retreat, whilst those who stood their ground could be won over. His country's enemies hoped that his superiors would rein him in before he descended upon them. Too often such hopes were rewarded for it was frequently to be those superior in rank to Keyes that were to prove his greatest adversaries. Writing to his friend Tomkinson, Keyes noted, 'I always seem to be fighting our own side to get on with the war.' Yet serving under and alongside Keyes invariably caused the flowering of a dedicated loyalty that was unshakeable in the face of the foe. The men who raced up the brows of the *Vindictive* and jumped down onto the mole wall did so because Keyes was their leader – a leader whose ardour for victory had burned into them the desire to win. Such men had come from every background, every social class and every degree of talent. But they all wanted a victory for Keyes and Britain. His detractors were not all bad men, but envy is an emotional corrosion that is difficult to overcome. Time and again, at Zeebrugge, in Belgium in 1940, and whilst in command of Combined Operations, Keyes demonstrated that, with the right men, there were no challenges that could not be overcome. Even the failures at Ostend brought to the enemy's attention the fact that the British and their allies were not going to give up, and the wreck of a light cruiser dumped on their doorstep was a constant reminder of the fact.

Unfortunately for Keyes, some of his contemporaries – and those critics who looked back at his career through the wrong end of a telescope – chose to disregard his achievements. There is no doubt that many of his generation tended to impose technology in place of courage in the belief that the enemy would fall back in the face of 'progress'. Keyes knew instinctively, however, that the fight could not be taken to the enemy by laying minefields across his own harbour entrance. It was aggression that gave victory, and that could only be delivered

The mole lighthouse extension at Zeebrugge as it is today.

directly to the enemy – not, as happened subsequently, to the enemy's women and children.

Keyes' later critics, who only knew their subject from books and preformed opinions, showed a deep lack of understanding of the environment and setting in which he and his men lived. They found it all too easy to follow the chorus of derision from those who earlier rushed to join the criticism of someone whose achievements they could never hope to emulate. The astonishment at what Keyes and his men accomplished in the face of appalling conditions and potentially overwhelming odds was replaced by shameful sneers. Such accounts should be disregarded as being little more than wilful misunderstandings and deliberate distortion.

Keyes personified courage, initiative, enterprise, magnanimity and example. That is why many who knew him and knew of his exploits considered him as the 'modern Nelson'. It was no exaggeration.

Select Bibliography

Aspinall-Oglander, Cecil, *Roger Keyes*, Hogarth Press, 1951.

Bacon, Sir Reginald H.S., *Britain's Glorious Navy*, Odhams, 1942.

Beesly, Patrick, *Room 40*, Hamish Hamilton, 1982.

Bennett, Godfrey, *Naval Battles of the First World War*, Pen & Sword, 1968.

Black, Nicholas, *The British Naval Staff in the First World War*, Boydell, 2009.

Boddie, R.C., 'The Blocking of Zeebrugge on St George's Day 1918', *Naval Review*, Volume 81, No. 3, July 1993.

Boyle, Andrew, *Trenchard*, Collins, 1962.

Bradford, Sir Edward E., *Life of Admiral of the Fleet Sir Arthur Knyvet Wilson*, John Murray, 1923.

Brisbane Courier, 24 April 1925.

Campbell, Gordon, *Sailormen All*, Hodder and Stoughton, 1933.

Carpenter, Alfred B., *The Blocking of Zeebrugge*, Herbert Jenkins Ltd, 1922.

Corbett, Sir Julian S., *Naval Operations Vols I–V*, Longmans, Green and Co., 1920.

Coxon, Stanley William, *Dover During the Dark Days*, General Books, 2010.

Cunningham, Viscount, *A Sailor's Odyssey*, Hutchinson, 1951.

Divine, A.D., *Deeds that Held the Empire – At Sea*, John Murray, 1939.

Evans, Martin Marix, *1918 – The Year of Victories*, Index Books, 2005.

Fisher, Lord, *Memories*, Hodder and Stoughton, 1919.

Fisher, Lord, *Records*, Hodder and Stoughton, 1919.

Halpern, Paul G. (Ed.), *The Keyes Papers Vol I*, Navy Records Society, 1979.

Halpern, Paul G. (Ed.), *The Keyes Papers Vol II*, Navy Records Society, 1980.

Halpern, Paul G. (Ed.), *The Keyes Papers Vol III*, Navy Records Society, 1981.

Hilton Young, E., *By Sea and Land*, Methuen & Co Ltd, 1924.

Holloway, S.M., *From Trench and Turret*, Constable, 2006.

Howard, Keble, *The Zeebrugge Affair*, George H. Doran Company, 1918.

James, Sir William, *The Eyes of the Navy*, Methuen & Co., 1955.

Jameson, William, *The Fleet that Jack Built*, Rupert Hart-Davis, 1962.

Keyes, Roger, *The Naval Memoirs*, Thornton Butterworth Ltd, 1935.

Keyes, Roger, *Outrageous Fortune*, Tom Donovan, 1990.

King-Hall, Stephen, *A North Sea Diary 1914–1918*, Newnes, 1936.

Klaxon, *Dead Reckoning*, Rich & Cowan Ltd, 1933.

Marder, Arthur J., *From the Dreadnought to Scapa Flow*, OUP, 1961.

McGreal, Stephen, *Zeebrugge & Ostend Raids*, Pen & Sword, 2007.

Mortimer, Gavin, *Fields of Glory*, Andre Deutsch, 2001.

Mumby, Frank A. (Ed.), *The Great World War Vol II*, Gresham.

Mumby, Frank A. (Ed.), *The Great World War Vol III*, Gresham.

Mumby, Frank A. (Ed.), *The Great World War Vol V*, Gresham.

Pitt, Barrie, *Zeebrugge*, Cassell, 2003.

Pollen, Arthur H., *The Navy in Battle*, Chatto & Windus, 1918.

Prince, Stephen, *The Blocking of Zeebrugge*, Osprey Publishing, 2010.

R.N.V., *Pushing Water*, John Lane, The Bodley Head, 1919.

Smith, Peter C. & Oakley, Derek, *Royal Marines*, Spellmount, 1988.

Stinglhamber, G.M., *The Story of Zeebrugge*, Zeebrugge Museum, 1932.

T 124, *Sea Power*, Jonathan Cape, 1940.

Tarrant, V.E., *Jutland – the German Perspective*, Cassell, 1995.

Thompson, Julian, *The Royal Marines*, Pan Macmillan, 2001.

Toland, John, *No Man's Land*, Eyre Methuen, 1980.

Warner, Philip, *The Zeebrugge Raid*, William Kimber, 1978.

Zemen, B.A.Z., *A Diplomatic History of the First World War*, Weidenfield and Nicholson, 1971.

Index

Adams, Bryan 95, 145–6, 155–62, 231, 252, 265–7

Alleyne, Sir John 203–4, 209–15, 219, 222, 231, 267–9

Annesley, John 139

Antell, George 155–7

Aspinall-Oglander, C. 53

Babb, Dudley 183

Bacon, Sir Reginald 23–41, 54–9, 64, 70–2, 80, 84–5, 91, 233, 248–52, 264–5, 287

Balfour, Arthur 50

Ballard, George 25

Ballot, Victoria Cross 230–1

Bamford, Edward 93, 154, 159–63, 230–2, 282

Battenberg, Prince Louise 43, 46

Bayly, Sir Lewis 36, 56, 70

Beatty, Sir David 16–7, 27, 38, 44, 54, 57, 80, 85, 103–4, 204, 264, 285–7, 310

Belben, George 176–7

Belgium 11, 29, 60, 65, 208, 237, 253, 240, 294–7, 307, 311

Beresford, Lord Charles 24

Billyard-Leake, E W 103, 123–4, 179–81, 185, 202, 233, 274–8

Bindall, Henry 152

Birdwood, William 51–2

Blake, Leslie 171

Blankenberge 67, 119, 126, 139, 146, 163, 198

Blockade 18, 26, 245

Boddie, Ronald 118, 172, 176

Bolsheviks 14, 53, 107, 266

Bonham Carter, S. 103, 110, 129, 177–86, 233, 261, 273–4, 277

Bourke, Roland 104, 119, 132–6, 220, 222, 231, 267–78

Bowlby, Cuthbert 172, 213–4, 272

Boyle, The Hon A. 59, 106, 114–7, 126, 130, 135, 190, 206, 210, 227

Bradford, George 95–6, 150, 158, 168, 231

Brady, Henry 117, 126–7

Bragg, William 125

Bramble, Frank 81, 96

Bremner, William 212

Brest-Litovsk Treaty 14

British Army 11–2, 26, 96, 206–8, 247, 296–9, 304, 307

Brock, Frank 61–3, 74, 79, 83, 88, 100–1, 108, 114, 118, 120, 127, 140–1, 155–6, 168–9, 215, 249, 261

Bruges 26, 32, 34, 64, 67, 90, 173, 206, 229, 234–8, 244, 247, 251, 253, 295, 297, 299

Bryant, Thomas 164–6

Bury, William 81, 97, 158, 167, 196, 203–4, 209, 217–25, 267

Campbell, Harold 99, 143, 161, 164, 166, 202, 231, 264

Campbell, Victor 115–7, 223

Carpenter, Alfred 74–5, 80, 94, 103–4, 109,

114–8, 121, 124–9, 141–6, 149, 157–68, 198–202, 206, 231, 250–2, 265, 281

Casualties in raids 238, 248

Chamberlain, Arthur 95, 142

Chamberlain, Neville 291-94, 300

Chappell, Lionel 165

Chater, Arthur 93, 138–42, 147, 159–63, 272

Chevallier, Felix 95

Childs, William 155–6, 161

China 41–3, 276

Churchill, Winston 25, 27, 43–7, 50, 112, 241, 249, 290–307

Cleaver, William 152

Clegg, William 99, 140, 146, 158

Cobby, John 114, 143, 163–7

Cochran, Thomas 168

Collins, Ralph 99, 165, 173

Colson, Henry 99, 160

Conybeare, Charles 93

Cooke, Theodore 147, 149, 159, 272

Corbett, Sir Julian 250

Cordner, Alexander 93, 140, 142, 163, 168

Coronel 16

Cory-Wright, Alan 183

Cowan, Walter 204

Crutchley, Victor 102, 134, 136, 203, 209, 215–6, 220-28, 231, 273, 277–8

Cunningham, A. B. 140, 227–8, 282, 302, 310

Dallas Brooks, R. 93, 156, 267

Dampier, Cecil 58

Dardanelles 25, 47–55, 249, 284

Dayrell-Reed, A. 212

De Robeck, John 47–53, 85, 204

Dean, Percy 182–6, 200, 231, 280, 282

Depth charge 31, 33, 61, 87, 88, 132

Dickinson, Cecil 95, 106, 155, 160

Director of Plans 36–8, 56–7, 71

Disenchantment School 11, 252

Dogger Bank 16, 46, 95

Dover Barrage Committee 36–7, 55

Dover Patrol 26–32, 40–2, 54–63, 88–90, 97, 106, 112, 196, 207, 225, 234, 248, 250–3, 287

Drummond, Geoffrey 220–4, 231, 278, 280

Dunkirk 26, 34–5, 59–60, 67, 73, 88, 90, 93, 99, 103–4, 107–8, 114–36, 171, 204, 207–13, 222, 227, 234, 268, 283–84, 296–98, 307

Eagles, Charles 93, 158, 164–6

Eastlake, Arthur L. 100, 140–41

Eaves, Harold 104, 161, 168

Edgar, William 164–5

Electric Launch Company 89

Elliot, Bertram 92–3, 98, 104, 140–2, 163, 168

Evans, Edward 59

Ferguson, Adam 97

Finch, Norman 147, 150, 230–2, 281–2

Fisher, Sir John 24–9, 40, 46–7, 56, 249–52, 265

Flanders Flotilla 43, 62, 67

France 12–3, 19, 26, 32, 57, 60, 69, 92, 95, 98–9, 106–13, 204, 207–8, 232, 244–5, 295, 307

Franks, Ivan 103, 123

Freyberg, Oscar 86

Gallipoli 25–9, 47–54, 59, 74, 85, 91–3, 96, 99–102, 115, 124, 185, 200, 204, 230, 267, 270, 285

Geddes, Lefroy 177

Geddes, Sir Eric 40, 57, 121, 229, 233, 265.

Gibbs, Valentine 98, 149, 158, 163–6

Godsal, Alfred 102, 131–6, 203–4, 209–15

Gore-Langton, H. 188–9

Grant, Herbert 80–1, 108

Haig, Sir Douglas 12–5, 20, 29, 112, 204, 207–8, 227, 244

Halahan, Frederick 60

Halahan, Henry 60, 93–4, 98, 106, 141–2, 168, 208

Hall, William 'Blinker' 39, 55–6, 63, 107, 228–9, 233

Hamilton Benn, I. 60, 99, 115, 119, 130–6, 211, 220–2, 270, 279

Hardy, Henry 102, 124, 131–6, 203, 207–9

Harner, Walter 152

Harrington Edwards, P. 96, 106, 142, 154, 201, 269–70

Harrison, Arthur 94–5, 142, 157–62, 168, 231, 252, 261

Harrison, Francis 130–4

Hartlepool 45

Harwich Flotilla 25, 36, 44, 47, 98, 112, 114, 121, 126

Hawkings, Claude 95

Heligoland Bight 15, 44, 46, 62, 95, 99

Helyar, Kenneth 186–9

Henderson, Oscar 98, 165–6, 202, 264, 271

Hercus, Eric 28–9

Hewett, Graham 77, 100, 140

Hill, Edward 127, 139, 142

Hilton Young, Edward 97–8, 127, 140–2, 146, 158, 166–7, 266–7

Hoare, Keith 119, 131–5, 222

Hood, the Hon. Horace 26–7, 32–3

Horton, Max 47

Howell-Price, J. 151–2

Hughes, Jonathan 168

Jackson, Henry 27, 29, 49, 51

Jackson, Rev F 208–9, 223, 225

Jellicoe, Sir John 16–20, 28–9, 38–9, 44–5, 54–7, 74, 250, 252, 264–5, 287, 310

Jutland 16, 54, 59, 95, 124, 264, 277

Keith Wright, J. 185–6, 200–1

Kerensky, A. 13–4

Keyes, Eva 43, 126, 172, 200, 208–9

Keyes, Geoffrey 284, 304, 306

Keyes, Roger 284, 304

Keyes, Roger John B.
    Director of Plans 36–40
    Early career 41–57

Dover Patrol 258–9
    Subsequent career 282–312

Kitchener, Lord 49–53

La Panne 208, 296, 299

Lake, Ferdinand 165, 282

Lambe, Charles 60, 108, 206, 234

Lambert, Francis 176

Lamplough, C. 160

Lenin, V. 14

Littleton, Hugh 177, 183

Lloyd George, D. 11–4, 20, 111, 276, 285, 292

Lloyd, Maurice 124, 185–6, 200–1

Lynes, Hubert 60, 115–6 119, 126, 130 136, 171, 203, 208–12, 225, 244, 270

MacLachlan, A. 203–4, 209, 217

MacMahon, Sir Henry 52–3

Maxwell, Gordon 146, 163, 198

Maxwell, Sir John 52

McBean, Russell 214–5

McCutcheon, James 99, 140

McKenzie, Albert 155–6, 161, 231, 252

Memorials 261–4

Mercer, Sir David 91–2, 105

Mines 14, 18, 25, 31–3, 39, 48, 56, 60–3, 71, 113, 124, 136, 278, 283

Monro, Sir Charles 50–3

Newbold, Aubrey 86, 137, 152, 198, 227

Oliver, Sir Henry 38, 40, 58

Osborne, Seymour 86, 96, 138, 141, 209, 223, 267

Ostend Raid (1) 130–6

Ostend Raid (2) 209–25

Outhwaite, Cedric 170–1

Palmer, John 162, 168

Payne, 'Jack' 99, 140, 145–6

Paynter, Charles 188, 261
Peshall, Rev Charles 101, 141, 146, 158, 270
Petrie, James 220, 222
Pocock, Frank 99, 165, 202, 272
Poland, Albert 212
Portable islands 28, 70
Pound, Dudley 54, 56, 74, 107, 301
Proctor, R. 213

Reed, Joseph 203, 219–22, 228
Rigby, Charles 138, 147
Rodman, Hugh 104
Rogers, Harold 99
Rosoman, Robert 81, 96, 110, 141, 143, 146, 163–4, 267
Ross, Gordon 220
Roxburgh, Allan 152
Royal Air Force 73, 76, 79, 107–8, 113, 116, 126–7, 130, 206, 233–4, 286–9, 295–9, 304, 307
Royal Navy 11, 15, 20–1, 25–7, 31, 38–9, 42–3, 46–8, 57–8, 63–4, 67, 75, 93–4, 98, 101, 107, 113, 119, 123, 129, 204, 227, 241, 244–5, 251–2, 266–7, 270–3, 276, 278, 285, 288, 290–3, 296, 301, 304, 307, 310
Rufigi River 71
Russia 11–4, 18, 43, 52–4, 71, 107, 244, 269–70, 282

Sandford, Francis 85–6, 106, 115, 137, 152, 210
Sandford, Richard 86, 151–2, 231, 261, 281
Scapa Flow 16–7, 21, 38, 72, 79, 96, 98, 103 277, 302
Scarborough 45–6
Schroeder, Ludvig V. 67
Schultz, Karl 238
Scott, Sir Percy 27
Seymour, Sir Edward 42
Smith, David 164–5
Sneyd, Ralph 102–3, 172–9, 202, 235, 273
Spencer, George 99, 164–6

Spencer, The Hon C. 215
Stinglhamber, G. M. 252
Straits of Dover 26–7, 32, 36, 39, 56
Stroom Bank Buoy 65, 90, 115, 119, 130–3, 136, 203, 211, 238
Sutton, William 143
Swin Deep 30, 108, 114–5, 120–1, 125

Tebbenjohans, Kurt 39, 56
Thatcher, John 149, 155
Tiffany Studios 88
Tirpitz, Alfred Von 238
Tomkinson, Wilfred 54, 59, 63, 99, 117, 129, 209, 283–4, 310
Tracey, Herbert 198, 200
Trumble, Frederick 223
Turkey 11, 47, 49, 51, 54, 285
Tyrwhitt, Reginald 25, 36, 40, 44–5, 56, 70–1, 74, 86, 114, 310

U-boat 12–21, 26–39, 45, 55–63, 67–70, 75, 88, 90, 99, 114, 124–5, 209, 234–7, 241, 244–7, 268, 273
USA 13, 56, 305

Vaux, Philip 124, 179

Walker, Harold 95, 146, 269
Weller, Bernard 93, 142, 147, 159–60, 163, 230
Welman, Arthur 60, 99, 139, 211–2
Wemyss, Sir Rosslyn 38, 48–58, 79–80, 107, 121, 200–3, 229, 231, 250
Whitby 45
Wilson, Arthur 27, 32
Wilson, Woodrow 13

Youlton, Edwin 163–4, 167
Young, Dawbarn 172–3, 177

Zeebrugge Raid 137–202

The White Ensign worn on HMS *Vindictive* during the Zeebrugge raid.

If you enjoyed this book, you may also be interested in ...

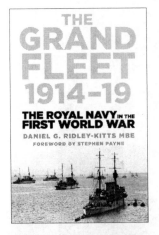

The Grand Fleet: 1914–19

DANIEL G. RIDLEY-KITTS MBE

During the First World War the reputation of the British Royal Navy was put on the line in its defence of the country, and, crucially, it was in those years, 1914–19, that the Grand Fleet became the single most potent weapon of war of any nation. In this comprehensive, illustrated history, Ridley-Kitts tells of the creation and development of the Grand Fleet under the drive of the energetic and charismatic Admiral of the Fleet 'Jacky' Fisher, who modernised the navy with the introduction of the revolutionary Dreadnought battleship.

978 0 7524 8873 8

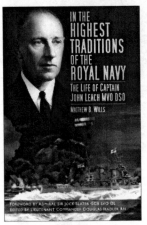

In the Highest Traditions of the Royal Navy

MATTHEW B. WILLS

On 10 December 1941, the Royal Navy battleship HMS *Prince of Wales* was sunk by Japanese bombers in the South China Sea. Amongst the several hundred men who went down with her was her captain, John Leach, who had fought against frightful odds and to the very end made the best of an impossible situation with courage and calmness. He truly embodied 'the highest traditions of the Royal Navy'. Author Matthew B. Wills analyses the influences that shaped John Leach and led him ultimately to his heroic end.

978 0 7524 9859 1

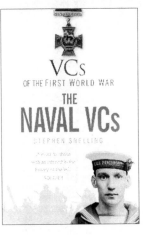

The Naval VCs

STEPHEN SNELLING

The Naval VCs is a complete record of almost fifty men who won the Victoria Cross while serving in the Royal Navy during the First World War. They include the conflict's youngest and oldest winners in operations ranging from the Atlantic to the coast of Africa and from the Straits of Otranto to the rivers of Mesopotamia. This book charts the lives and careers of the VC recipients and presents graphic accounts of their award-winning actions based on original material, much of it from eyewitness sources.

978 0 7524 8733 5

Visit our website and discover thousands of other History Press books.

www.thehistorypress.co.uk

Lightning Source UK Ltd.
Milton Keynes UK
UKOW04f1642130814

236877UK00001B/1/P